UNEQUAL

'Swati Narayan's fine book shows us that India's multiple layers of inequalities—social, economic, gender and more—have not only enabled the growing capture of its economy by billionaires (169 by last count on the *Forbes* list), but also has us trailing even those neighbours our elite so love to despise, Bangladesh and Nepal, on important indicators. Our entire policy direction of the past few decades has not only introduced new inequalities but further entrenched many old and existing ones. Narayan correctly sees that the pandemic further deepened these stark inequalities—that it just had to. The health mega crisis it thrust on us saw India notch up the highest number of COVID-19 excess deaths in the world. It also saw India's billionaire numbers move from ninety-eight to 160—and health sector billionaires (thirty-two) outnumber those from any other sector. Narayan explores the complex layers of our inequalities and also, at some levels, the moral economy of our elite.'

– P. Sainath, Founder Editor of The People's Archive of Rural India (PARI) and Author of *Everyone Loves A Good Drought* and *The Last Heroes*

'This immensely readable book invites India's smug elite to a journey to truth. The journey begins by confronting an inconvenient fact: Nepal and Bangladesh have long overtaken India in many key indicators of human development. Swati Narayan's relentless pursuit of a bold question—what can we learn from our 'poor little neighbours'?—turns this book into a travelogue in more senses than one. In a refreshing departure from the dull academic prose, she recounts anecdotes of her travels to the eighty randomly selected villages in Nepal, Bangladesh and Bihar. She does not lose sight of her questions as she travels across geographies, time periods and academic disciplines, as she reads economic data with the lens of developmental economics, historical sociology and political economy. The reader also travels across different genres—a lucid mix of travelogue, ethnographic stories, reporting of field surveys and data analysis. This journey finally takes us to the sober truth that India's massive and growing inequalities in class, caste and gender terms are at the heart of this collective failure. This travelogue for our times invites us to undertake a political journey to mobilize the bottom of India's social and economic pyramid.'

– Yogendra Yadav, political activist and
Author of *Making Sense of Indian Democracy*

'For a change, Swati Narayan's travelogue does not compare India to China or Brazil, but to neighbouring countries with similar history and social structure, to show that India is lagging behind many of them in terms of development. Why? Because of "layers of multiple inequalities compound", because no country can develop if it remains that badly affected by all kinds of hierarchy. Narayan's argument is very powerful and suggests that India will not be a great power till this societal issue is taken seriously.'

– Christophe Jaffrelot, Professor at King's College London,
Researcher at CERI-Sciences Po/CNRS and
Author of *India's Silent Revolution* and *Modi's India*

'Fascinating account of how reducing inequalities—especially of gender—has been key to social development in South Asia. Essential reading for policy makers in India and everywhere.'

– Jayati Ghosh, Professor of Economics,
University of Massachusetts Amherst, USA

'Swati Narayan takes us on a fascinating journey through the villages of India and her neighbouring countries, unearthing many sources of deep-rooted inequalities that still undermine the nutrition, health, education and livelihoods of the nation's poorest families today. Deftly combining statistical analysis with first-hand research and vivid storytelling, she highlights myriad policies, initiatives and practices that can transform the lives of children, women, families and communities. These are rich insights, for India and far beyond, on what it takes to turn economic resources into flourishing lives for all.'

– Kate Raworth, Senior Associate at Oxford University and Author of *Doughnut Economics*

'In this eminently readable book, Swati Narayan shows how combating class, caste and gender inequities is essential to ensure general economic progress translates into human development outcomes. Gender equality in particular, but also investments in schools and hospitals, should not be seen as the end prize of economic growth: they should be treated as essential ingredients of growth, if it is to make a difference in people's lives. This is comparative social science at its best.'

– Olivier De Schutter, UN Special Rapporteur on Extreme Poverty and Human Rights

'One of the most extraordinary, yet often ignored, stories of international development is how India has been steadily overtaken by its neighbours in crucial areas such as education, health and human rights. In this brilliant comparative analysis, Swati Narayan shows how that has happened, and what India can learn from its more successful neighbours.'

– Duncan Green, Professor in Practice in International Development at the London School of Economics and Political Science and Author of *How Change Happens*

'This book blew my mind as well as confirmed my belief and understanding. It is an inspiring book with live case studies, first-hand data evidence, analysis and practical tips; a true roadmap to enlightenment with equality, justice and freedom. Swati Narayan also challenges the normative economic paradigms here by presenting evidence of India in comparison with its poorer neighbours and how linear macroeconomic indicators of growth can be misleading in terms of socioeconomic development. The wisdom expressed here is presented with clarity and impeccability on what it means for men and women to live as peaceful warriors in the modern world. This is one of the most insightful books I have seen in ages, so a must-read one!'

– Saloni P. Singh, Economist and Member, National Planning Commission, Government of Nepal

'With this remarkable blend of scholarship and reportage from India's borders, Swati Narayan shows us the consequences of Indian policymaking on the lives of its citizens. This is *the* book on the ways South Asian neighbours are pulling ahead.'

– Rahul Bhatia, Journalist

'Swati Narayan's book is a gripping tale of transformational South Asia. It beautifully crafts why some nations in the region are able to move faster than others in this race, based on the author's own intensive village-based research in Bangladesh, India and Nepal. A must-read for people interested in the future of South Asia.'

– Ahmed Mushtaque Raza Chowdhury, Professor at the Mailman School of Public Health, Columbia University, former Vice-Chair, BRAC and Co-author of *Bangladesh at 50: Advances in Health*

Un

SWATI NARAYAN

EquAl

**WHY INDIA
LAGS BEHIND ITS NEIGHBOURS**

cntxt

First published by Context, an imprint of Westland Books, a division of Nasadiya Technologies Private Limited, in 2023

No. 269/2B, First Floor, 'Irai Arul', Vimalraj Street, Nethaji Nagar, Alapakkam Main Road, Maduravoyal, Chennai 600095

Westland, the Westland logo, Context and the Context logo are the trademarks of Nasadiya Technologies Private Limited, or its affiliates.

Copyright © Swati Narayan, 2023

Swati Narayan asserts the moral right to be identified as the author of this work.

ISBN: 9789357769983

10 9 8 7 6 5 4 3 2 1

The views and opinions expressed in this work are the author's own and the facts are as reported by her, and the publisher is in no way liable for the same.

All rights reserved

Typeset by SÜRYA, New Delhi

Printed at Parksons Graphics Pvt. Ltd

No part of this book may be reproduced, or stored in a retrieval system, or transmitted in any form or by any means, electronic, mechanical, photocopying, recording, or otherwise, without express written permission of the publisher.

For my grandmothers

'Courage calls to courage everywhere,
and its voice cannot be denied'
— Millicent Fawcett (1847–1929),
suffragette, artist and writer

CONTENTS

Foreword by Jean Drèze   *xiii*

1. A Human Development Puzzle   3
2. India Trumped?   19
3. Eastern Neighbours: Ear to the Ground   43
4. Bangladesh   71
5. Nepal   99
6. Bihar   131
7. Southern Supermodels:
   Sri Lanka, Kerala and Tamil Nadu   155
8. The Price of Inequality   193

Appendices   199
Notes   224
Bibliography   298
Acknowledgements   333
Index   337

Foreword

FEW OBSERVERS ANTICIPATED, in the early 1990s, that Bangladesh would have a lower child mortality rate than India ten years down the line. At that time, India's per-capita GDP was not only much higher but also growing faster than that of Bangladesh. Child mortality was lower in India and it looked like the gap was all set to widen in India's favour. Yet the opposite happened: India was neatly leap-frogged.

When evidence of this emerged, about twenty years ago, it looked like a temporary anomaly. India, with its higher per-capita GDP, faster growth rate, higher social spending and robust democratic institutions seemed bound to take the lead again sooner or later. Instead, more evidence kept emerging that Bangladesh was overtaking India in critical aspects of human development: not only child mortality but also child development generally as well as life expectancy, fertility, sanitation, school participation, gender equity and more. In some respects, the gap looked truly embarrassing for India. Sanitation is a prime example: by 2011, open defecation had virtually disappeared in Bangladesh, but it was still rampant in India.

The plot thickened when it turned out, about ten years ago, that Nepal too was rapidly catching up with India and even overtaking it in some of these critical fields. That, again, looked like a temporary anomaly, but it is yet to go away. There is something truly puzzling here, considering Nepal's minuscule per-capita GDP.

Efforts to understand these patterns have tended to focus on what is happening in Bangladesh or Nepal. For instance, Bangladesh has won much appreciation for its low-cost public-health interventions, from oral rehydration therapy to universal child vaccination. This is surely one part of the story. But what if the main clue lies in India more than in Bangladesh or Nepal?

When the attention turns to India, an elephant quickly enters the room: social inequality. India is mired in a unique morass of interdependent inequalities, starting with its pernicious caste system. Inequality, of course, permeates South Asia and not India alone, but India seems to be the champion. Can this explain why the progress of social development in India is so slow despite economic growth being so fast? It seems to help, at the very least. As recent research has shown, for instance, India's continued failure to eliminate open defecation has something to do with the difficulties of turning sanitation into a widely-shared social responsibility in a country where disposing of shit was traditionally considered to be the job of specific, despised castes. Similarly, the poor nutrition of Indian children clearly has a lot to do with the extreme disempowerment of young women in Indian society.

There are other adverse connections between social inequality and human development. For instance, we can think of human development as an outcome of various forms of social cooperation. And social cooperation can be quite difficult when the society is not only divided but also stratified in multiple ways. Just to mention one simple example, think of what India would be like if parents, teachers and administrators cooperated to ensure the best possible education for all the country's children. Our schools would be transformed. Given the wide-ranging personal and social roles of elementary education, this would also change the country and people's lives. The atmosphere of India's schooling system, however, is anything but cooperative. The system, curriculum included, is designed to pick and help the winners—the small minority of privileged children who are being prepared for India's elite institutions of higher education. Upper-caste teachers are not always convinced that education is important for underprivileged children. And the wide social distance between teachers and poor parents, especially mothers, also makes it difficult to foster active parent-teacher associations or school management committees. In that environment, it is perhaps not surprising that India is making slow progress towards universal quality education.

Swati Narayan has been exploring some of these connections for many years, based on careful research as well as intensive fieldwork in India, Bangladesh and Nepal. In this book, she presents a lively account of her findings, addressed to a wide audience. Her work sheds light on the price of inequality in South Asia, and India in particular, but it also points to the possibility of change: from Kerala to Nepal, struggles against social inequality have often proved rewarding.

Understanding comparative experiences of human development and their social context is not an easy task. Some pieces of the puzzle are bound to abscond, and there are many ways of arranging the rest. Still, the stifling effects of inequality on India's social achievements are hard to miss. Swati Narayan's book exposes this basic connection from many different angles. If you are hungry for 'causal evidence', your stomach may not be full by the end of it. But if you are after food for thought, this book is for you.

Jean Drèze
Visiting Professor, Department of Economics,
Ranchi University

Bangladeshi villagers blush as they recall the contrasts across the border fence

1

A HUMAN DEVELOPMENT PUZZLE

There is no man here poor and abject
Nor is there any, full of riches and money
Here some do not eat cast off rice-sweepings
And some all the cream and honey

– 'Shamyo' (Equality),
Kazi Nazrul Islam (1899-1976),
Bangladeshi Poet

ONE SUMMER AFTERNOON, we carefully crossed the mud ledge around picturesque, water-soaked Bangladeshi paddy fields. We headed towards the international border. After some time, a knot of curious local villagers in colourful lungis began to tail us. To break the ice, I casually asked them if they had ever noticed any interesting contrasts through the border fence between their Bangladeshi side and the Indian side. They burst out laughing. 'Every morning, we still see Indians take a dump in the open fields'.[1]

This bonhomie with absolute strangers was wholly

unexpected. As an Indian doctoral student, I was travelling in the remote Panchagarh district of Bangladesh.[2] My Bengali translator Safiq (pronounced Sho-phe-kh) was from Dhaka University.[3]

One of the remote villages we had moved into was so close to the Indian border that my Airtel mobile phone had suddenly beeped and come back to life. Still, initially, we had received a hostile reception there. No family was willing to host us, which was puzzling, as we had always been able to find friendly homes in other villages. Then the mystery unravelled. Local elections were a few days away and the villagers had heard through the grapevine that we were spies—that is, election observers. Still, I was determined to find a way to stay on. Public transport was patchy and our options few. The village had been selected at random from census records for my survey, so it had to be this one. Safiq and I just sat in the bazaar patiently with all our bags and waited for the tide to turn.

A hearty roadside meal of coarse rice, mosur dal (lentils) and aloo bhorta (spicy mashed potatoes) fuelled our spirits. A few hours later, a cyclist arrived with the good news that a widow was willing to host us in her spare room. From her home, in the clear night sky, we could see the flickering floodlights from the border watch towers.

Oddly, in this particular stretch, the international border fence had been built 50 metres inside Bangladesh. So, every morning, the Indian Border Security Force (BSF) guards would open the fence gates and let in a few Bangladeshi farmers whose fields fell on the Indian side. Every evening, after another headcount and thorough check at the gate, these farmers would return to their homes in Bangladesh.

Many villagers told us that they sorely missed an era when the border was fully open. The elder folk had cherished memories of crossing over to meet their relatives in nearby Siliguri city and Darjeeling hill station.

Now, at any border village that we were surveying from our list, when people learnt that I was an Indian, they immediately threatened to call the police. This was a common joke till I reassured them that I had a passport and visa and did not jump the fence illegally. Safiq was quite scared of going anywhere near the border. He kept quoting the poignant line from the popular Bollywood film *Bajrangi Bhaijan* starring actor Salman Khan, '*Pehle woh shoot karenge aur phir aatma ko poochhenge kaun se side se aaye thhe*' (first they [the border guards] will shoot and then ask the departed soul which side of the border it hailed from).

The contrasts between the two sides are visible in so many ways. However, Indians seem to have a deeply outdated and distorted idea about the achievements of our next-door neighbour because of these travel restrictions across borders.

Two-thirds of Indians and Bangladeshis live in villages. Unlike India, though, most Bangladeshi villages we saw in Panchagarh district usually had some agro-processing industries.[4] The last village we'd surveyed had a dusty jute mill, a smelly fertiliser factory and a production unit for organic manure. The village we were currently staying in had a poultry unit for eggs and chicken and another manufacturing plant with assembly lines to process tea. Unlike India, where tea is mostly cultivated in large estates, individual Bangladeshi farmers in this area grew tea in their small chai bagans (tea gardens). The driver of the 'van' (battery-operated cycle cart), who had driven us that morning to the processing unit, too had his own tea field. He was really happy with the money he had earned for the leaves he had sold the previous day. We also saw a stream of local farmers driving into the production unit in small trucks brimming with tea leaves. Two women immediately piled these fresh leaves into large coolers for preservation till the factory reopened in the peak season. As we entered the premises, the intoxicating aroma of tea enveloped us.

Another striking contrast, to my Indian eyes, was sanitation. Even the humblest of homes we stayed in had squeaky-clean toilets. Purchasing the cheapest toilets in Bangladesh costs even less than Chinese mobile phones. Local entrepreneurs have designed them to be odour-free, with simple mechanical trapdoors to seal the plastic pans from buzzing flies.[5] Most of these rural toilets do not have doors. Instead, lungis hang as curtains to reduce costs. The Bangladeshi local government also distributes free cement rings to build toilets, unlike India which gives modest and often insufficient cash grants. So, even poor Bangladeshi families are keen to build low-cost, hygienic toilets.[6]

Thus, a decade before prime minister Narendra Modi launched his 2014 Swachh Bharat Abhiyan[7] (SBA, or the Clean India Campaign), defecating in the open was largely a forgotten memory in Bangladesh.[8] On the other hand, in the twenty-first century, even with India's missions to the moon and superpower ambitions, the ground reality is that one in every four rural homes has no toilet.[9]

Since economic liberalisation in the 1990s, Indians have, on average, grown much richer than their Bangladeshi and Nepali neighbours in terms of purchasing power.[10] The Indian home minister has threatened that 'Not even a bird will be allowed from across the border'.[11] Puzzlingly then, in recent years, many poorer neighbours have quietly overtaken India on several social development indicators.

Until the 1980s, for example, Indian women on average lived longer than most of their South Asian sisters across borders. But, in the last twenty-five years, the tables have turned. By 2021, women in almost every country in South Asia—Sri Lanka, Bangladesh, Nepal, Maldives and even Bhutan—were expected to live longer than Indian women.[12]

This is an unexpected reversal of fortunes. Almost fifty years ago, most of these countries, except Sri Lanka, were worse off than India. Now, most neighbours have overtaken India in life spans and many other social indicators. For example, in every single South Asian country, except Pakistan, fewer children are too thin or too short for their age than in India.[13] Similarly, now more Bangladeshis are literate than Indians. A greater share of girls are also in secondary schools. Even Afghanistan, before the takeover by the Taliban, had a larger share of women in the workforce than India.[14] From healthcare to education and nutrition to gender equality, most Indian neighbours are sprinting ahead in social development, at least in their rapid speed of improvement.

1.1: **Number of years a newborn girl can expect to live**[15]

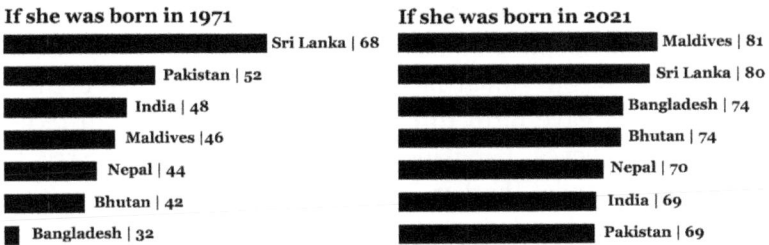

Source: World Development Indicators, 30 June 2023 version

Economist Jean Drèze, my doctoral co-guide, had spotted early signs of this puzzle nearly twenty years ago. In 2004, he wrote, 'India has been neatly leap-frogged, that too during a period when economic growth was much faster in India than in Bangladesh'.[16] With characteristic humour, his long-time co-author Amartya Sen even quipped that 'self-assured commentators who saw Bangladesh as a "basket case" not many years ago could not have expected that the country would jump out of the basket and start sprinting ahead'.[17]

This unique puzzle of India's poorer neighbours racing ahead in different aspects of human development is also a worldwide exception. Typically, for example, citizens in richer countries live longer.[18] But, both Nepalis and Bangladeshis, despite being poorer, do far better than expected. Even life spans in some regions of the United States with large African-American populations, such as the Mississippi Delta, is lower than in Bangladesh or Nepal.[19] In fact, Bangladesh has nearly doubled the average life expectancy of women in less than fifty years. To put this in context, England only achieved this feat at a glacial pace over the course of a century.[20]

Seventy-eight-year-old grandmother Haseena Khatun[21] has reaped the fruits of these sweeping changes. She was born in the Bengal province of British India. After the 1947 Partition, she told me that her village became part of East Pakistan. At the end of the bloody 1971 Liberation War, she became a citizen of the new country Bangladesh. Haseena also remembers the traumatic 1974 famine when her family survived only on gumar-bhat, or rice gruel. In her eventful life, Haseena gave birth to eleven children at home. In recent years, she believes, Bangladeshi healthcare has progressed by leaps and bounds. 'Earlier health facilities were so far. Now they are very close,' she believes.

In India, on the other hand, extreme contradictions flourish. Tall skyscrapers of opulent prosperity and dark rural hovels with intense poverty coexist. A newborn girl in the southern state of Kerala in 2018 could expect, like Haseena, to live to the ripe age of seventy-eight years—two years more than American men.[22] At the same time, girls born in the north Indian states of Bihar and Uttar Pradesh are likely to survive an entire decade less.

The pandemic has also deepened these stark inequalities within and across the borders. Even as most of the world shut down, Bangladesh ran its factories in shifts to record positive economic growth. The Nepali Supreme Court ordered all COVID-19 treatments to be free to protect the right to health.[23] Bhutan, of course, was a role model. The prime minister, a surgeon, ensured that there were only twenty-one pandemic deaths with one of the fastest vaccination drives in the world.[24]

In contrast, India is estimated to have had the largest number of COVID-19 excess deaths in the world.[25] The second wave, in particular, was catastrophic, with crematoriums in New Delhi running out of space and abandoned bodies floating on the Ganges. For those on the margins, the pandemic has been a tsunami that has battered both lives and livelihoods. With schools closed and hospitals overstretched,[26] the contagion has also single-handedly wiped away years of progress against poverty and turned back the clock on human development.[27]

The microscopic virus has also unmasked previously cloaked inequalities within India.[28] After the prime minister announced the abrupt lockdown, the upper and middle classes banged pots and pans in their high-rise balconies in appreciation. Still, the desperate exodus of millions of working-class migrants—stranded in cities without food, shelter and emotional solace—back to their villages on foot, cycle, buses and trains in appalling conditions, haunted even their conscience.

Natural calamities are typical stress tests that challenge the strength and soul of nations. Isn't it odd then that there was no panic-induced migrant crisis in any other country apart from India anywhere else in the world? So, the crux of the South Asian puzzle is: why have some countries lagged behind severely in human development while others have unexpectedly forged ahead? Could the historical burden of thick layers of inequalities cemented across generations be the reason for India's slow and lopsided social development?

EXTREME INEQUALITIES

Her sleeveless dress and quiet confidence were a breath of fresh air in the dusty, ramshackle home. Most of the other women in this family, from the Dom caste, were dressed in crumpled saris. Renu's husband, Jitu, too, in his smart shorts, looked completely out of place in this remote Bihari village.[29] After we struck up a conversation, I realised that the young couple had just crossed the open border, less than a kilometre away, from Nepal to Bihar on a day trip to visit their family.

The contrasts between these relatives who lived on different sides of the international border could not have been starker. In Kathmandu, Renu worked in a private canteen, while Jitu was a mechanic. The young couple were upwardly mobile and in good health and spirits. As a Nepali, Renu's education in government schools had been free until grade eight. Every time her nine-month-old infant fell ill, she confidently took her to a nearby government health post for free treatment. The brimming self-assurance of this bright, young Dalit couple was not an exception. Since the return of democracy in 2006, as my research even a decade later showed, Nepal has witnessed an unmistakeable improvement in caste and gender equations.[30]

Their Indian relatives, on the other hand, were struggling to eke out a living. Renu's sister-in-law Malati, who was born in Nepal and had shifted to India two decades ago after marriage, complained about the caste discrimination that her children faced in school. She also confided that she was petrified of her family falling ill. In this Bihari hinterland, there were no health centres nearby, nor were free medicines available. In fact, the larger family had gathered to mourn the death of her brother-in-law, who had died of liver cirrhosis. Though alcohol was banned in the state, spurious liquor flowed freely. In 2022, journalist M.N. Parth wrote about families in Uttar Pradesh who routinely cross the border to go to Nepal, as healthcare was cheaper and better there.[31] For these Indian families, the closure of the international border due to COVID-19 proved tragic.

This uneven progress in the quality of healthcare, education and life chances in India compared to its poorer neighbours like

A Human Development Puzzle

Nepal and Bangladesh was precisely the puzzle my five-year doctoral research aimed to probe. If the lowest tier of Dalits living in India's neighbouring countries were so clearly able to lead a healthier, more educated, better life, how had this historic transformation unfolded? Why had this progress not been replicated across India? Why do Bihari Dalits, especially most Doms and Musahars, at the bottom of the ladder, live in such grinding poverty?

I delved deeper into this question, with extensive fieldwork across India's borders. In time, it became obvious that the main culprits in India were the multiple layers of severe inequalities that aggravate one another. This book focuses on only three of the most extreme axes of these inequalities—class, caste and gender—to understand why India lags behind.

Wealth inequality in India is now, without a doubt, among the worst in the world.[32] The rich and the poor live in completely different Indias, and the twain rarely meet except, perhaps, at the traffic signal. Since 2016, when wealth tax was abolished, India has created more billionaires than France, Switzerland and Sweden combined. Despite the pandemic, Gautam Adani's—the richest Asian and Indian—fortune skyrocketed more than twelve times from $9 billion in 2020 to $120 billion in 2022. In these two years, his companies won handsome government contracts for mines, electricity, airports, expressways and ports. In 2022, *Forbes* and *Bloomberg* even crowned him the third richest person in the world ahead of Bill Gates and Jeff Bezos.[33] But, in early 2023, after serious allegations of financial fraud, the stock prices of Adani's companies tumbled.[34]

In this time, under one of the strictest lockdowns in the world,[35] up to 200 million Indians sank below the poverty line.[36] Eighty-four per cent of Indian families also saw a fall in their income.[37] In this 'other' India, a few years ago, eleven-year-old Santoshi died of starvation in Jharkhand, begging for 'bhat-bhat' (rice, rice) from her helpless mother, who could only offer her warm water with a few tea leaves.[38] Harrowing starvation deaths are reported with regular frequency in the Indian media. In 2018, a village I visited was still in mourning. Most of the neighbours, who also lived in straw huts covered with dried leaves and bits of plastic, were themselves on the brink of survival.[39] Inequality is now so skewed that the bottom half of India's population has to survive on only 6 per cent of the nation's wealth.[40]

For generations, the caste system has also magnified these extreme economic inequalities. At least 41 per cent of India's wealth is now in the hands of the forward castes, double their population share.[41] On the other hand, is it a coincidence that Santoshi's family is Dalit, with only a few doors to knock on for help?[42]

When a family belonging to a marginalised caste tries to live with dignity and manages to prosper, the backlash is swift and brutal. In Rajasthan, nine-year-old Indra Kumar Meghwal was recently beaten to death by his teacher for drinking water from an earthen pot reserved for upper castes.[43] A few months earlier, upper caste villagers had stabbed to death a Dalit health worker Jitendra Meghwal, only because they envied his stylish handlebar moustache and secure government job.[44] As Babasaheb Ambedkar, the architect of India's constitution, made clear, the caste system openly justifies this 'suppression of one class by another'.[45] Poverty in India largely remains hereditary along caste and religious fault lines, with limited social mobility.[46] The discrimination is so insidious that Dalits and Adivasis have also lived shorter lives, according to data for the last two decades (although this is perhaps true for centuries).[47]

Finally, and most crucially, there is extreme gender inequality. India is among the most unequal countries in the world for women.[48] Grisly murders and gruesome rapes dominate news headlines month after month. Patriarchy is so acute that gender discrimination begins even before birth. Forty-six million women are 'missing' from India's population, especially due to the sex-selective abortion of female foetuses in the last four decades and the neglect of girls as infants.[49] Since the turn of the millennium, low child sex ratios have also spread to the prosperous regions of western and southern India.[50] Even as adults, one of every four women in India cannot read and three do not earn an income. Their dependency on men is so extreme that few rural women get a chance to flourish outside the confines of the four walls of their kitchens or homes.[51]

This book argues that the main reason why India lags behind its neighbours is the vice-like grip of systemic and, at times, barbaric inequalities, which are now on the rise.[52] The differences in the life chances of the rich and the poor, men and women, Brahmins and Doms and, for that matter, Keralites and Biharis, Hindus and Muslims across India are so sharp that, until these inequalities are bridged, it is impossible for the nation as a whole to prosper, let alone be a world leader. Worse, these overlapping layers of multiple inequalities compound one another. For example, Dalit women in northern India face the most atrocities, with the highest incidence of rape.[53]

Of course, a few exceptions do break through the shackles. Of India's 166 billionaires, one is a Dalit.[54] Since the affirmative action of the 1990s, there has also been a 'silent revolution' of upward mobility among the educated backward classes.[55] But, structurally, the claws of casteism, patriarchy and feudalism have gripped India with such ferocity over generations that the majority of the population remains subjugated in one form or another.

In contrast, even South Asian neighbours that are poorer than India, such as Bangladesh and Nepal, have lower income inequalities.⁵⁶ Nepal has only one billionaire and Bangladesh none. In the last few decades, most of India's neighbours have also sped ahead in improving the lives of the majority of their citizens, particularly the poor. These relative successes have been achieved largely due to their ability to curb inequalities.

THE RIGHT TO EQUALITY

Among developed countries, citizens of more equal societies tend to have better rates of health, education and child development. The Scandinavian countries, such as Norway, Sweden, Finland and Denmark, not only have the least income inequalities but also score higher on human development.⁵⁷ On the other hand, highly unequal countries, such as the United States, tend to grapple with more social challenges—from homelessness and obesity to gun violence.⁵⁸ So high inequality often leads to low human development.⁵⁹ Inequality also undermines democracy in multiple ways. For example, 21 million largely illiterate, impoverished women are missing from India's electoral roles.⁶⁰ On the other hand, 90 per cent of Indian parliamentarians are millionaires. Forty-three per cent even face criminal charges.⁶¹

Babasaheb Ambedkar had warned that 'democracy is not a plant which grows everywhere'.⁶² He believed that democracies, by definition, should promote equality through 'a form and a method of government whereby revolutionary changes in the economic and social life of the people are brought about without bloodshed'.

But have democratic governments in South Asia been able to transform deeply entrenched caste, class and gender inequalities? The main argument of this book is that frontrunner regions in the neighbourhood, especially Bangladesh, Nepal and Sri Lanka, have been able to gradually, over centuries, dilute such inequalities. Three catalysts have fuelled their progressive transformations—public services, social movements and women's agency. Bangladesh has been a trailblazer in the doorstep delivery of welfare services, from healthcare to micro-credit (see chapter 4). Nepal has also slowly built its welfare state since the return of democracy in the 1990s (see chapter 5). Sri Lanka (see chapter 7), too, has long provided free healthcare. Education from schools to universities is also entirely free.[63]

For generations, radical social movements in South Asia have acted as catalysts to usher in greater social equality. This book also examines how three unique historical waves of elite displacement in Bangladesh have substantially reduced class inequalities. Nepal is also in the midst of transformative social change, especially after the Maoist People's War. In Sri Lanka, over a century from 1820 to 1920, left-wing trade union and religious reform movements have been influential agents of change.

Women are supposed to 'hold up half the sky'.[64] In modern Bangladesh, there has, without a doubt, been a distinct change in gender relations.[65] In Nepal, too, especially after the Maoist guerrilla army began to recruit women, traditional gender stereotypes have been quietly abandoned across the board.[66] Sri Lanka has had a rich history of gender transformations too. After all, Sri Lankan women were the first in Asia to earn the right to vote.[67]

India, on the other hand, is a land of extreme contrasts. In southern India, over the course of the century, a series of radical, anti-caste movements have been at the heart of Kerala and Tamil Nadu's transformation to reduce the 'elite bias'.[68] Women's movements have also been at the forefront of social change.

At the other extreme, backward states such as Bihar lie at the nadir of social spending.[69] As my travels confirmed at every bumpy turn, government schools, hospitals and public transport suffer from sore neglect.[70] Northern India also boils with caste discrimination. For generations, the forward castes have monopolised education and lucrative occupations.[71] Despite peasant movements, land reforms have been largely inadequate. The feudal hegemony of the elite classes remains unshaken, especially in the Gangetic plain, with its grinding poverty. Patriarchy dominates every sphere of life.

On an average, therefore, even after decades of a booming Indian economy, one out of every three preschool children is stunted in height,[72] more than 50 million students cannot read their school textbooks[73] and more than 250 million adults are illiterate.[74]

DECODING THE PUZZLE

In 1905, the visionary Bangladeshi feminist writer, Begum Rokeya Sakhawat Hossain, wrote *Sultana's Dream*. This futuristic short story is set in an imaginary 'Ladyland' where only women rule, and create fantastical inventions like solar ovens, while men care for the children at home.[75] Modern Bangladesh does not exactly mirror Sultana's dream. But India's poorer neighbours are quietly leading the way in bridging inequalities of class, caste and gender. Bangladeshi and Nepali women, for example, are more likely to work outside the home and hold seats in Parliament.[76] Their children are also less likely to be underweight and are expected to spend more years in school.[77]

There is much for India to learn from its poorer South Asian neighbours.

Local boats are one of the main modes of transport in Bihar's flood-prone Kishanganj district

2

INDIA TRUMPED?

> Ill fares the land, to hastening ills a prey,
> Where wealth accumulates and men decay:
> – *The Deserted Village*,
> Oliver Goldsmith[1]

THE HEALTH CENTRE was a joke. The only living beings on the premises were grazing in the courtyard. 'The sacred cows are the doctors,' laughed my research coordinator, Ismael. The entire building was dilapidated—floors broken, walls collapsing, paint peeling and weeds growing in the rooms and roof. In the village we were visiting, this was the only health centre within a kilometre radius.[2] The doctors and health workers had obviously abandoned this workplace despite continuing to draw a hefty government salary. The only other health facility was more than 14 kilometres away.[3] Bihar does have better health centres. But in the Muslim-majority Kishanganj district, most government services we saw were similarly in shambles.

We also went to the homes of two accredited social health activists (ASHAs) who worked in the village as doorstep health workers. Neither of them had received any medicines for two years and we heard a litany of complaints. Their kits only had old oral rehydration salt (ORS) packets and a few government brands of condoms and contraceptive pills.

I was even more shocked when I walked up to a neighbouring house. Peeping through the window, I saw a severely disabled boy huddled inside a dark room. I was heartbroken to find that he had been kept hidden away like this. His mother, with teary eyes, asked us if we could help in any way. Unfortunately, I had to tell her that neither of us were medical practitioners but that we would love to speak to her son. When Bhim was brought to the courtyard, he flashed an unforgettable smile. I impressed upon his mother that, ideally, he should be exposed to some sunlight daily.

Bhim's unspeakably poor parents were at their wit's end. There was no healthcare facility in the vicinity. They loved their son, but simply did not know what to do for him. I felt just as helpless. On the spur of the moment, I asked them to stand together for family photo. Later, I was able to print the grainy image along with a disability pension form to hand over to Bhim's mother. But I knew fully well that, at best, these were only symbolic gestures of comfort.

This was just one home. During our survey in Bihar, we met many families in similar or even worse predicaments, struggling with chronic ailments. They wage a daily battle against the criminal neglect of public healthcare in India. The poorest families pay the indescribably heaviest price.

To reach this distant village, we had crossed a river on a precarious boat that two men somehow rowed using only bamboo poles. The narrow deck of the dinghy had been packed with fifteen-odd bicycles and a few motorcycles (including our own). A bevy of weary villagers with their jute sacks, chickens and household wares had jostled for space. It was a miracle we hadn't toppled over. In the midst of the monsoon, such rickety boats were the primary means of transport across the flooded plains of Bihar.

Travelling in the hilly regions of Nepal was equally tricky. One of the randomly selected villages for my survey was said to be three hours away from the district headquarters. But the journey ultimately took seven hours. After two hours on the rickety bus, we came across the raging Kamlamai river, which had flooded due to the rains. The veteran driver calmly stopped the bus midstream. Two conductors stepped out and, walking with meditative steps in the rushing current, surveyed the riverbed. After three hours of these rudimentary explorations, the driver finally figured out the best route to navigate the bus across the river. As passengers stuck inside, we had our stomachs in knots. Finally, when the bus reached the shore, all of us broke into a spontaneous round of claps.

Despite the perilous terrain, this far-removed Nepali village had relatively good healthcare, in contrast to Bihar next door. When I suffered a sudden bout of severe vertigo, my Nepali translator Bijeta literally saved my life. The private pharmacy she took me to was a blessing, even with its limited stock of medicines. The shop even had beds in a room at the back to administer saline drips to patients. Later, when we finally reached the well-stocked government clinic an hour away, we met the health worker Gopal. Though he was not a doctor, he had seventeen years of experience under his belt. Gopal used his stethoscope and blood pressure instrument to check my extremely low BP. Both his medical skills and endearing pidgin English lifted our spirits instantly.

Many health posts in Nepal are also managed by junior doctors. Unlike India, the Nepali government insists that all private medical colleges offer some students free education with full scholarship. After completion of their degrees, these young doctors have to serve in rural areas as a part of their two-year mandatory government service bond.[4]

Equally impressive were the government 'birthing centres', which were open round the clock. At one centre, we met two midwives, Anita Dahal and Sujata Adhikari, each with an impressive twenty-two years of experience. As we sat there, I watched Anita give a contraceptive injection to a village woman. The centre had all the essential medical equipment on my checklist, except for oxygen supply. For the last two decades, this birthing centre had also been distributing free medicines. As I began to inspect their capsule strips, I realised that many of them had been made in India. Ironically, I had rarely seen these medicines in Bihari health centres only a few kilometres away across the border. As we were preparing to leave, Anita said something which also caught me completely off-guard. She reminded me that, as midwives, they were dedicated lifesavers, who had been gravely affected by the 2015 economic blockade of Nepal along the Indian border.[5] The stoppage of transport had crippled the Nepali economy for six months, disrupted the supply of medicines, affected 90 per cent of families with fuel shortages and severely endangered lives.

Her censure was true on so many levels. It often seems obvious that India has increasingly lost the plot, both across borders and within the country. Until the 1990s, fewer newborn children in India died as compared to its South Asian neighbours, except for Sri Lanka. Since then, the tide has turned. Nepal, Bangladesh, Bhutan and Maldives have raced ahead. Birthing centres are only one of the many practical, low-cost strategies that India's neighbours have invested in to save precious infant lives. These rapid improvements also clearly show that, even without fast economic growth, it is possible for poor countries to transform the quality of life of their citizens.[6]

But India's focus in the last few decades has largely been only on rapid—and, unfortunately, skewed—economic growth.

Thirty years ago, an average Indian earned at least 40 per cent more than a Nepali in purchasing power terms. By 2020, this had soared to almost double. Similarly, as per the Maddison Database, as early as 2008, an average Indian had the kind of real incomes that ordinary Bangladeshis could earn only in 2018.[7] Still, both these poorer countries, Nepal and Bangladesh, have surpassed India on several social indicators.

To make matters worse, recently, the Indian government seems to have plunged into a habit of knee-jerk denial.[8] They invariably criticise every international scorecard that paints India in a poor light. The government has rejected the Global Hunger Index as 'an attempt to tarnish the image of the country,'[9] and rubbished the World Health Organisation's estimate of excess deaths due to the pandemic.[10] They have questioned the motives of even the most reputed United Nations agencies.[11] Unless the doctor admits that the patient is sick, there is no hope of finding a cure. Still, the government has flatly refused to believe the clearly mounting international statistical evidence on the superior performance of India's neighbours on social development. Some economists have even dismissed the acceleration of India's South Asian neighbours on social development indicators as 'plain wrong'.[12] But their counter-claims that 'Indians and Bangladeshis enjoy the same life expectancy at birth' are absolutely factually incorrect. On the contrary, the World Development Indicators database clearly shows that, in every single year since 1988, both Bangladeshi men and women were expected to live longer than their Indian neighbours.[13]

SO CLOSE YET SO DIFFERENT

The South Asian enigma thus remains—why does India lag behind her neighbours on many social development indicators? Why has the Bangladeshi government consistently invested in healthcare? How have Nepali women in the Himalayan country raced ahead of Indian women in education and employment? Political sociologist Theda Skocpol emphasises the timing and sequence of landmark historical events that usually usher in social changes. Violent conflicts, regime changes, social movements and even humanitarian disasters, such as famines and pandemics, often mark turning points that could unexpectedly promote social equality.[14] So, my research maps the evolution of these types of social changes in India's neighbours over long historical stretches of time.[15]

For cross-country comparisons, the Mill's Method of Logic[16] helps to easily spot differences in comparable cases. For example, economists Acemoglu and Robinson, in the chapter 'So Close and Yet So Different' of their book *Why Nations Fail*, compared two cities—Nogales in America and its namesake Nogales in Mexico on the other side of the international border. They aimed to understand 'how could the two halves of what is essentially the same city be so different?'[17]

My analysis is similarly divided into two geographic comparisons of contiguous regions in specific time periods.[18] I have named them 'Eastern Neighbours' and 'Southern Supermodels'.

The differences between India and its Eastern Neighbours form the core analysis of this book.[19] The Indian state of Bihar shares similarities in history, geography and culture with next-door neighbours Nepal and Bangladesh.[20] Yet these neighbours have outperformed Bihar in the last half a century and raced ahead on several human development indicators. I travelled across these three neighbouring regions to conduct a one-of-a-kind primary survey of eighty villages. Apart from my translators, I also trained and supervised forty local women who spoke regional dialects to conduct the survey across these three countries.

However, northern and southern India are often poles apart.

2.1: Eastern Neighbours and Southern Supermodels

So, in the case of the Southern Supermodels, the comparison focuses on the 'similarities in similar cases' across borders.[21] The nagging question I was trying to answer was, historically how did these neighbouring regions of Sri Lanka, Kerala and Tamil Nadu progress nearly simultaneously in social achievements despite being part of entirely separate political regions?[22] This analysis compares Tamil Nadu (1916 to present), Kerala (1820–1975) and Sri Lanka (1830–1977), in the heydays of their human development acceleration, when this progress was most visible. For this largely historical research spanning two centuries, I pored over archives, old colonial reports and books in dusty libraries.

India and its Neighbours

At nearly every conference, I am asked how individual states within India can be compared with its neighbouring countries.

My response is simple. India is usually compared with China, as both these Asian giants have more than a billion citizens. Within South Asia, on the other hand, India's population is eight times greater than Bangladesh and forty-seven times greater than Nepal. So, comparing India as a whole with these smaller South Asian countries is like comparing watermelons with grapes. Hence, analysing individual states within India with neighbouring countries of similar size, geography, demography and culture, makes more logical sense.

So, the Eastern Neighbours research appropriately clubs together three geographically contiguous regions—Bihar, Bangladesh and Nepal—which share similar levels of average incomes. Bangladesh, like Bihar, also has one of the highest population densities in the world with families living cheek by jowl. Similar to Nepal, nearly 80 per cent of Biharis also live in rural villages.[23]

Historically, these neighbouring regions have also had porous borders. The Indo–Nepal Peace and Friendship Treaty signed in 1950 and the Nepalese Citizenship Act enacted in 1952 opened the doors for large-scale migration from India. Since then, hundreds of Bihari families have migrated, settled and acquired citizenship in the Nepali Terai region and are now called Madhesis. These border areas are so similar that my field notes from Nepal are filled with descriptions such as 'our hosts are Mahatos and they speak Maithili. It feels like we are in Bihar.'

Similarly, in the analysis of the Southern Supermodels, the

regions of Kerala, Tamil Nadu and Sri Lanka have 'entangled histories'. For example, the Malabar district which is now in Kerala, was once a part of the British colonial Madras province. The rest of the province was absorbed into Tamil Nadu.

Political scientist Yogendra Yadav and his colleagues have aptly described India as a 'state-nation'.[24] The Indian nation is, after all, a collection of diverse states with different languages, ethnicities and cultures.[25] Academic Prerna Singh also argues that Indian states with stronger regional solidarity and pride tend to have better human development.[26] Hence, comparing different Indian states with neighbouring countries makes much sense.

Bihar or West Bengal?

Another question that I am always asked is why do I compare the Eastern Neighbours with Bihar and not West Bengal. The main reason is that in 2014 (when this research started), Bihar's average income was similar to Bangladesh and Nepal, though slightly lower.[27] However, in terms of purchasing power parity, West Bengalis were, on average, nearly twice as rich as Nepalis and two-thirds as wealthy as Bangladeshis.

During my travels, I also saw these huge economic contrasts firsthand. In the middle of my travels in Bangladesh, I ran out of money and had to make a day trip to India to withdraw cash from an ATM. Starting from one of my survey villages, I changed three vehicles—a cycle cart, bus and electric rickshaw—and eventually crossed the new Banglabandha border at Zero Point on foot. It was a surreal experience, as that particular day also turned out to be the festival of Holi. On the Indian side, in the highly developed tourist city of Siliguri in West Bengal, even the border guards had colour on their faces and most tourists on the streets were drunk.[28] Apart from the differences in clothes, religions and festivities, the most striking contrast lay in West Bengal's economic prosperity. Shops, bank ATMs and even malls mushroomed in Siliguri. Cars, rickshaws and motorcycles were everywhere. In comparison, the rural landscape that I had left half an hour away in Bangladesh was immensely modest. West Bengal, after more than three decades of communist governments, is also an anomaly in the region, with distinctly better social indicators. On the other hand, Bihar is more comparable to both the Eastern Neighbours and similar to the Indian heartland BIMARU states.[29]

Also, though Bangladesh and West Bengal share a common language and history, Nepali culture in the Terai region is similar to the flat plains of Bihar. Nepal's international border with Bihar is also 'open' at numerous places, through which Indians like me can easily cross to either side without visas, on foot, rickshaws and horse carts—a priceless advantage for my research.

HUMAN DEVELOPMENT TO HAPPINESS

For starters, before I delve further into my travel adventures across borders, I will systematically analyse with hard facts whether India's neighbours indeed perform better. Do Nepal, Bangladesh and other South Asian neighbours overtake India on some or all indicators? Is their advantage absolute or only in terms of the speed of change? Also, do they surpass only some backward regions of India or the country as a whole? Equally importantly, is there lesser inequality in the quality of life of Bangladeshi and Nepali citizens?

First, let us examine a range of international statistical indicators to measure social well-being in India and its neighbours (table 2.2). But in this dusty terrain, as Albert Einstein observed, 'not everything that counts can be counted.'

Officially, on the United Nations' popular Human

2.2: South Asian Rank and Scores of Countries on Selected Indices

	Human Development Index (HDI), 2021	Multi-Dimensional Poverty Index (MPI), 2023	World Happiness Index, 2020-22	Gender Development Index (GDI), 2021	Global Hunger Index (GHI), 2023	Healthcare Access and Quality Index (HAQ), 2019
Sri Lanka	1 (0.782)	2 (0.011)	3 (4.442)	1 (0.949)	1 (13.3)	2 (60.54)
Maldives	2 (0.747)	1 (0.003)	-	4 (0.925)	-	1 (60.67)
Bhutan	3 (0.666)	-	-	3 (0.937)	-	4 (42.05)
Bangladesh	4 (0.661)	5 (0.104)	4 (4.282)	5 (0.898)	3 (19.0)	3 (44.09)
Nepal	6 (0.602)	4 (0.075)	1 (5.360)	2 (0.942)	2 (15.0)	6 (38.76)
India	5 (0.633)	3 (0.069)	5 (4.036)	6 (0.849)	5 (28.7)	5 (39.16)
Pakistan	7 (0.544)	6 (0.198)	2 (4.555)	7 (0.810)	4 (26.6)	7 (32.44)

Development Index (HDI), there is little difference across South Asia.[30] Predictably, the beautiful island tourist havens, Sri Lanka[31] and the Maldives, are considerably more affluent and also have the highest scores, while Pakistan ranks at the bottom. Nepal is still slightly behind India. But this is only because the HDI combines income and non-income measures. So, India scores well only due to its soaring economic growth rates since the economic liberalisation of 1991. But, due to the twin shocks of demonetisation[32] and the pandemic, in 2021, Bangladesh overtook India on both economic growth and HDI scores. Also, since the 1990s, Nepal and Bangladesh's HDI scores have improved faster than India's. Poorer neighbours are, without a doubt, very quickly catching up.

Within India, the southern states perform better on the sub-national HDI. Kerala, for example, ranks the highest and can be compared to Thailand and Brazil.[33] On the other hand, Bihar, Uttar Pradesh and Jharkhand, with the lowest scores, are similar to Zimbabwe, Angola and Congo in sub-Saharan Africa.[34] Clearly, India is a republic of extreme inequalities.

It is no surprise then that India has the world's largest multi-dimensionally poor citizens. The Multidimensional Poverty Index (MPI) measures a country's population that has been deprived on three parameters—poverty, education and essential services. In the global MPI index released in 2021, both Bangladesh and Nepal did better than India. But in the 2022 and 2023 versions, India had higher scores due to updated demographic data which was not made available by our neighbours.[35] Still, between 2006 to 2016, India was able to halve its MPI score. The poorest communities by geography, caste, religion and age saw the fastest improvement in the intensity of their poverty.[36] This was the result of progressive civil society movements that had pushed for a range of human rights-based laws to reduce deprivation. The National Rural Employment Guarantee Act 2005,[37] the Right to Education

Act 2009 and the National Food Security Act 2013[38] were pioneering statutes, which have had long-term impacts.

Within India, though, there remains a wide disparity in MPI scores. In the last two decades, less than 1 per cent of the population of Kerala and 4 per cent of the population of Tamil Nadu were multi-dimensionally poor, compared to 35 per cent of the population of Bihar. 'Graded inequality' due to caste also affects access to welfare services across India.[39] The most poignant examples are of those on the hunger frontlines. Consistently, for the last two decades, children from Adivasi, Dalit and Other Backward Class (OBC) families have been more likely to be stunted in height.[40] My preliminary analysis also indicates that in the 2015–18 period, three of every four victims of starvation deaths were Dalits, Adivasis or Muslims.[41] In Jharkhand, the daughter of one of the families I visited with fellow activists from the Right to Food Campaign told us, 'My mother had not eaten anything for three days before her death; she had nothing to eat and starved in the piercing cold.'[42] The family belonged to the Birijiya tribe, which has officially been recognised as a 'Particularly Vulnerable Tribal Group'. They were automatically eligible and should have been the first to receive an 'Antyodaya Anna Yojana' food grain ration card meant for the 'poorest of the poor'. But starvation deaths are only the tip of the iceberg. Scores of Indians with the greatest need are unable to demand their most basic rights to welfare lifelines for survival, due to extreme social inequalities. Even after decades of a booming Indian economy, for example, nearly forty per cent of eligible children, pregnant women and breastfeeding mothers do not receive any food from anganwadis (childcare centres).[43] Now, to obscure these inequalities, the Indian government has created its own national MPI, with new indicators, which are estimated to undercount around thirty-seven million poor people.[44] The ground reality, however, is that 74 per cent of Indians cannot afford a healthy diet.[45]

Ironically, despite being poorer, Nepalis, Bangladeshis and Pakistanis are also happier than Indians on the latest World Happiness Index,[46] released in the midst of the pandemic. Worryingly, since 2015, India has joined the club of the fifteen most unhappy countries in the world. On the other hand, after the end of the guerrilla war, Nepal has been among the top twenty countries worldwide which have seen the largest increase in the level of happiness.

Most of all, India is one of the countries that are the most unequal for women. In India, discrimination begins at the stage of the embryo. Because of sex-selective abortion of female foetuses, millions of women are 'missing' from India's population.[47] Since the turn of the millennium, India has also been one of the few developing countries where the percentage of working women has plummeted. In the 1990s, 30 per cent of Indian women earned an income, a figure that plunged to 19 per cent in 2021. Adult women are disappearing from the workforce in factories, offices and malls. Now, there are fewer working Indian women than even Saudi Arabia.[48] The #MeToo movement has also bared the pervasiveness of sexual harassment, from Haryana sports stadiums to Bollywood. The 2023 Global Gender Gap Index released by the World Economic Forum places India twentieth from the bottom, with Afghanistan being the lowest. The glass ceiling is also so rigid that women occupy only 17 per cent of seats in Indian boardrooms compared to 40 per cent in France.[49] On the other hand, the East Asian growth 'miracle' has been associated with large increases in the number of working women.

So, across the board, on thematic indicators from the Gender Development Index (GDI) to the Global Hunger Index (GHI) and the Healthcare Access and Quality Index (HAQ), India is a laggard—not a frontrunner in South Asia and far from being a world leader. There is no doubt that, despite all its wealth, India mostly performs far worse than its poorer neighbours.

It is true that each of these fancy measures is designed subjectively. But all of these long-established international indices could not have been deliberately created only to downscale India. The cold reality is that except for the MPI, India trails Bangladesh, Nepal, or both, on most of these indices.

Sri Lanka,[50] Maldives and Bhutan, also surpass India on several counts. Their citizens are also wealthier, on average. On the other hand, while Pakistan performs worse than India, most of its citizens are also poorer. So, the constant comparison of India with Pakistan in the media is a meaningless distraction. Instead, comparing India with its poorer Eastern Neighbours—Nepal and Bangladesh—would better capture the essence of the South Asian human development puzzle. Despite low incomes, the achievements of these Indian neighbours have been truly exceptional.

MILLENNIALS TO GENERATION Z

Our breathtaking morning walk was across valleys, mountain springs and rickety bridges under a gorgeous sky. With the bright, local village girl Rushilla as our guide, Bijeta and I reached the community-managed Nepali school perched on top of a hill. Many of the teachers and students we met there lived in the nearby Manjhi (Janajati indigenous community) hamlet. So, we walked to their homes to continue our survey. When we reached the hamlet, unlike with the other villages we had visited, we were taken aback. Many men, women and children were wearing torn, unwashed clothes. They had little access to water as the river nearby had run dry and the public tap often did not work. These families were visibly poor, living in tightly clustered houses. A villager showed us how she brewed liquor from rice and sold it in large vats kept outside her home. Even before noon, we'd met many local men who were already drunk on this cheap alcohol.

However, when we went door-to-door to conduct our survey, we were in for a pleasant surprise. Though extremely poor, all the families in this village had excellent access to essential services. Their children studied at the nearby community school and every house had a toilet. Innovatively, many of these toilets also produced biogas from human and animal waste to be used as cooking fuel—one of the most sustainable and cheap sources of energy. A local non-governmental organisation (NGO) had given them subsidised materials and helped them to construct these low-cost dual sanitation-and-fuel solutions. I remembered having seen this ingenious biogas experiment in my childhood at a science exhibition. This was the first time that I was seeing this concept actually being used in a village. I wonder why India's Swachh Bharat Abhiyan for sanitation and the Ujjwala Yojana for clean fuel have missed this golden opportunity to similarly hit two birds with one stone.

Even as they answered our survey questions, two mothers sitting outside their homes continued to breastfeed their children, oblivious to the presence of men. Many women also confirmed that Sudha Ma Tamang, the village health volunteer (swasthya sevika), unfailingly visited their impoverished hamlet every single month. Sudha had earlier told us that she deliberately prioritised the most disadvantaged homes due to their greater need, even if they were located farther away. The villagers also confirmed that she gave pregnant women iron tablets each month and diligently distributed contraceptives and medicines. With this assured access to a variety of essential services—education, healthcare, sanitation and clean fuel—at their very doorstep, it is no wonder that Nepalis, despite their poverty, are racing ahead in human development.

Still, to double-check the success of Nepal and Bangladesh's human development compared to India's, here is a quick glance at national statistics on four thematic areas.

First, the differences between neighbours are most visible in access to education.

There is not much difference between teenage girls of Generation Z in India, Nepal and Bangladesh. In this age group, all three countries have roughly 88–89 per cent literacy. Similarly, millennial women in their twenties also have similar levels of literacy: 68–74 per cent. Only Indian women above the age of thirty are substantially more literate than their Nepali and Bangladeshi sisters. Those in their fifties and sixties, in particular, are twice as likely to be literate.

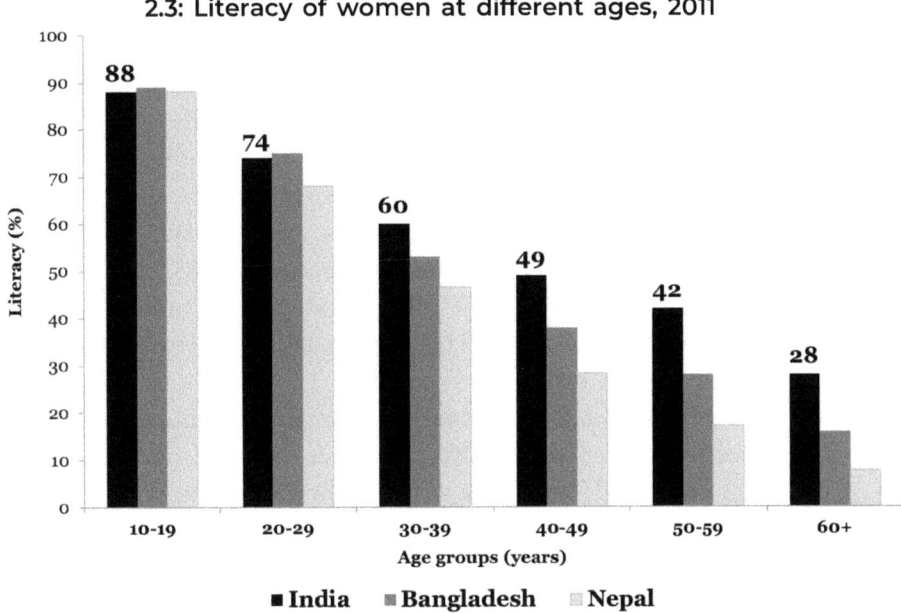

2.3: Literacy of women at different ages, 2011

Source: India, Bangladesh and Nepal: Censuses, 2011

This graph can also be read in the reverse direction, from right to left.[51] So, five decades ago, in the 1970s, when actor Amitabh Bachchan was still an 'angry young man' in his films, Indian teenagers were almost twice as literate as their neighbours. Bangladesh was a young country then, and Nepal was still a monarchy. Since then, Bangladeshi and Nepali women have quickly bridged the literacy gap with their wealthier neighbour. Education of children and adolescents has increased rapidly. Generation Z in these poorer South Asian countries has now quickly caught up with their Indian cousins.

I saw this thirst for education first-hand in rural Bangladesh. In every village home we walked into, invariably, there were children with their heads buried in textbooks, diligently learning their lessons. In the home of one of my hosts, Hillal bhai, every morning, his eight-year-old son Hasan, studying in the second grade, would wake me up from inside my comfortable mosquito net by reading aloud in his bellowing voice. Listening to him, I realised the depth of the scar that the 1971 Bangladeshi Liberation War had left. Hasan read from his history book about the brave battles of the thousands of Mukti Bahini freedom fighters who were martyred before the country finally won its independence. Since its birth fifty years ago, Bangladesh, as a proud, independent nation, has made undeniable progress. Hasan's reading skill was but one testament to this fact.[52]

On the other hand, the quality of Indian education is now so poor that, even before the pandemic, only 27 per cent of rural children of Hasan's age in grade three could read a simple paragraph of the level of grade two in their local language.[53] While in recent decades more children have enrolled in schools, there also remain vast educational inequalities between rich and poor families.[54]

The quality of learning in rural India is abysmal, even at the best of times.[55] On a rainy afternoon in a remote village of Bihar, a wizened grandfather sitting in the narrow porch of his mud house drove home this point to me simply. First, he asked his daughter-in-law, who had studied only till primary school, to read a paragraph, which she did fluently. Then, he asked his grandson, who was in grade 5, to read. The boy stumbled over the words, barely forming sentences, let alone grasping their meaning. Especially after one of the world's longest school closures of two years due to the pandemic, India has now plunged into a mass learning crisis.[56] The latest *Annual Status of Education Report* (ASER) based on a survey conducted by the non-profit Pratham confirms that, after the pandemic, more than half the rural students enrolled in grade 5 and a third in grade 8 aren't even able to read a grade 2 level basic paragraph.

Second, on the health front too, India's neighbours perform better. Of every 1,000 children born in Nepal and Bangladesh, around twenty-nine died before their fifth birthday.[57] In India, the number of deaths was thirty-three. Extraordinarily, since the 1990s, Nepal has been amongst the fastest countries of the developing world to reduce child deaths—even in the thick of a guerrilla war. Nepal and Bangladesh have also been more successful than India in bridging the gap between the rich and the poor in terms of infant mortality. Still, one area where India performs better is in the fewer number of deaths of mothers in childbirth. Since the government introduced cash incentives nearly two decades ago, Indian mothers are more likely to give birth in hospitals or health facilities.[58]

Third, the mysterious 'enigma' of high child malnutrition persists across South Asia.[59] Even Sri Lanka has more underweight children than sub-Saharan Africa. Still, India fares worse than most of its neighbours. Before their sixth birthday, 32 per cent of children in India were found to be too thin for their age as compared to only 22 per cent in Bangladesh and 27 per cent in Nepal.[60] Within India, too, there is extreme inequality in malnutrition. In the poorest families, 43 per cent of children are underweight, more than double than in the case of the richest.[61]

Malnutrition in India often begins even before birth since most Indian women are anaemic. After delivery, many Indian mothers also feed their infants inappropriately. In Bihar, for example, some families we spoke to told us that they give newborn babies cow's or goat's milk for the first three days after birth, due to age-old customs.

The Indian 'Mother's Absolute Affection (MAA)s' coy media campaign to promote breastfeeding, with actor Madhuri Dikshit as the brand ambassador, is a whimper compared to the campaigns across the border.

Bangladesh ran a five-year 'Doctor Apa' (Doctor Elder Sister) mass media campaign that provided information through infomercials on television and radio, loudspeakers, posters and wall paintings. The focus was to educate, especially mothers and mothers-in-law, on breastfeeding. As I saw in most villages, now it is culturally normal for multi-tasking Bangladeshi mothers to breastfeed their infants in public. In addition, a decade ago, in collaboration with some NGOs, the government had hired a temporary cadre of 'poushti apas' (literally, nutrition sisters), who had gone door-to-door to teach mothers how to feed their young children. Mahmuda Begum, one of my hosts, admitted that she, too, used to feed her first child suji (semolina) and maida (refined wheat flour) with honey. But now she knows that breastmilk alone is the best for the first six months. We also saw her feeding mashed food from small bowls to her two-and-a-half-year-old son. She explained, 'The government madam came when I was pregnant to teach us how to take care of and feed our children. We have also seen programmes on television that have educated us on how to feed children nutritious food.' When I asked why she had listened to their advice, she looked genuinely puzzled, 'Shouldn't we listen to the government health workers? The old traditions were not working—there were more deaths of mothers and infants. The children catch a cold if we follow our mother-in-law's wisdom. So, we started to listen to the health workers instead. They also gave us injections.' These poushti apas had taught mothers about the importance of breastfeeding. They had also demonstrated how to feed older children home-cooked complementary foods, that included mashed fish and eggs.

Fourth, rural Indians continue to use the great outdoors for defecation.[62] Women suffer the most from this indignity. The SBA had initially committed that India would be open defecation–free by 2018.[63] However, the government's latest National Family Health Survey (NFHS) conducted in 2019–21 exposes this false optimism, because despite cash grants, half of rural Indians in the northern heartland states of Bihar, Madhya Pradesh, Rajasthan and Uttar Pradesh still continue to defecate in the open.[64] The SBA's intimidation techniques have also been utterly insensitive.[65] In Madhya Pradesh, two Dalit children were beaten to death because they did not have a toilet at home and had, instead, gone into the bushes to defecate.[66] Notably, the SBA has been largely silent on the immense contribution of Dalits to sanitation work for generations.[67] In the last five years alone, 347 sanitation workers have died horrifically in sewers that they've had to plunge into to clean, without any protective gear. The Safai Karmachari Andolan (SKA) has launched a powerful nationwide 'Stop Killing Us' campaign.[68]

In contrast, in the last three decades, toilets have more than tripled in Bangladesh, including those in the poorest homes. Open defecation and foul disease environments, are known to reduce the absorption of nutrients in the human body and stunt growth in children.[69] So, despite similar genetic potential, in families with the same level of income, Indian children in West Bengal are shorter than Bangladeshi children due to poor sanitation.[70] In the last decade, Nepal, too, has had a quiet sanitation revolution.[71] By 2016, 85 per cent of homes had already built an improved toilet. To achieve this, the Nepali government had provided ceramic pans, cement bags, asbestos roofs and other materials to eligible poor and Dalit families. Initially, some families did not use the materials to build toilets, so the government had cracked the whip. In one village, I discovered that the local ward office had even started issuing 'toilet cards' to families who had functioning toilets at home. Without these draconian cards, no family could obtain any services from the local government—be it certificates for marriage or for birth or death.

Thus, while India's poorer neighbours are not paradises, they are clearly forging ahead if the statistical evidence on education, healthcare, nutrition and sanitation is anything to go by. Nepal and Bangladesh are performing better in female literacy, life expectancy, infant and child mortality, malnutrition as well as sanitation.

FOLLOW THE BREADCRUMBS

Still, while statistics confirm that many of India's neighbours have a clear edge, what do the realities on the ground reveal? This book investigates the Eastern Neighbours and the Southern Supermodels to make sense of this puzzle.

For starters, let us follow the trail of breadcrumbs in Bihar, Nepal and Bangladesh.

An exercise of 'Little Doctors' in a Bangladeshi school where a student tries to read an eye chart pasted on the wall at a distance.

3

EASTERN NEIGHBOURS: EAR TO THE GROUND

> The stars in the sky, they only
> seem stars there
> The eyes that see far,
> Failed to see the Stars around them,
> The Stars of this Earth
>
> – 'Akash Ka Tara Ke Tara',
> Hari Bhakta Katuwal (1935–1980),
> Indian–Nepali Poet and Lyricist[1]

ONE COLD AFTERNOON, as I was sipping sugary tea, sitting in the civil surgeon's office in a mofussil town of Bangladesh, Md Riauddin walked in with an air of purpose. I was really intrigued by his unusual job title, 'Health Education (In-charge)'. So, on a hunch, I tagged along with him on his motorbike to learn more about his work. This insightful trip was worth every minute.

Riauddin's first stop was the local primary school. The affable head teacher, Abdul Aziz, schooled me on the interlinked merits of human development. 'If a man has good education but no health, he cannot use his skills. Education and health are the real assets of both a person and a nation.' This salt-of-the-earth wisdom is not uncommon in a country with a long history of catastrophes.

The other school teachers, all women clad in burkhas, were equally enthusiastic. They invited me to witness the 'Little Doctors' initiative—a health education programme held twice a year in primary schools across Bangladesh. Abdul himself got down on his knees and helped some students button their sparkling white lab coats to dress up as 'Little Doctors'. The rest of the students stood in queues at a distance from an eye chart stuck on a wall. One by one, each child came forward, closed one eye and slowly read the alphabets. Their 'Little Doctor' classmates wrote out their prescriptions. This exercise in peer education and quick, large-scale health monitoring is genuinely innovative, not to mention adorable to watch. Children learn to conduct simple health check-ups on each other like testing eyesight and measuring height and weight. The Bangladeshi government has apparently learnt this technique from Japanese donors and schools.

This is such an invaluable intervention. I have had to wear spectacles since the tenth grade, and have often wondered how many children drop out of school simply because of their failing eyesight. Perhaps this is also one of the many reasons rural children in India struggle to read. Nowadays, in urban private schools, numerous children can be seen wearing spectacles, possibly due to excessive screen time. But in rural areas, access to an ophthalmologist or even an optician is a luxury.

The adoption of low-cost, novel ideas such as 'Little Doctors' in Bangladeshi public policy is a typical trait of high achievers in human development. They pay close attention to the little details.[2] To explore similar insights, my Eastern

Neighbours research systematically compared the Indian state of Bihar with Bangladesh and Nepal across the border.

The economist Ha-Joon Chang has said with much angst, '... since the 1980s ... a sea of ink was spilled in order to "prove" empirically that countries which had followed neoliberal policies did well.'[3] This book swims against that tide and also tries to move beyond dry statistics.

TRAVELLING ACROSS BORDERS

In the initial stages, I along with my doctoral co-guide, based on a comparable shortlist[4] from national censuses, selected the Muslim-dominated Kishanganj district in Bihar to compare with the Panchagarh district in Bangladesh, barely 50 kilometres apart as the crow flies.[5] Similarly, we chose the Hindu-majority Muzaffarpur district in Bihar to compare with Nepal's Sindhuli, which lies between the Terai plains and the Himalayan mountains. In each district, I hand-picked translators and an energetic team of ten women researchers who spoke the local dialects.

Across eighty villages in four districts in three countries, my various teams and I interviewed 1,600 village women,[6] especially mothers,[7] in three languages—Hindi, Bengali and Nepali.[8] To cross-check their responses, we also interviewed hundreds of health workers and teachers. For the first time, we also tested the reading and mathematics skills of many school-going children across borders.

With this wealth of data, we created four composite indices.[9] First, a unique 'Human Development' index.[10] The other three indices[11]—'Schools and Health Facilities', 'Social Equity' and 'Women's Empowerment'—are together called enabling factors or explanatory indices and they are expected to impact the outcome indicator of the Human Development Index. Also, as a standard disclaimer, I must mention that this data is representative of only individual districts, and not necessarily the region or country as a whole. The overall trends were unmistakable, though.

Apart from the door-to-door survey, I also conducted interviews with key policy shapers, largely in the capital cities of Dhaka, Kathmandu and Patna.[12] In Nepal, for example, I was able to interview both ex-Maoist rebels and government bureaucrats. But perhaps the most immersive process in my fieldwork was living in rural villages across borders with more than fifteen families of different castes, communities, classes, cultures, cuisines, nationalities, religions and languages.[13] I had my ears firmly to the ground.

Crossing international borders on a shoestring budget is as thrilling as it is gruelling. My modest doctoral travel grant ensured that largely I could not afford to take any luxurious shortcuts like flights, private taxis or cars. In the previous decade, working with non-profits, I had often visited countries across South Asia from Bangladesh to Afghanistan. Then, my stay had invariably been confined to hotel rooms and any insights were drawn only from the stale air of air-conditioned conference room echo chambers. For this doctoral research, though, I lived largely in the homes of villagers, crossed long distances and international borders on sleeper buses, overnight trains, rickety cycle rickshaws, public boats, horse carriages and on foot, and ate the most soul-satisfying street food. These were deeply enriching, immersive and eye-opening years, but they were not without their share of hiccups.

Especially in Bangladesh, during my fieldwork in 2016, there was a growing wave of violence by fringe elements rumoured to be from the Islamic State (IS). There was a spate of targeted killings of academics, students, secular bloggers, foreign aid workers and gay rights activists. In the first week of my fieldwork in Panchagarh district, we heard that a Hindu priest had been murdered in a nearby town. As an Indian with a Hindu name and with my academic and activist background, I could have been a target.

The night we heard this news, we were scheduled to stay in the home-cum-office of a tiny grassroots civil society organisation run by an old friend of mine, Farooq bhai. I had known him for a decade from my previous visits to Bangladesh. But, in the palpable air of tension and fear, his wife became extremely tense. That night she insisted that we all huddle together and sleep on the floor in the same room to protect one another. The next morning, wisely and politely, she also asked us to leave quickly for the next village as she did not want to invite trouble from the prashasan (officialdom) if anything happened to me. After Safiq and I left for the next village, at every turn, Farooq Bhai, with his large circle of friends, continued to open numerous doors for me.

A few months after I had left Bangladesh, a series of terrorist attacks terminated in the horrific Holey Artisan Bakery hostage shootout of twenty foreigners in the cosmopolitan Gulshan area of Dhaka, where I had briefly stayed with a Dutch host in an Airbnb.

Thanks to my team of dynamic, local women researchers, despite all the trepidation, the survey progressed well for more than a month without any mishaps whatsoever.

As an Indian, near the border areas, I often had to register with the local police station and the government detective branch. Some even offered me female bodyguards and police protection. But Safiq and I knew that we would be far safer working quietly on our own. I had unshakeable faith that the local villagers would protect us. Apart from a rudimentary hijab created from a folded dupatta, to blend in, I also had a local tailor stitch some kurtas for me with cloth bought from a village shop.[14]

Unlike other districts of Bangladesh, student researchers and foreigners were a rarity in Panchagarh. Every evening, as

I diligently wrote the day's notes on my computer, at least twenty to thirty visitors would show up at the homes we were staying in, just to see the 'madam from India'. It was overwhelmingly beautiful. One of the most moving gestures of affection, however, was from our elderly host Ruhanuma Apa. When we returned home one evening after completing our door-to-door survey in the village, we discovered that she had washed Safiq's clothes which he had left in the room—she explained simply that it was what she did for her son, a garment factory worker, whenever he came home from Dhaka. Her hospitality melted our hearts.

In Nepal, too, every trip turned into a feast of momos, dahi chiura (sweet curd with flattened rice) and noodles. But this changed dramatically. I usually stayed at a family-run guest house in a town called Sindhuli Madi, the capital of Sindhuli district, before travelling to the villages. But when I returned in late 2016, I sensed that my hosts were being unusually cold towards me. As they began to haltingly speak, I realised that the 2015 Indian economic blockade had led to grave food and fuel shortages across Nepal. Once the ice was broken, my hosts realised that, like me, most Indians were largely clueless about the extent of their hardship due to limited media coverage and that we, too, would not be in favour of the crippling economic sanctions. That afternoon, eating tasty chowmein noodles and watching a mind-numbing Hindi soap opera together on television, we silently bonded again.

In India, however, my concerns were of an entirely different nature. One of my fieldwork districts in Bihar, for example, was infested with dacoits, kidnappers and criminal gangs. At one juncture, my research coordinator and I had no choice but to cross a shallow river on a scooter, with me clutching at the handrails for dear life. The doctoral plan was to survey forty villages across two Bihar districts, twice as many as in Nepal and Bangladesh. But finding local women who had passed the tenth grade to conduct the survey was proving to be extremely difficult.

This difference in women's education and employment was perhaps the most telling contrast across borders. In one Bihar district, the women who eventually joined my team after much coaxing were all married. They had to juggle multiple responsibilities and return home early each day before sundown or face the wrath of their mothers-in-law. In the other district, we did finally manage to find unmarried female students to join the team at modest wages. But their parents were livid when they realised that the survey had questions on contraception and family planning.

In contrast, in Nepal, our team of young local researchers, who had recently graduated from high school, were not only more competent but also familiar with sex education.

HUMAN DEVELOPMENT

Bangladeshi preschool teacher Shaheen was only twenty-six, but she was a dynamo, brimming with energy. Married at the age of fifteen, despite all odds, she'd completed her studies. Her preschool students were able to read better than even second-grade students we had met in nearby schools. Shaheen employed a range of innovative teaching aids, including picture cards and abacuses. She showed her students multiple picture cards and combined different words phonetically making it easier for them to grasp. Most importantly, her students understood the meaning of every word they read, not only in Bengali but in English too. She was using a learning method called the Kajoli Early Childhood Education Model.[15]

This asbestos-roofed classroom with bamboo walls, virtually no ventilation and little sunlight, was buzzing with activity and joy. In Bangladesh, the government does not run pre-primary schools. Across the country, there are numerous such learning centres operated largely by NGOs, including BRAC (earlier called the Bangladesh Rehabilitation Assistance Committee). Most of them use different techniques of joyful learning. The Kajoli model is based on play and peer learning.

Shaheen's inspiring early childhood education centre was financed collectively. The mothers' committee of the village pooled money to pay her a modest honorarium. The school ran for only three hours a day, and the mothers brought 'khichuri' (a mixture of rice and lentils cooked together, often called 'hotchpotch' in Dhaka) by rotation for all the children to eat together.

The young teacher was ambitious about the future of her young students: 'You can't expect all five fingers of the hand to be the same. But I do hope that for some children who are intelligent, I am able to show them the right way. And for those who are laggards, it is my job to bring them ahead. A few days ago, I asked the children what their aspirations were. One girl wanted to be a female police officer and did dishum dushum [boxing moves]. Another wanted to be a doctor, the third a teacher. My students are so smart that the primary school teacher had to conduct a lottery to decide whom to give the most marks to, as she was flummoxed with their calibre.'

Most people are equally astonished when they see my survey results. Almost 90 per cent of the students in grade 5 whom we tested across twenty villages in Panchagarh were able to read at least a grade 2 level paragraph in Bengali. Even in Nepal, nearly two-thirds of the students we tested in grade 5 were equally competent. But in the two Bihar districts, less than half the students could read as fluently.[16] These results for Bihar were nearly identical to those in the *Annual Status of Education Report* that the NGO Pratham has been preparing for the last decade in India.[17] For the first time, with the same ASER tools, my survey tested children's learning levels across borders. The results were crystal clear—Bangladeshi children were strikingly ahead.[18]

In Bihar, amongst the children we tested, those from more affluent families scored markedly better than those from poorer ones. Poorer children had less than half the learning competencies.[19] This inequality is largely due to the additional money that wealthier families spend on private schools and private tuition. In contrast, family income did not influence learning levels in Nepal. Even better, the Bangladesh district had a high progressive ratio, with pupils from the poorest families turning out to be better learners than the wealthiest.[20] Competent and dedicated teachers trained in joyful learning techniques, timely availability of textbooks, scholarships for poor and female students as well as the Bengali cultural emphasis on education are all important factors in Bangladesh's educational successes.

In contrast, the repeated complaint of the parents we met in Bihar was that despite good intentions, chief minister Nitish Kumar's 'Degree Lao, Naukri Pao' (Get a Degree, Get a Job) scheme to recruit local teachers en masse had boomeranged and worsened the quality of education. Many upper caste teachers with fake degrees had usurped these plum jobs but were obviously unable to teach in the classrooms.[21]

In school after school in Bihar, we noticed clear signs of decay. In one government school, we saw two teachers in crisp saris sitting behind wooden desks, side-by-side, in the same classroom. They were apparently trying to simultaneously teach two different grades of students who sat on the floor in rows in front of them.[22] In another dimly lit classroom, possibly due to our presence, the teacher pretended to make the children 'read' in the darkness. Many students across schools also confided in us that their teachers beat them mercilessly, even though corporal punishment is strictly against the law.

In Bihar, we noticed that many children were officially enrolled in government schools, but did not attend classes. A recent 2023 post-pandemic survey by the Jan Jagran Shakti

Sanghatan found that, in government primary schools in north Bihar, 'only 23% of children enrolled were present' and dismally concludes that 'schools in Bihar seem to be in danger of mass displacement by private coaching centres'.[23] My survey also confirmed that 82 per cent of students enrolled in private schools and 44 per cent in government schools also went for several hours of private tuition. [24]

On the other hand, in Bangladesh, on an average only 35 per cent and, in Nepal, only 29 per cent of students paid for extra tuitions. In fact, the draft Bangladeshi Education Act, that has been under debate for the last decade, proposes an absolute ban on all private coaching centres, private tuition and even on the publication of guidebooks.[25]

The 'human development index' that I created with my survey data also measured basic knowledge of healthcare. We asked village women simple questions[26] such as whether milk was good for pregnant women, colostrum for infants and fluids for children with diarrhoea. On an average, 82 per cent of the women we interviewed in Bangladesh answered correctly compared to 66 per cent in Nepal. In Bihar, the level of awareness amongst the women we interviewed was 61 per cent, and their knowledge of ORS was the lowest.

Similarly, to indirectly measure nutrition, we asked women whether anyone in their family had slept hungry in the last three months. In Bangladesh and Nepal, they were truly puzzled by this question. More than 90 per cent of women we spoke to were positive that no one in their family had faced hunger. But in both the Bihar districts, women hesitated while answering this question. Their downcast eyes and silences spoke volumes of their own haunting deprivation.

We also asked women what they had eaten the previous night. They invariably giggled as they tried to jog their memories. Using their responses, we calculated a slightly modified version of the Women's Dietary Diversity Scores.[27]

As expected, Bangladesh scored the highest, with almost 91 per cent of the women telling us they'd eaten animal protein (mostly fish) the previous night. Nepal followed suit, even though only 30 per cent of the women had eaten meat (along with 20 per cent fish and 14 per cent eggs). Expectedly, women in the Bihar districts scored the least.[28]

The availability of toilets across borders was the biggest contrast. Almost 99 per cent of homes we visited in Bangladesh and 96 per cent in Nepal already had a toilet that they used regularly. In Bihar, at the time of my survey in mid-2016, only 14 per cent of households had a latrine. Despite the hype around SBA, toilets were few and far between.[29] Often, only the homes of local politicians had toilets as this was a mandatory eligibility criterion if they wished to stand for elections.[30] But the demand for latrines that we encountered among women was overwhelming. Around 97 per cent of the women who had to regularly defecate in the open complained to us of their discomfort, especially when they were unwell or menstruating. Almost 91 per cent of these interviewees also confirmed that they would certainly construct a toilet and regularly use it if the government provided adequate subsidy. Tellingly, 71 per cent of women who had used a toilet before gushed about how much they loved them. If only more women in Bihar earned an income or had more influence in household decisions how different the statistics would look.

Since 2008, on the other hand, Nepal has worked towards becoming open defecation-free (ODF). Every district has chalked out its sanitation plan. In Bangladesh, too, the levels of sanitation were very high. Islam is highly prescriptive about toilet hygiene and has its own set of rules known as Qadaa' al-Haajah. Even in India, before SBA, 65 per cent of Muslim homes had a toilet, compared to only 47 per cent of Hindu homes.[31]

But the real puzzle that foxed me for weeks was why so

many toilets in Bangladesh had toilet rolls, like in Western countries.[32] Every small village corner shop sold these locally manufactured, extremely cheap toilet rolls for as little as Tk 15 (about Rs 11). One roll even had the brand name 'Bangla' with a bar code. I wondered who bought these rolls in remote villages.

I had been chewing on this mundane puzzle for weeks, when Rehnuma, a local villager, helped me solve this mystery. She had her hands full, taking care of her infant twins, as we asked her a routine survey question about sanitation. Rehnuma suddenly beamed with pride and blurted out, 'I am a good Muslim mother as I wipe my children's bottom thrice with tissue paper and then use water as mandated by Islam.' Only then did I become aware that the Quran instructs utmost hygiene after 'relieving yourselves', and if 'you can find no water, take some sand and rub your faces and hands with it'.[33]

One day, our bus stopped at an unplanned open-air pitstop in the rural countryside. I was astonished when I saw from a quick sideways glance outside the window that the men were squatting to urinate. I nudged Safiq and asked him what was going on. He nonchalantly explained that this was recommended in the scriptures.[34] He said that his father would even get annoyed when he had to use western-style men's urinals. The specific Hadith on toilet hygiene also emphasised privacy. So, clean toilets dotted the landscape across rural Bangladesh.

Thus, across education, healthcare, nutrition and sanitation, my primary survey showed that Panchagarh district in Bangladesh had the best human development scores.[35] Both the Bihar districts lagged behind substantially.[36] Since there were minimal differences between the Hindu-dominated and Muslim-majority Bihari districts, I combined their scores. Obviously, in Bihar, state- and national-level public policies, rather than religious differences, were the main factors in determining social achievements.

SCHOOLS AND HEALTH CENTRES[37]

Classrooms need inspiring teachers. More than two-thirds of the mothers we met in the districts of Nepal and Bangladesh said that they were satisfied with the teachers who taught their youngest school-going child. In sharp contrast, only a third of mothers in Bihar held the same view.

Teachers often do not even show up in schools in Bihar. Teacher absenteeism or 'ghost teachers' are a chronic menace.[38] The 2006 policy of mass recruitment of local teachers also seems to have made no dent. Almost 75 per cent of the teachers we met confirmed that they lived in the same village.[39] But on the day of our unannounced visit, 41 per cent were absent from schools for one reason or another. In Nepal, on the day of our visit, 32 per cent of teachers were MIA (missing in action).[40] In contrast, in Bangladesh, only 18 per cent were away from duty.

Caste plays an important role in Bihar, both in the school attendance of teachers as well as students. In one village, when we entered a Musahar tola (hamlet), in the late morning hours, my jaw dropped. Barely clothed children were playing and running around everywhere when they should have been in school. We peeped inside the first mud house, which barely had a roof over it, and saw three children huddled in a corner. As we began our survey, a crowd of mostly women and children of all ages quickly surrounded us.

These families had been displaced by a flood that had washed away their homes a few months ago. As the children's names had not been deleted from their old school's register, the teachers in the government school near where they lived now had refused to enrol them. The discrimination, unspoken of course, was because of their caste. Musahars in Bihar are denigrated as rat-eaters, a necessary part of their diet for generations to subsist in the face of dire poverty and deprivation.

We asked the children to get ready so we could take them to school. It took some persuasion, but by the time we finished our survey, twenty-five eager youngsters were wearing their Sunday best. The school was barely two minutes away. As the children trustingly held hands and made a single queue to walk to school, my eyes welled up. After an hour of cajoling, the teachers in the school finally gave the children some plates to have the meal provided by the school. We also sang a few songs to shore up their spirits and to help them build bonds with their new classmates. The head teacher agreed that the children could attend this school until their previous school issued transfer certificates. During our fieldwork in the area, we followed up every single day with the teachers of both schools, but we knew that the destinies of these children from the lowest caste would continue to be mired in red tape and unspeakable depths of prejudice.

Another troubling trend that I saw in government schools in Bihar was that children were usually made to sit on the dusty floor of classrooms. If they were lucky, there would be a mat. Otherwise, most students would bring their own jute sacks from home to sit on. On the other hand, most teachers would sit on chairs behind wooden desks. This situation is a reflection on the low government investment in basic infrastructure in schools. But it is also an example of the wide physical and status gap that exists between teachers and students. In contrast, we found that 85 per cent of students in Nepal and 66 per cent in Bangladesh sat behind desks. Many of these desks were painted in bright colours to make the classroom atmosphere joyful. Another excellent initiative in Nepal was that classroom walls, staircases and playgrounds were painted with images of alphabets, multiplication tables, poems and various measurements. All it took was a bucket of paint and a few brushes, and the children were surrounded by learning material in every corner of the school. Thus, basic concepts would visually come to be etched in their memories.

The availability of textbooks, essential to learning the curriculum, was also another indicator we gauged. All students in government schools in India are guaranteed free textbooks based on the compulsory education law. Still, in two of every three Bihari schools we visited, textbooks were inexplicably delayed for as long as three to eight months after the start of the academic year. No wonder Bihari students struggled to learn.

I pleasantly discovered that Bangladesh and Nepal had employed ingenious solutions to ensure that 80 per cent of their students received these textbooks on time.[41] In Bangladesh, the new academic year starts on the first day of January. So, New Year's Day is also celebrated as National Textbook Day. A schoolteacher explained to me, 'We have to submit photographs to the education department to show that we are distributing textbooks to children on the 1st of January each year. Even if it is a holiday, we have to distribute on New Year's Day.'[42]

In Bangladesh and Nepal, more than two-thirds of the schools we went to also had good toilets. But in Bihar, more than half had no toilets at all. This made girls, in particular, more likely to drop out. In one school, students pulled me aside to show me the extent of the gender bias they faced. They took us with them to see the toilets for ourselves. Here's what I recorded in my field notes:

> The boys' toilet is clean as, apparently, the teachers also use it. With much difficulty, we open the girls' toilet, and the stench and filth are unbearable. The girl student who is showing us around tells us that this toilet is no longer used. The children confide to us that, worse still, only girls are made to clean the boys' toilet.[43]

Among Eastern Neighbours, only India provides free school lunches. These midday school meals are meant to enable malnourished children to catch-up in growth.[44] Sadly, in Bihar, though eggs are on the menu once a week, we rarely found them in the meals that the schools served.

We also measured access to healthcare in the three districts across borders.[45] More than half the homes confirmed that their nearest health facility was within 3 kilometres. Since 2009, in Bangladesh, the Awami League government's flagship initiative has been to construct Community Clinics 'to extend primary healthcare at the doorsteps of the villagers all over the country'.[46] Similarly, in Nepal, we found 'health posts' near most villages, and 85 per cent of them were open when we arrived. In contrast, in the far-flung Kishanganj district of Bihar, only nine of the twenty villages we visited had a health facility nearby, and we found that most were shut.

Free medicines are also the cornerstone of a well-functioning public health facility. Around 80 per cent of the health centres in Nepal and 65 per cent in Bangladesh had in stock at least half of the thirteen basic medicines on our survey checklist.[47] Bangladesh also has a thriving pharmaceutical industry for generic drugs that supplies most medicines on the Essential Drugs List (EDL).[48] At one Community Clinic, we saw that the local family welfare assistant Madina Begum's bag was brimming with contraceptive pills, condoms and injections. As we spoke, a village woman in her nightdress and without slippers walked up to Madina and casually asked for free, contraceptive 'sukhi bori' (happiness pills). In contrast in Bihar, 60 per cent of the health facilities we visited did not have even half of these basic medicines.

Both the districts in Bangladesh and Nepal emerged as frontrunners, based on the combined scores on the quality of schools and health centres. Bihar, though, was acutely deprived. In Kishanganj district, public services were so appalling that local villagers used the distraction created by our survey to heckle a corrupt anganwadi (government pre-school) teacher.[49]

Yet, the most common refrain from both Muslim and Hindu villagers we met, and especially from the Musahars and Doms at the bottom of the caste ladder, was, '*Hum aage badhenge jab log hamare saath badhenge. Teen log aage. Dus log peeche. Lekin koi saath mein nahi hai. Koi judna nahi chahate.*' (We will protest when other people unite with us. Three people in front. Ten behind. But nobody is with us. Nobody wants to join hands together).[50] Tellingly, the ability to demand better public services seemed to be stifled by a lack of social unity and solidarity.

SOCIAL EQUITY

Economists Amartya Sen and Jean Drèze, in their book *India: Development and Participation*, insightfully describe the impact of social distances:

> The problem of social distance arises from the fact that, compared with the pupils and their parents, teachers in government schools often come from relatively privileged social backgrounds in terms of caste, class and gender.[51]

Teachers are less likely to talk down to their students and their guardians if they belong to the same caste. Healthcare workers are also likely to be more caring towards their patients if they hail from the same social class or community.[52] When social distances are diluted, often there is better access to public services. This is particularly important in an India riven by caste and communal brutality and discrimination. A few years ago, in Uttar Pradesh, a Dalit student was beaten to death by his teacher for writing the wrong answers in the examinations.[53] In the same district, another Dalit student was beaten 'for not bringing a plate for food from home'.[54] More recently, in a viral video, one can see an upper caste teacher asking students to slap a Muslim boy repeatedly.[55]

Though both corporal punishment and caste atrocities are legally banned, these violent malignancies continue to plague India. In our survey we tried various indirect measures to capture these social distances.

More than half the mothers we met in the chosen districts of Bangladesh and Nepal, for example, confirmed that they had spoken at least once to a teacher who taught their youngest school-going child in the previous academic year. In Bangladesh, if a child was absent for more than three days, the teacher had to visit their home and then, submit an 'absenteeism form', containing detailed explanations, to higher authorities.[56] In contrast, less than a third of mothers we met in Bihar had the same level of interactions with teachers.

Mothers' education is often an important factor in how confident they are in their interaction with teachers. In the Bangladesh district, four out of every five mothers and in Nepal, more than half of the mothers we met were literate. In Bihar, less than half the mothers we met could even read the alphabet. Understandably, they were more diffident when speaking with teachers. This social distance was particularly acute in Musahar hamlets. Teachers in Bihar were also particularly dismissive of illiterate parents. One teacher in half-baked English mouthed the typical barb, '*Guardians tight nahin hote hai. Bacchon ko tayyar nahin karte hain*' (Parents don't impart discipline. They do not prepare their children for school), even as Musahar families agonised about the open discrimination their children face within and outside the classroom.[57]

On the health front, more than two-thirds of the women we interviewed in Bangladesh and Nepal had met a health worker in the previous three months, compared to only half in Bihar. We also asked villagers how long they usually had to wait in a health facility before a doctor or a nurse attended to them.

Nepal's health posts were the quickest. An important reason was that many of them were not managed by doctors but by well-trained 'health assistants' with long years of medical experience. In Bangladesh and Nepal, almost half the teachers and health workers we met also confirmed that at least one of the students they had taught or patients they had treated in the previous year was related to them. So, with emotional distance bridged by kinship bonds, these workers were likely to be more committed. In Nepal, in particular, 97 per cent of the swasthya sevikas we interviewed had treated their own relatives at some point or the other. Even though they did not receive a salary, swasthya sevikas were deeply respected as 'the backbone of society'.[58] In Bihar, too, more than two-thirds of the ASHA doorstep health workers routinely treated their own relatives who lived in the same village. On the other hand, doctors, nurses and other health workers, despite their hefty salaries, did not share the same bond with their patients. So, across the three countries, we found that most villagers were not comfortable visiting the homes of these senior healthcare workers for consultations.

Lastly, we found that teachers and health workers were usually amongst the few government employees in rural villages with steady incomes. Villagers often turned to them for loans. Predictably, almost half the teachers and health workers we spoke to in Bangladesh confirmed that they had, at some point or the other, lent money to someone in the village where they worked. Villagers in the remote Muslim-dominated Kishanganj district of Bihar were also more indebted to these welfare workers than in urbanised Muzaffarpur. But Nepali teachers and health workers were, by far, the most generous. Sixty-four per cent of Nepali teachers and half the health workers had lent money.

These unique responses were compressed into a 'social equality index'. The Bihar districts displayed the greatest social distance between teachers and health workers and the villagers they served. Bangladesh and Nepal clearly had greater social equality.

WOMEN'S FREEDOMS

Women's freedoms often hinge on education. In the past four decades, female education in Bangladesh has expanded to such an extent that, across classrooms, we found more girls than boys.[59] When I asked a bright fifteen-year-old boy whose mother was a school teacher what he thought about this trend, he solemnly quoted Napoleon Bonaparte, 'Give me an educated mother, I shall promise you [the birth of] a civilized, educated nation.'[60]

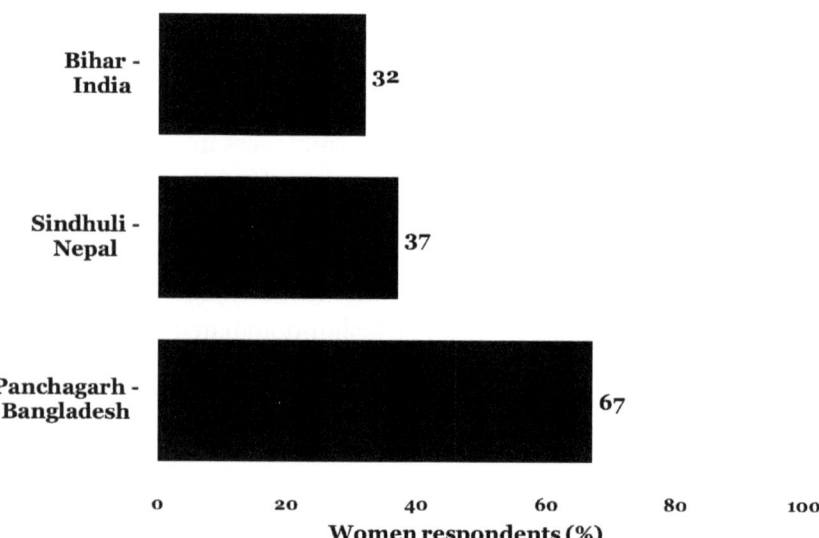

3.1: Wives who are educated for the same or more years than their spouses (%)

Source: Author's Household Survey, 2016

Surprisingly, 67 per cent of Bangladeshi women we met said that they had spent as many or more years in school than their husbands. Though, on average, these women had received only six years of education, even that was often more than their husbands. The 2006 World Bank Survey on Gender Norms in Bangladesh first detected this unique trend of 'educational hypogamy'.[61] This was contrary to the traditional South Asian aspiration for women to 'marry up' the social ladder. In Bihar and Nepal, for instance, more than two-thirds of the women we met were less educated than their husbands.[62]

Since childhood, I have watched women burdened with the primary responsibility to prepare food and feed their families every day in both rural and urban homes. Mothers, grandmothers, daughters-in-laws and aunts in India invariably slave away in the kitchen, cooking nearly every meal from scratch. The recent Malayalam film, *The Great Indian Kitchen*, touches a raw nerve on this subject. On top of that, in more than half the rural homes in northern India, women typically eat last after serving everyone else in the family.[63] So, in poor homes, women also often eat the least, as little food may be left for them after everyone else has eaten.

In Bihar, 58 per cent of women we met said that they ate only after other family members had eaten. In the home of one of my researchers, I saw this discrimination first hand and recounted it in my field notes with anguish:

> It is around 10 p.m. and finally, dinner is served. The father asks me to go to the next room to eat separately, but I will have none of it. He tells me that there is a parampara (tradition) that women must eat only after men. But since I am not budging, a plate of roti is kept in front of me as we sit on the floor to eat. But the women of the house are not yet being served. As soon as the men and the children finish their meal and the moment her husband gets up, the elderly mother hungrily drags his half-eaten plate of rice

that he has left behind, and starts eating from it in a hurry. The daughter-in-law bustles around cleaning, bent low. She has prepared all the food but is not allowed to eat until her father-in-law, husband, children and then mother-in-law finish. She will be the last to eat, sitting in a corner on the floor. I can also see from the corner of my eye my researcher's sister, who is studying in the tenth standard, sitting on a chair in the other room, seething with rage that I was offered food with the men simply because I am from the shehar (city). She is starving, has school tomorrow, but is still not permitted to eat. The men in the house are all rotund, while the women are weak and frail. Any guesses why? My blood boils.[64]

To my absolute surprise, I discovered that this cultural norm that I grew up with in India was uncommon in Bangladesh. Only 11 per cent of Bangladeshi women we interviewed said they ate after their husbands. In fact, 23 per cent, especially those with infant children, said that the previous night they had eaten even before their husbands had returned home. Throughout my fieldwork, across many host families too, we all ate our dinner together on the floor of the ranna ghar (kitchen) or in the courtyard. In the most unforgettable iftar meals that I have had in the humblest of homes, during the holy month of Ramzan, we would all sit together to eat muri and fruits, and drink glucose water when we broke our fast in the evening. Even for sehri, the morning meal before dawn, we would all sit together on a mat on the floor and gobble up our food with sleepy eyes. The world over, in Muslim families, commensality or eating together, sometimes from the same plate, is culturally cherished. In the Hadith, on the 'Etiquette of Eating', the Prophet urges, 'Eat together and mention the Name of Allah over your food. It will be blessed for you.'[65]

Even in Nepal, despite it being a largely Hindu society, 92 per cent of women said that they ate together as a family. In upper caste homes, there even appeared to be a range of strict eating customs. One day, as we sat together in the home of our Bahun (Brahmin) hosts, I tried to scoop some rice onto my elderly host Ram Bua's plate. I was promptly reprimanded by my Newari translator Bijeta: 'Only someone who has finished eating is allowed to serve someone who is still eating.'[66] These norms ensured that everyone served themselves; shared meals were encouraged. Bijeta told me that she had been trained in these customs since her childhood and practiced them strictly.

We also asked women if, based on traditional cultural practices, they wore a ghoonghat (veil), face scarf, sari pallu (sari end), hijab or burkha when stepping outside the home,[67] or going in front of elders. Expectedly, 88 per cent of Bangladeshi women said that they covered their heads with their saris or wore burkhas. In both Hindu and Muslim-dominated districts of Bihar, more than 70 per cent of women also had the same response. In Nepal, which has never encountered Muslim rule, the practice of purdah or even ghoonghat was virtually nonexistent. Only 21 per cent of women we met, largely those who lived in the Terai areas bordering India, covered their heads.

Even my Nepali researchers 'look[ed] like fashion models' in chic, well-cut Western clothes. My translator, Bijeta, walked with ease in the villages in shorts and a T-shirt, and no one blinked an eye. Even in the market squares, it was not unusual to see grandmothers wearing traditional Nepali saris, sitting on their haunches and casually smoking bidis with their heads immersed in a cloud of smoke.

Thus, the Nepal district had the highest levels of women's freedom, followed by Bangladesh. The Bihar districts were at the bottom, with the most stifling gender inequities.

THE COST OF INEQUALITY

Finally, for each of the eighty villages, we combined the information from both households and welfare workers.

Expectedly, villages that scored well on the 'human development index' created specially for my research were also more likely to have good quality schools and health facilities as well as better women's empowerment. Social equality, too, had a positive correlation, though that was slightly weaker. Overall, 56 per cent of the variation in human development could be explained with statistical significance by the three indices.[68] Sindhuli district in Nepal and Panchagarh in Bangladesh also clearly had better scores across the board than the two Bihari districts.

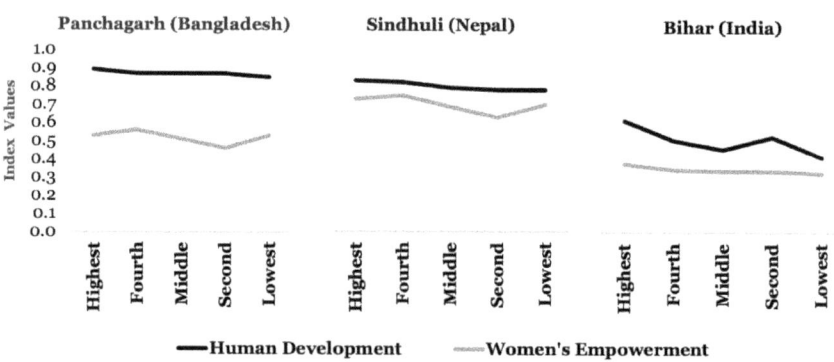

3.2: Wealth inequalities in human development and women's empowerment

I also divided the families into five quintiles based on their possession of simple assets—from beds and fans to pressure cookers and mobile phones. In the districts of Bangladesh and Nepal, human development scores were fairly evenly distributed across families. Women's empowerment scores displayed an even more progressive trend. Women from the poorest families in both countries had higher scores than richer families. On the other hand, in Bihar, there was clearly a regressive trend. The poorest households not only had the lowest human development scores but also fared the worst in women's freedom. Predictably, in Bihar, more affluent families were better off on all counts.

The inequalities between communities also cast an interesting picture.[69] In Bangladesh, minority Hindu families in my sample had higher human development scores than Muslim ones. The reverse was true for women's empowerment in the two communities. In Nepal, human development scores were fairly evenly distributed among different castes. Predictably, in the Bihar districts, Dalits recorded the lowest human development scores, while forward castes had the highest. But Dalit and Muslim women had higher empowerment scores.

NEIGHBOURS SHINE

All forty villages in Bihar trailed those in Nepal and Bangladesh on all parameters.

But this statistical analysis does not explain the underlying reasons for these differences across borders. Why, for instance, are social distances more compressed in Nepal than in Bihar? How has Panchagarh district in Bangladesh leapfrogged Kishanganj in Bihar, even though it is just a stone's throw away across the border? Why are women in Nepal more empowered than those in Bangladesh and Bihar? Why have the governments of Bangladesh and Nepal bothered to invest more in schools and health centres?

The key to success for India's poorer neighbours seems to clearly lie in their ability to dilute inequalities of wealth, caste and gender. So, I dug deeper to analyse how these social inequalities have gradually dissolved, over decades and centuries, across India's borders.

Even Rome was not built in a day.

An anti-terrorism sculpture at Dhaka University campus, where hundreds of students were murdered during the 1971 Bangladeshi Liberation War.

4

BANGLADESH

> Last year I was a Jolāhā (weaver),
> now I am a Sheikh,
> and next year, if the prices rise,
> I shall become a Saiyid.
>
> – Late nineteenth-century proverb
> *The Imperial Gazetteer of India*, 1881[1]

THE BUZZ WAS electric. In only twelve days, voters would choose their candidate for the local government. As we entered the local market square, a loudspeaker blared, 'Vote for the autorickshaw.' Predictably, the two main candidates in these elections were from the biggest national parties—Awami League (AL) and Bangladesh National Party (BNP). The rest of the dozen-odd candidates were independents. Their election symbols were unique to the rural countryside, from a loudspeaker to a sheaf of wheat and a humble autorickshaw.

One difference stood out. In every village, we saw women candidates, usually burkha-clad, going door-to-door asking for votes, even in the afternoon heat. But we rarely found men similarly on their feet. Instead, male candidates usually organised rickshaw or cycle rallies with boisterous slogan-shouting by tens of supporters on blaring loudspeakers. Veteran feminist Meghna Guhathakurta, whom I later met in Dhaka, confirmed that this was indeed a distinct trend.[2] One-third of the seats in the local government are reserved for women, the same as in India. But Bangladesh has an unusual indirect gender quota system.[3] Each voter has to vote for two candidates. A regular contestant of any gender in their constituency and a woman candidate who represents three constituencies. So, women from reserved seats had to seek votes from an electorate that was three times larger. However, money and muscle power were monopolised by men. Thus, women candidates, with fewer resources, usually had to walk long distances and ask for votes door-to-door.[4]

The bazaars, too, were caught up in the heady atmosphere. Men spent all night plotting election strategies over endless cups of lal cha (tea without milk). Even late into the evenings, we would hear vans driving down the highways and village bylanes, loudly appealing for votes on loudspeakers, announcing the names of their candidates and their unusual symbols.

On election day, our host, a widow, woke up early. For the first time, we saw her leave home wearing a full-length burkha. She had been chosen by one of the candidates as a representative. Her job was simple—to sign as a witness after the counting of the ballots. Of course, her main motivation was the modest honorarium that would follow.

The entire road leading up to the election booth in the local school was decorated with paper flags depicting election symbols. Voters wore their Sunday best. Near the polling booth, men and women stood in separate, solemn queues. Outside the school, it was a carnival. Vendors sold candy floss and peanuts in paper cones, while children played on the streets. This was indeed a festival of democracy.

The whole village seemed to have poured out of their homes into the bylanes around the school. We kept bumping into friends from the various homes we had surveyed. There was not a single vehicle on the streets, except that of an election observer who drove past with an officious siren on his car. We saw him enter the school to inspect the polling station. Later, as Safiq and I stood on the main highway trying to find some public transport, the officer kindly stopped his car and offered to give us a lift to the nearest town.

We gratefully entered the air-conditioned comfort of his official vehicle. Safiq was particularly thrilled. Like many of his classmates at Dhaka University, he dreamt of joining the government service, with all its pomp and prestige. But as we accompanied the officer on his tour of duty, the façade of this festive election melted away. At the next polling booth, rumours were rife that one of the main candidates had laid out a free banquet for the voters. Everywhere we heard murmurs of gifts and different inducements.

When the results were out, it was obvious that, across the district, wealthy candidates had won their seats hands down. After all, Bangladesh is amongst the most corrupt countries in South Asia and the world.[5]

In our village, there was a massive gaffe. The losing candidate's supporters thought that he had won based on a hand gesture by an official inside the counting hall. They had started celebrating. Then the election official declared that he had lost by a razor-thin margin. This miscommunication created a ruckus, which could have easily turned into a brawl. But the losing candidate beseeched his supporters to remain calm and avoid violence. The next day, we bumped into this gracious gentleman in the village street, but all he could give us was a dazed grin.

Elections seem to be hardwired into the Bangladeshi national consciousness. It is a hard-won symbol of democracy in a country that has a long history of military dictators, coups, murders and intrigue. Even government primary schools conduct annual student elections using ballot papers. Every school I visited had a board with photos of elected student council members.

Yet, the 2018 general elections were marred by severe allegations of vote rigging and violence. The previous elections in 2014 had been boycotted by the BNP, the main opposition alliance. Democracy in Bangladesh remains fragile. The 2022 Varieties of Democracy (V-Dem) Liberal Democracy Index (LDI), which measures how liberal a democracy is, ranks Bangladesh as one of the lowest in South Asia, lower than India.[6] Both countries along with Pakistan are now classified as 'electoral autocracies'. The 2024 Bangladeshi elections also promises to be marred by controversies.

Despite this turbulent polity, as evident from my on-the-ground survey, the commitment of all Bangladeshi political leaders to social welfare is exceptionally high. The key question that emerges is: why do even autocratic regimes bother to placate citizens with welfare? What forces have shaped this unique social contract between the citizens of Bangladesh and their ruling elites?

MONOPOLISTIC PARTYARCHY[7]

Sitting in an autorickshaw in rural Bangladesh, we passed by a hoarding that showed a smiling Prime Minister Begum Sheikh Hasina talking animatedly into her mobile phone. In the backdrop were women who seemed to be eager to enter a picket-fenced Community Clinic. I was so intrigued by this poster that I stopped the vehicle, took a photograph and had Safiq translate it for me later. The slogan proclaimed, 'Community Clinics are one of the best efforts to ensure healthcare, which makes Bangladesh the role model for the world.' There was even a chronology of events on the hoarding to support this claim:

1998: Sheikh Hasina established 10,600 Community Clinics to ensure health facilities for every person.
2001: Community Clinics were closed by the Bangladesh Nationalist Party.
2009: After 8 years, Sheikh Hasina has reopened Community Clinics.
2014: 12,815 Community Clinics have been opened, 900 Community Clinics conduct normal deliveries, 30 types of medicines are distributed and in tune with the slogan of 'Digital Bangladesh' laptops have been provided to every clinic.

The hoarding ended on a high note: 'The Awami League government ensures that Community Clinics, which provide health facilities for every person, fulfil the vision of Bangabandhu [i.e., Sheikh Mujibur Rehman] and Sheikh Hasina to make this dream come true.'

Well-functioning Community Clinics are indeed a sight to behold. We reached one at 10 a.m.[8] The health centre had not yet opened, but a group of men and several women carrying children were already waiting there to be immunised. The previous day, families had been informed on their mobile phones about their children's vaccination appointments. We waited outside the centre for a few minutes, when the sari and hijab-clad health assistant (HA) arrived in a sweat with a helper who was carrying the vaccines in an ice box. She opened the door of the clinic, and in a matter of minutes, about ten mothers and fathers swarmed around her with their infants and their vaccination cards. I clicked several photos and realised that there was absolutely no space or time to interview the HA. An excellent sign—nothing better than busy welfare workers who don't have time to chat.

Unfortunately, Community Clinics remain only a political project. Despite intense competition between the two main parties, as of 2016, Community Clinics had not been enacted as a legal right. So, HAs like the one we met did not have secure, permanent jobs on par with other government employees. They had launched a nationwide andolan a few months ago. Due to these protests, in another clinic we visited the supply of medicines had been temporarily stopped. Many families we met were angry as they had returned from the clinic disappointed and did not know where to lodge their complaints. These patients were also victims of this unsteady system.

Bangladesh's development has, without a doubt, happened in fits and starts. The country has been plagued by chronic corruption, unstable governance, simmering communalism and political instability in the last five decades.[9] Since the brutal assassination, in 1975, of the first prime minister, Sheikh Mujibur Rehman, Bangladesh has had ten heads of government.[10] Till the 1990s, power had been firmly held by a nexus of politicians, military officers and bureaucrats—the most powerful elites in the country. After democracy returned in 1991, a new form of patronage politics seems to have emerged.[11] Competition between the two main political parties has fuelled a race for populist welfare policies, such as Community Clinics.

Overt political support for education has led to the rapid expansion in the number of school enrolments.[12] In the 1980s, even General Ershad (1982–91), to gain popular support for his feeble military dictatorship, made primary education legally compulsory and introduced free tuition for girls in secondary grades. This right was enshrined in law in Bangladesh nearly two decades before India enacted the Right of Children to Free and Compulsory Education Act in 2009.

Political scientist Mirza Hassan has rightly described Bangladesh as a 'monopolistic partyarchy' with a 'winner

4.1: Primary and secondary enrolments by political regime in Bangladesh

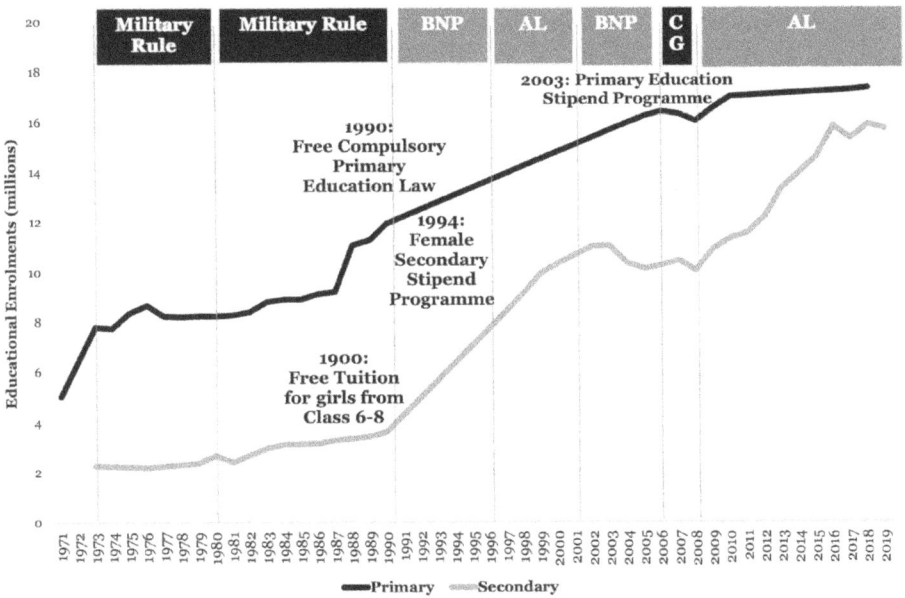

Source: Adapted from (Naomi Hossain and Naila Kabeer, 'Achieving Universal Primary Education and Eliminating Gender Disparity') with the latest data available from the UNESCO Institute of Statistics.

Note: AL = Awami League, BNP = Bangladesh National Party, CG = Caretaker Government, FSSP = Female Secondary Stipend Programme, PESP = Primary Education Stipend Programme

takes all' ethos.[13] Whenever a particular political party is in power, it controls and politicises trade unions, professional associations and civil society, based on party affiliation, through its nominees. One of my Bangladeshi surveyors told me that a close friend of hers was imprisoned only because the family were long-time loyalists of the opposition party. But despite their ideological and political differences, heart-warmingly the personal friendship between my surveyor and her close friend remained strong.

Despite the turbulence of alternating episodes of authoritarian and democratic regimes, in Bangladesh 'a distinct and durable political settlement has emerged'.[14] The political elites expand welfare policies to opportunistically safeguard their vote banks and gain popular support.[15] If they do not deliver, all regimes know that they can easily be replaced.[16] This is not an imaginary fear in a country that is legendary for its gigantic street protests.[17] The 2018 street protests for road safety initiated by school children grew so widespread across ages that they brought Dhaka to a standstill, hit international headlines and had to be quelled with tear gas.[18] The 2013 Shahbag protests were more overtly political, as old wounds from the atrocities committed during the 1971 Liberation War resurfaced.[19] With the 2024 elections around the corner, the political atmosphere has once again become charged.

Still, most of the political elites in Bangladesh also have a deep-seated commitment to social welfare. As feminist economist Naila Kabeer once vividly described, in Bangladesh even 'the urban elite are only one generation removed from life in the villages'.[20]

The foundation of this solid social commitment was laid in the 1970s. The 'spectral wound'[21] of the 1971 Liberation War and the 1970 cyclone Bhola cemented 'a social contract between the rulers and the ruled'.[22] Political sociologist Naomi Hossain has convincingly argued that the durable roots of this social contract became evident only after the 1974 famine. 'As many as 1.5 million people—2 per cent of the total population, overwhelmingly the rural landless proletariat—died in this catastrophe, having already been starved, displaced, terrorized, and otherwise harmed during the liberation war of 1971.'[23] Since then, the ruling classes have always been deeply aware that,

> Their own survival depended on human development and basic social protection. This ensured that protection against

natural disasters and food shocks was institutionalized as a state priority, helped protect key policies to transform the population through health and education against political competition and corruption, brought poor rural women to the forefront of development, and ensured the elite policed themselves to deliver these essential public goods.[24]

Our host Jahirunal Apa also distinctly recalled both the Liberation War in 1971 and the famine in 1974 as turning points in her nation's history. One night, in her kitchen, as she served us the most delicious spinach-and-beetroot dish I had ever eaten, she recalled the horrors of the Liberation War. She was unmarried then. Her father's house was 50 kilometres from her present home and a stone's throw away from the Indian border. Jahirunal Apa had tried to escape to India with her parents and siblings. But the camp was overflowing and they had to leave the day after they arrived, she recalled bitterly. The family spent seven long days and nights in an open field, sleeping under the stars. She did not witness the violence herself, but her future husband told her he had seen a decapitated body.

The 1974 famine made a more lasting impression on Jahirunal's memory. In that time of severe food scarcity, the Union Parishad (local government) chairman had organised a langar (soup kitchen) in his house. She vividly remembered how two thick rotis were all that they received, once a day. What bothered her the most was that there was no rice, which is what she was used to eating. She found the rotis too hard to chew. Even to collect these rotis, Jahirunal had to leave the house at 8 a.m. to return only by 1 p.m. She had to wait for hours in the queue on an empty stomach. There was absolutely nothing else to eat throughout the day. By the time the famine had occurred, she was married and had a 3-year-old son. She said that her husband would try to get work in the fields of wealthy landlords for a measly Taka 1.5 per day. Her son would also accompany her husband, but he was too young and the landlords would refuse to pay the boy. The only food she could afford to cook, on rare days at that, was an inferior variety of wheat pounded to make gruel for the family. When I asked her how things had changed since those dark days, her response was precise. She said that, in the 1970s, one bigha of land would produce, at best, five maunds (around 185 kilograms) of harvest. But after the Green Revolution, fertilisers and pesticides (aushad) were routinely applied to the fields. So, one bigha started yielding twenty-five maunds (925 kilograms) of rice. Even though they had little land, things had improved substantially for the family, especially after her son started to work and send money from Dhaka. Despite all the hardship that she had faced in her lifetime, Jahirunal and her husband (whom she always referred to in the third person as 'your chacha', your uncle) remained ever generous with their time, food and love.

Importantly, even at the peak of the famine, the heads of the local governments had organised community kitchens in villages. For the last quarter of a century, Begum Khaleda Zia and Begum Sheikh Hasina, as prime ministers elected in rotation, have also displayed their commitment to numerous social programmes. Apart from the increase in crop yield during the Green Revolution, this social contract between the ruling elite and Bangladeshi citizens has been crucial.

Still, Bangladeshi economists Wahiduddin Mahmud and Simeen Mahmud[25] have argued that Bangladesh's development experience is neither 'a typical case of large public social spending on welfare-oriented programmes nor economic growth-fuelled development'. Instead, for them, the country has been able 'to achieve rapid progress in many social development indicators ... by creating social awareness and using low-cost affordable solutions'.[26]

Since the multiple tragedies of the 1970s, an internationally celebrated driver of Bangladesh's success has been non-governmental organisations (NGOs), especially known for their culture of innovation. After the Liberation War, though Bangladesh was labelled a 'basket case',[27] foreign donors generously supported pioneering, home-grown NGOs. The breadth of their influence nationwide has been expansive. Gonoshasthaya Kendra, for example, built the first refugee hospital during the Liberation War. In the midst of the war, in Bangladeshi refugee camps, researchers discovered that ORS could be used to treat diarrhoea.[28] The medical journal *Lancet* hailed this solution as 'the most important medical discovery of the 20th century'.[29] Diarrhoea remains the second leading cause of child deaths worldwide.[30] But in Bangladesh, over the decade of the 1980s, BRAC, in a visionary initiative trained 12 million mothers, that's nearly every home across the country, on how to prepare ORS.[31]

More famously, the 2006 Nobel Peace Prize-winning NGO Grameen Bank popularised the spread of rural micro-credit.[32] Economist S.R. Osmani estimates that roughly 2 per cent of these micro-credit borrowers in rural Bangladesh escape poverty each year.[33]

In the 1970s, after the Liberation War and the famous 'Concert for Bangladesh' at Maddison Square Garden in New York, much of the foreign aid went to NGOs as 'service providers' rather than to the newly formed Bangladeshi government with its limited capacity. Since then, international assistance to Bangladesh has steeply fallen from 8 per cent of GDP in 1977 to only 1.4 per cent in 2020. In recent years, many Bangladeshi NGOs have, therefore, morphed into private social enterprises. BRAC, for example, which is one of the world's largest NGOs,[34] has eighteen social enterprises and numerous businesses.[35] These activities generate sizeable revenues which cross-subsidise their non-profit development activities.[36] Grameen Bank is another example. It has micro-credit members spread across more than 90 per cent of Bangladeshi villages.[37] Its telecom service Grameenphone's annual turnover of more than $1 billion, for example, is comparable to the box office revenues of popular Hollywood films such as Tom Cruise's latest *Top Gun: Maverick*.[38]

The role of NGOs in Bangladesh has also been quietly institutionalised.[39] In my fieldwork district, for example, the district collector regularly held monthly coordination meetings with all the civil society organisations who worked actively in his district.[40]

At the same time, in the 'unwarranted air of self-congratulation in the aid industry',[41] it is important not to over-exaggerate their accomplishments. For example, as a frustrated government primary school teacher complained to me, 'NGOs do less but show more.'[42] At this group meeting of school teachers, I asked them how many of their children studied in government schools. To my surprise, all of them raised their hands. Even in my sample, 59 per cent of students we tested at the primary level studied in government schools.

The international revenues of NGOs largely depend on amplifying their achievements. An exasperated fifty-four-year-old government health worker also lamented, 'It is a misconception that NGOs deliver free contraceptives door-to-door. That is what I have been doing in villages for more than three decades. The government supplies only one type of pills for free—sukhi bori—but NGOs have many brands. Some women prefer to pay and buy those pills which suit them better.'[43] In Bangladesh's highly competitive welfare delivery space, NGOs do expand citizens' choices. But, increasingly, Bangladeshi NGOs are less able to deliver services to poor households.[44] With the drying up of international donors in recent years, many NGOs have begun to change strategies. In schools, for instance, they have begun to charge high fees.[45]

Since the 1980s, the Bangladeshi political elites have also co-opted NGOs with government 'sub-contracts' to suppress radical social mobilisation. Most NGOs have tamely 'opted for service delivery and an advocacy strategy of apolitical nature'.[46] In contrast, progressive Indian civil society movements in the last few decades have successfully built social pressure to push political parties to enact a series of human rights-based laws, which ensures greater accountability.[47] But in Bangladesh, 'in the absence of any social movement initiated by NGOs or the poor themselves ... laws and policies have evolved as part of a top-down, elite-driven strategy to cope with poverty-related crises, rather than as outcomes of bottom-up political pressure'.[48]

Bangladeshi NGOs also actively encourage their vast network of members to vote in local elections and support chosen candidates.[49] In the 2011 Union Parishad elections, for example, 26 per cent of the elected leaders in the seats reserved for women were Grameen Bank members.[50] Still, there are clear limits to political adventurism in Bangladesh. Nobel laureate Mohammed Yunus faced a severe backlash for his quickly aborted ambitions to create a new political party and was even removed from the helm of Grameen Bank, the organisation he founded.[51] Still, due to the sheer scale of their micro-credit programmes and impressive financial muscle, Bangladeshi NGOs do have a limited 'countervailing influence'. BRAC, for example, has access to three of every four Bangladeshis as micro-finance borrowers. Grameen Bank has an even larger base of borrowers and 83 million Grameenphone subscribers, the largest national mobile telecom service.[52]

Foreign remittances have also boosted the sustainability of these NGOs. Before the pandemic, more than 6 million Bangladeshis worked abroad, mainly in India and the Middle East. In 2016, foreign remittances contributed to 5 per cent of Bangladeshi GNP.[53]

In sum, Bangladesh's development is dominated by two forces—the social contract of the State with its citizens and the apolitical NGOs. While both these players work side-by-side, Bangladesh's developmental success has 'depended more fully on the politics being right'.[54]

ASHRAFISATION

As a Muslim-majority country, Bangladesh has fewer caste-style hierarchies than Muslims in India.[55] Most Muslim village women we met in our door-to-door survey had no idea about their surnames. When Safiq probed further about their bongsha (family) or jati (clan) name, they still seemed clueless. In contrast, in the same villages, the Hindu residents were quite conscious of their caste and family lineage. One man even showed me his sacred thread and proclaimed loudly that he was a Kshatriya. But amongst the Muslims we met, only Jotdar (small landlord) families like Talukdars and Syeds seemed aware of their family lineage with a hint of unconcealed pride.

This also draws attention to a historical puzzle. Why did rural peasants in Bangladesh (previously East Bengal), oceans away from Arabia, convert to Islam?[56] Also, has religion alone shrunk social distances in Bangladesh?

For almost a millennium, Buddhism's 'egalitarian and universalist ethic' thrived in East Bengal.[57] In the third century BCE, Emperor Ashoka sent envoys to spread Buddhism across Asia. Soon after, East Bengal became the hub of two Buddhist empires—the Palas[58] and the Chandras. By the twelfth century, Buddhism flourished in Bengal, while most other kingdoms in India had reverted to Hinduism and its rigid caste hierarchies.[59]

Bengal's egalitarian culture was further strengthened by the advent of Islam. In 1204, the Turkish–Afghan military general Mohammad Bakhtiyar[60] swept into Bengal's 'frontier province'.[61] Since then, historians have been puzzled by the mass conversion of rural peasants to Islam in the eastern parts of Bengal. Even British officials were perplexed that 'it is not in the vicinity of the great Mughal capitals that we find the Muhhamadans most numerous'.[62] While there are many theories, historian Richard Eaton proposes that the 'indigenous' non-Hindu population were the main converts.[63] Over time, Sufis, as mystics from Central Asia, settled in Bengal and spread a syncretic variant of Islam.[64]

East Bengal developed its own distinctive religio-cultural worship. 'The worship of Buddha's footprints, for example, is believed to have been transformed into the veneration of the holy Prophet's qadam rasul (footprints).'[65] Egalitarianism was also at the heart of Sufi philosophy and Islam.[66] In one of the Hadiths, Prophet Muhammad declared, 'No Arab is superior to a non-Arab, nor is a white superior to a non-white, save through piety.'[67] The Turkish variant of Sufism, which flourished in Bengal, emphasised social mobility. The 1872 British Census administrators also found that a 'large number of Muhammadans ... occupy the same social position as their Hindu neighbours',[68] with fewer caste-style hierarchies.[69]

Sitting in the silence of the hallowed halls of London's British Library, while slowly tabulating columns from the Bengal Censuses of 1891 to 1931, I was struck by the fact that consistently around 85–95 per cent of Bengali Muslims considered themselves to be 'sheikhs'.[70] In contrast, in the rest of India, only 40–50 per cent of Muslims told census enumerators that they belonged to the same upper crust.[71] This self-perception of fluid social mobility was unique to Muslims in eastern Bengal. Perhaps, this was a form of 'ashrafisation',[72] similar to 'sanskritisation' amongst Hindus, where marginalised castes imitate those above them in the social hierarchy.

East Bengal's rich history of subaltern peasant movements has also been crucial in gradually diluting class hierarchies. After the 1757 Battle of Plassey and the advent of British colonialism in India, there was a change in East Bengal's rural elites. By 1765, the British East India Company had appointed agents to extract land revenues ruthlessly from small peasants. In protest, the Sannyasi and Fakir rebellion groups (1763–1800)[73] plundered East India Company's property and ran a parallel government.[74] Still, the exploitation of peasants was so extreme that the 1772 Great Bengal Famine claimed nearly 10 million lives.[75]

'Permanent Settlement', the new taxation system, both 'ruined the Muslim aristocracy in Bengal'[76] and impoverished the Muslim raiyats (peasants) who formed 70 per cent of the population.[77] A new Hindu zamindari class emerged as 'hereditary owners' of fertile land who paid only a fixed annual revenue to the British.[78] In the next twenty years, Bengali peasants lost at least one-third of their land as they were unable to repay land revenue arrears.[79]

This sharp social inequality also sparked four peasant movements in East Bengal—the Faraizi movement (1818–62), the Wahhabi uprising (1782–1931), the Santhal rebellion (1855) and the Indigo revolt (1860). These movements tried to bridge both caste and class hierarchies with slogans such as *'langol zar, zamin tar'* (land to the tiller).[80] 'One-third of the Muslim population of Dacca' joined these movements at one point of time or the other.[81] The prime minister of East Bengal A.K. Fazlul Huq (1937–43)[82] of the Krishak Praja Party (Peasants Party) attempted to abolish the zamindari system. But the draft law was sabotaged[83] by 'the power of big landlords and moneylenders'.[84]

Late one evening, in one of the upazilas[85], Farooq Bhai invited me to join an adda (discussion) with his friends at the newly minted Cultural Library. His friends were local academics affiliated with the Communist Party of Bangladesh. After many cups of lal cha, much to my surprise, one academic recounted that Panchagarh district, too, had been part of the 1855 Santhal rebellion. When I expressed some scepticism, he called his Santhali neighbour on the phone. On ringing off, he confidently asserted that, before Partition, in Panchagarh district alone, there were 6,000 Santhalis, but now only seventeen to twenty families remained. Despite all these peasant movements, it was only after the departure of the British, that the newly formed Pakistani government in East Bengal ultimately abolished the zamindari system.[86] The 1950 East Bengal State Acquisition and Tenancy Act set a thirty-three-acre ceiling. Many zamindars had to give up their land for redistribution to the landless. During fieldwork, I met eight-five-year-old Khairul Alam who recalled that 'previously we had 500–600 bighas of land. But in the fifties after the Pakistani government abolished zamindari, we had to surrender 400–500 bighas. We had only 20–25 bighas left.'[87] With this effective land redistribution in East Bengal in 1963-64, 83 per cent of cultivable land was of a size of less than 12.5 acres.[88] A former freedom fighter in the 1971 Liberation War whom I met also emphasised that, with this redistribution, 'feudalism disintegrated in the areas from the British zamindari system'. This erosion of the landed aristocracy also 'enabled the social structure of East Bengal to become more egalitarian'.[89] The latest 2019 Agricultural Census also confirms that only 8 per cent of rural households in Bangladesh are landless. However, only 55 per cent of rural families cultivate their own agricultural farms. In fact, now 22 per cent of rural Bangladeshis are sharecroppers or tenant cultivators and 30 per cent primarily earn their income as agricultural labourers.[90]

One of my hosts, Hilal bhai, was one such sharecropper who moonlighted as a rice trader. Everyone called him 'netaji' as he had all the traits of a budding politician. He explained that, despite the Tebhaga Andolan[91], sharecroppers had to hand over half the harvest to the landlord under the borga tenancy system prevalent in his village. But now, input costs were also shared in half. Also, after the Green Revolution that took place in the 1960s, land productivity increased so substantially that even tenant farmers became relatively prosperous. The alluvial soil of the Bangladeshi riverine delta, the world's largest, is immensely fertile. After the Green Revolution, a greater variety of crops could be cultivated in the district—rice, wheat, corn, tea, peanuts and vegetables. From then on, farmers could expect three good rice harvests: aman, boro and aush.

My research also revealed that, in the twentieth century, three historical waves of mass migrations in East Bengal had diluted class inequalities by displacing the traditional elites. In 1575, when Emperor Akbar conquered Bengal, Persian was adopted as the official court language. Two centuries later, the British imposed English as the official language. The Hindu elite of East Bengal welcomed this change. But the Muslim elite were hostile to English.[92] So, the British colonial administration employed very few Bengali Muslims. Instead, Hindus, who in 1871 formed less than half the population of the Bengal province, cornered 88 per cent of all the jobs available for Indians.[93]

The bhadralok[94] elite, thus, evolved as a predominantly Hindu, upper caste, professional and landowning class of 'gentlefolk'. Initially, this class of landowner 'Babus',[95] 'saw this as the essence of the social distance between himself and his social inferiors'.[96] By the twentieth century, as historian Joya Chatterji describes, being bhadralok also included 'possessing the goods of education, culture and anglicisation',[97] with 'one foot in the city and the other in the countryside'.[98] The East India Company was headquartered in Calcutta, which was also the political capital of the British Empire in India from 1757 to 1911. This Bengali Hindu bhadralok class was therefore a uniquely colonial phenomenon. But this elite class was expelled from East Bengal in three unique historical waves of mass displacement—in 1905, 1947 and 1971—which diluted the class hegemony of the bhadraloks.

First, in 1905, the British partitioned Bengal. In the aftermath of the 1857 Revolt, the British policy aimed to 'divide and rule' to quell potential mutinies. Eastern Bengal had a Muslim-majority. While this administrative partition had to be withdrawn within six years, it still managed to dilute the authority of the traditional Hindu bhadralok class in East Bengal to a certain extent. But Muslims still filled only 12 per cent of the appointments in Dhaka (then Dacca) in the British colonial administration.[99] By 1923, political leaders A.K. Fazlul Huq of the Krishak Praja Party and Chittaranjan Das of the Swaraj Party, representing their respective communities, signed the Hindu–Muslim Bengal Pact.[100] This treaty created separate Muslim electorates for the Legislative Council and reserved 55 per cent of seats for Muslims in government appointments.[101] The 1932 MacDonald Communal Award also shifted the political balance of power in favour of Muslims.[102]

The second division of Bengal took place as a part of the larger Partition of India at the time of Independence in 1947. With Muhammad Ali Jinnah emerging as 'the sole spokesman' of the Muslims,[103] the new nation-state of Pakistan included the Muslim-majority province of East Pakistan, i.e. East Bengal. In this bloody partition on religious grounds, three million refugees fled to India. In East Pakistan, earlier the majority of 'landlords and moneylenders were caste Hindus'. But, 'at the time of partition most of them migrated to India'.[104] So, not only did a large majority of the Hindu bhadralok class leave East Bengal, but the lands that they had left behind were also confiscated.[105]

However, newly formed Pakistan was an unstable country. Though Bengalis formed almost half the population, they were greatly underrepresented in the government of undivided Pakistan. Especially during periods of military rule in Pakistan, East Bengalis felt neglected politically, culturally and especially in terms of socio-economic development.[106]

To rub salt into their wounds, in his speech in Dhaka on

21 March 1948, Pakistani Governor-General Muhammad Ali Jinnah insisted on 'Urdu, and Urdu alone' being the official language across the territory of Pakistan.[107] In protest, a pro-Bengali 'Language Movement' erupted in East Pakistan.[108] Throughout the 1950s and 1960s, this 'cultural movement'[109] was deeply secular and had 'an equalizing influence across religions'.[110]

With this groundswell of Bengali popular support, Sheikh Mujibur Rehman's Awami League Party squarely won the 1970 general elections held in undivided Pakistan. But the Bengali leader was arrested instead of being invited to form Pakistan's new government. The Pakistan Army airdropped soldiers into East Pakistan and launched the brutal 1971 Operation Searchlight. Most Bengali-speaking people in East Pakistan supported the Mukti Bahini (Liberation Forces) guerrilla fighters. In this bloody nine-month 'Liberation War', the Indian Army extended external support to the Bengali guerrillas.[111] Hundreds of East Bengali civilians were killed in this genocide[112], and more than 200,000 women were raped.[113] Nearly 10 million refugees fled to India in conditions similar to those our host Jahirunal Apa had described. Journalist Salil Tripathi's book *The Colonel Who Would Not Repent* has one of the most bone-chilling descriptions of the mass murder of students in the hostels of Dhaka University.

> Eyewitnesses who survived have testified that on the day the troops took over the campus, soldiers went from bed to bed beating up students, killing most of them. The next day, Pakistani soldiers asked students to move the bodies of dead students, which many of them did for fear of being killed. Resistance would have been futile, but removing the bodies did not help them either. A grainy video smuggled out of Pakistan shows several students lined up to be shot. One of them, dressed in black, falls to his knees pleading for mercy. The pitiless soldiers shoot all of them.[114]

The Shaheed Minars (martyrs' memorials) constructed in many schools that now dot the rural Bangladeshi landscape are a constant reminder of the many lives lost during the Language Movement. In 1971, Bangladesh was born as a new country.

This turbulent civil war triggered the third wave of elite displacement. After the war, an estimated 1.5 million Bengali-speaking Hindu refugees, including those from erstwhile zamindari families, permanently stayed back in India, especially in the neighbouring Indian states of West Bengal, Tripura and Assam. On the other hand, most of the remaining wealthy Urdu-speaking Muslims migrated to West Pakistan.[115]

The new nation was born into tumult. Three years later, in a severe famine, 1.5 million Bangladeshis died due to starvation. Eight-five-year-old Khairul Alam told me, 'During the famine, there was hoarding of foodgrains by businessmen for profit. Some people did not have any food for ten–fifteen days. The government gave cooked food in langars [soup kitchens]. During the famine, many people perished on this Panchagarh road.'[116] Bangladesh's success today probably owes much to this painful birth. The devastation of the early 1970s was a turning point in the social transformation of the new country.

The elite displacement due to these three partitions and the devastation wrecked by the famine have inadvertently resulted in a high degree of social homogenisation, especially in rural areas.

But some social divisions continue to fester here as much as anywhere else. Today, Hindus form roughly 9 per cent of Bangladesh's population. Of them, a fifth are Dalits, who face double discrimination as marginalised minorities.[117] For example, in Dinajpur city, Dalits are so socially excluded that they are still not allowed to enter restaurants or barber shops.[118] Some occupations, too, continue to be dominated by oppressed-caste Hindus. In northern Bangladesh, for example, we discovered that Dalits were still hired to empty sanitation pits. Even in our survey, in Panchagarh district, half the homes confirmed that when a latrine pit filled up, in 94 per cent of the cases, they would hire Dalit cleaners, mostly Methors or Doms, to clean it up. Across borders, caste prejudices seem the hardest to sweep away.

SULTANA'S DREAM

Four of my surveyors in Panchagarh, who also worked with a local NGO, had planned a massive celebration to mark 8 March, International Women's Day. The chief guests they had invited were two senior district officials, ironically both men. The official from the police department delivered a patronising spiel on women's empowerment, but at least he ended on a high note by praising his wife, a gynaecologist who was professionally more qualified than him. The schoolgirls in the audience clapped uproariously.

The other invited speakers were a female freedom fighter, a female union nirbahi officer and the head of the local Women's Commission. The main event was a cycle rally by schoolgirls—quite appropriate as Panchagarh was the only district in Bangladesh where we saw schoolgirls routinely cycling to school, a rare sight in other districts.[119]

My primary survey also confirmed the unusual Bangladeshi trend of educational hypogamy: two of every three married women we spoke to were equally or more educated than their husbands. Feminist economist Naila Kabeer argues that, in recent years, there has been a rise of the 'daughter-in-law phenomenon'. The increase in female education, employment opportunities and women's empowerment has clearly improved the perception of the worthiness of young women in the eyes of their mothers-in-law. Within Bangladeshi homes, this has spurred an inter-generational shift in traditional power dynamics.[120]

But how has this country, with its turbulent history, renegotiated gender norms? Bangladeshi activists chronicle their women's movements in three distinct phases.

First, in the pre-Partition phase (1820–1947), the women's movement in East Bengal protested against the extreme forms of purdah, which literally caged women inside their homes and restricted their mobility. Bhadramahila—largely upper-class Muslim women along with some Hindus—lived in seclusion in the andarmahal (inner house) and were only permitted to travel in palanquins.[121] Sociologist Dagmar Engels has argued that this extreme sexual control of women increased their absolute dependence on men. Begum Rokeya launched a scathing attack on this barbaric seclusion,[122] justified by the symbolic 'veneration of women'.[123] By the late nineteenth century, with the advent of British 'Westernisation' and the influence of the Brahmo Samaj,[124] bhadramahila began to discard purdah norms.[125] By 1826, Christian missionaries had started schools exclusively for girls.[126] Within a century, women's empowerment and mobility increased to such an extent that in East Bengal they were in the frontlines of Mahatma Gandhi's 1920–21 Non-Cooperation Movement and the 1931 Civil Disobedience Movement against the British Empire.[127] Immediately before Independence, rural women, with great 'intensity of commitment', also joined the Tebhaga Andolan.[128] Ila Mitra, a fiery, communist leader,[129] led 50,000 women in the Nachnol revolt and is still considered a legend among the Santhals of East Bengal. But she was brutally tortured in police custody, and the movement was crushed.[130]

The second phase is the Pakistani period (1947–1971). In the heady 1960s, Bengali women joined with fervour the secular movement against the imposition of Urdu. On 21 February 1952, female students were the first protestors to defy the curfew at Dhaka University, which sparked the Language Movement.[131] For two decades after that, women regularly organised large numbers of university and school students to participate in protest marches.[132] At that time, simple freedoms, such as wearing a sari publicly, performing traditional cultural dances and publicly celebrating Pahela Baisakh (Bengali harvest festival) became potent symbols of rebellion.[133] Bengali women also challenged the Pakistani government's imposition of headscarves on them and the ban on Rabindra Sangeet on television.[134] By 1971, women had also taken up combat roles in the Mukti Bahini liberation force.[135] The Mukti Bahini even had a separate female battalion, the gun-carrying 'Naari Muktijoddhas' (female freedom fighters). These important contributions of women to the Language Movement, however, have been historically sidelined.

The nine-month Liberation War marked a turning point in Bangladeshi history and altered gender relations. As the veteran feminist Raunaq Jahan described to me, 'The war of independence was a shock to the social system of a non-violent rural society.'[136] The Pakistani army employed mass rapes as a weapon of war. This was one of the darkest chapters in the history of the conflict, and the new nation carried the trauma of the 200,000–300,000 birangana (war heroines)[137] and their unwanted pregnancies. Many of these 'war babies' were aborted or later given up for international adoption. On one of the many eye-opening days that I spent doing research at the Nehru Memorial Museum & Library in New Delhi, I chanced upon Nayanika Mookherjee's book *The Spectral Wound: Sexual Violence, Public Memories, and the Bangladesh War of 1971* and Yasmin Sakia's *Women, War, and the Making of Bangladesh: Remembering 1971*.[138] These books describe the horrors of these rape camps in military barracks, where hundreds of women were held captive and tortured. Instead of glorifying the 'faceless, essentialised' biranganas, these books give voice and agency to the women to narrate their own experiences in searing detail.

> I saw many girls in the bunker. There were 50 or 60 of us. My sister-in-law was there also, but she died. She died in the bunker. She died because of torture; three women died

there. I don't know till today how many women died after they were rescued.[139]

These books also empathetically chronicle the futures that these survivors have laboured to build in the five decades after the war.

The third phase started after Bangladesh's independence from Pakistan. In the new nation-state, women's empowerment became a national focus. The impact of these multiple social tragedies led to 'the beginnings of a feminist consciousness in the country'.[140] Raunaq Jahan described to me how the genocide and mass rape 'shifted the power structure and women's social status'. It 'unhinged women's role from being necessarily protected by men, to go out to earn an income'.

The famine in 1974 marked another turning point. This period dismantled the shadow of the purdah. Women renegotiated the old 'patriarchal bargain', which 'relinquished control of their mobility, assets and earning potential in return for male protection and provision'.[141] In the aftermath of the famine, 'NGO movements mushroomed and social change was in the air'.[142]

After the creation of Bangladesh, with the support of numerous NGOs, millions of women participated in micro-credit[143] schemes to expand their incomes. Also, in the quest for survival, scores of poor women broke purdah and searched for employment.[144] Thousands of women joined both NGOs and government organisations as developmental foot-soldiers, as teachers, health workers and social workers.

Since the turn of the millennium, 90 per cent of the workers recruited in the readymade garment sector (RMGS) sweatshops have also been women. Across the rural landscape, thousands of village women also toil in agro-processing industries, from jute mills to dairy units. Every morning, on any Bangladeshi rural highway, streams of women in cotton saris can be seen walking purposefully towards these factories with steel dabba lunch boxes in their hands. These economic opportunities have also helped women to renegotiate their control over public spaces.

One night after dinner at the factory canteen near our village, I quickly jotted my observations in my field notes:

> Outside the jute factory, on either side of the road, there was a line of teashops (arranged like American bars—with stools) with the owner (bartender) in the centre of a square arrangement of four tables and the customers on benches around him. The first thing that struck me was the number of women in saris, with their hair covered with the thin cotton pallu, who were busy sipping tea and eating shingaras (samosas) and cake. Most of them worked in the jute factory, often in night shifts. One woman wrapped a small muffin in a newspaper to carry home for her child. Partaking in these simple pleasures seems to be an early sign of empowerment, unthinkable across the border in rural Bihar.

Of course, women who work for wages also bear the double burden of housework. Worse, the conditions in the Bangladeshi factories and sweatshops are often appalling, as I saw first-hand during the night shifts. In 2013, the entire Rana Plaza factory building, which did not conform to safety norms, collapsed and made international headlines.

The precarious employment and low wages of Bangladeshi women at the bottom of the capitalist hierarchy is a double-edged sword: they reflect extreme exploitation, but the opportunity to work outside the home does offer a degree of economic security, mobility and empowerment.

SHONAR BANGLADESH

Thus, Bangladesh's development is a picture of contradictions. The warp and weft of its turbulent history has created Bangladesh's distinctive weave as a country with fewer social inequalities.

A typical Aama Samuha (mothers' group) meeting in Nepal with village women from different castes in a wooden gazebo

5

NEPAL

We have carried bags in our laps in place of baby,
We have carried gun in our hands in place of sickle.
– Women Fighters, Sudin,
Maoist song of the Tharu ethnic tribe[1]

After two hours on a very rickety road with our heads frequently bumping into the ceiling of the small bus, my translator Bijeta and I finally reached our destination. The picturesque village on the hills was worth the rough ride. A resourceful friend had arranged for us to live in a farmer's house.

This Nepali village in the foothills of the Himalayas was lush with greenery and numerous streams. A hanging bridge across a small river was so pretty, I could scarcely believe my luck. My urban lungs were on a picnic. The skies were clear blue, and the air pure and clean. Our hosts ate only the rice and vegetables they grew in their own fields. They drank milk from the cows and buffaloes in their backyard. Little was wasted. Every morsel of grain, even from plates set out for washing was eaten by animals—chickens, goats, cows and buffaloes—grazing around the house.

But beneath the tranquil surface lurked a darker truth. Walking through the village, we realised that the habitation was clearly segregated on caste lines. The Bahuns and Chhetris (Brahmins and Kshatriyas in Nepal), as the upper castes, lived near the road, owned fertile land, ran the village shops and possessed bullocks. The Janajatis and Dalits invariably lived in houses in remote hamlets on the upper reaches of the hillocks. Their homes were difficult to reach. Especially during the rains, I found myself on all fours, trying to climb up the steep dirt track. Because marginalised castes lived on the steepest slopes, their access to water was also minimal. Women spent gruelling hours fetching water in pots precariously balanced inside bamboo baskets which they carried on their backs.

The houses in the village looked nearly identical. They were two-storied wooden structures, designed for greater protection against floods and earthquakes. The ground floor usually had a kitchen with walls plastered with mud or thatch and a separate shed for animals. Most of the floors above, with tiled roofs, had bedrooms and rustic, wooden, open-air sit-outs.

The local schools were the real hubs of activity. Government schools usually began at 6 a.m. and closed by noon. For two months in the winter, the timings shifted to 10 a.m. to 4 p.m. The first school we visited had a simple wooden structure. The children sat on benches and desks, and the walls were covered with colourful drawings made by the students. Like Bangladesh, the teachers' room had many helpful flex posters describing human body parts, the national animal, Nepali leaders and multiplication tables. An NGO had provided some of these posters and the school had purchased the rest with its maintenance funds. Another NGO had donated a collection of toys. In the half-hour recess, we saw the students play football, ludo, snakes and ladders and jigsaw puzzles. The teachers themselves were engrossed in a game of chess. The children were all smiles when they saw our camera, and ran around excitedly, posing for pictures.

Peeping into the classroom and later cross-checking with the teacher, we realised that the seating arrangements did not reflect any bias based on caste or religion. But girls and boys sat on separate benches. Their parents had purchased the smart uniforms they were wearing. The government school did not charge any fees, except for a modest examination fee. All girls and Dalit children also received annual scholarships.

However, the students did not seem to understand the meaning of most of the words that they were reading in English in a singsong manner. Their English teacher did not seem to comprehend my spoken English either. But the English textbook was well-designed to reflect Nepali culture. For example, there were many simple stories of animals from the Jataka Tales, that is, the previous births of the Buddha, who was born in Lumbini in Nepal. There were also descriptions of Nepali Hindu festivals and even a vignette on the travails of street children.

The forty-five-year-old head teacher, Hari Paudel, was a serious, soft-spoken and warm-hearted person. Hari Sir, as the villagers called him, was a Chhetri and had lived and taught in that village for twelve years. He had cleared the Lok Seva exam and joined Nepal's exclusive teaching cadre. His youngest son had studied only in government schools and was now in the tenth standard. Hari complained that his salary was not enough. Later, we visited his home and met his wife, son and parents. Apart from an electric kettle, their mud home was bare of luxuries. Hari owned no vehicle and usually walked twenty minutes to the school. One day we even saw him awkwardly take a lift atop a local tractor on his way back home. His family owned seven kathas of land, which his wife and parents cultivated. They ate whatever they grew and did not need to buy rice from the market.

Hari informed us that, despite all the political turmoil in Nepal in the last two decades, school textbooks always arrived on time, at the start of each academic year. He had to go to the district headquarters to collect them, however.

At first, while testing the fifth-grade students, I was disappointed that they could not solve a simple carry-over subtraction problem. With twigs and Bijeta's assistance, I tried in vain to explain the method to them. Then Hari walked into the classroom and showed us the value of his sixteen years of experience. He used a simple visual technique, of adding a line above the numerals on the blackboard, parking the carry-over adjustments on this 'roof'. Everyone grasped the explanation in a jiffy. Hari told us that he had already taught them carry-over subtraction, but they had probably forgotten. The children currently in the third grade, whom we had tested earlier, could not do the calculation as they had just started the school year and this topic had not been covered.

Since Hari was also an elected ward member, his time was precious. The previous month, nearly 200 people had visited his home for help in filling out forms for registration of marriages, citizenship certificates, birth certificates as well as applications for government programmes. He met parents almost every day to discuss their children's performance. As expected, he had also lent money to many of them. Later, we bumped into him at a roadside meeting, and realised that he had also organised an enterprising local savings group.

We also learnt from the villagers that Hari Sir was a local leader of the Maoist Party. So, the next time we met him, we asked him a few questions about his political journey. Hari had joined the party in its founding years in 1994 as a student. During the long years of the People's War, he had to keep his affiliation a secret. Prachanda, the Maoist armed rebel leader who, in December 2022, became Nepal's prime minister once again, had also started his career as a village schoolteacher. Hari told us that his life had been threatened a few times. In fact, Sindhuli district had been a hotbed of Maoist activities in the early days. But he had never been imprisoned since he was a government servant.

The main question on which I wanted clarity from him was whether the Maoist People's War had, in any way, played a role in reducing caste inequality in Nepal. Hari gave me a vivid description of the contrast before and after the civil war. With a glint of rage in his otherwise calm demeanour, he said:

> Previously, the open discrimination against Dalits was so acute that they would not be allowed to sit in the same room as the upper castes. Later, even if Dalits were allowed to sit in the same room, once they left, the upper castes would symbolically purify the area with cow urine.

I distinctly remember that my Nepali colleague from the NGO Oxfam had given me an identical description nearly a decade ago. Hearing this again from Hari seemed to confirm that casteism and open discrimination in Nepal had indeed been far more widespread before the People's War than even in parts of northern India. In fact, until 1962, the Muluki Ain (Legal Code) of the Hindu kingdom of Nepal had even legalised and institutionalised casteism. Different punishments and fines were earmarked for the same crimes based on the caste of the perpetrator and the victim. For example, a Brahmin found guilty of premeditated murder would only have his property confiscated and might be publicly shamed, but all the other castes would face capital punishment.[2]

Hari stressed that caste equations had changed considerably. 'Now Nepal has passed a law against untouchability and discrimination. The People's War had certainly played a role in reducing social barriers. But some discrimination still exists.'

In his soft voice, he explained the transformation. 'Because of the War, people are more aware of their rights and are willing to fight for them.' But it took me many more conversations with villagers to truly understand how the guerrilla rebels had made a dent in age-old caste dynamics.

Just as we were leaving the meeting, Hari asked me if I was still associated with an NGO. He wanted help with improving the quality of education and creating employment opportunities in his village. I was struck by this request from such a reticent man. But being realistic about the limited time and resources at my disposal, I asked if procuring books for the school library would be sufficient. Hari jumped at the suggestion. Later, in Kathmandu, I met two owners of a chain of independent and second-hand bookshops that catered to foreign tourists. They readily agreed to donate many cartons of excess books in English, Nepali and Hindi to Hari's government school. Ever efficient, Bijeta even figured out a way to coordinate with a few bus conductors to transport these books to Hari's village for free. This exercise was, by far, the most joyous part of my Nepali fieldwork.

But it left me with a lingering question—why are even strangers in Nepal so willing to help one another? Why does the government invest so consistently in schools, textbooks and teachers? And as Hari had suggested, did the Maoist People's War really reduce caste inequalities? Was this the key to Nepal's human development successes?

NAYA NEPAL

The Maoist rebels and successive democratic governments have indeed built on the collective dream of 'Naya Nepal' (New Nepal)—a slogan that became popular towards the end of the People's War (1996–2006). The larger aim of the war had been to abolish the monarchy, dilute the dominance of elites and advocate for marginalised communities. With this vision, Nepal's new 2015 Constitution has made a solid commitment towards protecting human rights.

The post-war return to democracy, however, has not been smooth. In the past sixty years, Nepal has had fifty prime ministers[3]. The country has also had a long history of rebellions, palace intrigues and frictional alliances. Despite this turbulent polity, the developmental state has slowly managed to take root. My research shows that three factors have played an important role: the electoral successes of left-wing parties, traditional community organisations and foreign remittances to aid welfare investments.

First, let us consider the legacy of the Maoist People's War and successive post-democratic left-leaning governments. The main aim of the decade-long guerrilla rebellion in the last Hindu kingdom in the world was to topple the monarchy, end feudalism and restore democracy.[4] The rebels also tried to challenge social exclusion based on caste and ethnicity. But the war also extracted an incalculable toll. Within a decade, 13,000 Nepalis died, 200,000 were internally displaced, thousands migrated abroad and the economy lost an estimated US$ 315 million.[5] Yet, astonishingly, despite the intense conflict, Nepal's official HDI scores increased and the country moved from a low to a medium level of human development.[6] In this decade, poverty also fell from 42 per cent in 1995-96 to 31 per cent in 2003-4.[7] By 2010, even income inequality, which had increased initially,[8] fell to less than the pre-conflict levels.[9]

Post-conflict, too, the Nepali developmental state has been deeply influenced by left-wing parties, which have been in power for roughly ten of the fifteen democratic years in three distinct phases (2008–13, 2015–17, 2018–21) and again from year-end 2022. But the transition to a federal democratic republic has been somewhat rocky. More than ten prime ministers have taken oath in the last decade alone. Nepal's

Table 5.1: Regimes in Nepal's post-conflict political history, 2005–21

Timeline	Political position	Political Party	Prime Minister
2005–2006	Monarchy	Direct Rule by King Gyanendra Bir Bikram Shah	
2006–2008	Centre-left	Nepali Congress	Girija Prasad Koirala
2008–2009		Unified Communist Party of Nepal (Maoist)	Pushpa Kamal Dahal (Comrade Prachanda)
2009–2011	Left-wing	Communist Party of Nepal (Unified Marxist–Leninist)	Madhav Kumar Nepal
			Jhala Nath Khanel
2011–2013		Unified Communist Party of Nepal (Maoist)	Baburam Bhattarai
2013–2014		Independent	Khil Raj Regmi
2014–2015	Centre-left	Nepali Congress	Sushil Koirala
2015–2016	Left-wing	Communist Party of Nepal (Unified Marxist–Leninist)	Khadga Prasada Oli
2016–2017		Unified Communist Party of Nepal (Maoist)	Pushpa Kamal Dahal
2017–2018	Centre-left	Nepali Congress	Sher Bahadur Deuba
2018–2021	Left-wing	Communist Party of Nepal (Unified Marxist–Leninist)	Khadga Prasada Oli
2021–2022	Centre-left	Nepali Congress	Sher Bahadur Deuba
2022–	Left-wing	Communist Party of Nepal (Maoist Centre)	Pushpa Kamal Dahal

economic growth, too, has been slow. However, the frequent return to power of the left-wing parties has resulted in a firm commitment to social protection. The drafting of a new constitution has also cemented 'a set of defined rights which have had a strongly universal character'.[10] The budgets for social assistance and social pensions alone, for example, rose from 0.5 per cent in 2004-5 to 2 per cent of the GDP in 2014. These commitments were the result of:

> ... the expectations derived from the People's Movement of 2006 and the Interim Constitution of 2007. There is political pressure from the rank and file of political parties, civil society and trade unions for the government to deliver on this vision and meet the aspirations of the 'new Nepal'. There is also inter-party competition, which makes it politically attractive to opt for progressive social policies.[11]

Even before the People's War, the government of the Communist Party of Nepal (Unified Marxist-Leninist) had introduced a pioneering universal social pension.[12] After the war, in 2008, the former Maoist guerrilla rebels emerged as the largest political party in the Constituent Assembly elections. They not only increased the pension but also guaranteed universal coverage.[13] Nepal is now one of the few countries in the developing world where 80 per cent of the elderly receive a pension[14] in cash every three months.[15] In villages, we met many older men and women who depended on this lifeline.

Similarly, in 2008, a populist programme guaranteed free outpatient healthcare and essential medicines. In the Constituent Assembly elections, nearly all twenty-five political parties also promised universal healthcare as a fundamental right in their manifestos.[16] Nepal's extensive network of well-equipped primary health posts and hospitals are a testament to this commitment. The 2009 Aama Surakshya cash grant has also encouraged mothers to deliver in hospitals. Nepal's Child Grant for children under five years has also been successful.[17]

The vision of left-wing Nepali governments has always been to build an expansive welfare state. Though the two main left-wing political parties—the Maoist and the Marxist-Leninist factions—merged in 2018,[18] their union was short-lived. After the pandemic, with a new left-wing government assuming the reins of power, the expansion of social policies is likely to accelerate.[19]

The second factor is an unusual network of traditional community organisations which provide an extra layer of peer assistance to improve access in Nepal's public services. The two prominent community organisations are the Aama Samuhas (mothers' groups) and the community forestry groups.

The Aama Samuhas began in 1816 when the British Army began to recruit Gurkha soldiers. Their wives and mothers, left behind in the rural countryside, formed groups to support one another.[20] With the restoration of Nepal's democracy in the 1990s, Aama Samuhas have expanded nationwide. With the support of NGOs, these vibrant women's groups now engage in micro-credit, peace education, literacy programmes, healthcare peer support, infrastructure maintenance, women's rights and other welfare activities.

One sweltering afternoon,[21] Bijeta and I stumbled upon an Aama Samuha meeting. We saw women from different castes sitting in a circle in the cool shade of a beautiful wooden gazebo outside a health post. When we walked in, they were exchanging recipes, gossip and political updates. One woman complained that she had heard on television that government servants would receive a pay hike. She wisely argued that this could fuel inflation as sudden increases in disposable income could create supply constraints. In another village, an Aama Samuha we met had morphed into a micro-credit group, primarily to support pregnant women with medical emergencies in the rugged mountain terrain.

The revival of these Aama Samuhas is a visible fruit of

Nepal's peace dividend. Importantly, these groups are ideal training-grounds for women to gain experience for more prominent roles in public service.[22]

Similarly, community forestry groups have played a productive role. Community forestry has a long history in Nepal.[23] Many forests were nationalised and converted into national parks in the late 1950s.[24] In a policy shift in the late 1970s, amorphous forest 'user groups' were created. Still, it was only after the 1993 Community Forest Act that village groups began to harvest forest resources systematically. These forestry groups are often more dynamic and less politicised than local government bodies.[25] Most villages have a 'user group' that sells forest produce, from timber to herbal medicines, to earn handsome incomes. Nepal's community forest groups make more than US$ 10 million annually in revenues, which they usually invest back to cater to village-level priorities.[26] For example, one forestry group we met had innovatively used its funds to hire temporary teachers for the local school and also to light up the village with solar panels.[27]

The third—unexpected—pillar of Nepal's welfare investments has been foreign remittances. Nearly half of all Nepali homes have at least one person working abroad. Most of these international migrants are in India, across the open border. Before the pandemic, remittances contributed to 27 per cent of Nepal's GDP. In contrast, they fuelled only 6 per cent of Bangladesh's and 3 per cent of India's GDP. From 1996 to 2011, 33 per cent of rural Nepali families could climb out of poverty as remittances[28] were usually spent on 'non-food, human development investment and health'.[29] By 2017, for example, nearly every Nepali home had a toilet, even without government subsidies. But the post-pandemic after-shocks and its impact on international migration have been severe.

A remittance-fuelled economy also leads to some regressive repercussions. 'English medium' private schools, for example, have mushroomed across villages to cater to the booming demand from remittance-earning families. Colloquially, these non-residential schools are called 'boarding schools'. We saw that most of the children enrolled in these classrooms were boys.[30] This gender discrimination reflects a significant new trend in Nepali society, where remittances are disproportionately spent on boys.[31]

So, an unusual combination of factors have strengthened the post-conflict Nepali welfare state. But have social distances been bridged in Naya Nepal?

JAN ANDOLANS

When you board a bus in Nepal, the first question often asked is, 'What is your caste?' Even in northern India, while people try to guess your caste from your surname, the question is rarely this direct. Despite this odd cultural trait, there has been a visible melting of caste inequities in the country in the last decade.

Historically, the caste structure in Nepal, as a multi-ethnic, multi-racial and multi-lingual country, has been quite different from India. As a Dalit feminist Nepali activist explained to me, in India, only people who are employed in so-called 'unclean' occupations are considered to be Dalit. But in Nepal, people employed in several other occupations can also be classified as Dalit.[32] For example, in northern India, Bishwakarmas (blacksmiths) are officially classified as OBC. But in Nepal, Bishwakarmas are Dalit but of a higher order than Sarkis (cobblers).[33]

Nepal has had an uneven history of both assimilation and stratification. Gautama Buddha was born around the sixth century BCE in Lumbini which is now a province of modern Nepal. In his lifetime and for centuries later, Buddhism spread to Nepal and across Asia. But by the third century

BCE, the Lichhavi dynasty of Shaivite Hindu rulers began the rigid process of 'Hinduisation'. They adopted Sanskrit as the official language.[34] Then, the Malla dynasts, who ruled for the next five centuries, classified citizens into sixty-four sub-castes. These sub-castes with strict restrictions on social intercourse and mobility were more complicated than India's varna system.

In the eighteenth century, King Prithvi Narayan Shah of the Rajput lineage unified fifty-six princely kingdoms, in a process now referred to as 'Nepalisation'. He dreamt of a united Nepal as the epitome of 'asil Hindustan' (pure land of the Hindus).[35] The Shahs also brutally subjugated indigenous communities and worsened the stranglehold of upper caste domination. The Rana oligarchy, which ruled for the next century, was even more regressive. In 1854, the Ranas codified the Muluki Ain social code, which legalised a modified version of the Hindu Laws of Manu. The code institutionalised caste discrimination, and legalised untouchability and caste-based social hierarchies.[36] It unified criminal law and customary law based on an edifice of caste-based purity laws. For more than a century (1854-1963), the Muluki Ain formally divided Nepali society into the touchable (pure) and the untouchable (impure) castes.[37]

The upper castes were considered to be the superior Tagadhari (twice-born sacred-thread-wearing) castes. The Shudra (impure but touchable) and Achhoot (impure and untouchable) castes at the lowest rung had strict taboos against inter-dining and inter-marriage. Muslims, Buddhists and foreigners were considered low-caste and 'pani na chalne' (water-unacceptable). Indigenous tribal Janajatis were also divided into sub-groups as those who were 'touchable' or those who could be 'enslaved'.[38]

For the same crime, different castes would receive different punishments. In case of inter-caste sexual relations with a Brahmin woman, for example, the thread-wearing upper castes and liquor-consuming Matwali castes would only be imprisoned for up to six years. But the untouchable castes would be branded and all their property confiscated, while the enslavable castes would be imprisoned for four years and then enslaved for life.[39] Even uncontrollable farts in public elicited different fines based on the caste of the 'offender' and the 'victim', with the largest fines imposed on untouchables.[40]

For a century, the Ranas also restricted education. In 1942, only 0.7 per cent of Nepalis could read and write. The Ranas banned foreign travel as well, isolating Nepal from the rest of the world. In 1950, a multi-party armed revolution finally overthrew the Ranas. But after a short period of partial democracy, in 1960, King Mahendra of the Shah dynasty banned all political parties and introduced a regressive Panchayat system. The new 1963 Muluki Ain, however, finally banned untouchability. But Dalits continued to be prohibited from entering the Pashupatinath shrine.[41] The country remained acutely socially stratified. Even by the 1980s, the literacy rate in Nepal had increased to only 21 per cent.

Against this backdrop, my research shows that in the last four decades, four factors have played a vital role in diluting social inequalities: the two Jan Andolans, the Dalit movement, international migration and the Maoist People's War.

First, in the 1990s, thousands of citizens protested on the streets in the multi-party Jan Andolan I (Peoples' Movement). Eventually, the king abolished the Panchayat system and lifted the ban on political parties. However, in the politically tumultuous 1990s, six prime ministers formed nine different governments. In the midst of this turmoil, in 1996, the Maoist wing of the Communist faction launched a rural, armed guerrilla war—the People's War—to overthrow the feudal monarchy. In 2001, in the middle of this intense civil conflict, the monarch dismissed the elected government and declared a state of emergency. A few months later, the sensational massacre of many of the royal family members by the heir to the throne marked a turning point in shattering royal authority.

After these dramatic events, seven political parties collectively organised Jan Andolan II (People's Movement II). In April 2006, hundreds of thousands of Nepalis marched on the streets, clamouring for democracy. Chanting slogans, they surrounded the royal palace in Kathmandu until the monarch finally stepped down.

After the restoration of democracy in 2006, the Maoist rebels were the ones who won the elections and had the most representatives in the Constituent Assembly. In those stirring days, I happened to be in Kathmandu to attend an NGO conference. I still remember seeing trucks full of cheering Maoist supporters descending on the capital from the rural countryside to celebrate their victory. After nine long years of consultations in a country with sixty-five different ethnic groups, Nepal finally adopted a new secular constitution in 2015 with a strong emphasis on human rights.

The second factor in diluting social inequalities was Nepal's Dalit movement. Nepal's 3.6 million Dalits form only 14 per cent of the population.[42] Due to extreme social and economic exclusion, 42 per cent of Dalits live below the national poverty line,[43] and their literacy rate is 15 per cent lower than the national average.[44] Historically, Dalits have also faced severe forms of 'socially sanctioned apartheid'. In some regions, they continue to be denied access even to public water taps.

The Dalit movement in Nepal emerged in the 1950s. The genesis of it was the Samaj Sudhar Sangh's 1952 agitation for entry into the Pashupatinath temple. By the 1980s, Dalit activists began to demand affirmative action, akin to that in India. The 1990 Constitution, granted reservation quotas to fifty-nine castes and ethnic groups. In 2002, the government created the National Dalit Commission, and finally in 2011 enacted the Caste-Based Discrimination and Untouchability (Offence and Punishment) Act.

The 2015 Constitution also includes several specific clauses that protect the fundamental rights of Dalits. At the lowest tier of governance, for example, in an innovative step, a third of the budget of every Village Development Committee (VDC) is divided among various castes based on their numbers in the population.[45] In one village, we met the head of the Dalit committee. He informed me that they had decided to use their share of the budget to build a well and piped drinking water for the Dalit hamlet, along with a gravel road to the government school.

Third, international migration has also played a valuable role in bridging caste inequalities. Before the pandemic, remittances contributed to a quarter of Nepal's economy.[46] During fieldwork, we also interviewed unschooled Musahar and Dom men who had worked as labourers in the construction industry in the Middle East and South East Asia, and had acquired modest material prosperity. One day, in the home of one of our hosts, we met Birbal Thapa, an immigration agent. He said that although only 1 per cent of Nepali migrants that he recruited for jobs abroad were fully illiterate, only 5 per cent had completed the tenth grade. The rest had spent only a few years in school. When we probed further, he admitted that his work was illegal. He and his brother worked as agents for a 'manpower company'. They would 'liaise' between companies abroad and the Nepali government to obtain visas and tickets. He charged approximately Nepali Rupees 20,000–30,000 from each labourer to help them migrate abroad.

Birbal had worked for three years in Malaysia and five years in Iraq. He sent people primarily to Qatar, Saudi Arabia and Kuwait. The primary demand he said was in the construction business, especially in Qatar for both the 2020 Summer Olympics (which it did not ultimately win the bid) and the now-historic 2022 FIFA World Cup in Doha that the Argentinian team won in a cliff-hanger. Since there was no question of local Qataris doing physical labour, recruitment from abroad was essential to build the stadiums and world-class facilities. Birbal claimed that the labourers largely came from Myanmar, Vietnam, Bangladesh, Nepal and the Indian states of West Bengal, Bihar and Odisha. He estimated that each labourer earned about 20,000 to 25,000 Indian rupees per month, roughly Nepali Rupees 50,000, which the workers considered a fortune. In his experience, most men travelled on two-year visas and worked abroad for five to ten years. After that, they saved enough to buy land in their village, build a house and sometimes even shift to cities, especially to Kathmandu.

Birbal admitted that the working and living conditions on foreign shores were abysmal. Many employers confiscated the passports of migrants until the completion of work, though governments in the region have now begun to insist that labourers be allowed to retain their passports. Birbal felt that, despite these hardships,

> 'The condition of the Musahars has improved so much in this village. Previously, whole families were employed on other people's farms and received only two square meals daily as payment. Now they own farmlands.'

He also emphasised that when migrant labourers abroad work, eat and live together, 'caste barriers dissolve substantially'.[47] He also believed that migration had done a lot of good, if not for the labourers, then at least for their children and wives back home. According to Birbal, the only migrants who suffered were those addicted to alcohol who squandered away their savings.

Building on this newfound prosperity and social mobility, in the small town of Sindhuli Madi—the capital of my fieldwork district—the most expensive hotel and all the gold jewellery shops were owned by Dalits, based on the traditional occupation of Sunars as goldsmiths. Also, with limited land reform since the 1950s, in Nepal, 86 per cent of all families and 60 per cent of Dalit homes possess land. Unsurprisingly, Nepali forward castes have the largest size of holdings, while Dalits remain the most dispossessed.[48]

Figure 5.1: Caste-wise households which possess land and size of land holdings

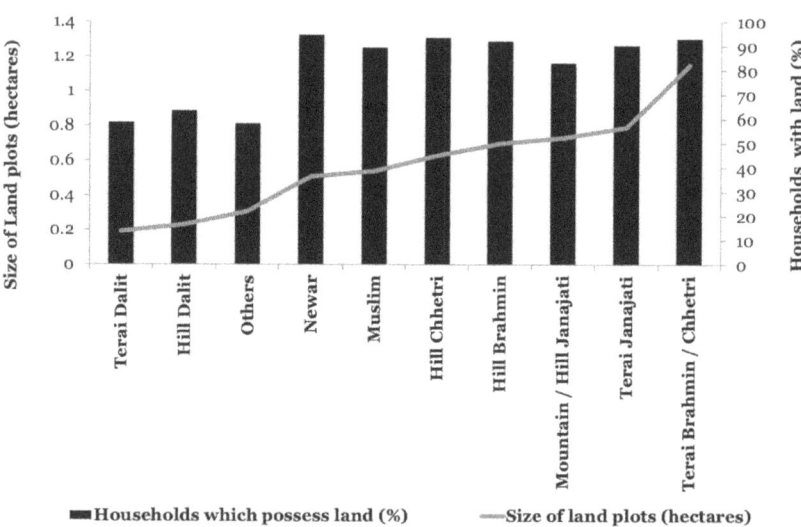

■ Households which possess land (%) ── Size of land plots (hectares)

Source: Yogendra B. Gurung et al., *Nepal Social Inclusion Survey 2012: Caste, Ethnic and Gender Dimensions of Socio-Economic Development, Governance and Social Solidarity*

Lastly, the decade-long People's War has played the most critical role in reducing social discrimination after centuries. On 13 February 1996, inspired by the Cultural Revolution in China and the Naxalite Movement in India, the Communist Party of Nepal (Maoist) faction declared a Jan Yuddha, or People's War.[49] Before the conflict began, the rebels submitted a forty-point charter of demands to the government. One of the important demands was that 'the system of untouchability must end once and for all'.[50] The rebellion actually began as a class struggle against 'the traditionally dominant feudal class', that is, the Thakuri Raj.[51] By 2001, across five districts, the 5,000–8,000 armed rebels had established jan sarkars (people's governments). In time, the cadres had a presence in almost all of the seventy-five districts of the rural countryside.[52] At the height of the guerrilla rebellion, the Maoists controlled over 80 per cent of the country's rural areas.

Political sociologist Uddhab Prasad Pyakurel argues that 'the Maoist Movement capitalized on the agenda of socially, culturally and economically marginalized people of Nepal especially women, the Dalits and ethnic groups'.[53] In essence, the Maoist rebellion was a caste war as much as a political struggle.[54] As the teacher Hari put it:

> ... before the Maoist movement, we were all fragmented and marginalised. The People's War united all the minorities and raised their voice from a single platform and created awareness about rights. We realised that we had been dominated and we should raise our voice.[55]

Apart from Dalits, the Maoists also drew into their ranks hundreds of supporters from the 'Man-gu-ra-li' (Magar, Gurung, Rai, Limbu) and other indigenous tribal communities.[56] Also, non-Hindu, non-Nepali speaking Kiratis, Tharus and Dalits joined their cadres. But the Maoist top-tier leadership was predominantly upper caste. Still, as a former foot soldier explained to me, the lower tiers of the guerrilla army, who came mainly from marginalised castes and tribes, cherished the fact that often they were given command over their upper caste colleagues.[57]

In addition, the Maoists also formed the Dalit Mukti Morcha, or Dalit Liberation Front, as a sister organisation[58] to advocate for affirmative action and compensation for historic atrocities. During the conflict, the rebels declared several occupied zones as 'untouchability-free areas'.[59] The guerrillas also encouraged Dalit marches into upper caste neighbourhoods. As the rebels took over landed estates and homes, the insurgency gradually shifted the rural balance of power. Their populist strategy included cancelling money lender interest[60] and 'Robin Hood-style redistribution'.[61]

One day in the village market, Bijeta and I met a Dom family selling beautiful bamboo baskets and mats. The Mallik family insisted that we visit their home in the Dom tola (hamlet). On the porch, we met the lady of the house, Bhakta. Next to her was a young mother breastfeeding her child. Her husband slept on a charpoy nearby. He reeked of alcohol, as did most of the other men in the village, across castes. The Mallik family were distinctly poorer than the others we had met in the village. But they were constructing a new home. The unfinished skeletal architecture of this new brick-and-cement structure formed the backdrop for our conversation.

The Malliks showed us the most intricately woven bamboo baskets and fans. This was their only source of income. They sold the fans at NPR 30 apiece and the basket at a mere NPR 50—a pittance for such exquisitely skilful craft. The women served us water they had fetched from the nearby hand pump. They proudly told us that they could now draw water from the village well along with all the other castes. Bhakta also informed us, 'Now we are served full meals in the eateries in the village without any discrimination. The Bahuns, Chhetris let us sit together with them.'

Earlier, during my recce of Sindhuli, I had interviewed a former human rights worker and radio presenter for a government channel. He had spoken of the Maoist movement's role in reducing caste discrimination, and I had scarcely believed him. But he had argued so fervently that his insights had expanded the course of my doctoral analysis. I now asked the Malliks if the Maoist guerrillas had made any efforts to reduce caste discrimination. To my surprise, they nodded in agreement: 'After the Maoist movement, untouchability stopped, as everyone listened to them since they had a high position in society.'[62]

The Dom family clarified that, though the guerrillas created a general atmosphere of fear, nobody was forced at gunpoint to end discrimination. Instead, the rebels used various tactics to increase social interactions between castes in a deeply stratified society. For example, they regularly held collective meetings in the village at night that included revolutionary songs and slogans such as 'Naya Nepal Nirman' (creation of a new Nepal), which was rooted in the vision of an egalitarian society.

The Malliks said that social relations and social power had changed during and after the People's War. Bhakta reminded me more than once that she could now go to temples to pray. In a classic sign of Sanskritisation, the walls of her house were full of posters of a range of gods—Shiva, Saraswati, Paravati, Ganesh, Vishnu and so on.[63]

Interestingly, many of our upper-caste hosts complained that the Maoist cadres had often insisted on being fed when they had spent the night in their homes. A Bahun shopkeeper complained that, during the rebellion, the Maoists had frequently demanded goats, cows and other animals to eat at night, without paying for them. Another Bahun health worker from a nearby village also grumbled, 'Maowadi (Maoists) came to our home at night and asked us to cook, then they disappeared into the jungle.'

But a former Maoist foot soldier from the Janajati community, whom I interviewed in another village, had a completely different narrative. He used gestures to emphasise the significance of marginalised caste rebels crossing the threshold to enter upper-caste kitchens. Such small acts broke centuries-old taboos against inter-caste dining.[64] The Maoists also encouraged inter-caste marriages[65] and feasts with an eye to increasing social interaction between castes.[66]

Changing the school curriculum was another distinct strategy that was used to influence the 'institutions of indoctrination'. Many teachers like Hari were themselves members of the party. Another Newari Maithili teacher recounted how the Maoists had 'kidnapped' him for a few days and taken him to a remote location to teach him the new syllabus. The guerrillas also opposed the teaching of the Sanskrit language, in order to erase overt symbols of upper-caste domination.[67] The cumulative impact of these multiple strategies was that caste discrimination reduced perceptibly in Nepal, especially in the Terai and hill areas. It has far from vanished, though, and the stranglehold of caste continues in Nepal's mountainous regions.[68]

While it is true that, after the conflict ended, the Maoists transformed into a democratic political party and won a landslide victory in the 2008 Constituent Assembly elections, the armed rebels also have a profoundly dark history. Generations of Nepalis have been traumatised by the socio-economic and psychological scars of the guerrilla violence. Almost 37 per cent of Maoist guerrillas were under the age of eighteen,[69] effectively being child soldiers.[70] There were reports of kidnappings, abductions and mass recruitment of underage children.[71] The Maoists also strongly encouraged at least one member of every family to join the armed conflict. In the throes of the conflict, many female cadres also faced sexual violence both from the Royal Nepal Army and the guerrillas.[72] Tellingly, after the war, most of the enlisted female combatants chose voluntary retirement.

I interviewed a high-ranking female government bureaucrat who was deeply critical of the Maoists. At the same time, however, she did acknowledge that, 'the Maoists did a lot to change the mindset and build social awareness to build an equal society. The Constituent Assembly was created due to them, and ganatantra [democracy] was also restored because of the Maoists.'[73] Another interviewee who was affiliated with the party told me about the egalitarian vision of the Maoists. 'The overarching aim of the party was to build an equal society which would be Savarna Bagun Mukti [Free of Oppressor Caste Hegemony] with Mahila Mukti [Women's Liberation].'

During the final leg of the People's War, the most influential female rebel leader Comrade Parvati, alias Hisila Yami, observed, 'Today Nepalese Dalits are way ahead of Indian Dalits in the field of breaking caste barriers.' However, she also acknowledged that, 'Maoist Dalits cadres can enter high caste houses without any obstruction, but local Dalits from the same village are often discriminated'.[74] Still, she believed that the 'transformation which would have taken centuries before the revolution have taken ten years'.[75]

Bourdieu's concept of 'habitus' focuses on new changes that societies adapt to in order to survive extreme circumstances. The People's War's explicit intent was to catalyse these profound cultural transformations. Anthropologist Ina Zharkevich, in her book *Maoist People's War and the Revolution of Everyday Life in Nepal*, documents how the Thabangi ethnic community in mid-western Nepal, which traditionally considered cows to be sacred animals and not to be killed, normalised beef-eating during the conflict years.[76] As the villagers explained to her, '*bani parepachi mitho lagyo* [once the habit was acquired, beef turned out to be tasty], and gradually became a part of the local diet'.[77]

DAUGHTERS OF THE EVEREST

Traditionally, in pahadi (mountain) cultures including in Nepal, women have enjoyed relatively greater freedoms. In the 1940s, the early Nepali women's organisations were born as offshoots of political parties. They mobilised women to overthrow the Rana monarchs and establish democracy. Only after women earned the right to vote, in the 1950s, were schools for girls opened. In the 1960s, under the new Panchayat system, the king banned all political parties. Hence, most women's organisations, too, had to go underground.[78] After the brief return of democracy in the 1980s, many international NGOs also began adult literacy classes and micro-credit programmes.[79] These changes transformed women's social capital, political engagement and cultural norms.

The decades of conflict and international migration have also altered the rural landscape of Nepal. In the years of the violent conflict, in whole villages in the western hill districts of Nepal, there were no men.[80] Now, women head one of every three Nepali households.[81] This is twice as many as in Bangladesh or India.

Though wars generally increase women's vulnerabilities, sometimes they can also empower women.[82] Usually, 'women living in communities directly affected by violent political conflict rated more highly on empowerment measures'.[83] They are more likely to work outside the home and also end up making more decisions within the home.[84] During the World Wars, for example, when men fought on the frontlines, women temporarily[85] took their place on factory shop floors across industrialised countries.[86]

In Nepal, too, especially after the conflict, women's employment has soared.[87] Nepal's Gender Inequality Index, too, has fallen and is now better than both India and Bangladesh.[88] Even in the midst of the conflict, Nepal's Gender Development Index rose from 0.77 in 1995 to 0.92 in 2015. The combined impact of Jan Andolans, international migration and the Maoist War has ignited a gender transformation in Nepal.

Women actively participated in the first Jan Andolan in the 1990s. Also, during the Maoist conflict years (1996–2006), many age-old regressive traditions dissolved. Many widows, for example, refused to wear white-coloured clothes.[89] The 'badge of resistance is the *sindoor* (vermillion) on the forehead and her *pothay* (red beaded necklace), symbols of a married woman, which she wears in defiance of her widowhood'.[90] These small but meaningful cultural changes symbolised the depth of the post-conflict transformation in women's lives.

In the Second Jan Andolan in 2006, which saw street protests to overthrow the monarchy and restore democracy, women from seven political parties formed the Inter-Party Women's Alliance (IPWA). Two years later, these feminists lobbied fiercely for reservations to be provided in the Interim Constitution. They ensured that Nepal became the first country in South Asia to earmark 33 per cent of seats for women at all levels of the executive, legislature and local bodies. The 2015 Constitution also has a specific quota to ensure women gain leadership positions in Parliament.[91]

In 2016, Nepal appointed its first female parliamentary speaker, Onsari Gharti Magar. Simultaneously, the first woman president, Bidhya Devi Bhandari, and the first female chief justice, Sushila Karki, also took their oaths of office. The progressive 2015 Nepali Constitution, amongst the youngest in the world, has enshrined the principle of proportional representation. So, in the 2017 local government elections held after a gap of seventeen years, women won 41 per cent of all elected posts.[92] Significantly, 47 per cent of these women were Dalit, due to a landmark intersectional sub-quota provided for in the Local Level Election Law 2016, which ensures that at least one of every five ward members is mandatorily a Dalit woman.[93] India's long-awaited Women's Reservation Bill though enacted by the Parliament after twenty-seven years, in September 2023, does not have similarly progressive sub-quotas for OBCs and is likely to be implemented only after another decade.[94]

In spite of these gains, women in Nepal largely continue to be appointed only to figurehead positions. Only 2 per cent of mayors are women. However, 91 per cent of the ceremonial posts of deputy mayor have been given to women to fulfil the quota. Of them, very few are Dalits[95]—a clear indication that, despite a robust feminist movement, women from marginalised communities continue to be deeply under-represented in positions of real power.

Since the conflict years, the mass migration of four million Nepali men abroad has also altered the country's gender landscape. For one, marriages have become more fragile. Across villages, we heard stories of men who had migrated abroad and abandoned their families. In one village, two of the three Dalit women we met said that their husbands worked in the Middle East, but had not visited for years and had also stopped sending money. Much to our surprise, in another village, one of our Bahun hosts in his sixties, also had his second wife living next door.[96] Though polygamy is now illegal, it has a long social history in Nepal. Again, in another village, we met two co-wives who lived in adjoining houses. Due to the prolonged absence of men and lack of alternative livelihoods, women have also started to perform traditionally male agricultural tasks, such as ploughing.[97] Clearly, Nepali society is in the midst of a profound gender transformation.

The ten years of the Maoist guerrilla conflict were another crucial historical turning point. The Maoist Party had submitted a forty-point charter of demands to the government before declaring the People's War in 1996. One of their key demands was the right of women to inherit property.[98] But the most significant aspect of the war was the recruitment of women guerrilla combatants.

Women formed 30–40 per cent of the frontline Maoist

cadres. During the People's War, 'poor, peasant, illiterate and Janjati women ... achieved a level of political visibility never before imaginable in Nepal's politics'.[99] Hundreds of women joined the Maoist Party and its sister organisations.

To learn more about their motivations, I took a bus to the Maoist headquarters in Kathmandu to interview a high-ranking woman leader. Suddenly, as I got off the bus it started to rain heavily and I had to stop to buy an umbrella. After many wrong turns, I found the Maoist headquarters—an imposing, fortified building with unmistakable red flags everywhere. Without a second thought, I pulled out my camera and started to take some photos. From the corner of my eye, I noticed a woman glaring at me from the first-floor balcony. This was my interviewee, and since I was late by a few minutes, she was waiting for me impatiently. After we waved at each other, she came downstairs to check my identity card, after which she greeted me with an unusually firm handshake. My mind raced, with a mix of unexpected fear, anxiety and excitement. This promised to be one fascinating interview.

We walked up to the first floor and then down a corridor with arresting oil-on-canvas paintings of fallen comrades bathed in red blood, on the wall. Once we had entered her room, with its comfortable cloth sofas, she slowly read out my surname from a notebook and asked about my caste. This was always the first question in Nepal before the inevitable one about my marital status. I usually managed to dodge, distract or refuse to answer. But this once, to put her at ease, I answered truthfully. She then said that I must have figured out from her surname that she was a Bahun, though frankly, I hadn't. I blurted out that I was surprised that a Bahun woman had joined the Maoist party, which had mainly fought for the upliftment of the oppressed castes.

That got us talking and she slowly opened up. Her own marriage was inter-caste, she said. Her parents were communists. From a young age, their rural house was filled with guests who would discuss left-wing ideology. So, she was always attracted to its core principles. The turning point in her life came when her father decided to re-marry. Her illiterate mother was left emotionally traumatised and economically vulnerable, with two daughters and two sons to care for single-handedly. The strong-willed mother decided that she would educate all her children, so they could stand on their own feet and never have to face such vulnerabilities. And, that's what she did.

Her family hailed from the Dang district, a hotbed of communist activity in the mountain region. They had joined the original 'Mashaal' group founded by Mohan Vaidya.[100] From the fourth grade onwards, she had started participating in communist events. With time, her commitment to political activism had organically grown stronger. When she turned eighteen, the top leaders in the party had decided that the time was ripe for her to get married. In keeping with their encouragement of inter-caste alliances,[101] her marriage had been 'arranged by the party' with a politically active leader from an indigenous community. More than twenty years ago, top-ranking party leaders had blessed her wedding, a celebration free of traditional rituals. Instead, there had been speeches, revolutionary songs and slogans.[102] To me, these janabadi bibahs seemed quite similar to the anti-caste, ritual-free self-respect weddings that happened in Tamil Nadu (described in later chapters).[103] Her husband had steadily risen to the top echelons of the Maoist central leadership. Recently, she too had won an election to become a parliamentarian.

I wanted to understand what motivated women to join the Maoist army in such large numbers. She explained, 'The first attraction for village women was the unique opportunity to change their roop [form] by wearing shirt-pant, carry the banduk [gun], and join the army as full-timers, or support from the outside as part-timers.'[104] In a conservative society, these gun-carrying women in khaki trousers challenged the 'image of womanhood'.[105] But many scholars have wondered whether this mass recruitment of women was an act of agency or exploitation. Anthropologist Lauren Leve argues that it is incorrect to attribute their decisions to the Western notion of rebellious choice, autonomy or agency. Rather, rural Nepali women joined the Maoist rebels to display their moral commitment to 'personal sacrifice' that is more valued in Eastern cultures.[106] In the course of the war, more than 3000 women guerrillas were martyred.[107]

In the thick of the battle, in 2003, the most prominent Maoist female leader, Hisila Yami (under the nom de guerre Parvati), had also published an insightful survey in the *Economic and Political Weekly*.[108] As per the survey, around 53 per cent of women combatants were from the exploited classes. Although two-thirds of the total women rebels were also unmarried.[109] So, the war may have also been an unspoken escape route for many women from the triple oppression of casteism, feudalism and patriarchy.[110] Some conflict zones even had women-only guerrilla squads.

In their heyday, the guerrilla army controlled 75–90 per cent of the rural Nepali countryside. They had established a parallel government in all seventy-five districts.[111] At that time, the Maoist rebels and their sister organisations also undertook a number of campaigns against abhorrent gender practices. In western Nepal, they advocated against chhaupadi pratha[112] and marriage-by-kidnapping. In the northwest, they denounced polyandry. In the south, they rallied against the regressive Teej festival[113] and the sexual trafficking of Tamang women.[114] The most popular campaign, however, was the 2001 movement against alcohol launched by the women's front of the Party. In a multi-ethnic, multi-lingual and multi-religious country, the rebels sought to build on this intersectionality of feminist struggles.

After the guerrilla war, the Nepali national army instituted specific quotas for women.[115] The majority of the female guerrillas, however, chose to voluntarily retire rather than be absorbed into the Royal Nepal Army. Many of these former Nepali combatants have silently redefined traditional stereotypes of gender and division of labour in other professions, due to the huge lack of stable post-war socio-economic opportunities and the absence of men.[116] In Kathmandu, I saw working women in several traditionally male-dominated occupations. Some ran street-food stalls, while others drove tempos.[117]

PEACE DIVIDEND

Lenin's idea that war can bring rapid social transformation, which would take much longer in times of peace, is debatable. But it does seem that the decade-long 'Maoist movement paved the way for a radical transformation of Nepali society'.[118] Still, the most crucial changes in Nepal have been visible only after the war. The peace dividend has enabled these evolutionary changes to ripen.

In most primary schools in Bihar, only girls are tasked with sweeping the premises each morning. The same gender division of

6

BIHAR

> As long as indignities without count
> Are visited on the untouchables' account,
> Surely their tormentors too must pay
> For the crimes they commit in every way.
>
> – 'Bechain' (Kalu Ram Jatia),
> Dalit poet and editor of *Adi-Hindu*[1]

BIHAR HAS A long history of violence against the oppressed castes. In one of my fieldwork districts, around the time that I was there in July 2016, two Dalit youths were beaten up and urinated on by forward castes.[2] Everyday discrimination in Bihar is rife too. Almost 41 per cent of Dalit families we interviewed in Muzaffarpur district admitted that even they would 'have a problem if a Musahar[3] were to eat in our home'.[4] These thick layers of 'graded inequality' prevent marginalised castes from forging unified class alliances to resist or overthrow their oppressors.[5]

In one village, we visited a school in the Paswan[6] hamlet first thing in the morning, but found it closed. The building was painted bright pink, but the rooms seemed to be on the verge of collapse. No classroom had a blackboard, benches or even a mat to sit on the floor. There was no child or teacher in sight. Worse still, we learnt from the cook that she had not served midday meals for months. We returned later in the afternoon. This time we saw some children. They were sitting on a mat on the veranda floor, hanging on to every word their teacher spoke. The teacher sat behind a rickety table on a high chair. This physical distance between the teacher and the student reflected the deep emotional distance between their caste positions in the social hierarchy.

In another school in the same village, we saw two children with blank faces and a few books neatly packed in plastic shopping bags waiting outside the gates. The school was yet to open and they were unsure if it was a holiday. Half an hour later, a teacher walked in, her sari pallu fastened with a big pin. We tried to call the head teacher (he was also the village head's husband and was locally called 'mukhiya pati'), but he did not answer his phone. As with most schools we visited in Bihar, there was a toilet each for boys and girls. But they were so dirty as to be unusable.

In the next village, we visited the Musahar hamlet, and the mothers we met complained bitterly to us that the anganwadi (pre-school) worker rarely served any food to their children. The worker was from the Telli caste, designated in Bihar as 'economically backward', but considered to be superior to the Musahars, who are at the bottom rung of the Dalits.

Even before we entered the anganwadi, we could hear the anganwadi worker yelling. She became even more irritated when she saw that we had come to pay a visit. We insisted that she feed the children as per the law. After a heated argument for nearly an hour, her helper finally showed up with an aluminium pot full of freshly cooked khichdi. The dishevelled children brought out their plates and ate hungrily. The mothers standing outside, were all smiles. This experience gave us a taste of their daily battles for the most basic of rights.

Research by social scientist Aparna John and her colleagues confirms that such disputes are not uncommon in Bihar. The caste of the anganwadi worker determines her social distance from the villagers she serves. Especially when food is scarce, these power differences become magnified and often cause 'perceptions of bias, physical violence episodes and create a hostile environment'.[7]

But why does Bihar suffer from such blatant caste discrimination? How pervasive and profound is its impact on access to public services? Why does Bihar, despite legendary experiments in socialism, have callous teachers, non-functional schools, classrooms without benches, crumbling hospital infrastructure and putrefying political will?

DEVELOPMENTAL STASIS

Walk into any cramped bus or auto stand in Bihar, and absolute strangers will strike up a conversation on politics. Most of these witty, earthy exchanges usually centre around poverty and welfare. For example, the 2015 state election campaign was fought entirely on the plank of 'development'. Three-time Chief Minister Nitish Kumar advocated for 'inclusive' development. On the other hand, Prime Minister Modi's right-wing Bharatiya Janata Party (BJP) promised a special 'development package' with sectarian undertones.[8] By 2020, these rival parties had joined hands to fight the next election in an alliance. In the midst of the pandemic, they even achieved a contested narrow victory but parted ways soon after. Through all of these changes, development continued to remain the most crucial electoral issue for Bihari voters.[9] Yet, travelling in Bihar often feels like taking a journey backwards in time.

In the last decade, Bihar has had stellar economic growth rates of more than 8 per cent, which would be the envy of any developing country. But this speed of change is an illusion, as Bihar has an extremely low base of economic development. Bihar's per capita income is the lowest in the country.[10] Similarly, while statistics on paper may indicate that Bihar has been the fastest in the reduction of multi-dimensional poverty, access to basic welfare services remains abysmal. For example, most of the anganwadis we visited in Kishanganj district were shut when we arrived. In one anganwadi, after three visits, finally, around noon, we met the anganwadi sahayika (helper), who got frightened when she saw us and hurried to wear her official sari-uniform. In the dusty mud room, her unwell husband was still sleeping. There was a parked motorcycle, a family cow and a pile of hay in front of a curtain where the children were supposed to sit. She explained that the designated anganwadi building next door was broken, so she often conducted classes in this overcrowded room. But, the blackboard on the wall looked unused and a pile of hay lay just below it. So we headed to the next room, which was equally in shambles with no teaching equipment.

The sahayika began to make khichdi in the corner of the room. With their mothers waiting outside, we taught the children a few words and sang nursery rhymes and songs to keep them occupied. We also played and pretended to make invisible rotis, till the kichdi was ready. Finally, the sahayika served the children the hot meal in small plates while they sat in a row on jute sacks. The mothers were relieved that their children were finally eating.

Later, when I informed the mothers that all children in Bihari anganwadis were also supposed to receive an egg once a week, they were genuinely perplexed.[11] Their children rarely received any food, let alone an egg. The sahayika, on her part, complained that the government had not paid her a salary or sent money for meals in months. Later, I complained to the supervisor-in-charge. He was extremely polite on the phone, but I seriously doubted that he intended to lift a finger on the matter.

The National Family Health Survey 2019–21 shows that three of every five children nationwide receive food from anganwadis. In Bihar, however, three of every five children do not receive any nutritious meals at anganwadis, let alone eggs. Similarly, nearly two of every four deliveries in Bihar take place at home instead of in a hospital or health centre.[12] Most crucially, 43 per cent of Bihari women are not literate, nearly double the national average.[13]

Despite the repeated electoral focus on socio-economic development, the question remains, why does Bihar perform so poorly when it comes to access to public services? Why do the majority of Musahar children shy away from schools? Why is corruption so rife and public transport negligible? And why are most women unlettered?

In the 1970s, socialist thinker Sachchidanand Sinha, in his treatise *The Internal Colony*, criticised the centralisation of power in Delhi. He argued that the Union government exercised excessive control on backward states like Bihar. Despite rich raw materials and cheap labour, Bihar often could not fund local priorities.[14] The central government's 'freight equalisation' policy,[15] its diversion of tax revenues and its meagre transfer of finances stymied Bihar's industrialisation and progress.[16]

Since the 1960s, agriculture has also been severely neglected in the eastern states. In contrast, the Green Revolution pioneers like Punjab and Haryana have received heavy public investment. To this day, only half the agricultural land in Bihar is irrigated, compared to 90 per cent in Punjab. Land is also very scarce in Bihar, and most rural homes are packed close together. With growing impoverishment, the proportion of agricultural workers who do not own any land in rural Bihar has increased from 42 per cent in 1971 to 53 per cent in 2011.[17]

In 1912, the British carved Bihar as a separate province from Bengal. But colonial power remained concentrated in

Calcutta. Economist Shaibal Gupta has argued that zamindari landlords were the 'worst elements' of Permanent Settlement in Bihar. 'Though Bihar was politically linked with Bengal, this (Bihari Westernised elite) class emerged very late in comparison to its Bengali counterpart'—the bhadralok.[18] Even before Independence, for most Biharis, caste was more important than a pan-Bihari identity.[19] While Bihar was active in the national independence movement, communities with roots outside the state dominated commerce and industry within.[20] Hence, despite rich mineral resources, Bihar remained underdeveloped.

Post-independence, feudal Bihari leaders preferred to attract capital from other states, but were staunchly 'opposed to any radical tenancy reform and ... indifferent to indigenous industrial development'.[21] So, an important contributor to Bihar's social, economic, political and industrial backwardness is a continued sense of 'retarded sub-nationalism'. In a society riven by caste divisions, there is a lack of socio-culture pride in a pan-Bihari identity.[22]

The 'quagmire of caste' has also impacted democratic politics.[23] Until 1977, the forward castes blocked genuine land reform. Over subsequent decades, oppressed castes gradually tilted the balance, especially through the reservation policy and their strength in numbers in democratic politics. The 'politicisation of caste' has cemented social solidarity among the marginalised castes. The tenures of former chief ministers Lalu Prasad Yadav (1990–97) and his wife Rabri Devi (2000–5), in particular, promoted social justice for the marginalised classes. But crime rates soared as job creation and public infrastructure were sorely neglected during their terms,[24] and the perception of Bihar's backwardness increased. Bihari migrants in industrial cities, in particular, routinely had to deal with this stigma.[25] However, the 2009 elections seemed to mark a shift from caste affinity[26] to 'clean development'.[27]

Since 2005, with chief minister Nitish Kumar's sushasan (good governance), Bihar has undoubtedly seen rapid economic growth.[28] However, this construction-led lopsided growth has resulted in the sore neglect of agriculture.[29] The smokescreen of 'development' has also side-lined caste injustices. Journalist M. Rajshekhar feels that even with widely-publicised development policies, such as distributing bicycles to girl students, in reality, Bihar has an 'absent state'.[30] In the corridors of power, the official mantra is 'inclusive growth'. But, in reality, poor people and marginalised communities remain excluded. Bihar continues to have India's lowest average income and the highest levels of poverty and malnutrition.[31] Improvements in education and healthcare have also been much slower than in other states. Ironically, public investments have also worsened existing social disparities. For example, cities, urban towns and villages near motorable roads have cornered most of the developmental spends.[32] On the other hand, the remotest corners of Bihar, like the Muslim-majority Kishanganj district, where I did my fieldwork, are threadbare, with few roads and utter neglect of public services.

Land reform has also been far from adequate in Bihar.[33] Around 86 per cent of Dalit families and more than half of OBC families do not own any land—amongst the worst kind of exclusion in the country.[34] In a classic pattern of graded inequality, marginalised castes and Muslims also have the least access to public services.[35] As the journalist Santosh Singh concludes about Bihar in his book *Ruled or Misruled*, 'The development card, in any case, is not the main text as it appears on the surface.' Instead, there is a surfeit of empty 'claims, counter-claims and resultant cacophony'.[36]

Despite Bihar being 'the cradle and the birthplace of socialism in India', it is stuck in a developmental inertia. Upper caste feudal hegemony,[37] an underdeveloped sense of sub-national Bihari identity, economic degradation as an 'internal colony' and non-inclusive growth have inflamed socio-economic inequalities.

SILENCED REVOLUTION

At every turn in Bihar, caste and religion raise their ugly heads. In Kishanganj, one evening, a progressive Muslim family informed us that they would have a problem if a Musahar were to share a meal with them. In another village, my Dalit researcher, who preferred to be called 'Harijan', said he could not stay with me in a Muslim home as they ate gau maas (cow meat), which many Hindus do not eat. It was with great difficulty that I convinced him that Muslims certainly do not eat beef at every meal.

In another Dalit home, a man displayed the same prejudice and even said that he would have a problem if a Muslim visited his home. His logic was that his family was Hindu and worshipped the cow, while Muslims ate only cows. 'So, how can we serve them food?'

The Hindutva lie has been spread so effectively that millions of Indians like him seem to assume that Muslims eat beef at every meal.[38] After dusk, in another conversation in a nearby village, with my OBC host, a Muslim researcher and his Dalit friend, I heard even more absurd tales of blatant prejudice. While they movingly spoke of their own struggles against discrimination, their own prejudices against the Musahars were appalling. The three men claimed that the Musahars, who lived across the river, did not want to progress. They were apparently so subservient that they bent low, called everyone 'sarkar' (landlord) and refused to sit on a chair. Of course, this victim-blaming is not uncommon in a country steeped in putrid caste prejudice.

Bihar, in particular, festers with extreme caste discrimination. Amongst the Dalits, Musahars are the most marginalised. Their population size is not insignificant. In Bihar alone, there are 2.7 million Musahars, which is more than the entire population of Botswana or Qatar. An equal number live in Uttar Pradesh. Though Jitan Manjhi, a Musahar, had a brief stint as the chief minister of the state, it appears to have made little difference to the condition of his community. Most continue to live in hamlets that reek of neglect. In 1901, only 0.1 per cent of Musahars were literate. More than a century later, only 22 per cent can read the alphabet.[39] In village after village, we met Musahar children playing at home rather than studying in school due to the bitter discrimination they face, both within the classroom and outside.[40] As anthropologist George Kunnath recollects in his insightful book *Rebels from Mud Houses*, most Musahar parents are resigned to the futility of their children's schooling due to the utter lack of social mobility. One mother rhetorically asked him, '*Musahar ka bachcha padhkar daroga banega?*' (Will going to a school make a Musahar child a police inspector?)[41]

The historical origins of the caste system are hazy. More than 3,000 years ago, in the late Vedic period, caste hierarchies were gradually cemented with the transition to settled agriculture across northern India. Each caste in the hierarchy was expected to concentrate only on their specialised occupation. In the second century, Kautilya's *Arthashastra* even suggested caste-specific punishment for the same crime.[42] By the fifth century, caste practices had become nothing short of appalling. Chinese traveller Fa-Hien (337–422 AD), who visited the ancient capital Pataliputra[43] (now Bihar's capital Patna), documented that Chandalas[44] who cremated corpses had to tap wooden sticks on the ground as they walked, so that high-caste Hindus could avoid even the sight of them.[45]

Bihar has also had one millennium of Buddhist influence and two centuries of Mughal rule. Unlike East Bengal, the local population did not convert en masse to Islam. Caste hierarchies have, therefore, remained rigid through generations. With the advent of British colonialism, the oppressed castes, however, did find new economic opportunities for social mobility,[46] but as sociologist M.N. Srinivas notes:

That is quite different from making progress towards an egalitarian society ... increased economic mobility, led to increased social mobility and the traditional process of Sanskritisation ensured that such mobility did not lead to revolution.[47]

Sanskritisation is a process where marginalised castes emulate the rituals, customs, rites and practices of the upper castes to claim a higher status.[48] One of my Dalit host families in Bihar, for example, had built a separate bhagwan ghar (shrine) in the courtyard that looked even better than his own home.

Still, Bihar has had its fair share of progressive social movements. Marginalised castes, Dalits and peasants have consistently fought for their rights. However, internal disunity and upper caste resistance have repeatedly silenced and quelled the embers of these rebellions. Two millennia of caste dominance have crushed meaningful social mobility.

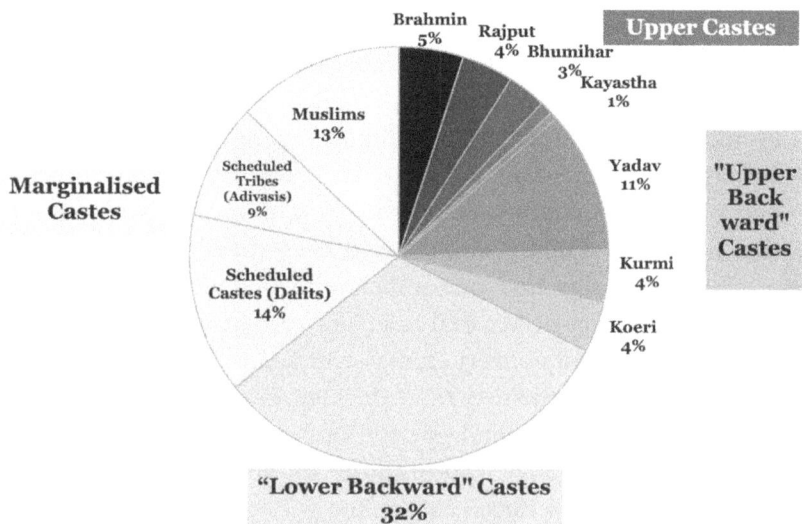

6.1: Main caste-groups in undivided Bihar based on the 1931 census

Source: Pradip Bose, 'Mobility and Conflict: Social Roots of Caste Violence in Bihar', in D. Gupta (ed.), *Social Stratification*

During the British Raj, there were two waves of Bihari marginalised caste movements. The British census, from its early days, inadvertently created an opportunity for caste mobility. The 1901 census in the Bihar province classified Bhumihars and Kayasthas as 'backward castes', lower than the Brahmins and Rajputs. To seek upward mobility, the Kayasthas set up caste associations that claimed descent from Emperor Chandragupta.[49] The Bhumihars even conducted a 1924 Purohiti Andolan to claim priestly status.[50] Both groups successfully upgraded their status to upper castes in the 1931 census.[51]

The second wave of caste movements by the 'upper-backward' castes, however, such as Yadavs, Kurmis and Koeris, was unsuccessful. The Kurmis started wearing the sacred thread. The Yadavs converted to vegetarianism and teetotalism,[52] and joined both the cow protection and Ahir movement against the zamindars.[53] But their status in the hierarchy was not elevated.

The British, through the 1919 Montagu–Chelmsford reforms, granted only two seats to the 'Depressed Classes'[54] in Bihar's legislative assembly, compared to ten in Madras.[55] Even before Independence, the Dalit leader Jagjivan Ram lamented that the Bihari 'Depressed Classes' were not only more backward, but also unable to create a united Dalit organisation.[56]

After independence, Babasaheb Ambedkar ensured that reservations for Dalits and Adivasis were introduced to reverse generations of social discrimination.[57] Marginalised castes in northern India have been less able to utilise these quotas due to their lower levels of education.[58] It is political quotas that have been more successful in ensuring representation in Bihar.[59] In the social sphere, however, caste remains deeply entrenched as a form of 'hidden apartheid'.[60] Though untouchability is legally banned, residential, social and economic segregation continue to be widely practised.[61] Around 47 per cent of rural households nationwide admitted in the recent India Human Development Survey that they still practise untouchability with northern India displaying the most prejudice.⁶² After all, as Babasaheb Ambedkar warned, anti-discrimination laws alone are ineffective without 'determined efforts on the part of government'.⁶³

As noted, political reservations have, to a certain extent, increased unity among the Bihari marginalised castes against the 'Brahmin–Bania Raj'.⁶⁴ In the 1970s, the All Indian Kurmi Mahasabha started a campaign to unite the marginalised castes using their strength in numbers for electoral advantage. For over three decades now, with the successive election of former chief minister Laloo Prasad Yadav and Chief Minister Nitish Kumar (both Kurmi), there has been a rise in the political clout of the 'other backward classes' in Bihar. Political scientist Christophe Jaffrelot argues that post-Independence, there has been a 'silent revolution' in India's socio-political landscape across northern India. Bihar, too, has seen the rise of the 'backward castes'.⁶⁵ But Dalits continue to remain on the margins.

In regions with competition for scarce resources, even the 'other backward classes' castes have also increasingly begun to commit atrocities against Dalits. As Human Rights Watch documents based on a police report, 'In rural areas in which the "backward classes" have been surging forward to take up positions of power and control in society, knocking down the upper castes who had held sway in such positions all along in the past … there is greater tension between structural neighbours in this hierarchy than between the top level and the bottom level.'⁶⁶ Needless to say, it is 'structural neighbours' that tend to have the greatest interaction as well as the need to vie for the same limited rural resources. In other words, the 'rise to power and dominance of the upper layers of the middle castes, especially the Kurmi, Koeri and Yadav communities, lead to a further intensification of Dalit exploitation.'⁶⁷

In the face of this oppression, in the late 1960s, the Naxalite movement germinated as a Maoist guerrilla movement to end feudal and caste exploitation. By the late 1990s, the Naxals had spread to thirty-six of the fifty-four districts of Bihar. In the initial days, the Naxals were considered to be fighting for the Dalit cause. Musahars 'since the eighties have formed a significant part of the rank and file of the Maoist movement'.[68]

In Nepal, the Maoist movement was able to realign caste equations to a certain extent within a decade. In stark contrast, the Naxals in Bihar faced a violent backlash from the upper and middle castes. In the 1990s, Bhumihars, especially, organised 'dominant caste sena or private caste militias or armies'.[69] These militias murdered, robbed and raped hundreds of Dalit peasants and landless labourers[70] with impunity. Central Bihar was a hotbed of caste violence.[71] Of these militias, the Ranvir Sena with a standing army of 12,000 was the most brutal. Between 1995 and 2000, they led twenty-seven gruesome massacres. Even the Naxals considered the 'Ranvir Sena to be the deadliest sena'.[72] In 1991, the Ranvir Sena beheaded Dalit and Adivasi labourers in Jehanabad district, who had demanded a minuscule wage increase. In the 1990s, more than 400 people were killed in conflicts between the various militias and the Naxalites.

By the turn of the millennium, the Naxals began to recruit guerrillas from all castes. Their own leadership and ranks, too, were no longer immune to caste prejudice. 'Dalit alienation was further accentuated', as the Naxals could no longer 'meet their socio-economic aspirations'.[73] Dalits in Bihar also did not have their own private militias.[74]

In 2007, the Nitish Kumar government created a new category of Mahadalits which has slowly expanded to include most of the Dalit communities in Bihar. My Bihari researcher explained it thus, 'We Harijans are the topmost in the Scheduled Caste list. Then there are Chamars and many other categories of Mahadalits. The Doms are at the bottom.'

Initially, the new category of Mahadalits created further rifts, as it only excluded the Paswans.[75] Despite their inclusion in 2018, caste gradations remain sharp in Bihar.[76] In 2014, after former chief minister Jitan Manjhi visited a temple, it was apparently 'washed' and 'purified'.[77]

LAND AND CONFLICT

Bihar is one of the most densely populated regions in the world. Hunger for land has also been one of the key reasons for these armed conflicts. Despite numerous peasant movements before Independence, land redistribution remains elusive.

In Mughal India, half the average farm produce was extracted as taxes.[78] In 1793, the British introduced the Permanent Settlement. This shift led to surplus extraction of taxes and such extreme exploitation of tenants by the zamindars that it altered feudal social relations.[79] After the Great Depression in the 1930s, with fewer peasants able to pay their taxes, land evictions increased. By the time of India's independence, the feudal hegemony of the zamindars had increased substantially.[80]

Unsurprisingly then, Bihar was once the crucible of peasant uprisings. The tribal-dominated areas rose up in the 1855 Santhal Rebellion, protesting against acute exploitation. The 1860 Indigo Uprising against the forced plantation of the cash crop was brutally repressed by the British.[81] In 1917, Mahatma Gandhi led the Champaran Satyagraha. By 1934, the Congress Socialist Party advocated for Kisan Sabhas (peasant associations) across Bihar.[82] After 1940, the sabhas even adopted a militant strategy due to communist influence.[83]

Since the 1930s, 'Bihar has also been the cradle and the birthplace of socialism in India', intermingled with caste politics.[84] The short-lived Congress Socialist Party (1934–39), born in Patna, was conceived of by socialists Acharya Narendra Dev and Jayaprakash Narayan, among others.[85] By the 1960s, Ram Manohar Lohia, a stalwart of the Socialist Party, was advocating for radical ideas such as compulsory inter-caste marriages and inter-caste dining for government servants. Karpoori Thakur, another socialist stalwart and two-time chief minister, introduced a sub-quota for the Most Backward Classes (MBCs).[86] In 1974–75, Jayaprakash Narayan led the Sampoorna Kranti (Total Revolution) movement in Bihar, which, as a powerful student protest movement, also emphasised the upliftment of the oppressed castes.

All these socialist movements were short-lived, and like the peasant and Dalit movements, never managed to alter the landscape of Bihar's developmental politics. The feudal hegemony of the upper and middle castes remained largely untouched for centuries.

On paper, after Independence, Bihar was the first Indian state to abolish the zamindari system. The landlords, however, actively opposed the 1950 Bihar Land Reforms Act with violence, court cases and other methods.[87] The government also delayed the 1957 Land Ceiling Bill to favour the landed elite, who subverted the loopholes to undertake tenant evictions and land grabs.[88] The upshot of all this was that, even decades later, extreme land inequalities have persisted and sharecroppers and landless labourers have been 'more often than not left out in the cold'.[89]

Despite numerous peasant movements and welfare laws, land distribution in Bihar has remained essentially unchanged. The upper castes have monopolised control—they form two-thirds (65 per cent) of the big landlords/peasants. On the other hand, 76 per cent of agricultural labourers without land, who largely survive hand-to-mouth, belong to marginalised classes and castes (Dalits, Adivasis and OBCs). Even families from marginalised communities who do own land have only small parcels. Almost 43 per cent of land holdings are of less than 0.4 hectares.[90] In 2009, one-third of the cultivated area was

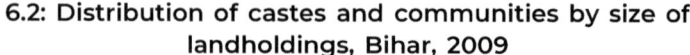

6.2: Distribution of castes and communities by size of landholdings, Bihar, 2009

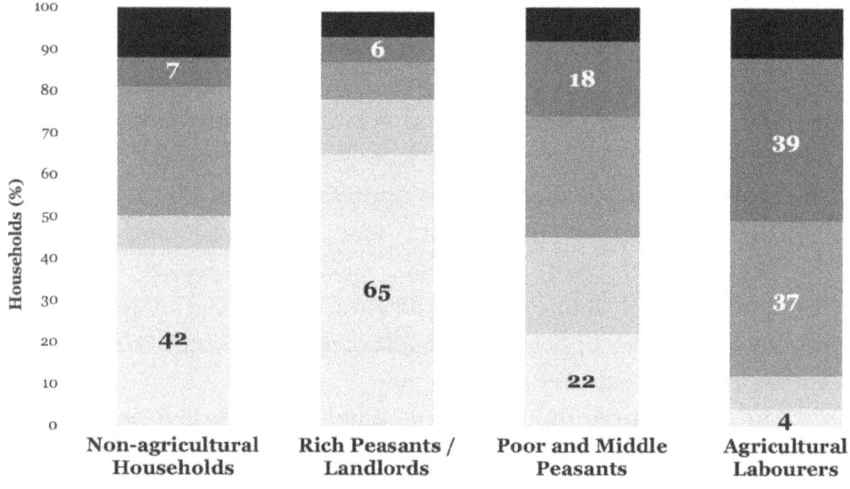

Source: Alakh Sharma and Jerry Rodgers, 'Structural Change in Bihar's Rural Economy'.

sharecropped by tenants. The pandemic lockdowns have been particularly brutal for those with scarce or no land, with minimal alternative safety nets to fall back on.

Fifteen million people were uprooted from their homes by India's 1947 Partition. Seventy years later, during the pandemic, India was in the throes of its worst reverse migration. This time, the population exodus was estimated to be more than double. For two months, India's national highways were filled with millions of migrants trudging hundreds of kilometres on foot, cycles, trucks and trains, back to their villages. For the ruling classes, these reverse migrants desperately walking home might as well have been ghosts. Most of them were returning from developed industrial cities and towns in southern and western India to their impoverished homes in the backward eastern states, Bihar among them. Due to poverty, unemployment, landlessness and hunger, more than half of Bihari households have at least one member who is a migrant, largely within India.[91]

NARI PUJA: WORSHIP OF WOMEN?

Ask any Bihari and they will tell you that Chhath is the most important festival on the calendar. Most of my female surveyors refused to work for a week before the festival. They said they had to prepare an array of sweets at home—from laddoos to thekuas. Outside many houses, we saw women pounding rice for the kheer, using large stone mortars and pestles. The excitement was palpable as families bought new clothes and migrants returned home in droves for the festivities. During one train ride, a Bihari migrant I met told me that, if he did not return home for Chhath, his family would mock him as an unworthy man.

When celebrations began in the village in Muzaffarpur district that we were in, I was stumped by how wide and visible the hold of patriarchy was. This was only an hour's drive from Patna. In most houses that I went to, women fasted for thirty-six hours at a stretch. The men did not fast. Twice a day, at dawn and dusk, these women walked to their local ponds, with men carrying baskets of fruits. Fully clothed, the women would take dips in these ponds to pray to the virile sun god.[92] Four of every ten Bihari women are underweight, and three of every five are anaemic.[93] Predictably, I saw many women faint during this marathon physical ordeal. In contrast, in Muslim homes in Bihar and across the border in Bangladesh, during the holy month of Ramzan (Ramadan), both men as well as women fast from dawn to dusk.[94]

In West Bengal and Nepal,[95] during the major Hindu festival of Dashien (Dussehra), the goddess Durga is worshipped for her warrior skills. Even a century ago, Begum Rokeya criticised this superficial worship of women (nari puja), which masks their routine subordination.[96] In Bihar, on the other hand, even the illusion of women's worship barely exists. Instead, poet Savita Singh, in her haunting poem about Bihari women, ponders, '*Kaun hai mera parmeshwar?* (Who is my god?)'.[97] In colloquial Hindi, husbands are often called 'parmeshwar' and equated to deities. In one of my fieldwork villages, my octogenarian host always referred to her husband as 'maalik' (master). She wouldn't think twice about eating leftovers from his plate. She explained to me that, since husbands are holy, foods tasted by them is like prasad (food blessed by the gods).[98] Across rural Bihar, many of my female researchers confirmed that this was indeed a common practice in their own homes too.

In most Bihari homes, as my survey recorded, women often ate last at every meal, and also invariably the least. Rural Bihari women rarely step out of the confines of their homes, and only 8 per cent earn an income. With high dependence on men, 43 per cent of married Bihari women also face domestic violence—double the Indian average.[99]

But why is the status of women in Bihar so dismal? What in its history explains it? Unlike Nepal or Bangladesh, why haven't radical movements for social change in Bihar addressed the 'women's question'?

In the second or third century, the ancient Hindu text Manusmriti codified traditional patriarchy: 'Though destitute of virtue, or seeking pleasure (elsewhere), or devoid of good qualities, (yet) a husband must be constantly worshipped as a god by a faithful wife.'[100] In Bihar, these words acquire a particular menace. Worse, the state practised one of the most extreme forms of 'sexploitation of the dalit women' with the barbaric ritual of Dola Pratha,[101] where the 'newly wed Dalit girl has to spend her first night with local upper/middle caste/class landlords'.[102]

In this climate of extreme feudal and patriarchal sexual violence, northern Indian social reform movements have been able to make only limited progress across centuries. In the nineteenth century, these emancipatory movements were primarily led by men. Raja Ram Mohan Roy fought against sati[103] and Ishwar Chandra Vidyasagar supported widow remarriage.[104] With the gradual spread of education, by the late nineteenth and early twentieth century, in various parts of India, Savitribai Phule, Fatima Sheikh, Sarala Devi Chaudharani, Pandita Ramabai, Swarnakumari Devi and other women pioneers began to lead these struggles for gender equality and education.[105]

However, even in the 1920s, a decade after Bihar was carved out as a separate province from Bengal, its purdah continued to be 'the most deplorable' in India.[106] Although their literacy rate was less than 1 per cent,[107] Bihari women launched a vibrant anti-purdah movement. In 1929, the All India Women's Conference held in Patna also passed resolutions against purdah and dowry, and in support of the Child Marriage Restraint Act enacted that year.[108] Thousands of Bihari women also actively participated in Mahatma Gandhi's Civil Disobedience Movement through the boycott of foreign cloth. It was largely married, semi-literate women from smaller towns who took part in these anti-government protests with the support of their husbands.[109]

By the 1940s, women's activist organisations had mushroomed across India. Unfortunately, the nationalist movement continued to glorify the virtues of self-sacrifice in the imagery of 'Mother India'.[110] After Independence, the Indian Constitution adopted universal franchise and legislated gender equality. In those early decades of the new nation, girls' and women's education spread rapidly. However, progress in terms of true empowerment was slow. Even women's movements focused primarily on empowerment in the domestic space. In 1973, for example, the left-leaning United Women's Anti-Price Rise Front conducted massive demonstrations against inflation.[111] 'Ten to twenty thousand women' went, 'to gherao (encircle) MPs and industrialists and offer them bangles as a token of their (the industrialists') emasculation'.[112]

In the more radical flaming fields[113] of Bihar, similar to Nepal, the Naxalite rebellion by Marxist–Leninist–Maoist armed guerrillas championed the struggles of the oppressed.[114] Since the 1960s, the Naxal movement was opposed to the patriarchies of feudal caste landlords, the nation-state and those that existed within the home. Women were estimated to form a third[115] of the Naxal cadre, most of them from marginalised castes and tribes. Many of these women had been displaced from their lands due to industrialisation, grinding poverty, upper caste sexual violence or oppressive patriarchy.[116] But unlike Nepal,[117] the agency and participation of women guerrillas in the armed struggle[118] was not socially transformative.

One crucial reason for this lack of progress was the brutal retaliation by upper caste private militias in Bihar. While previously militias would only target men, the ruthless Ranvir Sena, created in 1994 mainly by the Bhumihars, perpetrated femicide.[119] In the 1997 Lakshmanpur Bathe massacre, they raped girls and murdered pregnant women to symbolise 'killing the demon in the womb'. These men specifically targeted oppressed caste women[120] with full impunity.[121] A Ranvir Sena commander openly justified their atrocities on Dalits: 'Yes, we kill the women because they give birth to Naxalites … we have decided that if they kill two of us, we will ruin their whole *khandan* (clan); we will kill 15 of them.'[122]

Since 2005, with Nitish Kumar's rise to power as the chief

minister, violence by caste armies has reduced substantially.[123] Women voters have also enthusiastically supported his policies. In particular, the ban on alcohol has been the most popular, along with the reservation of 50 per cent of seats for women in the panchayat elections and 35 per cent in government jobs.

6.3: Armed private caste militias in Bihar

Year	Caste	Private Militia
UPPER CASTE		
1969	Rajputs	Kuer Sena
1979-1986	Rajputs	Kunwar Sena
1984	Rajputs, Brahmins	Kisan Sena
1988	Rajputs	Sunlight Sena
1981	Bhumihars	Brahmarshi Sena
1981	Rajputs	Samajwadi Krantikari Sena
1990	Bhumihars	Savarna Liberation Front (known as the Diamond Sena, later merged with Sunlight Sena to form Ranvir Sena)
1989-90	Rajputs	Kisan Sena
1990	Rajputs	Ganga Sena
1994	Bhumihars	Ranvir Sena
MARGINALISED CASTE		
1979	Kurmis	Kisan Suraksha Samiti
1983	Kurmis	Bhoomi Sena
1983	Yadavs	Lorik Sena
1983	Middle-class landlords	Kisan Sangh

Source: HRW, 'Broken People: Caste Violence against India's "Untouchables"'.

In this largely semi-literate and semi-feudal society, most Bihari women are still miles away from meaningful empowerment after millennia of subjugation.

Since the 1990s, the Dalit 'Feminist Standpoint', inspired by Marxism and Black feminism, has emphasised the overlapping layers of oppression faced by Dalit women in terms of class, caste and gender.[124] Musahar women, in particular, typify this triple, intersectional oppression.

The horrific rape and murder of three dozen orphaned girls in shelter homes in my fieldwork district of Muzaffarpur illustrates this diabolic imbalance of power.[125] The main accused, a business magnate, belonged to the upper caste. The impunity he enjoyed due to strong political, media and bureaucratic connections highlights the toxic stranglehold of patriarchy, feudalism and casteism in Bihar[126]—a hegemony that literally stunts the life chances of Bihari women.

ABSENT STATE

India, and Bihar in particular, are also among the world's laggards in social spending.

In his book *Last Among Equals*, M.R. Sharan documents the travails of the Samaj Parivartan Shakti Sanghathan (SPSS), a small, independent Bihari network, largely comprising women from marginalised castes and classes, that had sprung up to demand employment from the government under the Mahatma Gandhi National Rural Employment Guarantee Act 2005 (MGNREGA, or Manrega, as it is colloquially referred to). During my fieldwork in Muzaffarpur district, their mud-hut office became my second home. The women of the SPSS receive no government support, though one of every five Bihari women has joined the state-sponsored Jeevika self-help groups. Though Bihar remains one of the most impoverished states, of the 100 days of NREGA work guaranteed by law, the average days of employment provided to each participating household in 2022-23, was only 47 days.

So, SPSS women spend most of their time knocking on the doors of the apathetic Bihari state.

Children playing at a newly upgraded anganwadi with funds from the 'Smart City' initiative in Cochin municipal area in Kerala

7

SOUTHERN SUPERMODELS: SRI LANKA, KERALA AND TAMIL NADU

> Get a little more noisy and boisterous like the suffragettes in England and break a few glass windows.
>
> – A.M.K. Coomaraswamy, Secretary of the Diocese of Colombo, addressing the Ceylon Women's Franchise Union in 1928[1]

TALL WAVES LASHED the coconut tree-lined shore. In this serene village in Kerala, even the weathered fisherfolk were wary of plunging into the mighty Arabian Sea. Even in the midst of such majesty, the village's resilient social networks were truly awe-inspiring to me. In 2018, Kerala had been devastated by a flood. After two years of COVID-19, the overall mood in the state was distinctly grim. In God's Own Country, tourism had drastically declined. Income from fishing and other traditional occupations had fallen substantially. Many breadwinners had lost their jobs in the Middle East and other foreign shores, and had been forced to return home. Money was scarce all around. Despite these trials, the village had no dearth of the bare essentials for survival—food, shelter and social bonds.

Since the 1990s, Malayali women across Kerala have formed nearly 300,000 Kudumbashree (Prosperity to the Family)[2] neighbourhood groups with government support. Similar to the Jeevika self-help groups in Bihar and Aama Samuhas in Nepal, 4.6 million village women from every second home across Kerala meet with their Kudumbashree neighbours each week to chat, bond and pool their savings. Each group also specialises in producing simple goods for household consumption and sale. In the village where I was staying, I visited two Kudumbashree meetings which were being held within a few metres of each other. In one, the women had collectively made packets of very low-cost detergent powder and soaps. They had also filled used plastic water bottles with sweet-smelling liquid household cleaners and dishwashing liquid. These household necessities helped each family to save money and allowed the collectives to earn modest revenues. A family could purchase all their household cleaning products for two months with only a Rs 500 note. Branded, factory-made products at local shops would have cost at least twice as much.

The other Kudumbashree group I met was equally enterprising. These women had procured a strip of land by the beach from the local panchayat, and grew vegetables there. Since the land was not very fertile, the quality of these vegetables, in terms of shape, colour and texture, were not suitable for sale in the market. But they were more than sufficient for their own family needs, thus helping the women provide nutritious meals to their families and reducing household expenses. Similarly, across the length and breadth of Kerala, more than 40,000 Kudumbashree women's groups cultivate more than 10 million acres of what were earlier fallow lands.[3]

The Kerala government has not only actively supported these Kudumbashree groups from the very beginning, but has also encouraged their convergence with NREGA to increase women's employment. Now, 90 per cent of NREGA workers in Kerala are women, the highest in the country.[4]

The fair price ration shop in this village where I was staying was run by a woman as a family business. In Kerala, nearly every family is entitled to a ration card, even if one-third of them do not include any subsidy.[5] Families across classes purchase their grains from these ration shops. The poorest households receive twenty-eight kilos of rice absolutely free of cost every month. We saw some of these families walk barefoot to the shop with several neatly folded plastic bags tucked under their arms to carry back the rice. Wealthier families usually arrived on bicycles or motorbikes. The public distribution system across Kerala has become a shining symbol of food security, come what may—flood, sunshine, or indeed a pandemic.[6]

The anganwadis in Kerala are, equally, a class apart. I requested a few teenage girls who were returning from college to take me to the nearest anganwadi. As we entered, the teacher smiled, recognising them as her ex-students. Now she was teaching their younger siblings. She had also taught their parents, most of whom were fisherfolk in this village. Later, I requested the college-goers and their younger siblings to gather around for a group photo. They stood in the order of their heights to show me the different generations of students taught by the same anganwadi teacher. It was fascinating how one educated woman teacher could impact an entire village.

Similarly, in Tamil Nadu, I met many anganwadi workers who had worked for thirty to forty years as a part of the

Integrated Child Development Scheme initiated in 1975. These welfare workers were primarily women who had dedicated their entire lives to educating the young for a modest salary and had in the bargain shaped generations.

In anganwadis across Tamil Nadu and Kerala, I saw that, unlike Bihar, children were fed two small meals every day. It was like clockwork, punctual and without any fuss. On arrival in the morning, children usually received a healthy snack such as channa chundal (stir-fried chickpeas). Then, after some games and learning, they all ate a small lunch. Some would then lie on mats on the floor for a quick afternoon nap.

This anganwadi by the beach in Kerala was particularly well-resourced. It had marble flooring that an ecotourism resort nearby had laid as part of their corporate social responsibility initiatives. A five-star hotel had also donated many toys and games. Seeing the boys in the anganwadi casually play with dolls was a delight. I noticed that their teacher, too, looked on proudly.

Unsurprisingly, since the turn of the twentieth century, Kerala and its neighbour Sri Lanka have achieved levels of human development comparable to developed countries despite modest levels of per capita incomes. For this unique feat, they have been collectively hailed as the 'Kerala–Sri Lanka model'.[7] Decades later, their neighbour Tamil Nadu, too, caught up with these social development pioneers.[8]

The main question, however, is, how did these southern Indian states achieve similar human development as their neighbour Sri Lanka, when large parts of northern India have lagged behind? Why are anganwadi workers in Kerala so committed, unlike those in Bihar? Why do women of all castes and religions join the Kudumbashree groups and work together with such camaraderie? Like Bangladesh and Nepal, did the Southern Neighbours trio, too, invest in diluting inequalities?[9] Also puzzling is why Sri Lanka and Kerala, despite being politically different regions, had their human development acceleration at roughly around the same time—from 1820 to 1977? Also, why did Tamil Nadu take longer to develop to the same level?

Kerala, Tamil Nadu and their neighbour Sri Lanka share deep-rooted social, economic, historical and cultural ties. So, it is interesting that this southern triad has progressed in human development without rapid economic growth. Between 1911 and 1955, for example, when female life expectancy in Sri Lanka doubled from thirty to sixty years, per capita incomes were stagnant in the country. This experience is different from that of developed countries or even of newly industrialising 'miracle' Asian economies.[10] Jean Drèze infers:

> If Gujarat is a model, then the real toppers in development indicators, like Kerala and Tamil Nadu, must be supermodels.[11]

Since Gujarat is certainly not a model for human development,[12] the term 'Southern Supermodels' could be termed an exaggeration. But it does serve to highlight the exceptional performance of these southern states compared to the Indian average.

The advances of Bangladesh and Nepal are of more recent origin, both within the last half-century. The Southern Supermodels, on the other hand, were early achievers. Sri Lanka, Kerala and Tamil Nadu's successes date back to the pre-colonial period. This book examines the specific time periods when these regions experienced their respective human development acceleration: Sri Lanka (1830–1977), Kerala (1820–1975) and Tamil Nadu (1916–to date).[13] It does not, therefore, comment on their present socio-political scenarios.

COMMONALITIES

For millennia, the three Southern Supermodels have shared close ties due to their geographic proximity. For instance,

Kerala is named after its abundant coconut trees,[14] which probably came originally from Sri Lanka.[15] But, in fact, Sri Lanka and the two southern Indian states have entirely different histories, languages and cultures.

Mapping the chronological evolution of the distinct 'critical junctures' of these three regions helps to understand the period of their human development advances.[16] Interestingly, Sri Lanka and Kerala have roughly simultaneous development arcs. Tamil Nadu matured decades later.

Despite their differences, the Southern Supermodels as early pioneers share four overarching similarities which aided their human development advances.

1. Social Reform Movements

In the southern trio, the cumulative impact of successive social movements has considerably bridged inequalities. Sociologist Charles Tilly argues that social movements are a form of contentious politics. They enable marginalised communities to challenge the 'exploitation and opportunity hoarding' done by ruling-class governments and elites.[17] The strong influence of communist movements is another common feature in the southern trio.

Kerala

The slow ripples of Kerala's backwaters reflect an unusually turbulent social history. Most tourists cruise along these famous backwaters on tranquil houseboats. My experience of travelling in a diesel-powered commuter boat with a loud spluttering engine was entirely different. These journeys in Alleppey gave me a flavour of the local sights and sounds. As we waited at a boat-stop to pick up some local passengers, I noticed a huge, glass-encased statue of Mahatma Ayyankali, the anti-caste social reformer. The social history of Kerala is firmly anchored in its radical social movements.

Until the eighteenth century, Kerala had one of the worst forms of caste discrimination. Unlike the four-fold Varna system in the rest of India, the Nambudiri Brahmins of Kerala considered all other castes to be Shudras. They practised not only untouchability but also 'distance pollution' and 'unseeability'.

> An Ezhava must keep a distance of 36 steps from a Brahmin, and a Pulayan must not approach him within 96 steps. There are even castes so defiling that their mere sight alone is polluting ...[18]

Only after decades of anti-caste movements was there a 'loosening and levelling of the cultural soil'.[19] Kerala's evolution as a 'metaphor for a high HDI despite a low GNP' would have been inconceivable without these social justice movements.[20]

In the 1800s, two hundred Ezhavas[21] (Izhavas) attempted to enter the Vaikkom temple. But the protesters were attacked viciously, murdered and barred from all public roads.[22] In the nineteenth century, Christian missionaries in Travancore[23] began campaigns against agrestic slavery and for the empowerment of marginalised castes. The missionaries also influenced John Munro, the British resident in Travancore, to initiate government policies to expand education.[24] The main motive of the missionaries was evangelical. But by educating and uplifting the marginalised castes, they prepared the ground for future social movements.

The Mappila revolts (1836–1922)[25] also marked a distinct change in subaltern protests. Muslim tenants agitated against their severe economic exploitation.[26] By the time the British crushed the Mappila rebellion, the demands of various subjugated communities for social justice had begun in earnest.

Although the Ezhavas achieved some economic prosperity, education and social mobility, they continued to experience severe caste discrimination. In 1881, they formed 16 per cent of Kerala's population but held only 1 per cent of government jobs. By comparison, Nairs (Nayars), with roughly an equal population share, held 52 per cent of government jobs. Brahmins, who formed only 0.8 per cent of the population had cornered 18 per cent of these plum jobs.[27]

In 1891, therefore, 10,000 non-Brahmins issued the 'Malayali Memorial' petition accusing the government of favouring the Brahmins.[28] Political scientist Prerna Singh believes that this petition marked a turning point in the building of an overarching sense of Malayali 'we-ness' and sub-national pride in Kerala.[29] Soon after, in 1896, the caste-specific Ezahava (Izahava) Memorial was submitted which demanded greater equality of opportunity between castes.

Ezhava activism finally bore fruit only in the 1930s. The popular Sree Narayana Dharma Paripalana Yogam (SNDP), a religious and social reform movement in Travancore, enabled the 'transformation of caste consciousness to class consciousness'.[30] Sree Narayana Guru (1856–1928) preached an inclusive philosophy of 'One Caste, One Religion and One God'.[31] Since Ezhavas were denied entry into most temples, the movement built new temples open to all castes. Narayana Guru's followers also silently supported the landmark 1924-25 Vaikkom Temple Entry Satyagraha, led by the Congress party.[32] Even Mahatma Gandhi came to Vaikkom to negotiate with the temple management.[33] Even then, the government issued a legal proclamation permitting temple-entry for everyone only a decade later.

At the bottom of Kerala's social pyramid, the Pulayas and Parayas, as agrestic slaves, were even more marginalised than the Ezhavas.[34] Mahatma Ayyankali (1863–1941), whose shrines are so prominent across Kerala, emerged as a Pulaya leader in Travancore. He urged his followers to fight for their children's right to education, and their right to use public roads and wear dignified clothes.[35] These cumulative cultural revolts gradually eroded caste barriers.

At the turn of the twentieth century, the matrilineal Nair taravad[36] joint-family also collapsed.[37] Social scientist Robin Jeffrey argues that, in a society plagued by jarring inequalities, upper caste *déraciné* men were drawn to communist ideals to fill this social vacuum.[38]

After Independence, in 1956, modern Kerala was created through the merger of the princely states of Cochin and Travancore, along with the Madras Presidency district of Malabar. A year later, the state welcomed the first democratically elected Communist government in India (and the world). For more than ten of the twenty years until 1977, Kerala had Communist-led or Communist-majority coalition governments. By the 1970s, the 'Kerala model' of development was being eulogised, as the state had achieved a progressive reduction in caste and class inequalities with high human development outcomes.[39]

Academics have variously attributed Kerala's successes to its class struggles,[40] the matrilineal legacy[41] and the subnational 'we-ness' solidarity.[42] My research, however, indicates that the long arc of Kerala's evolution over the course of more than a century of social movements (including the oft-neglected 1813-1859 Channar Upper Cloth revolt can be placed largely before rather than after Independence.[43] From the first Vaikkom Temple Entry movement in the early nineteenth century, Kerala's evolution as a model of human development has been a hard-won achievement over centuries, even though caste prejudices have not entirely vanished. Academic V.K. Ramachandran lists out the wide range of movements which enabled Kerala to transform itself into a 'development model':

> The freedom movement, the radical and anti-caste sections of the social reform movement, the movement against landlordism, the movement against autocracy and monarchy, the movement for the linguistic reorganization of the region and the establishment of a unified Kerala, and, of course, the modern movement of workers, peasants and radical intellectuals ... Communists played a leading part in the literary movement and in the cultural movement (including the theatre movement) in Kerala.[44]

The left movement has also been one of the many catalysts of change in Kerala, in the later period. The first biography of Marx in an Indian language was published in Malayalam in 1912.[45] Post-Independence, Kerala democratically elected the first communist government in India.[46] This government implemented radical reforms in land rights, healthcare, education and food distribution. The communist parties in Kerala, unlike West Bengal,[47] had a mass political base of workers, peasants, agricultural labourers, students, teachers, youth and women.[48] Kerala has also had communist or communist-majority coalition governments in a series of short spurts: 1957–59, 1967–69, 1969–70 and 1970–77. Even when the left has not been in power, public services have remained at the centrestage of socio-political debates, which has led to the acceleration of human development.

Tamil Nadu

Tamil Nadu's human development gains, too, would have been inconceivable without its vibrant socio-political movements. These reform movements challenged stultifying caste practices. Previously, for many castes 'mere acts of going to school, drinking water, wearing footwear, sporting decent clothes, riding bicycles, entering a restaurant, finding a place to stay during travel have been a challenge.'[49]

Tamil Nadu's human development achievements, however, were largely visible only after Independence. They have been shaped by successive waves of predominantly identity-based anti-caste 'great social movements'.[50] The Non-Brahmin Dravidian Self-Respect movement and later the Dalit movement have diluted centuries of Brahminical hegemony. The fruits of this Tamil renaissance have also encouraged everyday 'decentralized collective action', for example, hunger strikes and mock funerals to demand and monitor public services such as NREGA employment.[51] So, successive political regimes have continuously been under pressure to fund welfare services, especially for marginalised communities.

I had my first taste of the flavour of these public services at the Amma Canteens in Chennai. In the boiling afternoon heat, the canteen I went to was packed with customers of all classes. Since there was no place to sit, we all stood around tall, stainless-steel tables. The sambar-rice and thayir sadam (curd-rice), prepared by the female cooks, each cost only 5 Indian Rupees and tasted like home-cooked food. Labourers, IT sector workers, migrants, students and even backpacking tourists flocked like bees to these subsidised canteens.

The late Tamil Nadu chief minister and former actor J. Jayalalithaa had started these populist Amma Unavagam canteens in the last few years of her life. They have since bridged class and political divides. Even Chief Minister M.K. Stalin of the rival Dravida Munnetra Kazhagam party has retained these popular canteens. These subsidised cafeterias, vote-catchers though they may be, embody the Dravidian spirit of public service.

A hundred years ago, even the existence of these innocuous eateries would have been unthinkable in Tamil Nadu. In the late nineteenth century, C. Iyothee Thass, a Dalit intellectual,[52] described the extreme social segregation between castes:

> If those who are known as Brahmins enter the villages and streets occupied by our people, who were the original Dravidians, but now called Panchamas by the Hindu high-caste-men, they (Brahmins) are driven out of the place in the most disgraceful manner amidst tumult and uproar on the ground that the spots stepped on by them have become polluted. The measure adopted to eradicate the impurity thus caused, is to cleanse the places trodden by these so called Brahmins by means of cow-dung, and the pots used for such purposes are destroyed beyond the limits of such towns. This treatment is similar to the one done when a person is dead and the body removed from the house ... Such is the hatred between the two classes of people ... I began to enquire into the cause for such animosity between the two classes from the time I could think myself.[53]

In this environment of acute caste stratification, Brahmins, who formed only 3 per cent of the population in 1886, 'held 42 per cent of all posts in the Madras Government'.[54] The Dravidian movement arose to challenge this hegemony. The first step was the 1916 'Non-Brahmin Manifesto'[55] published by prominent leaders of marginalised castes. Perhaps, Kerala's 1891 Malayali Memorial and the 1896 Ezhava Memorial were inspirations. Within a year, the ripples of change were visible.

The framers of the original Non-Brahmin Manifesto formed the Justice Party. E.V. Ramaswamy Naicker, later revered as Periyar,[56] also joined forces with them. In the face of this intense public pressure, two years later, the 1918 Montagu–Chelmsford Reforms reserved 28 seats for the non-Brahmin majority in the Madras Legislative Council. The Justice Party then went on to win the 1920 elections. In a first in India, they introduced reservation quotas for non-Brahmins in government.

But Dravidian activism was truly ignited when Periyar launched the radical Suyamariathai Iyakkam (Self-Respect Movement) in 1926. Initially, this social movement only promoted inter-caste dining and inter-caste marriage. Over time, the movement's goals became more radical, seeking to abolish caste and religion entirely. For at least three decades, this 'cultural project of emboldening people'[57] systematically diluted caste hegemony in Tamil society, polity, economy and even in the spoken word. In 1938, the anti-Hindi agitations opposed Hindi for being an alien language,[58] also pointing to its affinity to Sanskrit and Brahminism. This language rebellion united the Justice Party and the Self-Respecters towards building the Dravida Kazhagam, led by Periyar, as a mass organisation.

In the 1950s, Tamil Nadu was born as a separate linguistic state in independent India. At that time, the anti-Brahmin spirit was so potent that the 1954 Congress Chief Minister K. Kamaraj established his first cabinet without a single Brahmin. He also introduced universal education and free noon meals for school children.[59] Additionally, his government rolled out extensive rural electrification that boosted irrigation, agricultural productivity and industrialisation.

Interestingly, both the major political parties in Tamil Nadu today, the Dravida Munnetra Kazhagam (DMK) and All India Anna Dravida Munnetra Kazhagam (AIADMK), owe their birth to the Self-Respect Movement of the Dravida Kazhagam. For nearly five decades, these two Dravidian parties have traded power in every election, despite colossal corruption charges against each of them. With many larger-than-life film makers and artists from the Tamil film industry in their ranks, the two Dravidian parties have amplified the anti-caste ethos.[60] Artists, writers, poets, musicians and filmmakers have celebrated the spirit of Dravidian consciousness and Tamil pride. The second anti-Hindi agitation in the 1960s was the zenith of this Tamil cultural renaissance.[61]

In 1967, the DMK won the state elections with the former film scriptwriter M. Karunanidhi as the kingmaker. A decade later, M.G. Ramachandran (MGR), with his film hero image of a 'protector of the poor', rose to power with the breakaway AIADMK faction. The 1980s saw rapid improvements in the primary health care system, school education, nutrition, childcare and other public services. This also translated into improvements in life expectancy, infant mortality, maternal mortality and other human development outcomes.[62]

In 1990, when the Mandal Commission reforms ushered in reservations for OBCs nationally, only the Tamil Nadu assembly welcomed this historic initiative. Reservations had already been highly effective in Tamil Nadu. Non-Brahmins employed in gazetted government jobs rose from a mere 19 per cent in 1927 in the British Madras province to more than half in 1970 in post-Independence Tamil Nadu.

7.1: Administration of the Madras Province (and later Tamil Nadu) in Gazetted posts by caste and community, 1927–1970

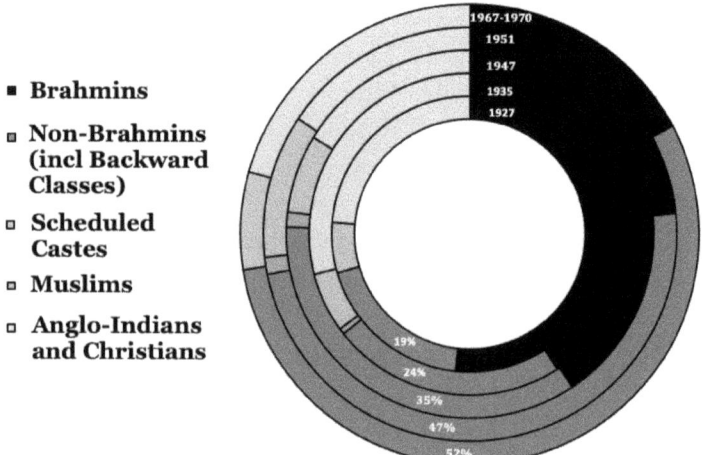

- Brahmins
- Non-Brahmins (incl Backward Classes)
- Scheduled Castes
- Muslims
- Anglo-Indians and Christians

Source: Christophe Jaffrelot, *India's Silent Revolution: The Rise of the Lower Castes in North India*, p. 240, Table 7.4

While marginalised castes gained upward mobility with the Self-Respect Movement, Dalits continue to remain extremely marginalised and oppressed. Caste violence against Dalits is rampant.[63] Villages in Tamil Nadu are highly caste segregated. Dalit colonies are usually located on the outskirts, with access to fewer public amenities. Even Dalit women elected as panchayat presidents face blatant discrimination.[64] The Dalit movement in Tamil Nadu has a long way to go to achieve equalities.[65]

In 1987, the Vanniyar agitations began,[66] but it was only in 2021 that the government set aside a specific quota for the sub-caste within the existing quota reserved for largely Dalits and Adivasis in the Most Backward Classes (MBC) and Denotified Communities (DNCs) Act 2021, though the Supreme Court in 2021 expunged the law.[67] In 2007, after agitations by the Muslim Munnetra Kazhagam, a 3.5 per cent exclusive reservation was carved out from the larger OBC quota for Muslims and Christians each.[68] Tamil Nadu has improved its social development outcomes primarily due to these concerted efforts at reservations in both the political and social spheres.

The left parties have never officially held power in Tamil Nadu. But when communist organisations were banned in 1924, the Self-Respecters sheltered them.[69] In the first state assembly elections held in 1951-52, the Dravida Kazhagam (DK) had also decided to extend support to the Communist Party. So, the influence of left ideologies in moulding Tamil Nadu's welfare state has not been entirely negligible.

Sri Lanka

In the third century BCE, Buddhism was introduced in the island nation by Emperor Ashoka's children Mahinda and Sanghamitra. In Ceylon (Sri Lanka since 1972), caste divisions, especially among the majority Buddhist community, have never been as stark as in India. The majority caste of agriculturalists was called the 'Goigama' in the Sinhalese-dominated areas and 'Vellalla' in the Tamil areas.[70] Also, as a Ceylonese suffragette highlighted in 1928:

> There is no untouchability in Ceylon ... unlike the people of India, the Ceylonese, both men and women, mix freely in society and have no scruples about mixed dining. Even interracial marriages are not anything extraordinary in modern Ceylon.[71]

Ceylon also has had a long history of colonisation—by the Portuguese (1505–1658), the Dutch (1658–1795) and the British (1795–1948).[72] The British considered Ceylon to be the 'senior colony of the new empire'.[73] The imperial administration tried to implement in Ceylon ideas of social liberalism, especially Fabianism, which was influential in Britain at the time.[74] The Ceylonese nationalist, trade unionist and suffragette movements also contributed significantly to the pressure to build a welfare state.

The vision of the Sri Lankan welfare state was initiated with the 1833 Colebrooke–Cameroon Reforms.[75] They ensured that Ceylonese received university education and were appointed in the bureaucracy.[76] However, the real breakthrough happened two decades before Independence. The Donoughmore Commission visited Ceylon in 1929 to introduce partial 'self-government'.[77] In 1931, Ceylon was the first Asian country to adopt universal franchise.[78] This was only two years after women in Britain earned the right to vote.[79]

Christian missionaries have also been prominent agents of change.[80] Mission churches insisted that converts of all castes should sit together as equals. Indeed, school education proved to be a great leveller. In 1893 and 1908, Theosophist Annie Besant, co-founder of the Fabian Society, also visited

Ceylon to advocate for women's education. Further, Anagarika Dharmapala,[81] founder of the Maha Bodhi society in 1891, led a Buddhist reform movement (1875–1933) to rekindle the spirit of egalitarianism.[82]

In the 1930s, the influence of the left ideology was also strong. Left-wing political parties built an urban trade union movement, influenced by the British labour movement, Fabian socialists and Trotskyism.[83] The anti-imperial Suriya Mal Movement of the 1930s against the sale of poppies to British veterans also politically supported a militant strike by textile workers. The Lanka Sama Samaja Party, an offshoot of this strike, was the nation's first socialist and later Trotskyite political force.

Since Sri Lanka's independence in 1948, the right-wing United National Party (UNP) and the centre-left coalition headed by the Sri Lanka Freedom Party (SLFP) have alternated in gaining electoral power.[84] During the period of accelerated human development, the SLFP was in power in three stretches: 1956–60, 1960–65 and 1970–77. The Trotskyite Lanka Sama Samaja Party (LSSP) and the Communist Party of Sri Lanka have both been part of these successive SLFP-led left-wing coalitions. Even when the left was out of power, governments have sought to maintain welfare subsidies to stem the left tide. In this post-Independence phase (1948–77), Sri Lanka substantially strengthened the welfare state. After the Second World War, the government provided all families with free rice rations.[85] The 1953 Health Services Act insisted on compulsory rural postings for doctors.[86] By the early 1970s, the government was spending 10 per cent of Sri Lankan GDP on welfare.

However, in 1977, the newly elected right-wing government liberalised the economy and rolled back the welfare state. By 1981, welfare expenditures fell to 4 per cent of GDP. The government even replaced the earlier universal free rice scheme with food stamps targeted only at the 'poorest of the poor'. In these years, the armed insurgency by the Tamil minority in the north also erupted. The Sri Lankan welfare state thus ebbed.

I saw the embers of the once mighty Sri Lankan welfare services after the 2004 tsunami. At that time, I was visiting the country to evaluate the state of schools for a civil society education coalition. The schools we visited were struggling with the availability of electricity and infrastructure. The most lasting impression etched in my memory is of a family I met in Galle. They continued to live in utmost fear in a home that had developed cracks. While they were grateful to be alive, the women showed me their idle sewing machines—all their raw materials had been washed away and international orders had dried up. On that trip, I also met the humanitarian A.T. Ariyaratne, the founder of the Sarvodaya Shramadana Movement. Rooted in Gandhian and Buddhist ideals, the movement focused on collective solidarity and played an important role in post-tsunami reconstruction to mitigate the dilution of Sri Lanka's welfare state.

2. Universal Public Services

In a school playground in Chennai, a group of boys were playing an unusual game during their recess. They had lined loose bricks together to resemble a small, open-air car, which they took turns to sit in and 'drive'. I felt myself smiling as I watched their joy in this simple game under the shade of trees in the hot, sultry Chennai summer. Creativity and resourcefulness, I soon realised, was also encouraged within the classroom. Most Tamil Nadu teachers are expected to plot students' milestones on an innovative chart designed as a game of snakes and ladders. This chart depicts all the necessary competencies a child needs to accomplish from grade 1 to grade 5, such as recognition of alphabets, learning multiplication tables and mastering carry-over subtraction.

Teachers map each child's progress, up a ladder as they gain some competencies or down a snake as they forget others. This evaluation enables teachers to quickly know which lessons to refresh till each student climbs all the appropriate learning ladders.

Tamil Nadu is one of the few states in India to adopt this model of continuous and comprehensive evaluation (CCE) as envisioned in the Right of Children to Free and Compulsory Education Act, 2009. Almost every classroom has plastic trays stacked in racks, filled with activity sheets for each child to complete during the year. Most of these activity sheets are innovative. For example, addition is taught with currency notes. Photos pictorially explain the meaning of words. Each day, after children complete the designated activities in the classroom, the teacher grades them. There are no end-of-term exams. With progressive learning, every day in the classroom counts.

In several schools, the four walls of the classroom have been converted into blackboards with a simple coat of black paint. These blackboards are divided into segments, and each child is assigned a slot with their name written in chalk. The children can freely doodle on their wall-space every day. Most children we met were very possessive of this space, proudly displaying their work on it. Schools in Tamil Nadu are certainly a cut above those in most of India.

A distinguishing feature of the southern trio has been their historical support for education as a universal tool to temper inequalities. For example, Travancore's Queen Gowri Parvati Bayi's Royal Rescript on Education is considered to be the Magna Carta of education. As early as 1818, she boldly proclaimed:

> The state should defray the entire cost of the education of its people in order that there might be no backwardness in the spread of enlightenment among them ...[87]

Among the southern trio, this history has led to a 'culture of public action' to demand public services with a sense of entitlement.[88] Tamil Nadu typifies this trait. On the one hand, politicians, mainly from the popular Tamil film industry,[89] have engaged in competitive populism to woo voters with freebies.[90] On the other hand, Tamil voters have also developed an aggressive sense of entitlement. Social scientist S. Vivek, in his book *Delivering Public Services Effectively*, describes how bureaucrats and politicians constantly face pressure from 'uncontrollable people'[91] who demand public services as a matter of right.[92] The political class in the largely Dravidian two-party state has been consistently committed to universal, rather than targeted, services. The majority of people in Tamil Nadu avail the services of government schools, primary healthcare centres, public distribution ration shops and other government services.[93]

Similar to other human development high-achievers, the southern trio also share three characteristics.[94]

Firstly, they tend to invest more as a proportion of GDP in 'equity-enhancing' policies for education, healthcare, nutrition and other essential services. In Sri Lanka, between 1959 and 1968, for example, expenditure on primary and secondary education was one of the highest in Asia. More than 4.5 per cent of GNP was spent to achieve a literacy rate of 85 per cent.[95] The government funded compulsory education, food subsidies and free healthcare through heavy taxation on the export of plantation crops.[96]

Secondly, the southern trio also focus more on primary rather than tertiary levels of care. In healthcare, for example, prevention is often better and cheaper than cure in hospitals.[97] Kerala's most impressive public health programmes focused on immunisation. Smallpox vaccination began in 1879 in Travancore and reached the entire population within six decades.[98]

7.2: Literacy rates (15+ years) in Kerala's erstwhile provinces of Travancore, Cochin and Malabar compared to Tamil Nadu and Sri Lanka, 1871–2011

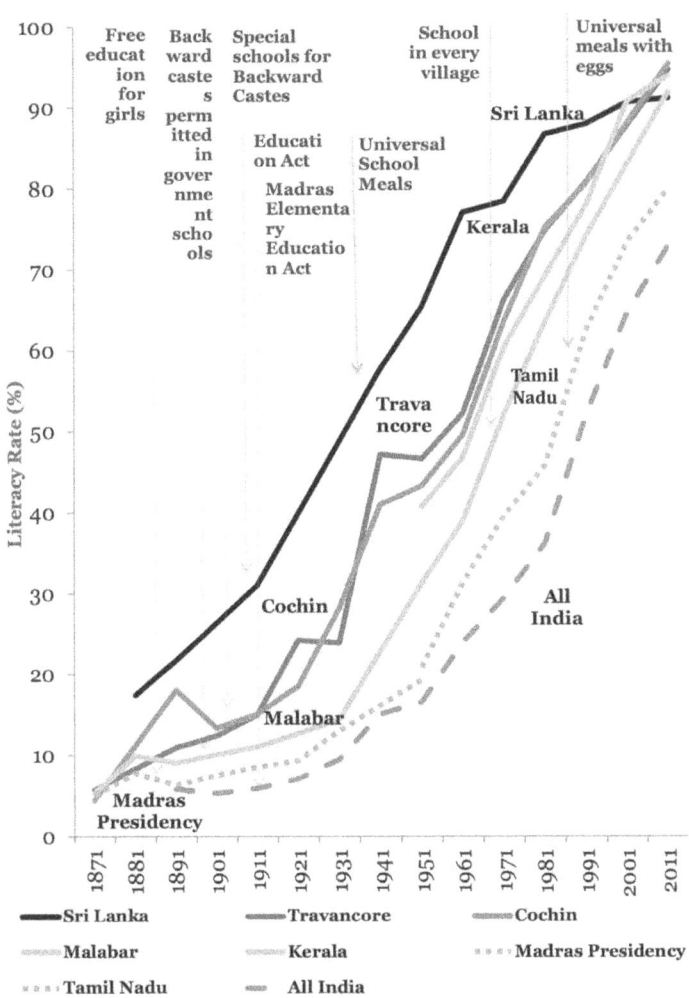

Source: Created by the author with data obtained for India, Kerala and Tamil Nadu from 1871–1991: V.K. Ramachandran, 'On Kerala's Development Achievements'; 1991–2011: Census of India. Data obtained for Sri Lanka from 1881–1981: James Warner Björkman, 'Health Policy and Politics in Sri Lanka: Developments in the South Asian Welfare State'; 1981–2011: World Development Indicators

Lastly, the three regions have also effectively tapped into synergies between health, nutrition and education.[99] During the Second World War, for example, apart from school meals, 'fair price' ration shops were also established in Kerala, a food-deficit state.[100]

Still, economist Surjit Bhalla has questioned, 'Is Sri Lanka an Exception?' in human development and even claims that 'it might have been a "failure"'.[101] But his analysis measures Sri Lanka's advances only in the limited time period of 1960–78. By then, the country was well past its prime acceleration. The 1970s actually witnessed 'a retreat from the expansionism of social welfare programs'.[102] Instead, 'the really fast expansion of Sri Lanka's social welfare programmes came much earlier, going back at least to the 1940s', when food distribution, school meals, malaria eradication and other public policies were expanded.[103] Bhalla's criticism, therefore, has been justly dismissed for the 'inappropriate' time period examined in his analysis and the lack of appreciation of the 'accumulated history of the expansion of social welfare programs stretching over many decades'.[104]

Still, to re-examine the superior performance of the southern trio, I have analysed education as an illustrative case during the entire period of the ascendency, from 1871 onwards.

I have compiled and created a unique graph with more than a century of comparative statistical data on literacy rates as available from 1871 to 2011. This illustration clearly shows that even as early as 1881, Ceylon was ahead of its neighbours Kerala and Tamil Nadu in terms of literacy. Within Kerala, the princely states of Cochin and Travancore performed better than British-governed Malabar. After the introduction of specific policies, distinct acceleration is evident. Importantly, the data also shows that rapid improvements in mass education in Kerala largely predate the post-independence left-wing governments by several decades.

Sri Lanka

In Ceylon, in the seventeenth and eighteenth centuries, the Dutch colonists established co-educational parish schools.[105] Christian missionaries also built several schools. By 1884, there was one school for every 900 Ceylonese.[106] In 1870, when India's first 'Lady Doctor' Anandibai Joshi was a mere child of 5 years—eventually she went to the United States to study medicine in 1885[107]—the Ceylon Medical College had already been established, and several women doctors had been trained.[108] In 1911, primary education was also made compulsory across the island.

The 1927[109] Donoughmore Constitution,[110] which had a clear vision that 'the Ceylonese peoples are now coming to a new independence',[111] marked the birth of the Sri Lankan welfare state.[112] In the 1930s, universal franchise 'stimulated the politically conscious minority to provide greater educational facilities for the rather apathetic majority.'[113] The education budget more than doubled from 1931 to 1945. The 1943 Education Act guaranteed all Sri Lankans free education in their mother tongues. In the 1940s, rural secondary schools were also opened across the island. Economically disadvantaged children even received state scholarships. Also 'the Minister of Education made a great contribution to public health when he succeeded against fierce opposition in introducing a system of school meals for children'.[114]

After Independence, Sri Lanka strengthened its welfare state. By the 1960s, education essentially became a state monopoly, with free education for all students from school to university.[115]

Kerala

As early as 1817, the Royal Rescript by the Queen of Travancore,[116] declared that the state would support the educational expenses of all citizens. The state would also fund two teachers in every primary school. This also aligned with Macauley's 1835 'Minute on Indian education' to promote English education and create an Indian elite to support colonial rule.[117] By 1866, across Kerala, vernacular schools had mushroomed.[118] With the increase in free schools for girls, enrolments trebled in the 1890s and more than doubled in the next decade.[119]

But why did the princely states invest so heavily in schools and universal public services? Sociologist Manali Desai argues that the monarchies of Cochin and Travancore wanted to prevent annexation by the British. The governor of Madras, for example, had threatened to annex Travancore when the spread of literacy was temporarily neglected during the reign of Raja Swati Tirunal (1829–47).[120] Christian missionaries also supported mass education and the monarchs adopted educational expansion as a 'preemptive response to British proximity and the threat of annexation as well as the threat of mass conversions to Christianity'.[121] Over time, these cumulative educational investments, in a deeply unequal society, ignited radical caste and class movements.[122]

7.3: Male Literacy Rates in Travancore by Caste, 1875–1931

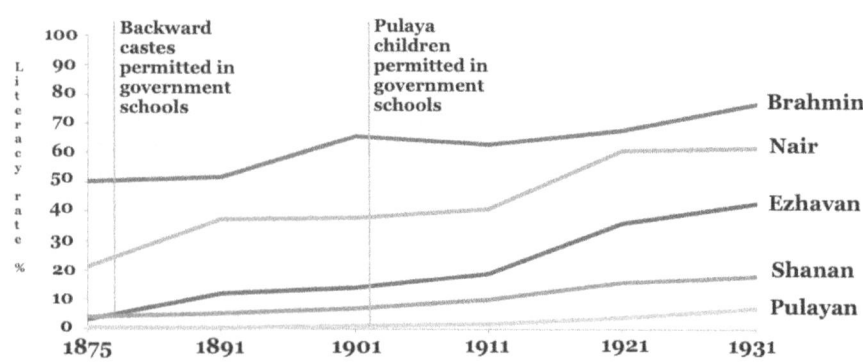

Source: Collated by the author from the Imperial Census of India data of many years especially that of Ayyar 1922 and Pillai 1932

In the nineteenth century, literacy in Kerala depended on caste and religion. Brahmin men had the highest literacy, followed in descending order by Nairs, Ezhavas and, finally, the so-called agrestic slaves.[123] Children of the marginalised castes were not even permitted to enter government schools.[124] Only the missionary schools offered free education to all.[125] Literacy rates of 'Christians were ahead of Muslims' and 'right behind the Nayars'.[126] Despite matrilineal traditions, in 1875, only 1.2 per cent of Nair women in Travancore could write.

There were a series of agitations by the oppressed castes to demand entry into state-run schools and public employment. Finally, in 1904, the government committed to funding the education of children from marginalised castes.[127] Special schools were also opened for oppressed castes and girls.[128] In 1911-12, the restriction on the admission of Pulaya children into government schools was removed. With the expansion of 'print capitalism', textbooks, newspapers and magazines were also published for mass consumption.[129] Public libraries were opened across cities and villages. These reading rooms built the foundation for a Malayalam literary and cultural renaissance.

By 1931, even before Independence, Kerala was the most literate region of India. Around 34 per cent of the population in Cochin district, 29 per cent in Travancore, and 14 per cent in Malabar could write, compared to 8 per cent in India as a whole. The first communist chief minister of Kerala, who was earlier with the Congress party, described in an interview:

> [O]ur effort was to have, in every village, a village Congress Committee, and, attached to it, a reading room and a night school.[130]

Tamil Nadu

In contrast, until 1951, the literacy rate in the Madras Presidency was not higher than the Indian average of 19 per cent. M.C. Rajah, a prominent Dalit leader in the Madras Legislative Council (1920–23), had powerfully argued that, for marginalised castes, subsidised tuition alone would not be sufficient. School meals, scholarships and other complementary policies would also be essential.[131] The Madras Elementary Education Act of 1920 devolved the responsibility for education onto local authorities.[132] With that, the enrolment of girls rose modestly.

Only after Independence did women's education in Tamil Nadu see a rapid increase. The first chief minister of Tamil Nadu, Rajaji, introduced a controversial system of caste-based education. In contrast, his successor K. Kamaraj (1954–63), also of the Congress, built a school in every village. His government also pioneered free noon meals for school children. Within a span of seven years, primary enrolments accelerated.[133] Subsequently, MGR (1977–87) universalised these meals across schools. Then, in the DMK years, nutritious eggs were added to the menu.[134]

The spread of education, including medical colleges, predated by several decades, improvements in health outcomes, such as decline in infant deaths. Over time, each advance has been mutually reinforcing, especially the progress in gender outcomes.

Two questions come up in this context. Why did the historical development of literacy rates in Kerala parallel that of Ceylon during 1830–1977? Why did Tamil Nadu develop only decades after Independence? The timelines of the three regions clearly indicate three significant developments.[135]

Firstly, Kerala's human development accelerated in the nineteenth century after a series of social movements by the subaltern classes. In Tamil Nadu, it was only after the 1920 Non-Brahmin Manifesto that the Dravidian Self-Respect Movement germinated. Secondly, the princely states in Kerala offered more significant avenues for social progress. The

Madras province, on the other hand, was governed by the British.[136] Lastly, the work of the Christian missionaries in education and social justice was greater in Kerala than in Tamil Nadu. This laid the foundation for the empowerment of oppressed castes and women.

3. Women's Agency

The advances of the Southern Supermodels are often credited to the greater freedoms enjoyed by women. Women's agency is usually displayed in their ability 'to earn an independent income, to work outside the home, to be educated, to own property'.[137] The ability to vote and be elected to political office are also equally important. Each of the three regions faced their own unique challenges in bringing women to the forefront.

My research highlights only three iconic turning points. Kerala's nineteenth-century Channar Upper Cloth Revolt for women to earn the right to dignified clothing, Sri Lanka's twentieth-century suffragette movement for women's right to vote and Tamil Nadu's Dravidian Self-Respect Movement, with women's emancipation at its core.

Kerala

The success of Kerala is often attributed to the matrilineal Nair community.[138] But the Nairs form only 16 per cent of Kerala's population. Women belonging to marginalised castes have had to fight for every inch of their freedom.

Barbaric customs did not permit women of oppressed castes[139] to clothe the upper parts of their bodies.

Only Brahmin and Nair women had the privilege to cover themselves when they went out, but not within the home.[140] Especially in the presence of the princely family and

Namboodiri Brahmins, all marginalised castes had to be semi-naked. 'The Namboodiri Brahmin women would bare their breasts only to the idols of deities; the Nairs would bare their breasts to the Brahmins; those lower in the caste order—the Channars, the Ezhavas and the Nadars, amongst others—had to bare their breasts to all the savarnas'.[141]

In the seventeenth century, an East India Company writer John Grose described even Queen of Attingal as being bare-chested at the Padmanabha temple procession. It is said that she even ordered the breasts of a Nair woman, who had dared to cover herself, to be cut off.[142] In 1788, the Muslim ruler Tipu Sultan outlawed this practice after his conquest of northern Kerala. In southern Kerala, the custom continued till 1865.[143]

This is an aspect of Kerala's history that has deliberately been erased from the public memory. In 2016, the revisionist BJP government even deleted a chapter dealing with this casteist, regressive custom from NCERT school textbooks.[144] The oral history of this appalling practice, however, remains alive. When I asked my grandmother, who grew up in Travancore, why she had not told me about this earlier, all she said was, 'You never asked.' As my enquiries widened, I realised that most Malayalis who grew up in Kerala are well aware of this history. A friend texted back, 'My great grandaunt was a victim of the breast tax.'

Sitting in the majestic reading rooms of the National Archives of India, a heritage building in the heart of Delhi,[145] I was stunned to read the book *A People's Revolt in Travancore: A Backward Class Movement for Social Freedom* by R.N. Yesudas, published in 1975 by the Kerala Historical Society. It is one of the few books in English that document in detail the four decades of the Maru Marakkal Samaram (Channar Upper Cloth Revolt) (1812–59) when oppressed caste women from the Shannar[146] (also referred to as Channar or Nadar) caste ardently fought for their right to wear dignified clothing.[147]

Keralopatti is an ancient multi-author Malayalam treatise, written on palm-leaves. It claims that the mythical Brahmin sage Parasurama created Kerala with the throw of an axe and prohibited women from covering their bosoms.[148] Even the thirteenth-century Venetian traveller Marco Polo has written about this unusual custom.[149] The Travancore kings even imposed a breast tax on women from oppressed castes who dared to cover themselves.[150] 'Baring breasts also meant acknowledging one's position in the caste hierarchy and amounted to paying obeisance to the upper castes.'[151] In a legend about the protest, it is believed that Nangeli, a poor Ezhava woman, cut off her breasts and bled to death rather than pay this unjust breast tax.[152]

In 1812, British Resident Commissioner Colonel Munro issued an order to permit at least Christian women to cover their upper bodies.[153] But even a decade after that, high-caste Hindus would violently attack Shannar Christian women who covered themselves. So, in 1828–30, there was a second revolt. In retaliation, upper caste Hindus burnt homes, chapels and schools.[154] Women were also forcibly stripped and assaulted in public. On 3 February 1829, Queen Rani Parvati Bai, a decade after her far-sighted Magna Carta on education, issued a regressive royal proclamation,

> … as it is not reasonable on the part of Shannar women to wear clothes over their breast, such custom being prohibited, they are required to abstain in future from covering the upper part of their body.[155]

The order went on to blame Shannar women who, 'in opposition to orders and ancient propriety are wearing their cloth over their shoulders, in consequence of which there are many disturbances in the country …'[156] Still, increasingly, Hindu Shannar women began to wear upper body clothes and kupayyam (jackets) in public places, similar to Christian,

Muslim and Upper caste Hindu women. The turning point was the third revolt of 1858–59. Upper caste Hindus, in collusion with the government, launched a series of violent mob attacks on Shannars, followed by counter-attacks.[157] Shannar women continued to face imprisonment and fines for the mere act of wearing a shoulder cloth.[158] At that time, the British government in Madras strongly admonished Maharajah Uthram Thirunal Marthanda Varma for these clothing restrictions 'unsuited to the present age and unworthy of an enlightened Prince'.[159] A few months later, Governor Charles Trevelyan reiterated:

> I have never met with a case in which not only truth and justice but every feeling of our common humanity is so entirely on one side. The whole civilized world would cry shame upon us if we did not make a firm stand on such an occasion.[160]

Under intense pressure from the British, the Maharaja issued a proclamation on 26 July 1859, 'We hereby proclaim that there is no objection to Shannar women ... covering their bosoms in any manner whatsoever, but not like women of high caste'.[161] Only six years later did the princely state end all clothing restrictions.[162] This iconic movement by oppressed caste women in Kerala demanding their right to wear dignified clothes predates even the first wave of the Western suffragette feminist movement.

This was only one of the many hard-won victories of women in Kerala over centuries. The Sabarimala temple entry[163] for women controversy, too, despite a 2018 Supreme Court verdict permiting entry to all women, continues to rage on with new challenges in the courts.[164]

Sri Lanka

In Ceylon, on the other hand, women have been joining the Buddhist monastic order as nuns since the third century. This offered an alternate lifestyle to male-dominated sexual control.[165] Besides, in pre-colonial times, Sinhalese marriages could be either diga (patrilocal) or binna (matrilocal).[166]

Sri Lankan women have also always been at the forefront of politics. They were the first in Asia to obtain the right to vote. Middle-class men in Sri Lanka had received the right to vote in 1912. By 1927, women leaders had formed the Women's Franchise Union. In 1929, the Union formally joined the International Women Suffragette Alliance.[167] The Union strongly argued with the Donoughmore Commission[168] that since 'women are entitled to hold property and deal with them as they like, they should be given a voice in making laws affecting such property'.[169] The Commission was suitably impressed and felt that 'it is difficult to deny the force of the argument'.[170] Thus, Ceylonese women secured the right to vote in 1931. At the penultimate hour, Fabian socialist Sidney Webb also agreed to their demands and reduced the voting age for women from thirty to twenty-one years.[171]

Three decades later, Sirimavo R.D. Bandaranaike became the first woman in the world to be elected as prime minister. This was partly the fruit of Sri Lankan women's early political evolution.[172] Despite these early successes, since preferential quotas have never been adopted, only 5.8 per cent of Sri Lankan parliamentarians in 2023 are women.[173]

Tamil Nadu

In Tamil Nadu, the women's movement evolved as a part of the radical Self-Respect Movement. Periyar even condemned monogamous marriage as an institution that sustained patriarchy. In one of his diatribes, he said:

> The concept of husband–wife relationship has been one of master–slave relationship. The essential philosophy of marriage has been to insist on women's slavery ... why should human being alone keep such contract of one-man-one-woman relationship ... until women are liberated from such marriages and from men, our country cannot attain independence.[174]

In the three decades of the movement, thousands of ritual-free Self-Respect weddings (suyamariyadai) were officiated without priests.[175] Instead of the tali,[176] considered to be a symbol of women's slavery, the newlyweds exchanged rings. Couples addressed each other as 'comrades' and took oaths of equality.[177] Periyar was also against 'chastity as an ideal for women'.[178] He supported property rights for children born out of wedlock.

Over the decades, the participation of Tamil women in the labour market also increased steadily. Former chief minister MGR significantly expanded women's employment to a range of welfare services such as anganwadi workers, school meal cooks, nurses, teachers and so on. This was also a populist measure to appeal to women voters as not only did they gain employment, but they also got access to a range of public services to supplement familial care responsibilities. J. Jayalalithaa, the erstwhile chief minister of Tamil Nadu, even reserved 30 per cent of jobs in the police for women. Textile hubs, such as Tirupur, also primarily employ women. Women's participation in the labour force of Tamil Nadu was 38 per cent in 2019-20, higher than the Indian average of 22 per cent.[179]

Across the Southern Supermodels, as more rural women have been educated, the opportunities to train and hire them as teachers, nurses and midwives have expanded. Women continue to be largely employed outside the home only in feminised professions such as nursing, teaching and textile manufacturing/production.[180] But gender stereotypes too have been gradually broken, especially with an increase in the number of 'the female labour migrants to the Middle East, female car park attendants, police women and female bus conductors'.[181]

4. Cultural Ties

Lastly, the cultural ties between the Southern trio have had a significant role in their progress in human development outcomes. These connections date back to pre-historic times.[182] Archaeological remains indicate similarities even during the early Iron Age.[183]

Emperor Ashoka's children introduced Buddhism in the third century BCE in Sri Lanka. In the eleventh century CE, the Chola empire is believed to have conquered Sri Lanka and established the Kingdom of Jaffna in the north.

Through generations, these historical and cultural ties enabled the diffusion of progressive ideals across borders. Tamil Nadu's Justice Party, for example, from the early days of the non-Brahmin movement, extended support to the 'untouchables' of Malabar province. Party journals supported the Thiyyas[184] and their right to use public roads, especially outside the Tali Temple in Malabar.

Periyar also often capitalised on these cultural ties. Politically, he cut his teeth at the 1924 Vaikkom Temple Entry Satyagraha in Travancore. He was arrested twice for his fiery, rhetorical, crowd-pulling speeches at the protest venue:

> [T]hey argue that pollution would result if we untouchables passed through the streets leading to the temple; I ask them whether the Lord of Vaikkom or the so-called Brahmins would be polluted by the presence of untouchables. If they say that the presiding deity at the temple would be polluted, then it could not be God, but a mere stone fit only to wash dirty linen with.[185]

The Self-Respect Movement inspired the Tamil Buddhist movement amongst the marginalised castes in Sri Lanka. The Tamil Buddhists also had 'close ideological cooperation with the Sinhalese nineteenth century Buddhist Renaissance' led by Anagarika Dharmapala.[186] In 1898, Pandit Iyothee Thass went from Tamil Nadu to Ceylon in order to convert to Buddhism, based on his faith in the historical Buddhist lineage of his Pariah caste. The significance of this conversion was that 'although they had been degraded to the lowest social level under the caste system in India, at the moment when they became Buddhists all these arbitrary social distinctions were stripped off their shoulders.'[187] Soon after, Iyothee Thass returned and founded the magazine *Oru Paisa Tamilian* which was the pivotal platform where 'the concepts of Dravidianism, anti-Brahmanism and rationalism came to be debated'.[188]

Sri Lanka was also a melting pot of ethnic communities. In the ancient times, Tamils of Indian origin had established a kingdom in Kandy. Between 1839 and 1843, one-and-a-half million Tamilians, especially Nadars from Tinnevelly (modern Tirunelveli district), migrated from Madras to Ceylon to work in the plantations. More than half returned to their homeland to purchase land and shops.[189] Migration from Tamil Nadu and Kerala to Ceylon continued steadily in the colonial period. Rummaging through papers at the British National Archives in Kew, I even chanced upon a pamphlet which showed that the Malayali associations of Colombo had advocated with the British government in 1928 asking them to recognise Malayalam as one of the official languages to qualify for the vote in Ceylon.[190]

There has been a steady exchange of progressive ideas across the southern borders. For example, the Channar Upper Cloth Revolt was sparked by Christian Nadar women in Travancore who were not allowed to cover themselves[191], only after they realised that their caste sisters across the border in Tamil-speaking areas of Tinnevelly did not face similar restrictions.[192]

The left movement in the three regions has also shared a common heritage. In the 1920s and 1930s, Kerala and Sri Lanka had waves of communist and labour movements. During this period, even the Self-Respect Movement in Tamil Nadu began to lean towards the left.

LAND REFORMS

The one main difference among the southern triad is that of land reforms. With the support of the left parties who had gained political power, Kerala and Sri Lanka implemented radical reforms. But effective land redistribution has eluded Tamil Nadu.

In 1957, Kerala democratically elected the first Communist government, which implemented radical 'land to the tiller' reforms by providing rights to the tenants. The number of landless households in Kerala fell from 31 per cent in 1962 to 13 per cent in 1982.[193] In 1983-84, 92 per cent of the rural population in Kerala owned land. The path-breaking Agricultural Workers Act 1975 also offered an unemployment allowance. Despite these advances, land distribution in Kerala remains greatly skewed. In 2011, 84 per cent of Dalit farmers in Kerala had to depend on wage labour for survival.[194]

On the other hand, Sri Lanka's 1972 land reform legislation ensured that the state acquired 20 per cent of all cultivable land. The law also nationalised plantation estates.[195] In 2002, only 6 per cent of Sri Lankans were landless, even though 22 per cent owned only their homes.[196] Sri Lanka's land laws also discriminate based on gender, and women have not yet secured equal property rights.

Of the Southern Supermodels, Tamil Nadu is the only one that has not legislated egalitarian land reforms.

Although 92 per cent of rural Tamilians own their homesteads, agricultural land ownership remains very skewed.[197]

DEVELOPMENT BEFORE GROWTH?

The Southern Supermodels analysis showcases that Sri Lanka and the Indian states of Kerala and Tamil Nadu have had long periods of accelerated human development, even in times of stagnant economic growth.[198] Their key similarity lies in their efforts to combat multi-dimensional inequalities—with investments in universal public services, progressive social movements, women's agency and cultural ties—in the course of more than a century.

Pohela Baisakh celebrations in Dhaka University with women wearing tiaras of flowers on their head

8

THE PRICE OF INEQUALITY

THE POHELA BAISAKH (Bengali New Year) celebrations in Dhaka are a riot of colour. The traffic comes to a grinding halt with traffic jams everywhere and large crowds on every street.

Dhaka University has the largest celebrations. At the end of our fieldwork, Safiq thoughtfully gifted me a white sari with a red border so that I could join in the revelry, suitably dressed. The main concert stage had Bangladeshi Bollywood singer James belting out rock songs in Hindi and Bengali in his distinctive voice. One of the songs was appropriate for me—the popular number *Alvida* (goodbye).

I had a whale of a time. The Rabindra sangeet, traditional dances, poetry, street food and theatre performances across the campus had created a joyous ambience, even in the clammy summer heat. Most of the women students unmindful of the sweltering weather, were dressed in red-and-white saris (sometimes with hijabs), bindis and tiaras of fresh flowers in their hair like Greek goddesses. Watching their enthusiasm brought home the import of how cherished and hard-won these festivities were. The Language Movement and Liberation War had paved the way decades earlier for this joyous celebration of the Bengali language and culture to take place today.

Historian Fernand Braudel highlights the *longue durée* in the gradual evolution of civilisations.[1] Like fine wine, social transformations, too, take long years and even decades to ferment, ripen, mature and get absorbed in a cultural context. Development pathways evolve differently depending on these transformations. Countries within South Asia have had diverse development journeys. But on an average Sri Lankans, Bangladeshis, Nepalese and Bhutanese tend to live longer than Indians.[2]

The persistent question for this research has therefore been—why does India increasingly lag behind in human development while most of its South Asian neighbours are speeding up their social achievements? Even Bangladesh and Nepal, despite being poorer, have overtaken India on many social indicators, from literacy and life expectancy to infant mortality and happiness. Their achievements prove that high economic growth is not a necessary precondition to improve the quality of life of ordinary citizens. These advances also challenge the claim that the only 'miracle' route to success is the East Asian mantra of 'the rising tide seems to have lifted all boats'.[3]

Studies on the contrasts within South Asia, however, are few and far between. The *Lancet*, for example, describes Bangladesh as 'one of the great mysteries of global health'. As political sociologist Naomi Hossain points out, 'Bangladesh punches well below its weight internationally.' So, its achievements are not sufficiently celebrated.[4]

In this potholed landscape, I worked on a pan-South Asian canvas with the spotlight on India's increasing slow-footedness.

The data from my unique cross-border primary survey across eighty villages also clearly shows that India's poorer Eastern Neighbours Bangladesh and Nepal performed better on a range of human development indicators. Villages that scored better were also more likely to have good quality schools, better health facilities, greater women's agency and compressed social distances. The advantage of these Indian neighbours seems to clearly lie in their concerted welfare investments and ability to dilute deep-rooted multi-dimensional inequalities.

In Bangladesh, my research shed light on social, religious and women's movements that have cumulatively, over long decades and even centuries, altered social hierarchies. For example, during fieldwork in Panchagarh district, I saw archaeological excavations underway in the ancient sixth-century Bhitorgarh fort, which unearthed Buddhist stupas, temples and viharas built along the Silk Route. This reminded me that East Bengal, which was once a part of the ancient Pala and Chandra empires, had more than one millennium of egalitarian Buddhist influence before the advent of syncretic Islam in the twelfth century. So, even before the mass conversion of the population to Islam in East Bengal, there had long been fewer caste-style disparities.

This book also traces how class hierarchies shrank after three unique historical waves of elite displacement. After the 1905, 1947 and 1971 partitions, the Hindu zamindar and bhadralok classes largely shifted to India. So, rural Bangladeshis who were left behind had fewer social divisions among them. Especially after the 1974 famine, a unique social contract developed between the Bangladeshi ruling classes of all hues and the ordinary citizens to prioritise welfare services—come cyclone or sunshine.

In contrast, in Nepal, the process of Hinduisation, from the third century BCE, institutionalised crippling caste inequalities and discrimination. But the combined influence of social movements and a progressive 2015 democratic constitution, to a certain extent, tempered these caste inequalities. Equally significantly, in Bangladesh and Nepal, women's movements succeeded in expanding women's freedoms both within and outside the home.

The Southern Supermodels analysis also reaches similar conclusions. From the mid-nineteenth to the mid-twentieth centuries, Sri Lanka and Kerala evolved along similar arcs. Sri Lanka had fewer class, caste and gender disparities. But social change in Kerala, which was once a 'madhouse of caste', was a hard-won victory after centuries of progressive movements. Similarly, Tamil Nadu's human development progress in the last century would have been inconceivable without the anti-caste movement that cemented a lasting commitment to social welfare.

In many ways, the frontrunner regions in both groups—Northern Neighbours and Southern Supermodels—resemble the ethos of the Scandinavian 'social democratic' welfare states. Usually, the more equitable a country is, the more likely it is to build a universal welfare state. After all, democracies depend on populist policies for votes.[5] Based on the 'paradox of redistribution',[6] Sri Lanka, Tamil Nadu and Kerala have also largely prioritised universal benefits instead of only narrowly targeting poor people. With its universal old age pensions and healthcare, this is true for Nepal as well, to a greater extent than even for Bangladesh.

Another similarity across these high-performing regions is that of land reforms. In Bangladesh, only 8 per cent of rural households are landless, due to land reforms that took place when it was still a part of Pakistan. However, due to the high population density and decreasing farm sizes, only a third of rural families now primarily depend on agriculture. In Nepal, 86 per cent of rural families and 60 per cent of Dalit homes own land. Similarly, in both rural Kerala and Sri Lanka, where substantial land reforms took place, more than 90 per cent of households own agricultural land, although sharp caste differences persist.[7] Rural land reforms, however, have eluded Tamil Nadu, which is now one of the most urbanised states in India.[8]

In contrast, in northern India, land is the prized possession of a few. On the porch of her modest home, a Bihari widow, Sakshi Devi, whom I was chatting with, blurted out proudly, 'Nobody has a damaad [son-in-law] as rich as mine. He has eight kathas land and earns Rs 15,000 every month selling medicines.' Of course, women's ownership of land in Bihar continues to be abysmal.

NORTH VERSUS SOUTH INDIA

Within India, there is a 'vast difference between the North and the South' in the social contract of the state which impacts the lives of ordinary citizens—women, men and children.[9] In Babasaheb Ambedkar's words:

> The North is conservative. The South is progressive. The North is superstitious, the South is rational. The South is educationally forward, the North is educationally backward. The culture of the South is modern. The culture of the North is ancient.[10]

The conclusions from my research are less sweeping in their generalisations, but stark nonetheless.

Political scientist Christophe Jaffrelot pertinently points out the significant contrasts which have made north India lag behind the south.[11] The northern caste movements, including those in Bihar, relied mainly on emulation and 'Sanskritisation'. As sociologist M.N. Srinivas has pointed out, in northern India, the 'low castes concentrated on acquiring the symbols of high status'. In contrast, the belligerent southern movements focused more on differentiation and assertion. These ambitious movements aimed to overthrow caste entirely.[12] In south India, the spotlight was always on 'the real sources of high status, that is, political power, education and a share in economic opportunities'.[13] Importantly, the upper castes have always been greater in numbers and more confrontational in northern India than in the south.[14] Bihar typifies these northern states.

The quality of life in northern India, especially Bihar, is particularly stunted. Multiple layers of inequalities of income, caste, religion and gender compound one another. They worsen across time and generations as 'inequality traps'.[15] The pandemic, which magnified these inequalities, has been an eye-opener.

The achievements of Sri Lanka, Bangladesh and Nepal, on the other hand, share some key similarities: higher investments in public services and progressive social movements have, to an extent, bridged overlapping vertical and horizontal inequalities. India, the sleeping giant, should learn from their impressive social progress.

Within India, the inspirational southern states of Kerala and Tamil Nadu also prove that consistent commitment to social welfare and social reform can dilute even intergenerational inequalities. So, transformative progress in the lives of citizens, even in the backwoods of northern India, is definitely within reach—in our lifetimes.

APPENDICES

Appendix A1: Comparison of select South Asian countries and Indian states on population parameters in 2016

	Sri Lanka	Nepal	Bangladesh	Pakistan	India	Bihar	Uttar Pradesh	West Bengal	Odisha	Kerala	Tamil Nadu
Population (millions), 2016*	21	29	163	193	1324	117	200	91	41	35	72
Population density, 2016*	338	202	1251	251	445	1106	829	1028	270	860	555
Urban population (%), 2016*	18	19	35	39	32	11	22	31	17	48	49
Gini Index, 2016	39.8	32.8	32.1	30.7	35.1	-	-	-	-	-	-
Electricity (%), 2016**	96	91	76	99	85	59	70	94	86	99	99

Appendix

Sources: Population, Population Density, Urban Population, Electricity, Gini Index (WDI, June 2016 version)

*For Indian states: Bihar, Tamil Nadu, Kerala, Uttar Pradesh, West Bengal, Odisha: [Census of India 2011, *Population Enumeration Data (Final Population)*]

**For Indian states: Bihar, Tamil Nadu, Kerala, Uttar Pradesh, West Bengal, Odisha: National Family Health Survey 2015-2016 (IIPS and ICF, 2017, 'National Family Health Survey (NFHS-5), 2019-21: India Report')

Notes: In the gini index 0 represents perfect equality and 100 implies perfect inequality in the distribution of incomes while the population density is defined as people per sq. km of land area

Appendix A2: South Asian average incomes in purchasing power parity (current international $), 1990–2019

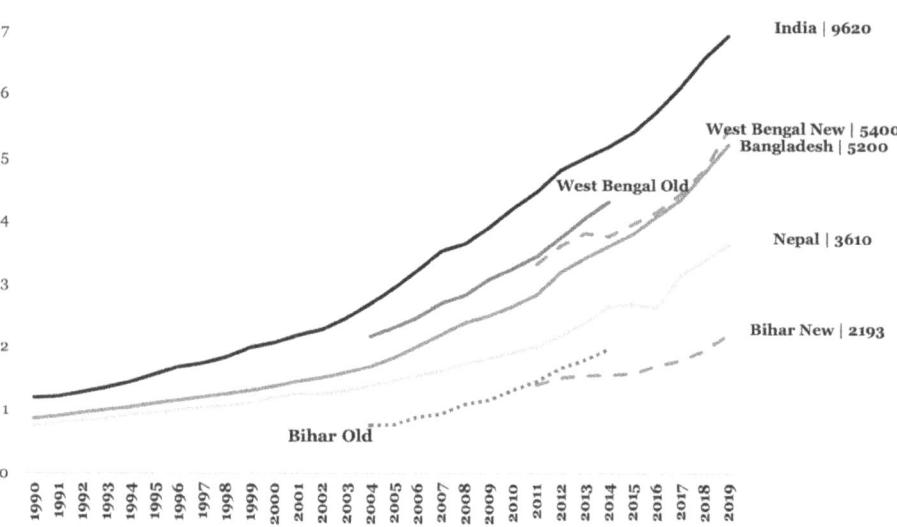

Source: Author calculations based on World Development Indicators 1990-2019, GNI per capita, PPP (current international $) and PPP conversion factor, GDP (LCU per international $) and Press Information Bureau India, Ministry of Statistics & Programme Implementation, 2017

Note: For Indian states, GNI per capita has been calculated by converting per capita income in Indian rupees to purchasing power parity in US dollars by dividing it with the GDP conversion factor which indicates the number of local currency units required to buy the same amounts of goods and services in the domestic market. (Arabinda Ghosh, Dean Spears and Aashish Gupta, 'Are Children in West Bengal Shorter Than Children in Bangladesh?')

Appendix A3: Evolution of social changes to reduce caste, class and gender inequalities

CLASS INEQUALITY	GENDER INEQUALITY High → Low	CASTE INEQUALITY HIGH	CASTE INEQUALITY LOW
HIGH		Bihar / Kerala, Tamil Nadu	Sri Lanka, Bangladesh
LOW		Nepal	

Appendix A4: Population with essential welfare services and amenities (%)

Country (DHS year)	HEALTH Children under 23 months who received all 8 basic vaccinations	NUTRITION Children with diarrhoea treated with Oral Rehydration Therapy (ORT) or recommended home fluids	SANITATION Population with no open defecation	EDUCATION Literacy in women aged 15-49 years	AMENITIES Population with electricity
Sri Lanka (2016)	99*	80	99	94	97**
Maldives (2016-17)	77	84	100	100	100
Bangladesh (2022)	89#	76	99#	73#	99**
Nepal (2022)	80	77	93	74	97
India (2019-21)	77	67	81	71	97
Pakistan (2017-18)	66	39	91	50	92

*In Sri Lanka, age-appropriate measles vaccines are provided at 24 months

**Households with electricity

#Bangladesh 2017-18; only preliminary data for the 2022 DHS has been released so far

Source: Latest available Demographic and Health Surveys (DHS)

Appendix A5: Share of pre-tax national income between the top 10% and bottom 50% of adults

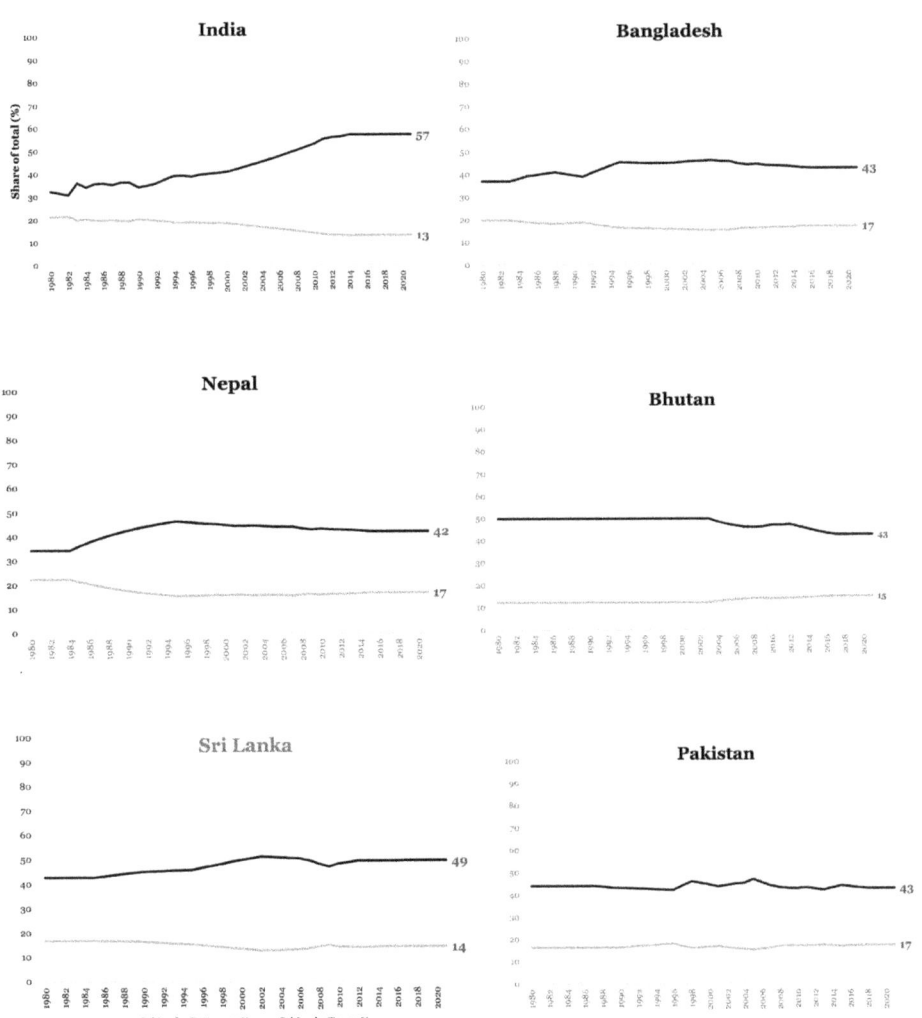

Source: Chancel, L., Piketty, T., Saez, E., Zucman, G. et al. World Inequality Report 2022

Appendix A6: Some selected gender and development indicators of South Asian countries

	Female life expectancy at birth (years) 2021	Underweight children under 5 years, female (%) 2016-2022	Women working in the labour force aged 15+ years (ILO estimate) (%) 2021	Women parliamentarians (%) 2022
Sri Lanka	80	21	33	5
Maldives	81	15	43	5
Bangladesh	74	22	38	21
Bhutan	74	13	54	17
Nepal	70	21	29	33
India	69	31	24	15
Pakistan	69	22	25	20

Source: WDI June 2023 version

Appendix

Appendix A7: Caste-based 'Graded Inequality' in access to essential services in India

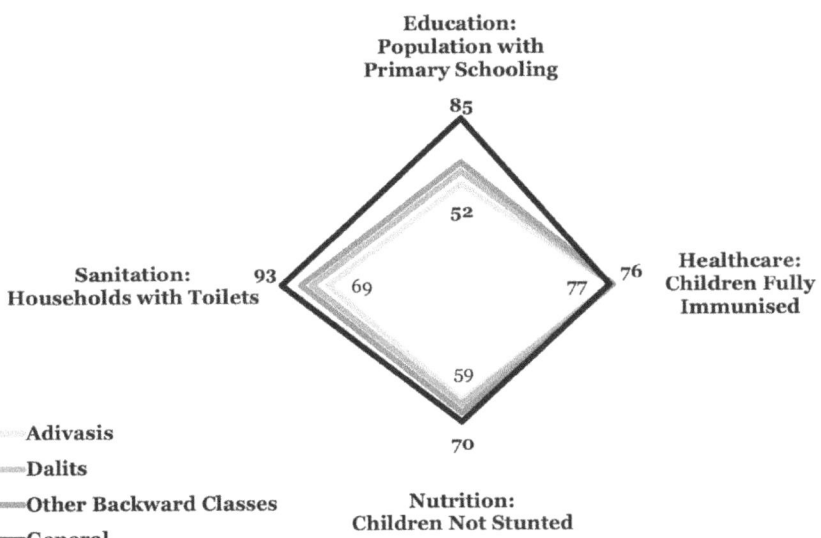

(In the National Family Health Survey, population with primary schooling is defined as the percentage distribution of household populations above age six who have completed less than five years of schooling)

Source: IIPS and ICF, 'National Family Health Survey (NFHS-5), 2019-21: India Report'

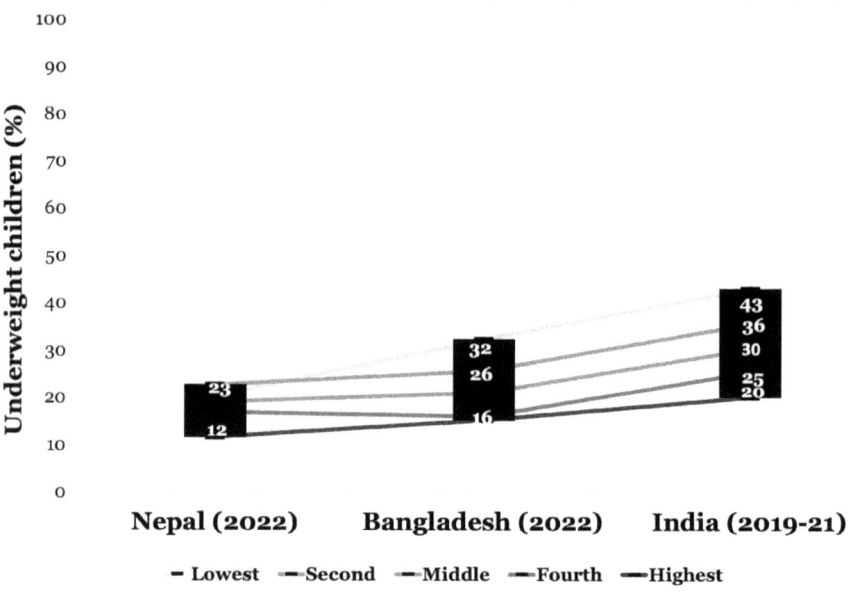

Appendix A8: Underweight children among rich and poor families, 2019–2022

Source: Demographic and Health Surveys

Appendix A9: Selection of sample districts in the Northern Neighbours

	Cultural	Social	Economic	Geographical
	Majority Religion (% of population)	Female Literacy (% of population)	Electricity (% of households)	Proximity to the Border
Bangladesh				
Panchagarh	83 [Islam]	45	27	Adjoining Siliguri corridor (India, Bangladesh and Nepal border)
Bihar				
Kishanganj	68 [Islam]	37	18	Adjoining Siliguri corridor (India, Bangladesh and Nepal border)
Muzaffarpur	85 [Hinduism]	45	19	150 kms from the Nepal border
Nepal				
Sindhuli	64 [Hinduism]	52	38	In the hills between terai and the mountains

Source: GoI, Census of India 2011, *Population Enumeration Data (Final Population)*, GoN, *Nepal – National Population and Housing Census 2011, Marks 100 Years of Census Taking in Nepal* and GoB, *Population and Housing Census, 2011*.

Appendix A10: Sample districts in Nepal, Bangladesh and Bihar

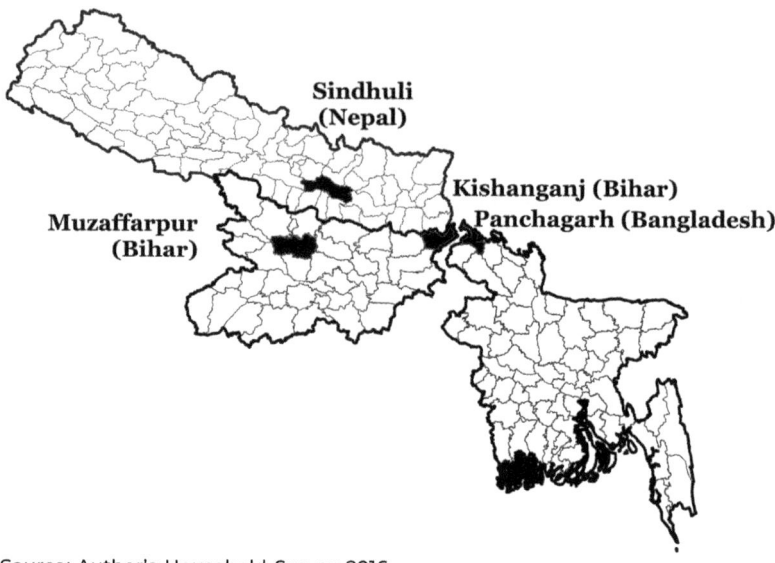

Source: Author's Household Survey 2016

Appendix A11: Four indices created with survey data from 80 villages

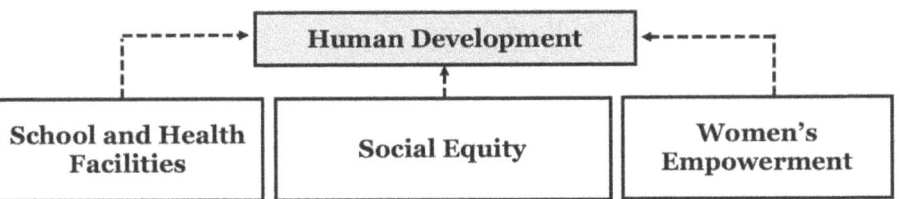

Source: Author's Household Survey 2016

Appendix A12: Students in Grades 1 to 5 with minimum* educational competencies by wealth quintiles

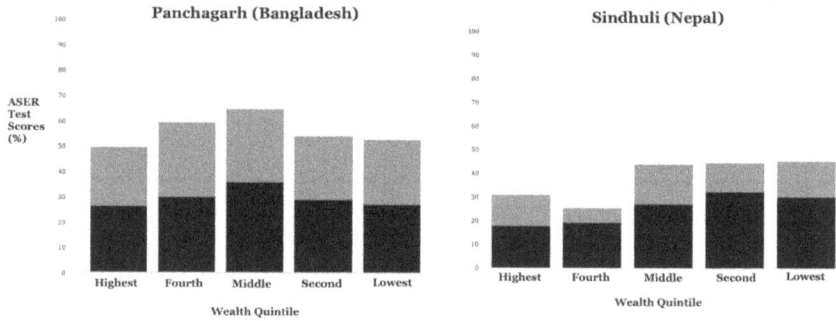

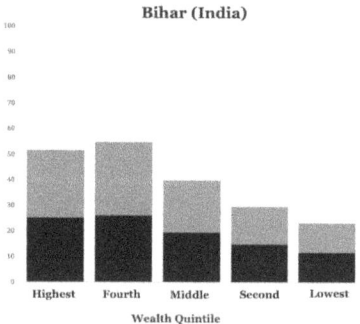

Note: *The minimum ASER test competencies in language and mathematics assumes that children in grades 1 to 4 are able to achieve at least grade 1 level competency and those in grade 5 at least grade 2 level educational attainment

Source: Author's Household Survey 2016

Appendix A13: Households with Toilets That Work (%)

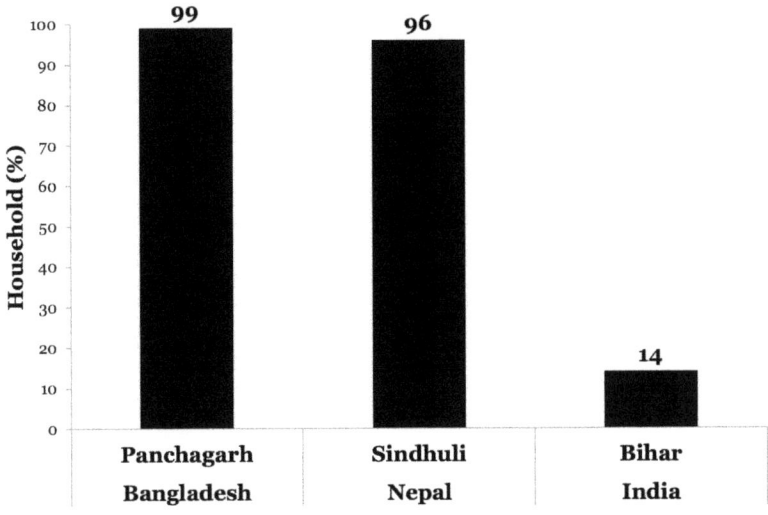

Source: Author's Household Survey 2016

Appendix A14: Inequalities in indices by caste and religion

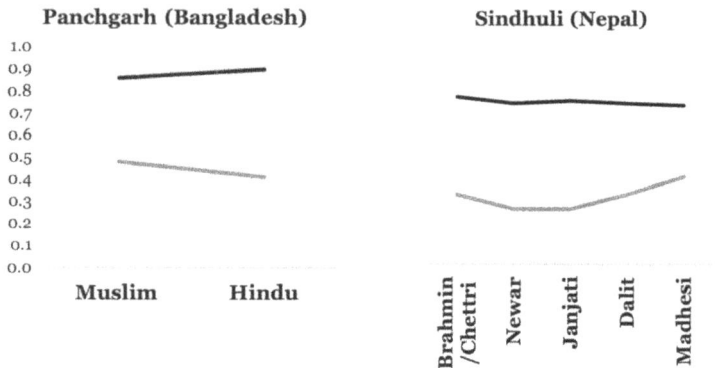

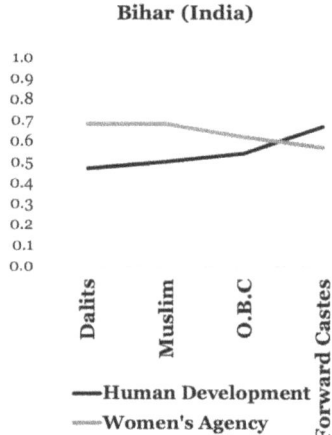

Source: Author's Household Survey 2016

Appendix A15: Scatter Plot of the Human Development Composite Indices in 80 villages

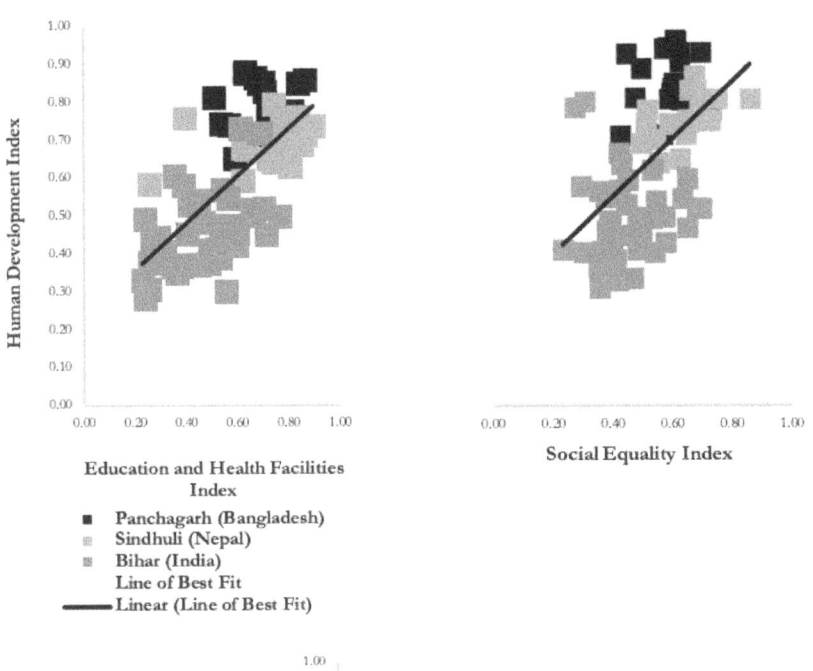

- Panchagarh (Bangladesh)
- Sindhuli (Nepal)
- Bihar (India)
- Line of Best Fit
- ——— Linear (Line of Best Fit)

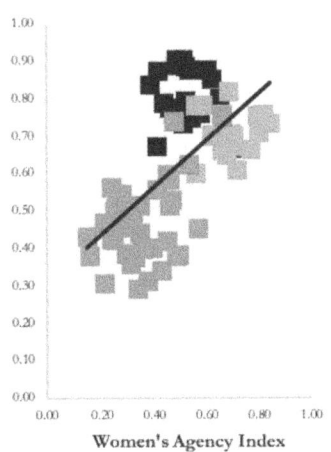

Source: Author's Household Survey 2016

Appendix A16: Nepali caste system hierarchy as per the Muluki Ain, 1859*

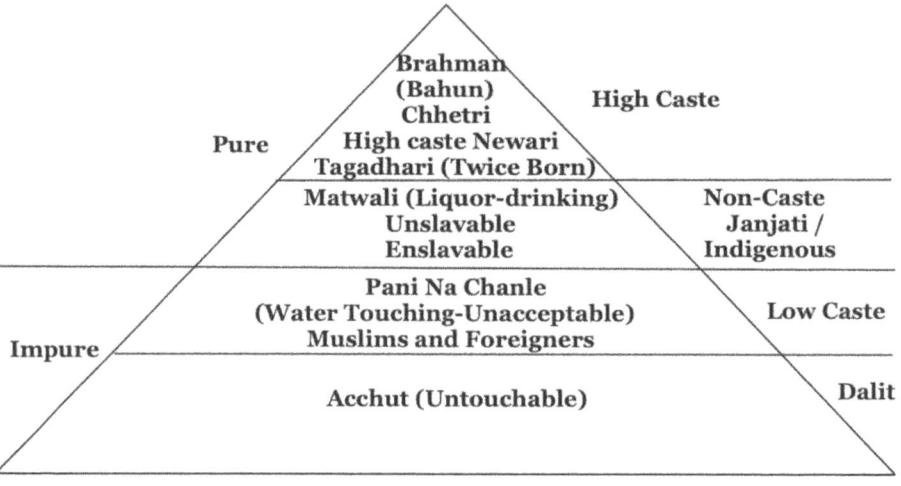

*This is a representative figure of the layers of the hierarchy, not of demographic composition

Source: Ishtiaq Jamil and Hasan Muhammad Baniamin, 'Representative and responsive bureaucracy in Nepal: a mismatch or a realistic assumption?'

Appendix A17: The punishment for public flatulence, Article 62, Muluki Ain, 1854

§	Offender	Victim	Rupees	Fee for expiation in ānā (16 ānā = 1 Rupee)
1	Every caste (jāta)	Same or lower caste	5	4
2	Rajapūta, Sacred Thread-wearers	Higher caste	7,5	4
3	Non-enslavable alcohol-drinker	Sacred Thread-wearers	10	8
4	Enslavable castes	Sacred Thread-wearers	15	1
5	Enslavable castes	Non-enslavable alcohol-drinker	5	4
6	Impure, but touchable or untouchable castes	Higher castes from whom water can be accepted	20	1,5
7	Untouchable castes	Impure, but touchable castes	5	4

Source: Rajan Khatiwoda, Simon Cubelic and Axel Michaels, 'The Muluki Ain of 1854: Nepal's First Legal Code', Table 9, p.43

Appendix A18: Timeline of Sri Lanka's socio-political developments after the advent of British colonialism

Year	Events	Description
1833	Colebrooke-Cameroon Reforms	Foundation for a liberal democratic political system.
1905-1919	Temperance Movement	Popular mass-based movement with the creation of a decentralized network of political temperance societies.
1927	Donoughmore Commission	Appointed by Sydney Webb to draft a new constitution for Ceylon.
1931	Universal Suffrage	Introduction of universal adult franchise.
1939	Poor Laws	Laws introduced that attempted to deal with poverty through state assistance.
1943	Free Education	Kannagara Report, which recommended universal and compulsory free education from kindergarten to university and the passage of the Education Act.
1944-1948	Independence	Soulbury Commission and Independence.
1950	Right to Healthcare	The Cumpston Report based on the principle of the right to health.
1953	Health Service Act	Passage of Health Service Act, which abolished private practice for doctors employed in the state sector.
1972-1975	Land reform	Land Reform law of 1972 and nationalization of plantations in 1975.
1977	Economic Liberalisation	The UNP government comes to power and introduces the new economic policy based on economic liberalisation.

Appendix A19: Timeline of Kerala's significant social and political developments

Year	Events	Description
1800s	Christian Missionaries	Christian Missionaries began to establish schools for disadvantaged communities such as the Ezhavas.
1800	First Vaikkom temple entry attempt	Ezhavas attempt to enter the Vaikkom temple but are brutally attacked.
1817	Royal Rescript on Education	Queen of Travancore issues a Royal Rescript declaring state responsibility for mass education.
1836 - 1921	Mappila Uprisings	33 Mappila Revolts (Moplah Uprising) in Malabar culminate in the Mappila Rebellion by Muslim tenants.
1858	Channar Upper Cloth Revolt	Nadar Christian women in Travancore protest for their right to cover the upper parts of their bodies and violence breaks out in several places.
1891	Malayali Memorial	10,000 non-Brahmins accuse the government of discrimination in employment in government jobs in favour of Brahmin outsiders.
1896	Ezhava Memorial	13176 signatories demand that the administration adopt socio-political egalitarianism within the state to include excluded castes.
1924-5	Second Vaikkom Temple-entry Satyagraha	Indian National Congress-supported Vaikkom satyagraha in Travancore, backed by the Ezhava leader Shree Narayana Guru, brings both E.V. Ramaswamy (later Periyar) and Mahatma Gandhi to Kerala.
1936	Temple entry proclamation	Temple entry proclamation in Travancore to open temples to all castes.

1948	Universal suffrage	Universal suffrage in Travancore and Cochin—Congress wins the elections.
1956	First Communist government	E.M.S. Namboodiripad becomes the Communist Chief Minister of the new Kerala.
1967	Left-led government	CPI (M)-led United Front government (UF) formed with Chief Minister E.M.S. Namboodiripad.
1969	Land Reforms	Kerala Land Reform (Amendment) Act passed.
1973	Gulf migration	Oil crisis, large-scale Gulf emigration begins.
1975	'Kerala Model'	Report produced by the Centre for Development Studies, Trivandrum hails Kerala's achievements as a 'Model'.

Source: Adapted from Robin Jeffrey, 'Politics, Women and Well Being: How Kerala Became a Model' and other sources

Figure A20: Timeline of Tamil Nadu's significant social and political developments

Year	Events	Description
1916	Non-Brahmin Manifesto	Prominent nationalists from the Madras Presidency issue the 'Non-Brahmin Manifesto'.
1920	Justice Party comes to power	The Montagu-Chelmsford Reforms provide non-Brahmins with separate representation in the Madras Legislative Council and the Justice Party comes to electoral power.
1921-22	Reservations for non-Brahmins	The Justice Party institutionalizes reservation in government service for non-Brahmins as Backward Castes.
1925	Self-Respect Movement	E.V. Ramasamy (EVR for short and later revered as Periyar) launches the Self-Respect Movement.
1938	First anti-Hindi agitations	The anti-Hindi movement sees the Justice Party and the Self-Respecters unite. EVR is elected president of the Justice Party in 1938. He organises a separatist agitation for Dravida Nadu to unite Tamil Nadu, Karnataka, Andhra Pradesh and Kerala.
1949	DMK formed	Leaders break away from the Dravida Kazagham (new name of the Justice Party) to form the Dravida Munnetra Kazagham (DMK).
1951	Reservations for Non-Brahmins	After agitations in the Madras state the first amendment to the Indian constitution is passed to ensure reservation of seats for non-Brahmins in educational institutions and government jobs.
1953	Madras state formed	Madras state is formed along linguistic lines.

1954	Kamaraj's First Ministry without Brahmins	Under Chief Minister K. Kamaraj, Madras is the first state to not have a single Brahmin in its ministry.
1954-63	Universal education	Universal free education is introduced in Kamaraj's tenure along with the introduction of school meals.
1965	Second anti-Hindi agitations	Widespread agitations in response to the Central Government's directive making Hindi the National Language.
1969	Renamed Tamil Nadu	Madras state is renamed as Tamil Nadu by the DMK government.
1977	AIADMK formed and MGR comes to power	M.G. Ramachandran (MGR), a film actor, wins his first term as chief minister after leaving the DMK, to form a new party, the Anna Dravida Munnetra Kazhagam (later AIADMK preceded by All India).
1987	Reservations for marginalised communities	An agitation by the Vanniyars. The government in a 2021 law sets aside 20 percent out of the total 50 percent BC reservation, but the Supreme Court annuls the law in 2021.
1990	Mandal Commission welcomed	Tamil Nadu state assembly is the only Indian state to pass a resolution welcoming V.P. Singh's Mandal Commission reforms with 27 per cent reservation for the backward classes in Government jobs.
2007	Reservations for Muslims	After agitations by the Muslim Munnetra Kazhagam, a 3.5 percent separate reservation within the 30 percent backward caste quota is reserved for Muslims.

2013	Amma Canteens	A year before her death chief minister Jayalalithaa of the AIADMK launches the Amma Canteens and a range of other subsidised welfare programmes under the brand name 'Amma'.
2021-3	School Breakfasts	The newly elected DMK chief minister Stalin announces that the Amma Canteens will retain their name and be expanded; and that all schools would also serve breakfasts to children.

NOTES

1. A HUMAN DEVELOPMENT PUZZLE

1. Field Notes, Panchagarh district, Bangladesh, June 2015. The Government of India began the Swachh Bharat Abhiyan in October 2014 and declared India open defection–free in 2019. But even in 2019–21, as the latest 5th National Family Health Survey indicates, 26 per cent of all rural households and 16 per cent in rural West Bengal do not have a toilet (IIPS and ICF, 'National Family Health Survey (NFHS-5), 2019–21: India Report'; Aashish Gupta and Sangita Vyas, 'Is Open Defecation Still Prevalent in Rural North India?'). Earlier Demographic and Health Surveys (DHS) from 2015-16 showed that while in rural India '55% of households report defecating in the open, open defecation has been almost eliminated from Bangladesh'. (Diane Coffey and Dean Spears, 'Open Defecation in Rural India, 2015–16: Levels and Trends in NFHS–4'). Even in 2011, less than 5 per cent of households in Bangladesh practiced open defection.
2. As a doctoral student, between 2015 and 2016 alone, I made three separate trips to Bangladesh to conduct the recces and fieldwork in Panchagarh district and to attend a South Asian conference in Dhaka.
3. Field Notes, Boda and Tetulia upazilas, Panchagarh district, Bangladesh, 12 February–29 March 2016.
4. Bangladesh's agro-food processing industry contributes to around 1.7 per cent to GDP. It employs about 2,50,000 people

and contributes to 20 per cent of the country's manufacturing output.
5 iDE, 'A New Standard for Sanitation'.
6 Diane Coffey and Dean Spears, *Where India Goes: Abandoned Toilets, Stunted Development and the Costs of Caste.*
7 Swachh Bharat Abhiyan (SBA), or Clean India Campaign, was initiated by Prime Minister Modi in 2014 with much fanfare, including public oath-taking ceremonies to eliminate open defecation and improve solid waste management, along with overall cleanliness in public spaces.
8 Demographic and Health Surveys compiled at www.statcompiler.com.
9 Nineteen per cent of all households and 26 per cent of all rural households did not have any toilet facilities (IIPS and ICF, 'National Family Health Survey (NFHS-5), 2019-21: India Report').
10 Since the 1970s, Indians have consistently been richer than Bangladeshis in GDP per capita in purchasing power parity terms. But especially in the wake of the pandemic, during 2019–22 Bangladesh's average incomes (GDP per capita) has overtaken India in current USD in nominal terms. Sri Lanka, Bhutan and Maldives also have higher per capita incomes than India (GDP per capita, PPP [current international $], in WDI, World Development Indicators, June 2023).
11 News reports. See, for instance, Scroll Staff, 'West Bengal: "Not Even a Bird Will Be Allowed from Across the Border If BJP Wins," says Amit Shah'.
12 World Development Indicators, June 2023 version.
13 Prevalence of underweight, weight for age (% of children under 5), Prevalence of underweight, weight for age (% of children under 5), Prevalence of stunting, height for age (% of children under 5), in WDI, World Development Indicators, June 2023.
14 World Development Indicators, June 2023 version.
15 To be precise, the graph depicts, as per demographers, the expected life expectancy 'in prevailing mortality conditions' experienced in 1971 and in 2021 respectively.
16 Jean Drèze, 'Bangladesh Shows the Way'.

17 Amartya Sen, 'What's Happening in Bangladesh?', p. 1966; Jean Drèze and Amartya Sen, *An Uncertain Glory: India and Its Contradictions*.
18 Angus Deaton, *The Great Escape: Health, Wealth, and the Origins of Inequality*.
19 Angus Deaton, 'The U.S. Can No Longer Hide from Its Deep Poverty Problem'; Fox, 'Is Mississippi Worse Off than Bangladesh?' There are nearly fifty counties in the United States heavily populated by African–Americans, Native Americans and non-Hispanic Whites which in 2014 had a lower life expectancy than Bangladesh's seventy-four years in 2020 based on the health profiles created by the Institute for Health Metrics and Evaluation at healthdata.org.
20 Office for National Statistics, 'How Has Life Expectancy Changed over Time?'; Life expectancy at birth, female (years), in WDI, World Development Indicators, June 2023. Of course, due to technology diffusion, recent life expectancy improvements across countries worldwide have been faster than in the past on the Preston curves.
21 All names of villagers have been changed.
22 Life expectancy for women in Kerala is based on Sample Registration System data for 2016–20 with 2018 as the mid-year by the Office of the Registrar General & Census Commissioner, India, released in November 2022. Life expectancy for men in the United States was seventy-six years in 2018 (Life expectancy at birth, male and female [years] in WDI, World Development Indicators, June 2023).
23 ICJ, 'Unprepared and Unlawful: Nepal's Continued Failure to Realise the Right to Health during the COVID-19 Pandemic'; Golam Rasul, et al., 'Socio-Economic Implications of COVID-19 Pandemic in South Asia: Emerging Risks and Growing Challenges'.
24 Bhutan has one of the lowest case fatality rate for COVID-19 at 0.03 per cent, which is significantly lower than the WHO's global case fatality rate of 1.02 per cent and India's average of 1.19 per cent as of 7 February 2023, based on data

from Johns Hopkins University CSSE COVID-19 dashboard, https://coronavirus.jhu.edu/map.html.
25 Most independent estimates range from 6.3 million to 2.7 million excess deaths compared to the Indian government's statistic of 0.5 million COVID-19 deaths. The WHO estimate is 4 million, which the Indian government has disputed (Murad Banaji, 'Why India's Response to WHO on Excess COVID-19 Deaths Doesn't Hold Water'; Murad Banaji and Aashish Gupta, 'Estimates of Pandemic Excess Mortality in India Based on Civil Registration Data').
26 India imposed the second-longest duration of school closures in the world, after Uganda, during the COVID-19 pandemic. For more, see UNDP, *COVID-19 and Human Development: Assessing the Crisis, Envisioning the Recovery, Human Development Reports*.
27 Post COVID-19, in the latest 2021 Human Development Index, India has slipped two places to the 132nd rank among 191 countries. The World Bank estimates that COVID-19 has reversed poverty decline and pushed 56 million Indians into poverty (World Bank, *Poverty and Shared Prosperity 2022: Correcting Course*).
28 Sociologist Paolo Gerbaudo argues that the pandemic, as an unprecedented period of worldwide crisis and heightened mobilisation of the state apparatus, has also escalated social confrontations by exacerbating old grievances to the extreme to trigger pre-modern, spontaneous protests such as toppling statues to banging pots and pans (Paolo Gerbaudo, 'The Pandemic Crowd: Protest in the Time of COVID-19').
29 Field Notes, Kishanganj district, Bihar, 8–11 September 2016.
30 Please see Chapter 5 on Nepal. Also, Punam Yadav, *Social Transformation in Post-conflict Nepal: A Gender Perspective* and Dhruba Kumar, *Social Inclusion, Human Development and Nation Building in Nepal*.
31 M.N. Parth, 'In Kheri: Changing Sides for Health'.
32 *World Inequality Report 2022* states that 'India is amongst the most unequal countries in the world', 'exhibiting extreme' and

'spectacular increases in inequality', due to an obscene 'increase in private wealth' from 290 per cent in 1980 to 560 per cent in 2020, higher than Russia and China. (Lucas Chancel, et al., *World Inequality Report 2022*, pp. 3, 11)

33 Based on Forbes, *Real-time Billionaire List* and *Bloomberg Billionaire Index* (accessed 26 December 2022). Also see Berkhout Esmé, et al., *The Inequality Virus*; *How India Lives 2021*; Asit Manohar, 'Indian Billionaire Made More Money than Elon Musk, Jeff Bezos, Bill Gates in Q4'.

34 Niha Masih, 'Who Is Gautam Adani? Asia's Richest Man Is Rocked by Fraud Claims'.

35 Oxford *Covid-19 Government Response Tracker*, https://covidtracker.bsg.ox.ac.uk/.

36 APU, *State of Working India: One Year of Covid-19*; World Bank, *Poverty and Shared Prosperity 2022*.

37 Oxfam, 'Inequality Kills: India Supplement 2022'.

38 Manish Kumar and Deepshika Ghosh, 'No Aadhaar, No Food? 11-Year-Old Girl Died "Begging for Rice", Says Jharkhand Family'.

39 Swati Narayan, 'In Jharkhand, Suspected Starvation Death Sheds Light on Deprivation of a Whole Settlement'.

40 Nitin Tagade, Ajaya Kumar Naik and Sukhdeo Thorat provide a wealth estimate based on the All India Debt and Investment Survey, 2013 conducted by the National Sample Survey Organisation (Nitin Tagade, Ajaya Kumar Naik and Sukhadeo Thorat, 'Wealth Ownership and Inequality in India: A Socio-Religious Analysis'). In 2020 Oxfam estimated that the wealth share of the bottom 50 per cent of India's population was only 3 per cent (Oxfam, 'Survival of the Richest: The India Story').

41 Nitin Tagade, Ajaya Kumar Naik and Sukhdeo Thorat estimate that Dalits and Adivasis who comprise 22 per cent of India's population own only 11 per cent of the wealth. Hindu OBCs, who constitute approximately 36 per cent of the total population, possess 30 per cent of the wealth, while Muslims with a 14 per cent population share possess only 8 per cent wealth share. In contrast, the Hindu forward castes with a

22 per cent population share monopolise around 41 per cent of wealth (Nitin Tagade, Ajaya Kumar Naik and Sukhadeo Thorat, 'Wealth Ownership and Inequality in India').
42 Swati Narayan, 'Aadhaar-for-food Can't Be a Mandatory Requirement'; Rahul Bhatia, 'How India's Welfare Revolution Is Starving Citizens'.
43 Wire Staff, 'Rajasthan: Nine-Yr-Old Dalit Boy Passes Away After Alleged Assault by Schoolteacher'.
44 *The Quint*, 'Dalit Youth Killed in Rajasthan for His "Good Looks", Say Kin; Cops Cite Rivalry'.
45 B.R. Ambedkar, *Annihilation of Caste*, in BAWS Collection, 1(1), p. 61.
46 Jhilam Ray and Rajarshi Majumdar, 'Snakes and Ladders: Intergenerational Income Mobility in India'; Sam Asher, Paul Novosad and Charlie Rafkin, 'Intergenerational Mobility in India: New Methods and Estimates across Time, Space, and Communities'.
47 Aashish Gupta and Nikkil Sudharsanan, 'Large and Persistent Life Expectancy Disparities between India's Social Groups'.
48 WEF, *Global Gender Gap Report 2021*.
49 Between 2013 and 2017, about 4,60,000 girls in India were 'missing' at birth each year. According to an UNFPA report, gender-biased sex selection accounts for about two-thirds of the total missing girls, and post-birth female mortality accounts for about one-third (UNFPA, *Against My Will: State of the World Population 2020*).
50 Prabhat Jha, et al., 'Trends in Selective Abortion of Female Foetuses in India'.
51 Half of rural women in India have not even completed nine years of education, and only 26 per cent were employed outside the home in 2019–21.
52 This argument has also been made lucidly in Jean Drèze and Amartya Sen, *An Uncertain Glory*.
53 Rajiv Kumar, 'On an Average, India Reported 10 Cases of Rape of Dalit Women Daily in 2019, NCRB Data Shows', based on National Crime Records Bureau, Ministry of Home Affairs, Government of India.

54 Shikhar Yadav, 'Dalit Billionaires & "De-Sanskritisation": Is India Ready to "Rap"?'
55 Christophe Jaffrelot, *India's Silent Revolution: The Rise of the Lower Castes in North India*; Christophe Jaffrelot and A. Kalaiyarasan, 'Dominant Castes, from Bullock Capitalists to OBCs? The Impact of Class Differentiation in Rural India'.
56 See A5 for comparisons of pre-tax income inequalities in South Asian countries.
57 UNDP, *Human Development Report 2020: The Next Frontier—Human Development and the Anthropocene*.
58 Richard Wilkinson and Kate Pickett, *The Spirit Level: Why Greater Equality Makes Societies Stronger*.
59 UNDP, *Human Development Report 2013: The Rise of the South—Human Progress in a Diverse World*; UNDP, *Human Development Report 2019: Beyond Income, beyond Averages, beyond Today: Inequalities in Human Development in the 21st Century*
60 Prannoy Roy and Dorab R. Sopariwala, *The Verdict: Decoding India's Elections*.
61 Mosiqi Acharya, 'India's Newly Elected MPs: Almost 90 Per Cent Are Millionaires and 43 per Cent Face Criminal Charges'. This research is by the Association of Democratic Reforms.
62 B.R. Ambedkar, 'Condition Precedent for the Successful Working of Democracy: Speech at the Poona District Law Library on 22nd December 1952' in BAWS Collection, 17(3), p. 485; also quoted in Yogendra Yadav, 'Ambedkar Said Tyranny of Majority Is No Democracy. Indians Must Read Him Again'.
63 World Bank, 'Treasures of the Education System in Sri Lanka: Restoring Performance, Expanding Opportunities and Enhancing Prospects'.
64 Popular quote by Chairman Mao Zedong during the Chinese cultural revolution to promote gender equality.
65 Naila Kabeer, 'The Rise of the Daughter-in-Law: Why Son Preference Is Weakening in Bangladesh'.
66 Punam Yadav, *Social Transformation in Post-conflict Nepal*.

67 Kumari Jayawardena, *Feminism and Nationalism in the Third World*.
68 A. Kalaiyarasan and M. Vijayabaskar, *The Dravidian Model: Interpreting the Political Economy of Tamil Nadu*. This insight is based on their elucidation in the online book discussion 'The Dravidian Model: Interpreting the Political Economy of Tamil Nadu' on 4 March 2021 organised by Kings College, London.
69 The 'high growth-rising inequality phenomenon' in the state further worsens social segregation (Sukanta Bhattacharya, Sarani Saha and Sarmila Banerjee, 'Income Inequality and the Quality of Public Services: A Developing Country Perspective', p. 1).
70 Travelling in northern India, there often 'lingers a sense of decay, despite the customary presence of the state' (Shobhit Mahajan, 'Decay and Darkness in Bihar', p. 79).
71 Ashwini Deshpande, *The Grammar of Caste: Economic Discrimination in Contemporary India*; Surinder Jodhka and Ghanshyam Shah, 'Comparative Contexts of Discrimination: Caste and Untouchability in South Asia'.
72 IIPS and ICF, 'National Family Health Survey (NFHS-5), 2019–21: India Report'.
73 Author calculations based on Pratham, *Annual Status of Education Report (Rural) 2022 Provisional* and MoE, *Report on Unified District Information System for Education Plus (UDISE+)*, 2021-22 (English).
74 Author calculations based on Government of India, 'Population Enumeration Data (Final Population)', *Census of India 2011*.
75 Rokeya Sakhawat Hossain, *Sultana's Dream* and *Padmarag*.
76 Proportion of seats held by women in national parliaments (%) and Labour force participation rate, female (% of female population ages 15+) (modelled ILO estimate), in WDI, World Development Indicators, June 2023. Oddly, Nepal's female labour force participation, which was estimated at more than 80 per cent by the WDI in their online tables for the last decade, has now been reduced to 29 per cent in 2022 in the June 2023 version and the back series have also been altered.

The reasons for this substantial change is unclear, without transparency. Still Nepali women's workforce participation remains more than India.

77 Prevalence of stunting, weight for height (% of children under 5) in WDI, World Development Indicators, June 2023; HDI 2021-22 dataset, expected years of schooling, in UNDP, *COVID-19 and Human Development*.

2. INDIA TRUMPED?

1   Irish poet quoted in Kofi Annan, 'Kofi Annan on Economic Inequality: "People Are Seduced by the Siren Songs of Cynical Populists"'.
2   As per the latest Rural Health Statistics for 2020-21 in rural Bihar, on average, sub-centres are located at a 1.7 km distance, while the national average, which includes hilly areas, is 2.5 km, (GOI, *Rural Health Statistics, 2020-21*).
3   Field Notes, Tehragacch block, 22–29 August 2016, Kishanganj district, Bihar.
4   A. Mahat, et al., 'Medical Scholarships Linked to Mandatory Service: The Nepal Experience'.
5   The 2015 blockade lasted about six months, and created a political, economic, social and humanitarian crisis in Nepal. Then Nepali prime minister K.P. Sharma Oli in a televised address called on India to end the crisis: 'Nepal is passing through a serious humanitarian crisis which should not happen even during the wars. The blockade imposed by our southern neighbour has underestimated the feeling of the Nepali and Indian people. Imposing a blockade to a landlocked nation is a breach of international treaties, norms and values.' Nepal has accused the Indian government of supporting the Madhesi ethnic community of Indian origin with the undeclared blockade against the new Nepali constitution. Nearly 95 per cent of Nepal's population was affected by crippling shortage of cooking fuel, leading to illegal logging of forests for firewood, shortage of life-saving drugs and blood bags, delay in the printing of 15 million textbooks and post-

earthquake rebuilding (BBC, 'Nepal Blockade: Six Ways It Affects the Country'; *Firstpost*, 'Nepal PM Oli Urges India to Lift Economic Blockade, Says It's Causing a "Humanitarian Crisis"'; Saif Khalid, 'India's "Blockade" Snuffs Out Nepal's Medical Lifeline').

6 Anil Deolalikar, 'Poverty and Child Malnutrition in Bangladesh'; Jean Drèze, 'Bangladesh Shows the Way'; Jean Drèze and Amartya Sen, *An Uncertain Glory*; Swati Narayan, *Serve the Essentials: What Governments and Donors Must Do to Improve South Asia's Essential Services*; UNDP, *Human Development Report 2005*, *Human Development Report 2016*.

7 The Maddison Project Database, version 2020 (Bolt Jutta and Jan Luiten van Zanden, 'Maddison Style Estimates of the Evolution of the World Economy: A New Update').

8 Aakar Patel, *Price of the Modi Years*.

9 Jagriti Chandra, 'Global Hunger Index Attempt to Tarnish India's Image: Centre'. In 2023, India has again slipped four places on the GHI and now ranks lowest in South Asia, but the government has once again criticised the methodology as 'flawed' and 'erroneous'.

10 Banjot Kaur, 'WHO Is Disputing India's COVID Death Numbers, So Govt Wants to Bury Global Report'; Jammi N. Rao, 'Inconvenient Truth: Why the Modi Govt Is Choosing "Denial" as Its Response to WHO's Covid Death Toll'; WHO, '14.9 Million Excess Deaths Associated with the COVID-19 Pandemic in 2020 and 2021'.

11 Rukmini S., 'India's Objections to WHO COVID-19 Mortality Estimates Are Misleading, Experts Say'; Murad Banaji, 'Why India's Response to WHO on Excess COVID-19 Deaths Doesn't Hold Water'; Bindu Shajan Perappadan, 'WHO Has Released the Excess Death Estimates Without Adequately Addressing India's Concerns: Health Ministry'; Rahul Shrivastava, 'WHO "Excess Covid Death" Report: Govt Lens on Pharma Firms Denied Entry to India'.

12 Jagdish Bhagwati and Arvind Panagariya, *India's Reforms: How They Produced Inclusive Growth*, p. 58.

13 Life expectancy at birth, male and female (years), in WDI, World Development Indicators, June 2023.
14 Theda Skocpol, 'Historical Institutionalism in Contemporary Political Science'.
15 F. Mackay, M. Kenny and L. Chappell, 'New Institutionalism through a Gender Lens: Towards a Feminist Institutionalism?'
16 British philosopher John Stuart Mill, in his 1843 book, chalks out five methods. The five Mill's Methods are the method of agreement, method of difference, joint method of agreement and difference, method of residue and the method of concomitant variations (John Stuart Mill, *A System of Logic Ratiocinative and Inductive: Being a Connected View of the Principles of Evidence and the Methods of Scientific Investigation*, p. 388).
17 Daron Acemoglu and James A. Robinson, *Why Nations Fail: The Origins of Power, Prosperity and Poverty*, p. 9.
18 Arend Lijphart, 'Comparative Politics and the Comparative Method'.
19 Based on the 'Method of Difference'. Mill describes this method as one with 'two instances resembling one another in every other respect, but differing in the presence or absence of the phenomenon we wish to study' (John Stuart Mill, *A System of Logic Ratiocinative and Inductive*, p. 483).
20 Bihar shares a 726 km border with Nepal. West Bengal, at 2,217 km, shares the longest border with Bangladesh. The Banglabandha Zero Point border crossing in Bangladesh's Panchagarh district is connected to the Siliguri Chicken's Neck. This is a small strip of land in West Bengal that connects India's northeastern states to the mainland and is less than 50 km as the crow flies from Bihar's Galgalia village and Thakurganj town in Kishanganj district. Siliguri is also less than 20 km from Nepal's open border with India and Bhutan's Jaigaon land border.
21 Mill's 'Method of Concomitant Variation' (John Stuart Mill, *A System of Logic Ratiocinative and Inductive*, p. 495).
22 Rex Casinader, 'Making Kerala Model More Intelligible: Comparisons with Sri Lankan Experience'; Thomas Timberg,

	'Regions in Indian Development'; S. Vivek, *Delivering Public Services Effectively: Tamil Nadu and Beyond*
23	See Appendix A1.
24	Alfred Stepan, Juan J. Linz and Yogendra Yadav, *Crafting State-Nations: India and Other Multinational Democracies*.
25	Yogendra Yadav, *The Rise of State-Nations—Lecture Transcript*.
26	Prerna Singh, 'We-ness and Welfare: A Longitudinal Analysis of Social Development in Kerala, India'.
27	Bihar's average income in 2014 was also four-fifths that of Nepal and three-fourths that of Bangladesh. So, comparisons on the human development front amongst these three regions then were not unnecessarily skewed due to differences in average incomes. But, since 2014, the Indian government has controversially changed the methodology for the calculation of economic growth. This change seems to have substantially depressed West Bengal's and Bihar's average incomes. On the other hand, Bangladesh's economic growth has soared and inched much closer to West Bengal after 2014. The World Development Indicators estimate that, especially in the wake of the pandemic, from 2019–22 Bangladesh's average incomes (GDP per capita [current international \$]) have overtaken India, and in 2019, 2020 and 2022, also in terms of growth rates. However, in terms of purchasing power parity (GDP per capita, PPP [current international \$]), Bangladeshi income has always remained lower than India's since 1990s. See Appendix A2.
28	Siliguri Chicken's Neck is a small strip of land in West Bengal that connects India's northeastern states to the mainland and is a mere 50 km as the crow flies from the Banglabandha Zero Point border of Bangladesh, Nepal's open border with India and Bhutan's Jaigaon land border.
29	BIMARU is an acronym of the first alphabets of the Indian states of Bihar, Madhya Pradesh, Rajasthan and Uttar Pradesh (before their bifurcations and now would include Jharkhand and Chhattisgarh) coined by demographer Ashish Bose in the

1980s to refer to backward states. The Hindi word 'Bimar' means 'sick'.
30 UNDP, *Human Development Report 2021-22, Uncertain Times, Unsettled Lives: Shaping Our Future in a Transforming World*.
31 UNDP, *Sri Lanka Human Development Report 2012*.
32 On 8 November 2016, Indian Prime Minister Narendra Modi announced that, within four hours, all Rs 500 and Rs 1,000 banknotes in circulation would lose their value as legal tender with the issuance of new bank notes.
33 Tadit Kundu, 'Why Kerala Is Like Maldives and Uttar Pradesh, Pakistan'.
34 UNDP, *Human Development Report 2021-22, Uncertain Times, Unsettled Lives: Shaping Our Future in a Transforming World*.
35 India's MPI scores in 2022 and 2023 were updated with the latest 2019–21 Demographic and Health Survey (DHS) data. But Nepal and Bangladesh's latest 2022 DHS survey data is not yet fully available, so the MPI used Multiple Indicator Cluster Surveys for 2019 were used as substitutes. Sabina Alkire, Usha Kanagaratnam and Nicolai Suppa, 'A Methodological Note on the Global Multidimensional Poverty Index (MPI) 2022 Changes over Time, Results for 84 Countries'.
36 Sabina Alkire, Christian Oldiges and Usha Kanagaratnam, 'Examining Multidimensional Poverty Reduction in India 2005/6–2015/16: Insights and Oversights of the Headcount Ratio'.
37 Stefan Klonner and Christian Oldiges, 'The Welfare Effects of India's Rural Employment Guarantee'.
38 Andaleeb Rahman, 'Universal Food Security Program and Nutritional Intake: Evidence from the Hunger Prone KBK Districts in Odisha'.
39 See Appendix A7 for caste-based 'graded inequality' in access to essential services.
40 Swati Narayan, 'Towards Equality in Healthcare: Trends Over Two Decades'.

41 Swati Narayan, 'Aadhaar-for-food Can't Be a Mandatory Requirement'; Rahul Bhatia, 'How India's Welfare Revolution Is Starving Citizens'.
42 Abhinash Dash Choudhury, 'Jharkhand's Starvation Deaths Raise Questions About India's Welfare Schemes'.
43 IIPS and ICF, 'National Family Health Survey (NFHS-5), 2019–21: India Report'.
44 K.D. Maiti and Santosh Mehrotra, 'The Curious Case of India's Millions of "Missing" Poor People.'
45 Estimates from the FAO, 'The State of Food Security and Nutrition in the World 2023'.
46 The World Happiness Index constructed largely from the Gallup World Poll of life evaluations is based on national averages of individuals' own assessments of their lives. The data from 137 countries is averaged over the years 2020–22. The index score is primarily based on answers to the single-item Cantril ladder life-evaluation question. The question asks respondents to evaluate their current life as a whole using the mental image of a ladder, with the best possible life for them as a 10 and the worst possible as a 0. Typically, around 1,000 responses are gathered annually for each country and then weighted for population representativeness.
47 Deniz Kandiyoti powerfully argues that there are largely two distinct forms of patriarchy. In the sub-Saharan African pattern, the insecurities of polygyny are matched with relative autonomy for women. In the belt of classic patriarchy in South Asia, East Asia and the Middle East, based on patrilocality and patrimony, women's subordination to men is offset by the control older women attain over younger women (Deniz Kandiyoti, 'Bargaining with Patriarchy').
48 WDI, World Development Indicators, June 2023.
49 WEF, *Global Gender Gap Report 2023*.
50 However, in the penultimate chapter, the heydays of Sri Lanka's historical human development trajectory (1830–1977) are analysed at a time when its economic growth rates were modest.

51 Jean Drèze and Mrilalini Saran, 'Primary Education and Economic Development in China and India: Overview and Two Case Studies'.
52 Hasan in grade 2 was easily able to read a paragraph from his textbook. In my 2016 survey in Panchagarh, 90 per cent of students in grade 5 in Panchagarh district of Bangladesh were suitably competent in language skills to be able to read at least a standard grade 2 level paragraph in Bengali. Fifty-eight per cent of students in grades 1 to 4 also had grade 1 language skills.
53 See Pratham, *Annual Status of Education Report (Rural) 2022 Provisional*. The 2016 ASER survey also uncovered that less than half the children in grade 5 in rural Bihar (42 per cent) and rural India (48 per cent) could read a grade 2 curricula paragraph in their medium of instruction. The competency for arithmetic was even more dismal at 27 per cent in rural Bihar and 26 per cent across rural India.
54 As per the latest 2022 ASER survey, after the pandemic the proportion of children (age 6 to 14) enrolled in free government school has increased sharply from 65.6 per cent in 2018 to 72.9 per cent in 2022. Further, amongst Indian children in the same grade the gap between those from the poorest 40 per cent of households and the richest 20 per cent is 34 per cent in numeracy and 44 per cent in literacy (Maryam Akmal and Lant Pritchett, 'Learning Equity Requires More than Equality: Learning Goals and Achievement Gaps between the Rich and the Poor in Five Developing Countries').
55 From 2012 to 2018, the ASER surveys found that less than half of students in grade 5 could read a grade 2 level text. After the pandemic, the latest 2022 national ASER survey has reported a reduction in reading levels to pre-2012 levels. The proportion of these children with reading skills in grade 5 fell from 50.5 per cent in 2018 to 42.8 per cent in 2022.
56 Jean Drèze, et al., *Locked-out: Emergency Report on School Education*.
57 The 2020 child mortality rates are based on the World Development Indicator estimates developed by the UN Inter-

agency Group for Child Mortality Estimation (UNICEF, WHO, World Bank, UN DESA Population Division) at https://childmortality.org/.
58 As per the World Health Organization's modelled estimates, for every 1,00,000 live births, in 2017, 145 mothers in India died compared to 173 in Bangladesh and 186 in Nepal. And in Sri Lanka, there were only thirty-six deaths.
59 V. Ramalingaswami, U. Jonsson and J. Rohde, 'Malnutrition: A South Asian Enigma'.
60 Based on the latest Demographic Health Surveys. Please see A8.
61 See Appendix A8 for underweight children among rich and poor families, 2017–22.
62 As per the preliminary NFHS 2019–21, 30 per cent of homes in India do not have improved sanitation facilities and 19 per cent no toilets. Also see Diane Coffey and Dean Spears, *Where India Goes*; Avani Kapur and Devashish Deshpande, 'Swachh Bharat Mission (Gramin) 3 Years On'; Nikhil Srivastav, 'Labelling versus Outcomes: On Swachh Bharat Mission'.
63 The Government of India's Swachh Bharat Mission had a self-imposed October 2019 deadline to make the country open defecation-free (ODF), and on its website, https://swachhbharatmission.gov.in, makes the controversial claim that 95.7 per cent of rural households have a toilet. Instead, the semi-autonomous Swachh Survekshan Gramin 2017 survey pegs the figure at a more modest 62.5 per cent (Rashmi Verma, 'Swachh Survekshan Gramin Reports 62% Toilet Coverage, Surveys 0.72% Villages in India'; IPE Global, *National Annual Rural Sanitation Survey Data 2017-2018: Provisional Summary Results Report*), and the latest National Family Health Survey 2019–21 also reach a similar conclusion based on preliminary data.
64 Aashish Gupta and Sangita Vyas, 'Is Open Defecation Still Prevalent in Rural North India?'.
65 T.G. Ajay, 'How "Swachh Bharat" Is Being Forced Upon Chhattisgarh Villagers'.

66 The Wire Staff, '2 Dalit Children Beaten to Death For Defecating in Public in Madhya Pradesh'.
67 Vidya Subrahmaniam, 'There Can Be No Swachh Bharat Without Ending Institutional Discrimination against Dalits'; Bezwada Wilson, 'Will Swachh Bharat Abhiyan Be a Success?'; Swagata Yadavar, 'Casteism Will Not Allow Swachch Bharat Abhiyan to Succeed'.
68 Newclick, 'Women Sanitation Workers Protest Against Govt "Lies" on Sewer Deaths'.
69 Dean Spears, 'Exposure to Open Defecation Can Account for the Indian Enigma of Child Height'; Coffey, et al., 'Stunting among Children: Facts and Implications'; Diane Coffey and Dean Spears, *Where India Goes*; Robert Chambers and Gregor Von Medeazza, 'Sanitation and Stunting in India: Undernutrition's Blind Spot'.
70 Arabinda Ghosh, Dean Spears and Aashish Gupta, 'Are Children in West Bengal Shorter Than Children in Bangladesh?'
71 GoN, New ERA and ICF, *Demographic and Health Survey 2016: Key Indicators Report*.

3. EASTERN NEIGHBOURS: EAR TO THE GROUND

1 This poem is included in the syllabus of the Central Board of Secondary Education in India. The translation is by Nissim and available on the website https://nepalgo.de/ (last accessed 1 August 2023).
2 Santosh Mehrotra and Richard Jolly, *Development with a Human Face: Experiences in Social Achievement and Economic Growth*.
3 Ha-Joon Chang, 'Rethinking Development Economics: An Introduction', p. 4.
4 The choice of the four districts was based on four comparable criteria: cultural similarities, economic development, social attributes and proximity to the border. See Appendix A9.
5 See Appendix A10 for the map on the sample districts in Nepal, Bangladesh and Bihar. This border at Zero Point was opened only at the tail end of my fieldwork. As a result, each trip to

reach Panchagarh for the survey fieldwork and recce required a circuitous journey of two nights in buses from Kolkata via Dhaka.

6   In every district, based on a random selection from respective national censuses, twenty villages were selected for the survey. Further, in every village, twenty households were selected based on the 'every fifth household rule' adopted by the ASER survey across four hamlets in each village to ensure random selection attuned to rural realities (Pratham, 'Survey Process—ASER Centre'). The method involved creating a village map and then dividing the population into clustered hamlets based on geography, caste or other universal and easily identifiable markers. From these, four hamlets were randomly chosen with an eye to ensure the representation of diverse castes and communities. Then, from the centre-point of each hamlet, five households were selected based on the 'every fifth household rule' by traversing in a circular manner and selecting every fifth household on the route. If a house was shut or unoccupied, then the next house on the lane was selected. Additionally, for the survey we only selected households which had at least one child pursuing an education, and in most cases, the respondent was a mother in the reproductive age.

7   The questionnaires drew inspiration from a number of established surveys—*Annual Status of Education Report (ASER)* (Pratham, *Annual Status of Education Report (Rural): 2017 Beyond Basics*), India Human Development Survey (IHDS) (Sonalde Desai and Reeve Vanneman, *India Human Development Survey-II (IHDS-II), 2011-12*), Demographic and Health Surveys (DHS) (IIPS and ICF, 'National Family Health Survey (NFHS-5), 2019–21: India Report'), Public Evaluation of Entitlement Programmes (PEEP) (Jean Drèze and Reetika Khera, 'Recent Social Security Initiatives in India'; Kritika Goel and Reetika Khera, 'Public Health Facilities in North India: An Exploratory Study in Four States') and Sanitation Quality, Use, Access and Trends (SQUAT) (Diane Coffey, et al., 'Revealed Preference for Open Defecation').

8   The questionnaires were designed, fine-tuned and translated into three languages by translators based in Kolkata (Bengali), Kathmandu (Nepali) and Ranchi (Hindi).
9   See Appendix A11 the four indices created with survey data from eighty villages and Appendix A15 for the scatter plot.
10 Though the HDI inspired this index, the variables were completely different and based on my primary survey in the village, not on national data.
11 The methodology for constructing each composite index consisted of three identical steps—aggregation, normalisation and calculation of geometric means, in that specific sequence.
12 upazilas in Bangladesh are the second-lowest tier of governance at the sub-district level. In the Indian context, they are the equivalent of a 'block' and in Western countries a county or borough. The lowest tier in Bangladesh is referred to as a 'union parishad' which is equivalent to a 'panchayat' in India.
13 The Merriam-Webster dictionary defines participant observation as 'a research technique in anthropology and sociology characterized by the effort of an investigator to gain entrance into and social acceptance by a foreign culture or alien group so as better to attain a comprehensive understanding of the internal structure of the society.'
14 During my initial recce in Bangladesh during the month of Ramzan, one of my Muslim hosts gently requested me to cover my head with a dupatta as a hijab. She confided that, despite naysayers in her village, she had, with much trepidation, taken a leap of faith to host us. Since then, I made it a point to cover my head throughout my travels in Bangladeshi villages, which helped in blending in and also in winning the trust of the villagers (Field Notes, Panchagarh district, Bangladesh, 17–27 June 2015).
15 The Kajoli model has been developed by Research Initiatives Bangladesh (RIB).
16 To compute the human development index from my survey data, the scores of the entire sample of 1,404 students from grades 1 to 5 whom we tested were aggregated. A total of

58 per cent of tested students in Bangladesh and 48 per cent in Nepal possessed the minimum language skills compared to only 29 per cent in Bihar. In mathematics, half the children in Bangladesh, less than a third in Bihar and less than a quarter in Nepal passed the rudimentary test. The evaluation was whether children in grades 1 to 4 could demonstrate at least grade 1 level competencies and those in grade 5 who could fulfil at least grade 2 level proficiencies. The reason for the low benchmark was that the syllabus varied marginally across the countries. For example, carry-over subtraction that we tested, which was taught in Indian schools in grade 2, was taught in Nepal in grade 3. Therefore, a majority of children in grade 3 were unable to solve it at the time of the survey in May 2016, as they had just started the school year.

17 Pratham, *Annual Status of Education Report (Rural): 2017 Beyond Basics*. Even before the pandemic, in 2019, the all-India survey showed that less than half the children in grade 5 could read a simple paragraph. In Bihar, the situation was even worse, where only a third of the students had learnt this simple skill. The 2016 ASER survey discovered that less than half the children in grade 5 in rural Bihar (42 per cent) and rural India (48 per cent) could read a grade 2 level paragraph in their medium of instruction. The competency for arithmetic was even more dismal at 27 per cent in rural Bihar and 26 per cent across rural India.

18 However, in mathematics, while Bangladeshi students far outshone those in Bihar, Nepalis trailed behind both. One reason for the unusually low scores in mathematics in Nepal may be an error in the administration of our survey—the test was printed in Devanagari script which is the basis of the Nepali written language. Later, we realised that in schools across Nepal, for mathematics alone, teachers preferred to use the Roman script. We detected this flaw at the orientation training itself and surveyors were instructed to handwrite the Roman script on the testing sheet. There may have been an error in the administration of the test in some villages.

19 The ratio of competent pupils in the lowest income quintile to the highest income quintile is 1.07 in the Bangladeshi district indicating a highly progressive ratio, 0.87 in Nepal which is near parity and an abysmal 0.45 in Bihar. Therefore, in the Nepali and Bangladeshi districts there is minimal disparity in ASER test scores based on wealth, while in Bihar educational achievement is regressively influenced by wealth. See Appendix A12.

20 As per my survey data, competent pupils in the lowest income quintile were better learners than those in the highest income quintile.

21 Abhay Kumar, 'Over 3,000 Teachers Surrender Fake Degrees in Bihar'; '"Fake" Degree Probe in Bihar: For 53,000 Contract Teachers, "Last Chance" to Prove Degrees Real'.

22 Field Notes, Tehragacch block, Kishanganj district, Bihar, 22–29 August 2016.

23 Amitava Paran and Kanika Sharma, 'Where Are the Kids? The Curious Case of Government Schools in Bihar'.

24 In my survey, students in both Bihari government and private schools that we tested were more likely to enrol for private tuitions (44 and 82 per cent respectively) than Nepal (26 and 67 per cent) and Bangladesh (27 and 31 per cent). But it must be noted that only 14 per cent of students in Bihar were enrolled in private schools, NGOs or madrassas compared to 41 per cent in Bangladesh (largely in NGO-run schools) and 31 per cent in Nepal.

25 *Bangladesh Post*, 'Draft Law Forbids Private Tuition'; Wasim Bin Habib, 'Jail, Fine for Pvt Tuition'.

26 They were queried regarding seven rudimentary healthcare factors—whether consumption of milk was good for pregnant women, colostrum for the nutrition of infants, and consumption of fluids for diarrhoeal patients. Further, they were asked to identify typhoid as a water-borne disease, the period of the greatest likelihood of pregnancy during menstruation cycles, to confirm the harmful effects of open defecation on health and their ability to prepare oral rehydration salts (ORS) as a hygienic sugar–salt therapeutic solution.

27 FAO, *Guidelines for Measuring Household and Individual Dietary Diversity*. Across a range of food groups, except starchy staples. Also, 'oils and fats' replaced the second category of vegetables, as we did not expect rural respondents to eat two different varieties of vegetables in a single meal. Weights were attached to each food group based on their respective calorific density (calories derived per gram) to calculate final scores. The calories per gram were defined based on the toolbox available in the Google search engine created by the United States Department of Agriculture (USDA) Food Composition Databases.

28 Only 15 per cent of women we spoke to ate meat the previous night, 18 per cent fish and 18 per cent eggs with consumption on all counts being double in Muslim-dominated Kishanganj district compared to Muzaffarpur.

29 As per the latest NFHS survey, in 2019–21, only 49 per cent of Bihari homes have improved sanitation facilities. In 2015-16, during the period of my fieldwork, it was only 25 per cent. Also, please see Appendix A13.

30 Field Notes, Tehragacch block, Kishanganj district, Bihar, 22–29 August 2016.

31 Sonalde Desai and Reeve Vanneman, *India Human Development Survey-II (IHDS-II), 2011-12*. Calculations by Aashish Gupta (personal communications).

32 Field Notes, Maidan Dighi union, Boda upazila, Panchagarh district, Bangladesh, 22–29 February 2016.

33 Maulana Wahiduddin Khan, *Quran: A Simple English Translation*, chapter 5, verse 6.

34 Field Notes, Pradhangachh, Bhojanpur Union, Tetulia upazila, Bangladesh, 23–26 March 2016.

35 The human development scores were created by integrating all the four indicators with equal weights and normalising the final scores across the villages.

36 On a range of 0 to 1, where 1 implied the highest level of human development, Panchagarh district in Bangladesh was ahead (0.78) of Sindhuli district in Nepal (0.61), while both

the Bihari districts (Muzaffarpur 0.38 and Kishanganj 0.32) lagged behind.
37 For education, four key indicators were merged—teachers, seating arrangement, educational material and basic amenities. For health the indicators were functional facilities, basic medicines and reproductive and child health.
38 A multi-country World Bank survey in 2004 documented that 25 per cent of teachers in government primary schools in India (and 38 per cent in Bihar) and 15 per cent in Bangladesh remained absent from work on any given day. On the other hand, a survey led by Azim Premji University across six states found a substantially lower absenteeism rate of 3 per cent. Still, they too noted that in reality often 19 per cent of teachers were not present in the classroom for a variety of reasons (Anurag Behar, 'The False Narrative of Teacher Absenteeism').
39 While the intent behind this policy was progressive, many of the teachers were recruited by the local panchayats based on fake certificates involving massive corruption, which has adversely affected the quality of education (Satyavrat Mishra, 'Bihar's Bitter Lesson in Teacher Recruitment'); Field Notes, Bihar, 29 August–14 September 2016.
40 Field Notes, Sirthouli VDC, Nepal, 25–31 May 2016.
41 The Bangladesh education ministry has also created a series of fifty colourful educational posters that we unfailingly found in every school, neatly covered in plastic to prevent wear-and-tear. Most of the posters are designed by UNICEF and a range of donors such as USAID, Wateraid, etc., in partnership with the Ministry of Education. In schools in the Indian state of Tamil Nadu, similar visual activity sheets were used in the classroom for children of different competencies.
42 Field Notes, Maidan Dighi Union, Boda upazila, Panchagarh district, Bangladesh, 22 January– 9 February 2016.
43 Field Notes, Tehragacch block, Kishanganj district, Bihar, 22–29 August 2016.
44 Abhijeet Singh et al., 'School Meals as a Safety Net: An Evaluation of the Midday Meal Scheme in India'.

45	The lowest tier of the health infrastructure in India is referred to as the primary 'sub-centre', in Nepal it is called 'health post' and in Bangladesh as 'community clinic.'
46	MoHFW, *Community Clinic Based Health Care (CBHC), DGHS*.
47	Antibiotic tablets for adults and syrup for children, paracetamol, eye ointment, iron tablets, vitamin A, vitamin B, vitamin C, deworming doses, oral rehydration salt (ORS) sachet packets, anti-allergy products, anti-acidity tablets and anti-bacterial ointments.
48	Omar Haider Chowdhury and S.R. Osmani, 'Towards Achieving the Right to Health: The Case of Bangladesh'.
49	Aparna John, *Performance of India's Community Nutrition Workers: Anganwadi Workers of the Integrated Child Development Services Scheme in Bihar*. Anganwadis are government-run pre-schools which are expected to provide early childhood care and education (ECCE). India has more than a million such anganwadis which cover more than 80 million children under the age of six. Each anganwadi under the National Food Security Act, 2013 is expected mandatorily feed children freshly cooked snacks in the morning and 'supplementary nutrition' or a small meal in the afternoon.
50	Field Notes, Kishanganj district, Bihar.
51	Jean Drèze and Amartya Sen, *India: Development and Participation*, p. 181.
52	Swati Narayan, 'Towards Equality in Healthcare: Trends Over Two Decades'; Gobinda Pal, 'Caste and Access to Public Services'; A.K. Shiva Kumar et al., 'Inequities in Access to Health Services in India: Caste, Class and Region'; Anand Teltumbde, 'No Swachh Bharat without Annihilation of Caste'.
53	Mayank Kumar, 'Dalit student dies after being beaten by teacher in U.P., Opposition mounts pressure on government'.
54	News 18 Team, 'School Teacher Trashes Dalit Boy for Allegedly Not Bringing Plate from Home'.
55	'"Jitne bhi Mohammedan bachche hai..." UP teacher makes kids beat fellow student'.

56 Field Notes, Maidan Dighi Union, Boda upazila, Bangladesh, 22–29 February 2016.
57 Field Notes, Musahar Tola, Muzaffarpur district, Bihar, November 2016.
58 Field Notes, Hatpate VDC, Sindhuli district, Nepal, 1–3 June 2016.
59 Maitreyi B. Das, *Whispers to Voices : Gender and Social Transformation in Bangladesh*.
60 Field Notes, Maidan Dighi Union, Boda upazila, Panchagarh district, Bangladesh, 22–29 February 2016.
61 In Bangladesh the World Bank Gender Norms survey in 2006 found that 36.3 per cent of women in the 15–25 age group married men with less education; Niels-Hugo Blunch and Maitreyi Bordia Das, 'Changing Norms about Gender Inequality in Education: Evidence from Bangladesh'.
62 This is also a growing trend in India with IHDS and NFHS survey data from 2005-06 also indicating that 30 per cent of women in the 15–45 years age group married men with less education than them. Munoz Boudet, et al., 'On Norms and Agency: Conversations about Gender Equality with Women and Men in 20 Countries'.
63 See the 2015-16 India Human Development Survey results (Sonalde Desai and Reeve Vanneman, *India Human Development Survey-II (IHDS-II), 2011-12*). The 2015 Social Attitudes Research India (SARI), too, concludes that women who live in households where men eat first are more likely to be underweight (Diane Coffey, et al., 'Revealed Preference for Open Defecation').
64 Field Notes, Dighalbank block, Kishanganj district, Bihar, 1–6 September 2017.
65 These verses are quoted in the Hadith by Wahshi bin Harb on the 'Etiquette of Eating', Book 3, Hadith 743 (Abu Dawud).
66 Field Notes, Bhimstan VDC, Sindhuli district, Nepal, 16–22 May 2016.
67 In Kishanganj district, we came across a hamlet of Shersabadi Muslim families who still practice an extreme form of purdah.

Married women are not allowed beyond the walls of the household. Working outside the home is strictly prohibited, except in the madrassa to teach children. Yet, as a pleasant surprise, they were well educated and, in some homes, had spent more years in schools or madrassas than even their husbands. One 22-year-old mother aced all the questions on healthcare in our survey, the only one in her village (Field Notes, Dighalbank block, Nepal, 14 September 2016).

68 For more details on the standard linear regression analysis, please see Appendix A15 and my doctoral thesis, Swati Narayan, 'India Surpassed: The Price of Inequality in South Asia'.

69 Please see Appendix A14.

4. BANGLADESH

1 There is a similar Persian couplet, 'The first year we were Jolāhās, the next Shaikhs; this year, if prices fall, we shall become Saiyads' (Quoted in Asim Roy, *The Islamic Syncretistic Tradition in Bengal*, p. 62). Saiyads are considered to be direct descendants of Prophet Mohammad and accorded the highest honour, Sheikhs are Muslims of Arab origin, while Jolāhās are weavers.

2 Personal interview with Meghna Guhathakurta, Director, Research Initiatives, 11 April 2016.

3 According to Article 9 of the Fundamental Principles of State Policy of the Constitution of Bangladesh, and through the Local Governmental (Union Parishad) Act of 1997, three directly elected seats are reserved for women in the Union Parishads (one from each of the three wards), the lowest level of councils in the sub-national administration. As per Article 65 (3A) of the Constitution, of the 350 seats in Parliament, fifty are reserved for women (International IDEA, *Gender Quotas Database*).

4 In India, due to the rotational nature of the gender quota system, men are more likely to be vested in ensuring that female family members are elected to reserved seats that they may have previously occupied to ensure proxy representation.

But in Bangladesh, qualitative interviews seem to indicate that 'Bangladeshi women members do not act as proxies of their husbands' (Mahbub Alam Prodip, 'Cultural Obstacles to Women's Political Empowerment in India and Bangladesh: A Comparative Perspective'). But, the larger constituency size for reserved women members in Bangladesh is an institutional constraint which diminishes their ability to both serve their constituents and influence decisions in the Union Parishad (Mahbub Alam Prodip, 'Exclusion Through Inclusion: Institutional Constraints on Women's Political Empowerment in India and Bangladesh').

5   Transparency International's 2022 Corruption Perceptions Index ranks Bangladesh in 147th place out of 180 countries and the worst in South Asia, apart from Afghanistan.
6   The 2022 V-DEM liberal democracy index released in March 2023 ranks Bangladesh as lower than Pakistan in South Asia. Since then, with the recent political developments in Pakistan, the ranks are likely to change substantially in the next annual report (Evie Papada, et al., 'Defiance in the Face of Autocratization', Democracy Report 2023').
7   Partyarchy is a term coined in political science and often used in the context of Bangladesh to describe socio-political domination whereby 'political parties monopolise the formal political process and politicise society along party lines' (Michael Coppedge, *Strong Parties and Lame Ducks: Presidential Partyarchy and Factionalism in Venezuela*, p. 24).
8   Field Notes, Maidan Dighi Union, Boda upazila, Bangladesh, 22–29 February 2016.
9   Naomi Hossain, *The Aid Lab: Understanding Bangladesh's Unexpected Success*, p. 4.
10 Salil Tripathi, '*Bangladesh's Quest for Closure*'.
11 Mirza Hassan, 'Political Settlement Dynamics in a Limited-Access Order: The Case of Bangladesh'.
12 Naomi Hossain and Naila Kabeer, 'Achieving Universal Education and Eliminating Gender Disparity in Bangladesh'.
13 Mirza Hassan, 'Political Settlement Dynamics'. The alternating monopoly that the Awami League and the Bangladesh

Nationalist Party exchange determines the nature of party–state relations, as well as those between the state and the society, with the characteristic of monopoly (winner takes all).

14 Mirza Hassan, 'Political Settlement Dynamics', p. 33.
15 Mirza Hassan, 'Political Settlement Dynamics', p. 33.
16 Naomi Hossain, *The Aid Lab*, p. 5.
17 Bangladesh has had a spate of student protests since the Language Movement in the 1950s and against the military dictators on the 1990s (TRT, 'Bangladesh's History of Student Protest Movements').
18 BBC, 'Bangladesh Protests: How a Traffic Accident Stopped a City of 18 Million'; N. Tanjeem and R.E. Fatima, *The 2018 Road Safety Protest in Bangladesh: How a Student Crowd Challenged (or Could Not Challenge) the Repressive State*.
19 Haroon Habib, 'At Shahbagh, Bangladesh's Fourth Awakening'; Saimum Parvez, 'Understanding the Shahbag and Hefajat Movements in Bangladesh: A Critical Discourse Analysis'.
20 Naila Kabeer's remark at the launch of Naomi Hossain's book *The Aid Lab: Understanding Bangladesh's Unexpected Success* at the event 'Out of the Basket: Lessons from Bangladesh's Development Successes' at the London School for Economics, 7 March 2017.
21 Nayanika Mookherjee, *The Spectral Wound: Sexual Violence, Public Memories, and the Bangladesh War of 1971*.
22 Naomi Hossain, *The Aid Lab*, p. 6.
23 Naomi Hossain, *The Aid Lab*, p. 5.
24 Naomi Hossain, *The Aid Lab*, pp. 5–6.
25 Simeen Mahmud was a wonderful source of knowledge during my PhD. I met her in her office in Dhaka in 2016 and in Brighton in 2017 when we had attended a conference on Bangladesh at IDS Sussex. Sadly, she passed away suddenly in 2018.
26 Wahiduddin Mahmud and Simeen Mahmud, 'Development, Welfare and Governance: Explaining Bangladesh's "Development Surprise"', p. 70.
27 Former US Secretary of State Henry Kissinger despairingly described Bangladesh in 1972 as an 'international basket case'.

28 Atul Gawande, 'Spreading Slow Ideas'.
29 The Lancet, 'Water with Sugar and Salt'.
30 Child deaths under five years. IHME, *Global Burden of Disease, 2019*.
31 Fazle Hasan Abed, 'Bangladesh's Health Revolution'; A.M.R. Chowdhury and Richard Cash, *A Simple Solution: Teaching Millions to Treat Diarrhoea at Home*; Amy Yee, 'Profile: The Icddr,b—Saving Lives in Bangladesh and Beyond'.
32 Muhammad Yunus, *Banker to the Poor: The Story of the Grameen Bank*.
33 Hence 'overall poverty would have been close to 5 per cent higher without the spread of micro-credit' mainly by NGOs. Siddiqui Osmani, 'Has Microcredit Helped the Rural Poor of Bangladesh? An Analytical Review of the Evidence So Far'.
34 BRAC is one of the world's largest in terms of the number of employees. In 2019, it employed more than 1,10,000 development workers. BRAC works not only in every one of the sixty-eight districts of Bangladesh but also in Kenya, Liberia, Afghanistan, Myanmar and other developing countries. (Jenny Lei Ravelo, 'The World's Largest NGO Rethinks Its Future').
35 BRAC's social enterprises include handicrafts, poultries, dairies, fisheries and nurseries, and they also have additional investments including tea estates, low-cost housing, banks, stock-brokerage, mobile money remittances, life insurance, etc.
36 The 2021 BRAC Annual Report indicates that only 14 per cent of BRAC's revenues are generated from external development grants compared to 66 per cent from microfinance and 15 per cent from social enterprises. From the total revenues, 20 per cent of BRAC's expenditures are allocated for 'development programmes' (BRAC, *Annual Report 2020-21*.)
37 GB, About Grameen Bank' (blog).
38 The Tom Cruise starrer was estimated to have earned $1.440 billion globally.
39 Anu Muhammad, *Rise of the Corporate NGO in Bangladesh*.
40 Field Notes, Panchagarh town, Bangladesh, 20 June 2015.
41 Naomi Hossain, *The Aid Lab*, p. 17.

42 The teachers had gathered from across the upazila for a meeting. Field Notes, Maidan Dighi Union, Boda upazila, Bangladesh, 22–29 February 2016.
43 Field Notes, Salbahan Union, Tetulia upazila, Bangladesh, 9 March 2016.
44 NGOs cater to around 1.3 million children. Of these, 70 per cent are enrolled in BRAC primary schools alone (BANBEIS, 'Table 3.5.6: Number of Schools with Different Activities, 2016').
45 BRAC has started a new form of 'Shishu Schools' where each child has to pay Tk 200 per month as fees. In one school we visited with thirty-two students, the teacher was paid a salary of Tk 2,600, i.e., one-tenth that of a government school teacher (Field Notes Panchpir union, Boda upazila, Bangladesh, 1–4 March 2016).
46 Mirza Hassan, 'Political Settlement Dynamics in a Limited-Access Order', p. 18.
47 Jean Drèze, 'Democracy and the Right to Food'; Alf Gunvald Nilsen, 'India's Turn to Rights-Based Legislation (2004–2014): A Critical Review of the Literature'.
48 Mirza Hassan, 'Political Settlement Dynamics in a Limited-Access Order', p. 35.
49 Shamsul Haque, 'The Changing Balance of Power Between the Government and NGOs in Bangladesh'.
50 GB, About Grameen Bank' (blog).
51 Mohammed Yunus attempted to form a political party in 2007 which was quickly rescinded in a few months, but by 2011 he was removed as the managing director of Grameen Bank and the High Court confirmed the dismissal.
52 Grameenphone is a joint venture enterprise between Telenor (55.8 per cent), the largest telecommunications service provider in Norway, and Grameen Telecom (34.2 per cent), a non-profit organisation of Bangladesh.
53 The multiplier effect of foreign remittances in Bangladesh is estimated to range from 1.35 (World Bank, 'Migration and Remittance Flows: Recent Trends and Outlook, 2013-

2016') to 3.3 per cent of GNP (K.A.S. Murshid, K. Iqbal and M. Ahmed, 'A Study on Remittance Inflows and Utilization).
54 Naomi Hossain, *The Aid Lab*.
55 India's Constitution recognises several Muslim communities as 'Other Backward Classes' (OBC) based on their social and educational disadvantages. Families are often keen to make a claim for these certificates, which offer affirmative action in educational institutions and employment. In Bihar, the central list consists of thirty and the state list of twenty-three identified Muslim communities including Momin, Kasab (Kasai), Idrisi (Darzi), Dhobi, Dhunia and several others.
56 Richard Eaton, 'The Rise of Islam and the Bengal Frontier, 1204–1760'.
57 Richard Eaton, 'The Rise of Islam and the Bengal Frontier, 1204–1760', p. 9.
58 Historian Panikkar contends that the Palas were Shudra in origin (M.N. Srinivas, 'Mobility in the Caste System').
59 In the eighth century, in India the Pratiharas ruled in the North, the Rashtrakutas in the Deccan and the Pandyas and Pallavas in the South—all espousing Hindu religious theology. The 1881 census records only 2,00,000 Buddhists in India and of these 1,55,809 were in Bengal.
60 Mohammad Bakhtiyar was initially under the suzerainty of the Delhi Sultan Muhammad Ghuri, until he rebelled.
61 Richard Eaton, 'The Rise of Islam and the Bengal Frontier, 1204–1760'.
62 H. Beverley, *Report of the Census of India 1872*; W.W. Hunter, *The Indian Mussalmans*.
63 Richard Eaton, 'The Rise of Islam and the Bengal Frontier, 1204–1760', pp. 133–34.
64 While the Chishtiya Sufi order from Afghanistan with Moinuddin (Ajmer), Qutubuddin (Delhi), Nizamuddin (Delhi) and Fariduddin (Pakpattan) was more influential in northern India, the Suhrawardi Sufi order was more popular in Bengal.
65 Abdul Momin Chowdhury, 'Reflections on Islamisation in Bengal', p. 48.

66 Imtiaz Ahmad, *Caste and Social Stratification among the Muslims*.
67 These verses are quoted in the Hadith included in the confirmed collection by Al-Bukhari and published in Volume 8 of the book by Musnad Imam Ahmad Bin Hanbal in 2012.
68 H. Beverley, *Report of the Census of India 1872*, p. 132.
69 Imtiaz Ahmad, *Caste and Social Stratification among the Muslims*; A.R. Momin, 'Muslim Caste: Theory and Practice'. In the seventeenth century, East Bengal had essentially four types of elites—the intellectual elite or the alim (Arabic scholars), the governing elite including the kazi (judges), the priestly elite such as the mullah, and the spiritual elite consisting of the fakirs, pirs and the murshids (R.K. Dasgupta, *Revolt in East Bengal*, pp. 8–9). By the nineteenth century, Muslims in India were largely divided into only two main social divisions. The upper crust of ashraf were assumed to have foreign ancestry. On the other hand, the ajlaf or atrap were considered to be converts of indigenous origin. Dr Ambedkar further highlighted a third invisiblised 'lowest of all' class of arzal who were forbidden to enter the mosque and even use the public burial ground (B.R. Ambedkar, 'Social Stagnation').
70 Saiyads are considered to be direct descendants of Prophet Mohammad and accorded the highest honour; Sheikhs are Muslims of Arab origin; Mughals are Muslims of Central Asian origin; and Pathans are of Afghan origin (Padmanabh Samarendra, 'Between Number and Knowledge: Career of Caste in Colonial Census'); Imperial Census of India, various years compiled by the author (Swati Narayan, *India Surpassed: The Price of Inequality in South Asia*, Figure 6.6, p. 152).
71 Asim Roy, *The Islamic Syncretistic Tradition in Bengal*, p. 62.
72 Imtiaz Ahmad, *Caste and Social Stratification among the Muslims*.
73 Joya Chatterji, *Bengal Divided: Hindu Communalism and Partition, 1932–1947*; Girilal Jain, 'Response to the West: Hindu-Muslim Divergence in India'.
74 Atis Dasgupta, 'Variations in Perception of the Insurgent Peasants of Bengal in the Late Eighteenth Century'.

75 Amartya Sen, 'Imperial Illusions'.
76 R.K. Dasgupta, *Revolt in East Bengal*, p. 13.
77 Muntassir Mamoon and Mo Māhabubara Rahamāna, *Material Conditions of the Subalterns: Nineteenth Century East Bengal*.
78 Karl Marx, *Notes on Indian History*, p. 116–20.
79 Peter Hardy, *The Muslims of British India*, p. 44.
80 Iftekar Iqbal, 'The Political Ecology of the Peasant: The Fairaizi Movement between Revolution and Passive Resistance', pp. 78–82.
81 A.L. Basham, *A Cultural History of India*, p. 385.
82 A.K. Fazlul Huq, later the Prime Minister of East Bengal province, was a Muslim who belonged to an elite family of jotedars.
83 Dilip Kumar Chattopadhyay, 'The Ferazee and Wahabi Movements of Bengal'.
84 Shaikh Maqsood Ali, *From East Bengal to Bangladesh: Dynamics and Perspectives*.
85 Upazilas are sub-districts in rural Bangladesh which were previously called thanas. It is similar to a 'county' or 'borough' in Western countries and 'block' in India.
86 Under this legislation, the State became the owner of all land, abolishing all intermediaries, with compensation paid over a period of time. The law fixed the ceiling at 33.3 acres of land per family (Shaikh Maqsood Ali, *From East Bengal to Bangladesh: Dynamics and Perspectives*).
87 Field Notes, Bura Buri Union, Tetulia upazila, Bangladesh, 21 March 2016.
88 Shaikh Maqsood Ali, *From East Bengal to Bangladesh*, pp. 102–4.
89 'East Bengal therefore did not have feudal landed aristocracy in the West Pakistani sense'. Further, '[h]istorically, there was no caste/biradari or tribal division in East Bengal in the pattern of West Pakistan. Most important, the institution of marriage was mostly exogamous (as against large endogenous pattern in the West)'. So, 'the main criteria for social advance in East Bengal was money and education'. (Shaikh Maqsood Ali, *From East Bengal to Bangladesh: Dynamics and Perspectives*,

pp. 102). With the rise of the middle farmers (Jotdars) after the 1950 land reforms elite reorientation increased rural vertical social mobility. Still, East Bengal society was somewhat divided between the lives of the upper classes with 'the former Choudhuries (revenue collectors) and Talukdars (small landholders), the Kazis (marriage registrars)' in contrast to the 'Zolahas (weavers), the Kulus (oil grinders), Dai (mid-wives)' (M. Rashidnzzamn, 'Election Politics in Pakistan Villages').
90 BBS, *Preliminary Report on Agricultural Census 2019*.
91 Muhammad Sanaullah, *A.K. Fazlul Huq: Portrait of a Leader*.
92 The 1943-44 Bengal Famine led to mass de-peasantisation, landlessness, and increased the dependence on sharecropping. In the early years of the twentieth century, Bengali sharecroppers were expected to not only bear all the costs of production but also hand over half their harvest to the landlords. The Tebhaga Andolan in pre-partition Bengal in 1946-47 was the 'three-shares' movement. Sharecroppers demanded from the zamindar landlords and the British administration that atleast a third of the produce be retained by the cultivators of land.
93 Muhammad Sanaullah, *A.K. Fazlul Huq: Portrait of a Leader*.
94 Under the British colonial empire, which was headquartered in Calcutta as the capital from 1757 to 1911, an elite English-speaking Bengali social class emerged initially in urban centres, which included petty officials, nouveau riche, zamindars and entrepreneurs, all colloquially referred to as bhadralok or gentlemen. Marxist historians compare the bhadralok to the 'bourgeois' or 'middle class', but Sumit Sarkar and S.N. Mukherjee argue that rather than a social class, they were simply the educated class in a largely illiterate society (S.N. Mukherjee, 'Class, Caste and Politics in Calcutta 1815–38').
95 'Babu' is a colloquial Bengali term for a man from this gentrified class.
96 Joya Chatterji, *Bengal Divided*, p. 4.
97 Joya Chatterji, *Bengal Divided*, p. 5.
98 Joya Chatterji, *Bengal Divided*, p. 13.
99 Muhammad Sanaullah, *A.K. Fazlul Huq: Portrait of a Leader*.
100 Gopal Maju Mukherjee, 'C.R. Das and the Bengal Pact'.

101 Muhammad Sanaullah, *A.K. Fazlul Huq: Portrait of a Leader*.
102 Joya Chatterji, *Bengal Divided*, p. 15.
103 Ayesha Jalal, *The Sole Spokesman: Jinnah, the Muslim League and the Demand for Pakistan*.
104 Shaikh Maqsood Ali, *From East Bengal to Bangladesh: Dynamics and Perspectives*, pp. 102–4.
105 The Vested Property Act (earlier Enemy Property Act) originally enacted in 1948 during the partition of British India allows the Bangladeshi government to confiscate property from any person deemed to be a state enemy.
106 Rehman Sobhan, *Bangladesh: Problems of Governance. Governing South Asia*. On the other side of the border, in the late 1960s, West Bengal was at the epicentre of the left wing, militant Maoist Naxalite movement, which sought to combat extreme socio-economic inequalities.
107 Syed Badrul Ahsan, 'When Mr Jinnah came to Dhaka'.
108 Bangladeshis have convinced the United Nations to declare 21 February as International Mother Language Day, which coincides with the day when students in Dhaka opposed the imposition of Urdu as the national language in East Pakistan. This day is celebrated with much fanfare across rural and urban Bangladesh.
109 Interview with a Marxist academic who had led a battalion of armed men of the Mukti Bahini (Freedom Army) in the 1971 war (Field Notes, Boda upazila, Bangladesh, 21 February 2016).
110 Interview with a Hindu academic (Field Notes, Boda upazila, Bangladesh, 21 February 2016).
111 Journalist Salil Tripathi, in his book *The Colonel Who Would Not Repent: The Bangladesh War and Its Unquiet Legacy*, depicts the utter brutality unleashed during this civil war, based on interviews with several eye-witnesses and participants on all sides of the conflict.
112 In the US Congress on 14 October 2022 a historic resolution was introduced to recognise that a genocide had occurred in East Pakistan in 1971 (H. Res. 1430 - Recognizing the

Bangladesh Genocide of 1971, 117th Congress). It has already been recognised by the the Lemkin Institute for Genocide Prevention and Genocide Watch.

113 The National Board of Bangladesh Women's Rehabilitation received 22,500 applications from raped women, of whom 86 per cent were illiterate and two-thirds rural. Countless cases remained unreported as families preferred secrecy (Yasmin Saikia, *Women, War and the Making of Bangladesh: Remembering 1971*, Thaslima Begum, '"We Lay Like Corpses. Then the Raping Began": 52 Years On, Bangladesh's Rape Camp Survivors Speak Out'.

114 Salil Tripathi, *The Colonel Who Would Not Repent: The Bangladesh War and Its Unquiet Legacy,* pp. 77–78.

115 After partition of British India in 1947, thousands of Muslims from Bihar migrated to East Bengal, which became East Pakistan. They largely supported the Pakistani administration as middle-level government officials. After Bangladesh's independence in 1971, more than a million Urdu-speaking people were stranded in the newly formed Bangladesh and also faced deep stigma as Urdu-speaking 'Biharis'. Until 2008, most remained 'stateless' and lived in appalling conditions, when the government of Bangladesh recognised only their children born after Bangladesh's independence in 1971 as citizens. Between 1973 and 1993, 1,78,069 'Biharis' were also repatriated to Pakistan.

116 The narrative of the famine in the air-conditioned NGOs in Dhaka were very different from the recollections of ordinary villagers I met. The NGOs waxed eloquent about the work of the UN and donors in a war-ravaged country. However, octogenarians we interviewed in the villages had an entirely different tale. They recollected that the only relief they received was from their own local elected leaders who organised langarkhanas (Field Notes, Bangladesh, February–April 2016).

117 Surinder Jodhka and Ghanshyam Shah, 'Comparative Contexts of Discrimination: Caste and Untouchability in South Asia'.

118 Personal communication with Megha Guhathakurta, Director, Research Initiatives, 11 April 2016.

119 But across household interviews, even in Panchagarh, we found an unwritten gender rule—as soon as girls are married, around the age of sixteen, they usually stop riding bicycles unless they have a job. Only paid employment seems to enable married women to secure permission from their families to ride bicycles.
120 Naila Kabeer, 'The Rise of the Daughter-in-Law'.
121 Sonia Amin, *The World of Muslim Women in Colonial Bengal, 1876–1939*.
122 Begum Rokeya Sakhawat Hossain, 'The Worship of Women'.
123 Dagmar Engels, *Beyond Purdah? Women in Bengal, 1890–1939*, p. 1.
124 Brahmo Samaj, which commenced in 1828, was a monotheistic reform movement of the Hindu religion. It flourished during the nineteenth and the early twentieth century and was a part of the Bengal Renaissance.
125 Meredith Borthwick, *The Changing Role of Women in Bengal, 1849–1905*, p. 228.
126 Sonia Amin, *The World of Muslim Women in Colonial Bengal, 1876–1939*.
127 Dagmar Engels, *Beyond Purdah?*, p. 1.
128 Kavita Punjabi, 'Otiter Jed or Times of Revolution: Ila Mitra, the Santals and Tebhaga Movement', p. 58.
129 Ila Mitro, the feminist, who was the leader of the Nachol revolt, shifted to Kolkata after Independence. She acquired a legendary status through the oral traditions across generations of the East Bengali Santhals (Kavita Punjabi, 'Otiter Jed or Times of Revolution', p. 58).
130 One lakh Santhals from across Bangladesh gathered to meet Ila Mitra when she visited the country on the fiftieth anniversary of the Tebhaga Andolan. The tribal community, through their oral tradition, consider the Santhal Rebellion of 1855 to be connected to the Nachol Tebhaga revolt of 1948 (Kavita Punjabi, 'Otiter Jed or Times of Revolution').
131 Martina Mondol, 'Women's Contribution in Language Movement'.
132 E.A.M. Asaduzzaman, 'Women Language Movement Heroes of Nilphamari'.

133 Nayanika Mookherjee, 'Gendered Embodiments: Mapping the Body-Politic of the Raped Woman and the Nation in Bangladesh'.
134 Hameeda Hossain, 'Women's Movements in Bangladesh: The Struggle Within – Europe Solidaire Sans Frontières'.
135 Nayanika Mookherjee, 'Gendered Embodiments'.
136 Interview with Raunaq Jahan, Centre for Policy Dialogue, 2 December 2015.
137 'Birangana' means 'war heroines' and was a term coined by Bangladesh's first Prime Minister Sheikh Mujibur Rahman to refer to the estimated 2,00,000–3,00,000 rape survivors and acknowledged their 'sacrifice' for the freedom of the nation. 'Nari jodha' is a more dignified term coined by women's activists, which means women fighters (Laxmi Murthy, 'The Birangana and the Birth of Bangladesh').
138 Nayanika Mookherjee, *The Spectral Wound*.
139 Yasmin Sakia, *Women, War, and the Making of Bangladesh*, p. 146.
140 Naila Kabeer, *Minus Lives: Women of Bangladesh*, p. 5.
141 Naila Kabeer and Naomi Hossain, 'Achieving Universal Primary Education and Eliminating Gender Disparity', p. 4095.
142 Interview with Raunaq Jahan, Centre for Policy Dialogue, 2 December 2015.
143 Micro-credit involves lending credit in the form of small loans with no collateral largely to women as borrowers. As the borrowers return the loan with interest, in instalments, the repayments are often employed to provide larger loans. Women are often encouraged to form self-help groups to engage in both micro-credit and micro-savings. Self-help groups are also often savings groups, where women collectively pool their savings at regular intervals in order to create a corpus of financial reserves for extending micro-credit, with or without external sources of funds.
144 Shelley Feldman and Florence E. McCarthy, 'Purdah and Changing Patterns of Social Control among Rural Women in Bangladesh'.

5. NEPAL

1. A collection of Maoist songs translated by Matthew W. Maycock, matthewmaycock.com/file/Maoist_Tharu_songs.html, last accessed 17 July 2023.
2. Sujit Mainali, 'How Discriminatory Was the First Muluki Ain against Dalits?'
3. The Print Staff, 'Nepal's Latest Crisis and Its Unstable Political History with 49 PMs in 58 Years'.
4. Yurendra Basnett, *From Politicization of Grievances to Political Violence: An Analysis of the Maoist Movement in Nepal*.
5. Gyan Pradhan, 'Nepal's Civil War and Its Economic Costs'.
6. GoN and UNDP, *Nepal Human Development Report 2014 Beyond Geography—Unlocking Human Potential*; UNDP, *Human Development Report 2005*.
7. Data from the Third Nepal Living Standards Survey quoted in IMF, 'Nepal: Poverty Reduction Strategy Paper Progress Report'.
8. Bishwa Nath Tiwari, 'An Assessment of the Causes of Conflict in Nepal'.
9. As per the SWIID database, Nepal's Gini index increased from 0.40 in 1996 to 0.41 in 2006 but fell to 0.38 in 2010.
10. Stephen Jones, 'The Politics of Social Rights', p. 262.
11. Bandita Sijapati, 'The Quest for Achieving Universal Social Protection in Nepal: Challenges and Opportunities'.
12. Robert Palacios, 'Universal Social Protection: Universal Old-Age and Disability Pensions, and Other Universal Allowances in Nepal'.
13. Nepal's social pension benefit amount is equivalent to 16 per cent of GDP per capita, compared to only 8 per cent in Bangladesh and 5 per cent in India of GDP per capita, respectively.
14. B. Babajanian, 'Tackling Old Age Poverty and Vulnerability'. Nepal's social pension benefit amount is equivalent to 16 per cent of GDP per capita, compared to only 8 per cent in Bangladesh and 5 per cent in India, respectively (Stephen Kidd, Rebecca Calder and Emily Wylde, 'Assessing Targeting Options for Nepal's Social Grants—What Does the Evidence Tell Us?').

15 The Village Development Committee (VDC) conveniently hands over the money to pensioners. However, many Musahars and Doms whom I met during fieldwork near the border areas, though acutely impoverished, do not receive this pension. One eligible and malnourished Dom lady, as many others, said that she did not receive the pension as she did not have a citizenship card. Her application was not processed as she does not have a letter from the VDC where she was born to testify her citizenship. The Nepali government is highly wary of the claims of citizenship of Doms and many communities in the Terai belt and suspect that they may be from India. So, as highly marginalised Dalits, they often face even more discrimination (Field Notes, Sirthouli VDC, Nepal, 25–31 May 2016).
16 Stephen Jones, 'The Politics of Social Rights'.
17 In 2009, Nepal's government initiated the Child Grant, a monthly cash transfer, for up to two children per family under the age of five. Initially, the grant targeted the Karnali region and Dalit families living in poverty in the rest of the country. But it was quickly extended to cover all children aged under five in twenty-five or seventy-seven districts. In 2023, the Child Grant covers around 40 per cent of children under the age of five with NPR 532 (US$4) paid per month per child.
18 Biswas Baral, 'What Is Delaying the Landmark Left Merger in Nepal?'.
19 For example, if Nepal were to lower the age criterion for the universal pension to sixty years and also universalise the child grant to all children under five years of age, then the programme would cover three-fourths of the population and 88 per cent of the poor at 1.5 per cent of GDP (Stephan Kidd, Rebecca Calder and Emily Wylde, 'Assessing Targeting Options for Nepal's Social Grants').
20 Keshav Acharya, 'Evaluating Institutional Capability of Nepali Grassroot Organisations for Service Delivery Functions'.
21 Field Notes, Sirthouli VDC, Nepal, 25–31 May 2016.
22 Sangita Thebe Limbu, 'Nepal's House of Cards: Are Women Included or Co-opted in Politics?'

23 Y.B. Malla, 'Changing Policies and the Persistence of Patron-Client Relations in Nepal: Stakeholders' Responses to Changes in Forest Policies'.
24 John Whelpton, 'The Quest for "Development": Economy and Environment, 1951–1991'.
25 Murari Raj Joshi, 'Community Forestry Programs in Nepal and Their Effects on Poorer Households'; John Whelpton, 'The Quest for "Development"'.
26 Ridish K. Pokharel, 'Pro-poor Programs Financed through Nepal's Community Forestry Funds: Does Income Matter?'.
27 Since the school principal was an active member of both the school management committee and community forest user group (Field Notes, Bhimstan VDC, Nepal, 16–22 May 2016).
28 World Bank, *Moving Up the Ladder: Poverty Reduction and Social Mobility in Nepal*.
29 Shridhar Thapa and Sanjaya Acharya, 'Remittances and Household Expenditure in Nepal: Evidence from Cross-Section Data', p. 11.
30 Field Notes, Sirthouli VDC, Nepal, 25–31 May 2016.
31 Ann Vogel and Kim Korinek, 'Passing by the Girls? Remittance Allocation for Educational Expenditures and Social Inequality in Nepal's Households 2003–2004'.
32 Interview with Feminist Dalit Organisation (FEDO), Kathmandu, Nepal, 15 June 2016.
33 Prakash A. Raj, *Maoists in the Land of Buddha*.
34 Uddhab Pyakurel, *Maoist Movement in Nepal*; John Whelpton, 'The Quest for "Development"'.
35 Harka Gurung, 'The Dalit Context'.
36 The code classified people into five groups, 'Tagadhari (those wearing the sacred thread called Janai across their torso), Masinay Matuwali (enslavable liquor drinkers), Namasine Matuwali (unenslavable liquor drinkers), Pani Nachalne Chhoichhito Halnu Naparne (Impure but touchables including foreigners, Muslims and Christians also fall under this category), and Pani Nachalne Chhoi Chhito Halnu Parne (Impure and Untouchable, upon touching whom one needed to purify

themselves by sprinkling gold-dipped water)'. Sujit Mainali, 'How Discriminatory Was the First Muluki Ain against Dalits?'
37 Please see Appendix A16.
38 Harka Gurung, 'The Dalit Context'. See Appendix A17.
39 Krishna Kant Adhikari, 'Criminal Cases and Their Punishments: Before and During the Period of Jang Bahadur'.
40 Rajan Khatiwoda, Simon Cubelic and Axel Michaels, 'The Muluki Ain of 1854: Nepal's First Legal Code'; Amish Raj Mulmi 'Codifying the Breaking of Wind'. Please see Appendix A17.
41 John Whelpton, 'The Quest for "Development"'.
42 GoN, *Nepal – National Population and Housing Census 2011, Marks 100 Years of Census Taking in Nepal.*
43 GoN and UNDP, *Nepal Human Development Report 2014: Beyond Geography.* Inequalities also have a geographic dimension. In 2010, the average income of a pahadi Brahmin in the hills was twice as high as a Dalit in the Terai plains (GoN 2010).
44 GoN and UNDP, *Nepal Human Development Report 2014: Beyond Geography.*
45 In Ward 1 of Sirthouli VDC, for example, 5 per cent was reserved for Dalits (Sarki, Khami, Musahars), 5 per cent for Janajatis (Dhanuar, Magar, Bhote), 5 per cent for Adivasis (Mahato), 10 per cent for women, 5 per cent for children and adolescents and 5 per cent for the differently abled (Field Notes, Nepal, 25–31 May 2016).
46 ILO, *Labour Migration for Employment: A Status Report for Nepal 2014/2015.*
47 Field Notes, Sirthouli VDC, Nepal, 25 May 2016.
48 Yogendra B. Gurung, et al., *Nepal Social Inclusion Survey 2012: Caste, Ethnic and Gender Dimensions of Socio-Economic Development, Governance and Social Solidarity.*
49 'People's War' was a term coined by Chairman Mao Tse Tung who founded the People's Republic of China.
50 Prakash A. Raj, *Maoists in the Land of Buddha.*
51 Baburam Bhattarai, *Monarchy vs Democracy: The Epic Fight*

       in Nepal. The ruling families in the hills of central and western Nepal are known as Thakuris, who claim descent from Indian Rajputs from Mewar (Krishna Hachhethu, 'The Nepali State and the Maoist Insurgency, 1996-2001').
52   Yurendra Basnett, *From Politicization of Grievances to Political Violence*.
53   Uddhab Pyakurel, *Maoist Movement in Nepal*.
54   My sample district Sindhuli in the eastern hills was also one of the hotbeds of the Maoist movement from its early days. On 8 September 2002, the rebels attacked and killed forty-nine policemen at the police post in one of my sample villages at midnight. They used women and children as human shields. A teachers in one of the other villages narrated how their school playground was converted into a rebel camp (S.D. Muni, *Maoist Insurgency in Nepal: The Challenge and the Response*).
55   Field Notes, Sirthouli VDC, Sindhuli district, Nepal, 25 April–1 May 2016.
56   Alpa Shah and Judith Pettigrew, *Windows into a Revolution: Ethnographies of Maoism in India and Nepal*.
57   Field Notes, Ranibas VDC, Sindhuli district, Nepal, 3–6 June 2016.
58   Hisila Yami, *People's War and Women's Liberation in Nepal*, pp. 121–22.
59   Prakash A. Raj, *Maoists in the Land of Buddha*.
60   Michael Hutt, *Himalayan People's War: Nepal's Maoist Rebellion*.
61   Sara Schneiderman and Mark Turin, 'The Path to Jan Sarkar in Dolakha District: Towards an Ethnography of the Maoist Movement'.
62   Field Notes, Sirthouli VDC, Sindhuli district, Nepal, 25–31 May 2016.
63   Field Notes, Sirthouli VDC, Nepal, 25–31 May 2016.
64   Even in village homes, we experienced abhorrent inter-dining taboos. In one Bahun home, we saw an orphan Dalit adolescent boy whom they had 'adopted' (more as a child labourer rather than a son). He was not permitted to eat within the house.

He had to wait until the rest of the family finished their meal and after he had washed their dirty dishes. In another Bahun home that we stayed in, my translator and I were not permitted to enter the kitchen while the lady of the house was cooking, although we ate there afterwards, sitting on the floor with the rest of the family (Field Notes, Sindhuli district, 5–10 April 2015 and Bhimstan VDC, 16–22 May 2016).

65 Hisilia Yami, *People's War and Women's Liberation in Nepal*, p. 122.
66 Ina Zharkevich, *Maoist People's War*.
67 Michael Hutt, *Himalayan People's War*.
68 Jeevan Sharma, *Political Economy of Social Change and Development in Nepal*.
69 In the midst of the guerrilla war, the most powerful woman leader of the guerrillas published the findings of a survey for an international audience in the *Economic and Political Weekly* even though it had a number of unsavoury revelations such as the acute need felt by women cadres for 'family planning' and 'menstrual hygiene', and the preponderance of sexual violence even within the force (Parvati, 'Women in the People's War in Nepal').
70 As per international law, under the Optional Protocol to the Convention on the Rights of the Child, non-state guerrilla rebels are forbidden from recruiting anyone under the age of eighteen years.
71 HRW, 'Hidden Apartheid'.
72 HRW, 'Silenced and Forgotten'.
73 Interview with female head of a government body to monitor transparency (Field Notes, Kathmandu, 15–16 June 2016).
74 Hisila Yami, *People's War and Women's Liberation in Nepal*, p. 124.
75 Hisilia Yami, *People's War and Women's Liberation in Nepal*, p. 9.
76 Ina Zharkevich, *Maoist People's War*.
77 Ina Zharkevich, *Maoist People's War*, p. 141.
78 Keshav Acharya, 'Evaluating Institutional Capability of Nepali Grassroot Organisations for Service Delivery Functions'.

79 Lauren Leve, '"Failed Development" and Rural Revolution in Nepal: Rethinking Subaltern Consciousness and Women's Empowerment'.
80 Shobha Gautam, Amrita Banskota and Rita Manchanda, 'Where There Are No Men: Women in the Maoist Insurgency in Nepal', p. 214.
81 Female Headed Households (% of households with a female head), World Development Indicators.
82 Cardona Justino, R. Mitchell and C. Müller, 'Quantifying the Impact of Women's Participation in Post-conflict Economic Recovery'.
83 Patti Petesch, 'Women's Empowerment Arising from Violent Conflict and Recovery: Life Stories from Four Middle-Income Countries'.
84 Cardono Justino, R. Mitchell and C. Müller, 'Quantifying the Impact of Women's Participation in Post-conflict Economic Recovery'.
85 Penny Summerfield, *Women, War and Social Change: Women in Britain in World War II*.
86 Pilar Domingo, et al., *Assessment of the Evidence of Links between Gender Equality, Peacebuilding and Statebuilding: Literature Review*.
87 Cardono Justino, R. Mitchell and C. Müller, 'Quantifying the Impact of Women's Participation in Post-conflict Economic Recovery'.
88 Nepal's Gender Inequality Index improved from 0.71 in 1995 to 0.45 in 2021. In contrast, India's value was worse at 0.49 and Bangladesh at 0.530 in 2021.
89 Punam Yadav, 'White Sari: Transforming Widowhood in Nepal'.
90 Shobha Gautam, Amrita Banskota and Rita Manchanda, 'Where There Are No Men', p. 233.
91 The 2015 Constitution, revised in 2016, guarantees gender quotas both in reserved seats and legislated candidate quotas. Article 91(2) of the Nepali Constitution specifies that there must be 'one woman out of the Speaker and the Deputy Speaker' in the Parliament.

92 Sangita Thebe Limbu, 'Nepal's House of Cards'. The law mandates that in each ward, there will be one chair and four ward members—two of whom must be women, including one Dalit woman.

93 The share of Dalits in Nepal's population is estimated to be between 18 and 20 per cent as per the just released 2021 census. So the proportional representation sub-quotas negotiated by Dalit and feminist activists in Nepal does represent a landmark policy of social inclusion. In India, one-third of the seats of panchayati raj institutions (at the lowest tier of governance) and one-third of the chairperson posts are reserved for women. Within these reserved women's seats, one-third are reserved for Dalit/Adivasi women, unlike Nepal's higher sub-quota of half (50 per cent) for Dalit women.

94 India's Women's Reservation Act (The Constitution [128th Amendment] Bill, 2008) has been enacted in September 2023. Women currently represent only 14 per cent of Indian parliamentarians. Amongst feminists the lack of inter-sectional 'quotas within quotas' has been an important point of debate and contention which 'seemed to set (mainly upper caste) feminists against (mainly male) OBC leaders' (Gail Omvedt, 'Women and PR'; Meena Dhanda, 'Representation for Women: Should Feminists Support Quotas?'; Nivedita Menon, 'Elusive "Woman": Feminism and Women's Reservation Bill'; Surbhi Karwa, 'Intersectionality, The Missing Link in the Women's Reservation Bill'). However, the newly enacted law neither has sub-quotas for OBCs, nor minority religions. Further, the rotational constituencies for women have also been criticised.

95 Bhola Paswan, 'Data Reveals Local Elections a Disaster for Gender Equality'.

96 Field Notes, Bhimstan VDC, 16–22 May 2016.

97 Shobha Gautam, Amrita Banskota and Rita Manchanda, 'Where There Are No Men'; Punam Yadav, 'White Sari'.

98 Urmila Aryal, 'All Nepal Women's Association'; Hisila Yami, *People's War and Women's Liberation in Nepal*.

99 Shobha Gautam, Amrita Banskota and Rita Manchanda, 'Where There Are No Men', p. 215.

100 Journalist Aditya Adhikari lucidly explains this genesis of the Nepali communist movement in his fascinating book *From the Bullet to the Ballot Box: The Story of Nepal's Maoist Revolution*.
101 Punam Yadav, *Social Transformation in Post-conflict Nepal*.
102 Conversation with leading women cadre member of the Maoist party, Field Notes, Kathmandu, Nepal, 15–16 June 2016.
103 Often women or men could have more than one proposal put forward by the party as documented in the interviews with former combatants (Punam Yadav, *Social Transformation in Post-conflict Nepal*, p. 109). Yet, after the war, several couples, especially with Dalit brides, faced opposition when they returned to their village (Interview with a member of the Feminist Dalit Organisation—FEDO—on 13 June 2016). Still, after the conflict, the Nepali government institutionalised a 1,00,000 Nepali Rupee ($1,270) cash reward to encourage inter-caste Dalit marriages (AFP, 'Nepal Introduces Grants for Inter-Caste Marriages').
104 Interview with a high-ranking women Maoist party official, 13 June 2016.
105 Punam Yadav, *Social Transformation in Post-conflict Nepal*, p. 103.
106 Lauren Leve, '"Failed Development" and Rural Revolution in Nepal', p. 127.
107 Hisila Yami, *From Liberation to First Lady*.
108 The survey was spearheaded by Comrade Parvati, which is the nom de guerre of Hisila Yami, the most influential female combatant amongst the Maoist guerrilla rebels. She also summarised the survey in her 2021 memoir, *Hisila: From Liberation to First Lady*.
109 Parvati, 'Women in the People's War in Nepal'. The survey also specifies that 'while unmarried women outnumbered married ones, when it came to having children, those bearing children out-numbered those without'.
110 Hisila Yami, *People's War and Women's Liberation in Nepal*, p. 3.

111 Yurendra Basnett, *From Politicization of Grievances to Political Violence*.
112 Chhaupadi Pratha is a traditional custom where menstruating women are considered untouchable and have to live in communal sheds away from their homes. Although the Nepali Supreme Court declared the practice illegal in 2005, it continues to be practised in the far western region.
113 Teej is a Hindu festival where women fast for the long life of their husbands, and to find suitable husbands.
114 Hisila Yami, *People's War and Women's Liberation in Nepal*.
115 Punam Yadav, 'White Sari'.
116 Punam Yadav, 'White Sari'.
117 K.C. Luna and Gemma Van Der Haar, 'Living Maoist Gender Ideology: Experiences of Women Ex-combatants in Nepal'.
118 Punam Yadav, 'White Sari'.

6. BIHAR

1 S. Sheoraj 'Bechain', *Voices of Awakening*.
2 In July 2016, the viral video of the public flogging of Dalit youth in Una block led to the anti-caste Dalit Asmita Yatra led by Jignesh Mewani in Gujarat which dominated the newspaper headlines for weeks. The Bihari incident however did not lead to any anti-caste protest. Mohammad Sajjad, 'Atrocity against Dalits in Bihar'.
3 Musahars, traditionally denigrated as 'rat eaters', are amongst the most discriminated Dalits and are at the bottom of the caste hierarchy.
4 Survey Data and Field Notes, Bihar, August to November 2016. In contrast, in Kishanganj only 15 per cent of Dalit households expressed the same prejudice in my survey.
5 Christophe Jaffrelot, *India's Silent Revolution*.
6 The Paswans, also known as Dusadh, are Dalits who in urban spaces often find employment as security guards.
7 Aparna John, *Performance of India's Community Nutrition Workers*, p. 75; Aparna John, et al., 'Factors Influencing the

Performance of Community Health Workers: A Qualitative Study of Anganwadi Workers from Bihar, India'.

8   Though the incumbent chief minister Nitish Kumar, in a grand coalition, won the 2015 election with a landslide, two years later the coalition dissolved and his party joined hands with the right-wing BJP to retain power as a regional satrap. In 2022, Nitish Kumar announced that the alliance with the BJP was over and he has now aligned with the Indian National Developmental Inclusive Alliance (INDIA) coalition for the forthcoming 2024 polls.

9   In both the 2015 and 2020 post-poll Bihari surveys, 31 and 36 per cent of voters respectively identified development as the most important issue. Cumulatively, with unemployment, poverty and hunger, the proportion was 46 and 61 percent respectively as per Lokniti-CSDS (Shreyas Sardesai, et al., 'Decoding the Close Bihar Election 2020 Verdict').

10 The per capita income of Bihar in 2021-22 was even lower than other impoverished states of Uttar Pradesh, Odisha, Jharkhand and Madhya Pradesh at INR 54,383 or approximately USD 652 per person per year on an average. IANS, Bihar per capita income is lower than Jharkhand, UP and Odisha: CAG.

11 Government Order (ICDS/40025/25-2012/4636 dated 13/08/2014).

12 IIPS and MoHFW, 'National Family Health Survey (NFHS-5) India Report'. In Bihar, 76 per cent of deliveries overall and 71 per cent among Dalits take place in a health facility compared to 89 per cent, the national average.

13 The National Family Health Survey 2019–2021 is based on a representative sample of women in the 15–49 years age group at the national, state and district levels. The 2011 census also indicated that 46 per cent of women above the age of fifteen in Bihar were illiterate compared to the national average of 35 per cent.

14 Girish Mishra, 'Review of the Internal Colony'; Sachchidanand Sinha, *An Internal Colony: A Study in Regional Exploitation*.

15 Under the policy of 'freight equalisation' introduced soon after

India gained independence, the central government guaranteed uniform prices nationwide for essential commodities, which included minerals such as coal, steel and cement. As a result of this protectionist policy which heavily subsidised the transportation of minerals within the country, private industries preferred to locate their factories and industries nearer the ports in western, eastern and southern India for onward international trade. Till this policy was abandoned with economic liberalisation, it severely hampered the economic incentive for industrialisation especially in the mineral-rich, landlocked areas of Jharkhand, Bihar, Chhattisgarh and Madhya Pradesh which had no port facilities.

16 Golam Rasul and Eklabya Sharma, 'Understanding the Poor Economic Performance of Bihar and Uttar Pradesh, India: A Macro-Perspective'.
17 Census of India 2011, *Population Enumeration Data (Final Population)*.
18 Shaibal Gupta, 'Non-development of Bihar: A Case of Retarded Sub-nationalism', p. 1496-1502
19 Prerna Singh, *How Solidarity Works for Welfare: Subnationalism and Social Development in India*.
20 Shaibal Gupta, 'Non-development of Bihar', p. 1500.
21 Shaibal Gupta, 'Non-development of Bihar', pp. 1496–1502.
22 Shaibal Gupta, 'Non-development of Bihar', p. 1496.
23 Shaibal Gupta, 'Non-development of Bihar', p. 1500.
24 Rajni Kothari, *Caste in Indian Politics*.
25 Awanish Kumar, 'A Class Analysis of the "Bihari Menace"'.
26 Awanish Kumar, 'Where Is Caste in Development?'.
27 Sanjay Kumar and Rakesh Ranjan, 'Bihar: Development Matters'.
28 Chirashree Das Gupta, 'Unravelling Bihar's "Growth Miracle"'.
29 Gerry Rodgers, et al. *The Challenge of Inclusive Development in Rural Bihar*
30 M. Rajshekhar, *Despite the State: Why India Lets Its People Down and How They Cope*.
31 Gerry Rodgers, et al., *The Challenge of Inclusive Development in Rural Bihar*.

32 Yuko Tsujita, Hisaya Oda and Prabhat Ghosh, 'Development and Intra-state Disparities in Bihar'.
33 Yuko Tsujita, Hisaya Oda and Prabhat Ghosh, 'Development and Intra-state Disparities in Bihar'.
34 In Bihar, 86 per cent of Scheduled Caste households do not own land compared to the highest in the Green Revolution states of 87 per cent in Punjab and 92 per cent in Haryana based on the 70th round of the National Sample Survey in 2013 (Ishan Anand, 'Dalit Emancipation and the Land Question').
35 Swati Narayan, 'Towards Equality in Healthcare'.
36 Santosh Singh, *Ruled or Misruled: Story and Destiny of Bihar*, p. 328.
37 Christophe Jaffrelot, *India's Silent Revolution*, p. 256.
38 Eram Agha, 'Hindu Right Wrongly Says Muslims Brought Beef-eating—Hindutva History Is a Mystery: D.N. Jha'.
39 Census 2011: Table SC-08: Educational Level by Age and Sex for Population Age 7 and Above.
40 In Patna, we were informed that the Nitish government had appointed shiksha mitras (education supporters), tola sewaks (hamlet volunteers) and vikas mitra (development assistants) from among Musahar communities themselves on handsome stipends, to ensure that children attend schools, but there was no sign of them in schools in the hamlets we visited.
41 George J. Kunnath, *Rebels from the Mud Houses: Dalits and the Making of the Maoist Revolution in Bihar*, p. 56.
42 For example, 'A Kshatriya who commits adultery with an unguarded Bráhman woman shall be punished with the highest amercement; a Vaisya doing the same shall be deprived of the whole of his property; and a Súdra shall be burnt alive, wound round in mats' (Shamasastry, *Kautilya's Arthashastra*).
43 Pataliputra refers to modern Patna, the capital of Bihar.
44 Dalit caste—they are tasked with cremating corpses.
45 B.S. Verma, *Socio-Religious, Economic and Literary Condition of Bihar*.
46 M.N. Srinivas, 'Mobility in the Caste System'.

47 M.N. Srinivas, *Caste in Modern India and Other Essays*, pp. 17–18.
48 M.N. Srinivas, 'A Note on Sanskritization and Westernization'. French sociologist Gabriel Tarde has also described similar 'laws of imitation' by the socially inferior classes; B.R. Ambedkar, 'Social Stagnation'.
49 Christophe Jaffrelot, *India's Silent Revolution*; Pradip Bose, 'Mobility and Conflict: Social Roots of Caste Violence in Bihar'.
50 Pradip Bose, 'Mobility and Conflict', p. 373.
51 Pradip Bose, 'Mobility and Conflict', p. 373.
52 Pradip Bose, 'Mobility and Conflict', pp. 196–97.
53 Pradip Bose, 'Mobility and Conflict'.
54 Since the 1850s, the British government used the term 'Depressed Classes' to refer to the former untouchable castes and indigenous tribes. In the 1935 Government of India Act, the term 'Scheduled Castes' and 'Scheduled Tribes' replaced the generic classification.
55 Christophe Jaffrelot, *India's Silent Revolution,* pp. 175 and 206. In 1923, M.C. Rajah led a delegation to the Madras government to complain that the non-Brahmins who got twenty-eight seats in the Madras Legislative Assembly after pressure from the Justice Party had benefited only the elite non-Brahmins, and not Untouchables. So, the Depressed Classes category was enhanced separately.
56 Prakash Louis, 'Lynchings in Bihar: Reassertion of Dominant Castes'.
57 Katherine S. Newman and Sukhdeo Thorat, *Blocked by Caste: Economic Discrimination in Modern India.* Initially, only Hindus were defined as Scheduled Castes (SCs) under the Constitution, but in 1956, Sikhs were included and in 1990 Buddhists too, but Christians and Muslims were never considered for inclusion in the lists. In October 1994, the Kerala state government decided to include the state's entire Muslim population in the OBC category by identifying them as 'Mappilas', thus making them eligible for reserved positions in employment and education institutions.

58 Babasaheb predicted that 'in politics we will have equality and in social and economic life we will have inequality' (B.R. Ambedkar, Speech at the Constituent Assembly, 25 November 1949, in BAWS Collection, 13, p. 1249)
59 Christophe Jaffrelot, *India's Silent Revolution*.
60 HRW, 'Hidden Apartheid: Caste Discrimination against India's "Untouchables"'.
61 OI and ANSISS, 'Mapping Inequality in Bihar'; G.R. Sahay, 'Substantially Present but Invisible, Excluded and Marginalised: A Study of Musahars in Bihar'.
62 Sonalde Desai and Reeve Vanneman, *India Human Development Survey-II (IHDS-II), 2011-12*.
63 B.R. Ambedkar, *What Congress and Gandhi Have Done to the Untouchables*, in BAWS Collection, 9(3), p. 380.
64 Christophe Jaffrelot, *India's Silent Revolution*, p. 235.
65 Christophe Jaffrelot, *India's Silent Revolution*.
66 HRW, 'Broken People: Caste Violence against India's "Untouchables"', p. 39.
67 George Kunnath, *Rebels from the Mud Houses*, p. 18.
68 George Kunnath, *Rebels from the Mud Houses*, p. 54.
69 Prakash Louis, 'Bihar: Class War Spreads to New Areas', p. 2206.
70 Ashwani Kumar, *Peasant Unrest, Community Warriors and State Power in India: The Case of Private Caste Senas (Armies) in Bihar*.
71 HRW, 'Broken People'.
72 Ashwani Kumar, *Peasant Unrest, Community Warriors and State Power in India*, p. 192.
73 George Kunnath, *Rebels from the Mud Houses*, p. 136.
74 Mohammad Sajjad, 'Atrocity against Dalits in Bihar', p. 21.
75 In 2007, the Nitish Kumar government created the Mahadalit category to signify the poorest amongst the Dalits. He set up the Mahadalit Commission which classified twenty-one of twenty-two Dalit castes in Bihar as Mahadalits. The Dusadhs (Paswans) are the only Dalit caste who were left out who constitute 30 per cent of the Dalit population in Bihar. However, this has been criticised as an electoral ploy to marginalise popular politician

Ramvilas Paswan with a Dusadh vote bank (George Kunnath, 'Compliance or Defiance? The Case of Dalits and Mahadalits').
76   IE, 'Explained: Who are Mahadalits?'
77   Manish Kumar, 'Temple Cleaned, Idols Washed after Bihar Chief Minister's Visit'.
78   Tirthankar Roy, *The Economic History of India, 1857–1947*.
79   Pradip Bose, 'Mobility and Conflict'.
80   Under the Permanent Settlement since the British only demanded a fixed quantum, by the time of India's independence, the zamindars on an average paid to the British only one-tenth of the gross rental they charged tenants and seized the rest. Arvind Das, *Agrarian Movement in India: Studies in 20th Century Bihar*.
81   Subhas Bhattacharya, 'The Indigo Revolt of Bengal', p. 13.
82   Christophe Jaffrelot, *India's Silent Revolution*, p. 256.
83   R.K. Barik, *Land and Caste Politics in Bihar*, p. 41.
84   Christophe Jaffrelot, *India's Silent Revolution*, p. 265.
85   Ram Sewak, 'Congress Socialist Party in Bihar—1934-39'.
86   Jagpal Singh, 'Karpoori Thakur: A Socialist Leader in the Hindi Belt'.
87   Peter Robb, 'Peasants' Choices? Indian Agriculture and the Limits of Commercialization in Nineteenth-century Bihar'.
88   R.K. Barik, *Land and Caste Politics in Bihar*, p. 149; Indu Bharti, 'Bihar's Bane: Slow Progress on Land Reforms'.
89   GOI, 'The Causes and Nature of Current Agrarian Tensions'.
90   Alakh Sharma and Jerry Rodgers, 'Structural Change in Bihar's Rural Economy'.
91   Archana K. Roy, et al., *A Report on Causes and Consequences of Outmigration in the Middle Ganga Plain*.
92   Field Notes, Bihar, August–September 2016. The cult of Chhathi Mai, the Mother Goddess who 'ensures the perpetuation of vansha (lineage) by granting the boon of having sons' is a more recent introduction (K.S. Singh, 'Solar Traditions in Tribal and Folk Cultures of India').
93   IIPS and ICF, 'National Family Health Survey (NFHS-5), 2019-21: Bihar.
94   Field Notes, Bangladesh, June 2015.

95 Dashien, referred as 'Durga Puja', is the biggest festival in the Indian state of West Bengal which was socio-culturally, linguistically and political integrated with Bangladesh prior to Independence.
96 Begum Rokeya Sakhawat Hossain, 'The Worship of Women'.
97 Parmeshwar (God) is also a wordplay for husband as the colloquial Hindi term 'Pati-Parmeshwar' implies that husbands are considered to be equivalent to God. *Main kiski aurat hun?* (Whose Woman Am I?), a poem by Savita Singh, Bihari feminist poet and academic. Quoted in Vaishnavi Mahurkar, 'Feminist Poetry: Contemporary Woman Poets Who Challenge Patriarchy In Hindi & Urdu' with the rendition of the original poem (Savita Singh, 'Hindi *Kavita*: *Main Kiski Aurat Hun*').
98 This social norm apparently goes back to the nineteenth-century Bengal (Dagmar Engels, *Beyond Purdah?*, p. 20) and was also confirmed by ten of my Bihari surveyors as prevalent in their own homes among the elder generation.
99 GoI, 2016, National Family Health Survey 4, 2015-16, State Fact Sheet Bihar, Mumbai: International Institute for Population Sciences and Bangladesh (2007 DHS) and Nepal (2016 DHS) compiled from statcompiler.com for the question 'Physical or sexual violence committed by husband/partner in last 12 months'.
100 George Bühler, 'The Laws of Manu'.
101 Dola literally means the palanquin in which women were carried to their husband's homes.
102 Sumit S. Srivastava, 'Violence and Dalit Women's Resistance in Rural Bihar', p. 35.
103 Sati was the traditional custom to burn widows on their husband's funeral pyre. It was banned in 1829.
104 Saroj Kumari, *Role of Women in the Freedom Movement in Bihar, 1912–1947.*
105 By 1848, Savitribai Phule with her husband Jyotiba Phule and Fatima Sheikh had opened the first school for girls in Bhide Wada Pune. In 1882, Swarnakumari Devi (sister of Rabindranath Tagore) founded the Ladies Society in Calcutta

to support widows. In 1889 Pandita Ramabai, herself a widow from an inter-caste marriage, started the Arya Mahila Samaj in Pune to oppose child marriages and Sharada Sadan in Mumbai largely to educate child widows. Sarala Devi Chaudharani founded the Bharat Stree Mahamandal in Allahabad in 1910, the first national-level women's organisation, apart from editing a women's magazine, founding a girl's school and participating in the freedom movement.

106 Saroj Kumari, *Role of Women in the Freedom Movement in Bihar*, p. 55. The observation was by Kamala Nehru, a prominent freedom fighter, and also Jawaharlal Nehru's wife and Indira Gandhi's mother.

107 Suruchi Thapar-Bjorkert, *Women in the Indian National Movement: Unseen Faces and Unheard Voices, 1930–42*, p. 59.

108 Popularly referred to as the Sarda Act was passed by the Imperial Legislative Council in 1929. The law fixed the age of marriage at fourteen years for girls and eighteen for boys. Suruchi Thapar-Bjorkert, *Women in the Indian National Movement*, p. 59.

109 Suruchi Thapar-Bjorkert, *Women in the Indian National Movement*.

110 Radha Kumar, *The History of Doing: An Illustrated Account of Movements for Women's Rights and Feminism in India, 1800–1990*; Sheila Rowbotham, *Women in Movement: Feminism and Social Action*.

111 Radha Kumar, *The History of Doing*, p. 103.

112 Radha Kumar, *The History of Doing*, p. 103.

113 The Naxalite violence in central Bihar has been characterised as 'flaming fields'.

114 Indu B. Sinha, '"Escape" and "Struggle": Routes to Women's Liberation in Bihar'.

115 Abhishek Bhalla, 'Women Flock to Naxal Cause: Government Figures Reveal 60 Per Cent of Active Maoists Are Female'; Pratibha Singh, 'Women's Role in the Naxalite Movement'.

116 Alpa Shah, 'Humaneness and Contradictions'.

117 Hisila Yami, *People's War and Women's Liberation in Nepal*.

118   Kusum Lata, 'The Women's Question in the Naxalite Movement in Bihar: Experiences of Women Leaders of Nari Mukti Sangharsh Samiti (NMSS) and Nari Mukti Sangh (NMS)'.
119   Indu Sinha and Arvind Sinha, 'Ranveer Sena and "Massacre Widows"'.
120   Sumit S. Srivastava, 'Violence and Dalit Women's Resistance in Rural Bihar', p. 37.
121   On 9 October 2013, the Patna High Court set all the accused free citing 'lack of evidence'. On 1 April 2010, the trial court had convicted twenty-six of whom sixteen were to face the death penalty and ten life terms.
122   Quoted in Ashwani Kumar, *Peasant Unrest*, p. 196.
123   Rajesh Kumar Nayak, 'Naxalism, Private Caste-based Militias and Rural Violence in Central Bihar'.
124   Sharmila Rege, 'Dalit Women Talk Differently: A Critique of "Difference" and towards a Dalit Feminist Standpoint Position'.
125   Mohammed Tarique, 'How the Muzaffarpur Sex Scandal Was Unearthed'.
126   Mohammad Sajjad, 'The Shocking Silence of Muzaffarpur'.

7. SOUTHERN SUPERMODELS: SRI LANKA, KERALA AND TAMIL NADU

1   TOI, 'Imitate the English Suffragettes: Advice to Colombo Women'.
2   Kerala State Poverty Eradication Mission, https://www.kudumbashree.org/pages/7.
3   Pranab Choudhury, Rana Roy and Aswani Munnangi, 'Group Leasing Approach to Sustain Farming and Rural Livelihoods: The Journey of Women Farmers in Kudumbashree Kerala'; Hyfa M. Ali and Leyanna S. George, 'A Qualitative Analysis of the Impact of Kudumbashree and MGNREGA on the Lives of Women Belonging to a Coastal Community in Kerala'.
4   Consistently over the last fifteen years, due to low NREGA wages, women have constituted more than half of all NREGA workers based on self-selection by rural households. However, it is the southern states of Kerala (90 per cent in 2002-

23) and Tamil Nadu (86 per cent) which have consistently had the highest participation of women compared to the impoverished states of Uttar Pradesh (38 per cent), Odisha (48 per cent) and Bihar (56 per cent). This feminisation of the government-run public works programme contrasts sharply with the fact that India has amongst the lowest female labour force participation rates in the world in paid employment, which has declined substantially in the last two decades (from around 30 per cent to 20 per cent). (Swati Narayan, 'Breaking New Ground: Women's Employment in India's NREGA, the Pandemic Lifeline').

5 The National Food Security Act as a matter of legal right guarantees two of every there Indians ration cards to purchase subsidised foodgrains. The Kerala government has expanded this programme to ensure near-universal coverage though many ration cards here for wealthier families offer limited or no subsidy.

6 Anto P. Joseph, 'How Kerala is Feeding Its 3.48 Crore Residents, Migrants amid the COVID-19 Lockdown'.

7 Rex Casinader, 'Making Kerala Model More Intelligible'; Thomas Timberg, 'Regions in Indian Development'.

8 S. Vivek, *Delivering Public Services Effectively: Tamil Nadu and Beyond*.

9 The focus of the second part of this book is to map the commonalities between the progressive Southern Triad. Mill's 'Method of Logic' forms the basis of this analysis to draw lessons from 'similarities in similar cases'.

10 In East Asia, the first tier Newly Industrialising Countries (NICs) which industrialised between the mid-1960s and 1980s are considered to be Japan, South Korea, Taiwan, Hong Kong and Singapore. The second tier in Southeast Asia which industrialised in the 1990s are Thailand and Malaysia, and some have included China and Vietnam, which in the 1980s moved away from Communism (Ha-Joon Chang, *The East Asian Development Experience*).

11 Jean Drèze, 'The Gujarat Muddle'.

12 Jean Drèze, 'The Gujarat Muddle'; P.K. Viswanathan and Chandra Sekhar Bahinipati, 'Growth and Human Development in the Regional Economy of Gujarat, India: An Analysis of Missed Linkages'; Himani Baxi, *Social Expenditure and Human Development in Gujarat*.
13 The secondary data on the Southern Supermodels has for decades indicated their superiority in human development compared to other Indian states. So, a primary survey would not only have been superfluous, but also required translation in three additional languages with dear financial expenditure for a doctoral student.
14 The earliest references to coconuts in Kerala appears in the tenth century in a temple inscription which describes the fruit as 'tengai', where 'ten' means south, as it was introduced either from Sri Lanka or the South Sea Pacific islands (Helaine Selin, *Encyclopaedia of the History of Science, Technology, and Medicine in Non-Western Cultures*). According to oral folk tradition, the Ezhavas, the largest caste group in Kerala, strongly associated with coconut trees through their traditional occupation as toddy tappers, also identify themselves as originally from Ceylon and as erstwhile Buddhists (Filippo Osella and Caroline Osella, *Social Mobility in Kerala: Modernity and Identity in Conflict*).
15 The island has had many names throughout its history. To Tamils, it has always been known as Eelam while to the Sinhalas as Lanka. For Arabs it was Serendib (from which the English word serendipity is derived) and to the British, Ceylon. After independence the Sinhala-dominated government officially changed the name to Sri Lanka in 1972 (John Holt, *The Sri Lanka Reader: History, Culture, Politics*).
16 Please see the timelines in Appendices A18 to A20.
17 Charles Tilly, *Durable Inequality*, p. 193; *Social Movements*.
18 Robert L. Hardgrave Jr, 'Caste in Kerala: A Preface to the Elections'.
19 G. Aloysius, *Interpreting Kerala's Social Development*, p. 5.
20 G.K. Lieten, 'The Human Development Puzzle in Kerala', p. 47.

21 Ezhavas were the upper tier of the marginalised castes, who were a buffer between the Brahmins and Nairs and the 'untouchables'. Their hereditary occupation was extracting coconut and palm wine and managing breweries.
22 G. Aloysius, *Interpreting Kerala's Social Development*.
23 The Maharaja of Travancore signed a treaty with the British East India Company in 1788 to protect his kingdom from Tipu Sultan, which opened the doors for the entry of the Christian missionaries. The first congregation was formed in 1685 (R.N. Yesudas, *A People's Revolt in Travancore*).
24 R.N. Yesudas, *Colonel John Munro in Travancore*; *The History of the London Missionary Society in Travancore, 1806–1908*.
25 In Malabar district, over 90 per cent of the land was owned by the Namboodri Brahmins or Nairs (as janmis), and the Muslim Mappilas were frequently evicted as tenants. The 'Moplah Outrages', as it was called by the British administration at that time, occurred between 1836 and the final rebellion in 1921-22. The majority of the protests were in the first sixteen years. Each of these uprisings culminated with the 'suicide of all the Mappilas involved, in an attempt to become shahids (martyrs for the faith)' (Stephen F. Dale, 'The Mappila Outbreaks: Ideology and Social Conflict in Nineteenth-century Kerala', p. 86).
26 Stephen F. Dale, 'The Mappila Outbreaks'.
27 V.K. Ramachandran, 'On Kerala's Development Achievements'.
28 Dick Kooiman, 'The Strength of Numbers: Enumerating Communities in India's Princely States'; Yesudas, *The History of the London Missionary Society*, p. 197.
29 Prerna Singh, 'We-ness and Welfare'.
30 Rex Casinader, 'Making Kerala Model More Intelligible', p. 3091.
31 V. Thomas Samuel, *One Caste, One Religion, One God: A Study of Sree Narayana Guru*.
32 S. Osmana, *Shree Narayana Guru*.
33 Mahatma Gandhi's negotiations with the Nambudiri Brahmin trustee of the Vaikkom temple at the time of the satyagraha reeked of orthodox Hindu values. He apparently argued, 'No

doubt they are suffering for their karma by being born as Untouchables. But why must you add to the punishment? Are they worse than even criminals and beasts?' (Eleanor Zelliot, 'Gandhi and Ambedkar: A Study in Leadership', p. 198).

34 R.N. Yesudas, *The History of the London Missionary Society*.
35 M. Nisar and Meena Kandasamy, *Ayyankali: A Dalit Leader of Organic Protest*; T.K. Oommen, 'Development Policy and the Nature of Society: Understanding the Kerala Model'.
36 In the nineteenth century, Nairs lived in matrilineal joint families. Generally, a man lived in his mother's house (taravad) and was permitted to form liaisons (sambandhams) with women in nearby houses. The children born were the responsibility solely of their mother's taravad. A man's legal heirs were his sisters' children, rather than his own. Under this system, by custom, Namboodiri men, apart from the eldest, were permitted to enter into sambandhams with Nair women. In 1912, Trivandrum passed a new law to recognise Nair marriages. For more details, see Robin Jeffrey, 'Matriliny, Marxism, and the Birth of the Communist Party in Kerala, 1930–1940'.
37 Robin Jeffrey, 'Matriliny, Marxism, and the Birth of the Communist Party in Kerala, 1930–1940', p. 77.
38 Robin Jeffrey, 'Matriliny, Marxism, and the Birth of the Communist Party in Kerala, 1930–1940'.
39 United Nations 1975. The then newly established Centre for Development Studies in Trivandrum (now Thiruvananthapuram) in partnership with the United Nations published the acclaimed report 'Poverty Education and Development Policy', which analysed case studies based on Kerala's unusually progressive social development.
40 Patrick Heller, *The Labor of Development: Workers and the Transformation of Capitalism in Kerala, India*.
41 Robin Jeffrey, *Politics, Women and Well Being: How Kerala Became a Model*.
42 Prerna Singh, 'We-ness and Welfare'.
43 J. Ratcliffe, 'Social Justice and the Demographic Transition: Lessons from India's Kerala State'.

44 V.K. Ramachandran, 'On Kerala's Development Achievements'.
45 Robin Jeffrey, 'Matriliny, Marxism, and the Birth of the Communist Party in Kerala, 1930–1940'.
46 G.K. Lieten, 'The Human Development Puzzle'.
47 Manali Desai, 'Party Formation, Political Power, and the Capacity for Reform: Comparing Left Parties in Kerala and West Bengal, India'.
48 V.K. Ramachandran, 'On Kerala's Development Achievements'.
49 S. Vivek, *Delivering Public Services Effectively: Tamil Nadu and Beyond*, p. 85.
50 K. Nambi Arooran, *Tamil Renaissance and Dravidian Nationalism, 1905–1944*.
51 S. Vivek, *Delivering Public Services Effectively: Tamil Nadu and Beyond*.
52 G. Aloysius, *Iyothee Thassar and Tamil Buddhist Movement*.
53 This quote is verbatim from a letter written in 1898 by C. Iyothee Thass to Henry Olcott, seeking support to revive Buddhism in the Madras Presidency. M.S.S. Pandian, *Brahmin and Non-Brahmin: Genealogies of the Tamil Political Present*, p. 105.
54 M.S.S. Pandian, 'Notes on the Transformation of Dravidian Ideology: Tamilnadu, c. 1900–1940', p. 85.
55 The Manifesto argued that India was not ready for self-rule due to the excessive hegemony of the Brahmins, who formed a mere 3 per cent of the population in the erstwhile Madras Presidency, but disproportionately dominated most political parties, the bureaucracy, the academia, journalism and the bar.
56 'Periyar' roughly translates from Tamil as 'the Great One'.
57 S. Vivek, *Delivering Public Services Effectively: Tamil Nadu and Beyond*, p. 87.
58 Tamil is one of the world's oldest languages from the Indo-Dravidian family which dates back several millennia, with perhaps Sanskrit and Pali as contemporary languages. Hindi developed only in the sixteenth century in the Indo-European family of languages. For more details, please see Tony Joseph, *Early Indians: The Story of Our Ancestors and Where We Came From*.

59 Conversations with school teachers during field visits in Tamil Nadu between 2013 and 2015.
60 Vaasanthi, *Cut-outs, Caste and Cine Stars: The World of Tamil Politics*.
61 K. Nambi Arooran, *Tamil Renaissance and Dravidian Nationalism: 1905–1944*.
62 S. Vivek, *Delivering Public Services Effectively: Tamil Nadu and Beyond*.
63 Arun Janardhanan, 'Tamil Nadu's Caste Fields: In 1 Year, over 100 Murders in Two Southern Districts'.
64 Johanna Deeksha, 'The Caste of a Chair'.
65 D. Karthikeyan, Hugo Gorringe and Stalin Rajangam, 'Dalit Political Imagination and Replication in Contemporary Tamil Nadu'.
66 The Vanniyars, numerically the largest caste in Tamil Nadu, were formerly known as Palli and were agricultural labourers traditionally. After their successful agitation in the 1980s, they were classified as 'most backward castes'.
67 In Tamil Nadu, the Backward Castes (BC) category refers to Other Backward Castes (OBCs). The Tamil Nadu government has also created a category of Most Backward Castes (MBC) which refers largely to Scheduled Castes and Dalits. Denotified Communities (DNCs) are those communities denotified from the reprehensible colonial Criminal Tribes Act of 1871. In Pattali Makkal Katchi v. A. Mayilerumperumal the Supreme Court, on limited grounds of unavailability of quantifiable demographic data on the Vanniyakula Kshatriya community, struck down the Most Backward Classes and Denotified Communities Act, 2021 as unconstitutional.
68 The Tamil Nadu Backward Class Christians and Backward Class Muslims (Reservation of Seats in Educational Institutions Including Private Educational Institutions and of Appointments or Posts in the Services Under the State) Act, 2007.
69 Miwako Shiga, 'The Non-Brahmin Movement'.
70 K.M. de Silva, *Social Policy and Missionary Organisations in Ceylon, 1840–1855*.

Notes 287

71 Mrs G. de Silva providing evidence at the Special Commission on the Constitution of Ceylon (Donoughmore Commission): on behalf of the Ceylon Women's Franchise Union, Witness Number 141 (Colonial and Dominion Office Records, The National Archives, Kew, pp. 268–69).
72 Harshan Kumarasingham, 'The Jewel of the East Yet Has Its Flaws'. The British occupied the Dutch territories of Ceylon in 1796. Initially, the Madras Government of the East India Company was expected to administer the newly occupied territories, but due to their inexperience in the region, there were a series of violations of local conventions. This resulted in a rebellion in 1797 and the Company was compelled to share administration with the Imperial Crown under a system of 'Dual Control' from 1802 (K.M. de Silva, *Social Policy and Missionary Organisations in Ceylon, 1840–1855*).
73 Harshan Kumarasingham, 'The Jewel of the East Yet Has Its Flaws'.
74 Laksiri Jayasuriya, *Taking Social Development Seriously: The Experience of Sri Lanka*.
75 Charles Jeffries, *Ceylon: The Path to Independence*, p. 29.
76 Laksiri Jayasuriya, *Taking Social Development Seriously*.
77 The Donoughmore constitution, the only one in the British Empire aside from Australia, South Africa and Canada, introduce universal adult franchise for elevtion of members to the State Council, which had both executive and legilsative functions, but Ceylon remained a British colony. Sri Lanka attained Independence from the British only in 1948. Dominion status within the British Commonwealth was retained till 1972 when Sri Lanka was finally renamed as a republic (K.M. de Silva, *A History of Sri Lanka*).
78 In 1931, the franchise was granted to every citizen over the age of twenty-one and in 1959 the age was reduced to eighteen.
79 James Warner Björkman, 'Health Policy and Politics in Sri Lanka: Developments in the South Asian Welfare State'.
80 K.M. de Silva, *Social Policy and Missionary Organisations in Ceylon, 1840–1855*.

81 K.M. de Silva argues that Dharmapala's 'propaganda bore the remarkable similarity to that of the great champion of Hindu resurgence in Western India, Tilak', with its 'blend of religious fervor and national pride, of a sophisticated internationalism with a coarse insularity' (K.M. de Silva, *A History of Sri Lanka*, p. 374).
82 Unfortunately, though it led to 'the erosion of caste fissures among the Sinhalese but contributed to ethnic consciousness' (Rex Casinader, 'Making Kerala Model More Intelligible', p. 3092).
83 K.M. de Silva, *A History of Sri Lanka*.
84 James Warner Björkman, 'Health Policy and Politics in Sri Lanka'.
85 Richard Goode, *Government Finance in Developing Countries*.
86 Laksiri Jayasuriya, *Taking Social Development Seriously*.
87 G. Ananthakrishnan, '200th Anniversary of Kerala's "Magna Carta of Education" Marked in Delhi'.
88 Jean Drèze and Amartya Sen, 'Public Action for Social Security: Foundations and Strategies'.
89 Vaasanthi, *Cut-outs, Caste and Cine Stars*.
90 The Amma unavagams (subsidised canteens), chains of pharmacies and packaged drinking water by the earlier chief minister J. Jayalalithaa were but the latest avatars of this embedded cultural phenomenon, which previously included offers of free-of-cost mixers, wet grinders, colour television sets, gold for mangalsutras, laptops, rice, bicycles, spectacles, and kits for newborn babies, in addition to subsidised iodised salt, departmental stores and even the announcement of low-cost cinema theatres. The new government of M.K. Stalin has also carried forward this distinct Tamil Nadu legacy with a cash transfer to all families and free bus transport for women.
91 Apart from the Dravidian, Dalit, communist, and other 'great social movements', S. Vivek documents how 'decentralized public action' in Tamil Nadu has been ubiquitous in the form of marches, meetings, sit-ins, hunger strikes, gheraos, petitions, postcard campaigns, mock funerals, blocking roads, burning

effigies, *pattai-namam* protest, pot breaking and other methods of protests (S. Vivek, *Delivering Public Services Effectively: Tamil Nadu and Beyond*).
92 S. Vivek, *Delivering Public Services Effectively*, p. 42.
93 S. Vivek, *Delivering Public Services Effectively*.
94 Santosh Mehrotra, *Integrating Economic and Social Policy: Good Practices from High-achieving Countries*.
95 K.M. de Silva, *A History of Sri Lanka*.
96 K.M. de Silva, *Social Policy and Missionary Organisations in Ceylon, 1840–1855*.
97 Santosh Mehrotra, *Integrating Economic and Social Policy*.
98 P.G.K. Panikar and C.R. Soman, *Health Status of Kerala: The Paradox of Economic Backwardness and Health Development*.
99 Santosh Mehrotra, *Integrating Economic and Social Policy*.
100 Barbara H. Chasin and Richard W. Franke, *Kerala: Radical Reform as Development in an Indian State*.
101 Surjit Bhalla, 'Is Sri Lanka an Exception?'.
102 Surjit Bhalla, 'Is Sri Lanka an Exception?'.
103 'Food distribution policies (e.g. free or subsidised rice for all, free school meals) were introduced in the early 1940s, and health intervention was also radically expanded (including taking on the dreaded malaria). Correspondingly, the death rate fell from 21.6 per thousand in 1945 to 12.6 in 1950, and to 8.6 by 1960 (all this happened *before* the oddly chosen period 1960–78 used in Bhalla's much-publicized "international comparisons" of expansions).' (Amartya Sen, 'Food, Economics, and Entitlements', in Jean Drèze and Amartya Sen, *The Political Economy of Hunger, Volume 1: Entitlement and Wellbeing*, p. 48).
104 Sen also criticises the methodology used by Bhalla as 'the "level-level" approach is confused with the "level-change" approach!' (Amartya Sen, 'Appendix: Sri Lanka's Achievements: How and When', in Pranab Bardhan and T.N. Srinivasan (eds), *Rural Poverty in South Asia*).
105 Kumari Jayawardena, *Feminism and Nationalism in the Third World*.
106 John Ferguson, *Ceylon in 1884*.

107 Kavitha Rao, *Lady Doctors: The Untold Stories of India's First Women in Medicine*.
108 Kumari Jayawardena, *Feminism and Nationalism in the Third World*.
109 The Commission was appointed by Sidney Webb who, as Lord Passfield, the Fabian Socialist, was the first Labour Secretary of State for the Colonies during 1929–31. The Donoughmore Commission was constituted before he assumed office (K.M. de Silva, *A History of Sri Lanka*). Nonetheless, two of the commissioners, Sir Drummond Shiels, a Scottish Fabian who later served as Webb's under-secretary, and Sir Geoffrey Butler, an expert on the League of Nations, were veteran Labour Party members. Lord Donoughmore was a Liberal peer, previously chairman of the committees of the House of Lords known for championing women's rights. The Commission spent four months interviewing 140 people including the women's movement (K.T. Rajasingham, *Sri Lanka: The Untold Story*).
110 Beatrice Webb, in her diary, notes that Ceylon's Donoughmore Constitution is 'said to be the work of Drummond Sheils', the Fabian socialist (Beatrice Webb, *Typescript Diary, 30 May 1929-25 December 1931*, p. 68).
111 Charles Jeffries, *Ceylon*, p. 50.
112 Laksiri Jayasuriya, *Taking Social Development Seriously*.
113 Colonial Office, *Report of the Commission on Constitutional Reform: Presented by the Secretary of State for the Colonies to Parliament by Command of His Majesty*, p. 34.
114 Colonial Office, *Report of the Commission on Constitutional Reform*, p. 35.
115 K.M. de Silva, *A History of Sri Lanka*.
116 The Queen Gowri Lakshmi Bayi Rani acceded to the throne at the age of twelve years following the untimely death of her father. The *Imperial Gazetteer of South India* claims she 'confided the administration of the State to Col J. Munro, the Resident, and from that date Travancore commenced a fresh career of peace, progress, and prosperity' (W. Francis, et al., *Gazetteer of South India*, p. 407). Yesudas, in his hagiography of the British resident, claims that she 'entrusted everything

connected with Travancore into the hands of Munro' and considered him to be 'her elder brother' (R.N. Yesudas, *Colonel John Munro*, p. 11). In a letter urging him to accept a salary at least that of a Diwan, she exudes that she is 'continually impressed with a sense of the invaluable benefits that have resulted to my Government and country from your labours and exertions.' (R.N. Yesudas, *Colonel John Munro*, p. 60).

117 Munro wrote in a letter in 1817, 'The diffusion of English literature among the people is one of the most effectual means of eradicating their errors, improving their minds and attaching them to the British nation.' (R.N. Yesudas, *Colonel John Munro*, p. 53).

118 Sir Herbert Hope Risley, *The Imperial Gazetteer of India*.

119 Sir Herbert Hope Risley, *The Imperial Gazetteer of India*.

120 Desai highlights that after the 1857 mutiny these threats on native states increased with poor governance and political instability as an overt justification (Manali Desai, 'Indirect British Rule, State Formation, and Welfarism in Kerala, India, 1860-1957', p. 466).

121 Manali Desai, 'Indirect British Rule, State Formation, and Welfarism in Kerala, India, 1860-1957', p. 473.

122 Manali Desai, 'Indirect British Rule, State Formation, and Welfarism in Kerala, India, 1860-1957'.

123 V.K. Ramachandran, 'On Kerala's Development Achievements'.

124 Samuel Mateer, *Native Life in Travancore*.

125 R.N. Yesudas, *The History of the London Missionary Society in Travancore, 1806–1908*, p. 159.

126 V.K. Ramachandran, 'On Kerala's Development Achievements', p. 264.

127 Nine castes were listed and the government declared that even a change of religion would not affect their commitment to the child originating from a backward caste (R.N. Yesudas, *The History of the London Missionary Society in Travancore, 1806-1908*).

128 P.K. Michael Tharakan, *History as Development Experience: Desegrated and Deconstructed Analysis of Kerala*.

129 Robin Jeffrey, 'Testing Concepts about Print, Newspapers, and Politics: Kerala, India, 1800–2009'.
130 V.K. Ramachandran, 'On Kerala's Development Achievements'.
131 S. Vivek, 'Understanding Public Services in Tamil Nadu: An Institutional Perspective'.
132 Santosh Mehrotra, 'Well-being and Caste in Uttar Pradesh: Why UP Is Not Like Tamil Nadu'.
133 S. Vivek, *Delivering Public Services Effectively*.
134 R. Kannan, *MGR: A Life*.
135 Please see Appendices A18 to A20.
136 Manali Desai, 'Indirect British Rule'.
137 Amartya Sen, *Development as Freedom*, p. 193.
138 S. Vivek, *Delivering Public Services Effectively*.
139 Only Brahmin women had the privilege of covering themselves when they went out, but not within the home. Nair women also covered themselves when they went out but those more underprivileged were prohibited from covering their bosoms (R.N. Yesudas, *A People's Revolt*; S.N. Sadasivan, *A Social History of India*).
140 R.N. Yesudas, *A People's Revolt*.
141 Lavanya Shanbhogue Arvind, 'When Women Paid Tax to Cover Their Breasts'.
142 S.N. Sadasivan, *A Social History*.
143 S.N. Sadasivan, *A Social History*.
144 In 2019, the National Council of Educational Research and Training (NCERT) deleted from the Class 9 history textbook a section on the Channar Upper Cloth Revolt from the chapter 'Clothing: A Social History' based on the curriculum rationalisation exercise without any public consultation (T.A. Ameerudheen, 'NCERT Decision to Remove Chapter on Caste Struggle in Kerala from History Textbook Draws Criticism').
145 The National Archives of India (NAI) built by architect Edwin Lutyens is being refurbished as part of the Central Vista project. The British Library in London also has a copy of the book.
146 In Tamil-speaking areas the caste was referred to as 'Shannars' or 'Channars'. In Travancore they were considered to be

'Nadars', though the words are used interchangeably in border areas. Nadars were a sub-caste which historically had the occupation of toddy tappers and made a living by climbing palmrya coconut trees, though many converted to Christianity in the nineteenth century.
147 R.N. Yesudas, *A People's Revolt*.
148 R.N. Yesudas, *A People's Revolt*.
149 R.N. Yesudas, *A People's Revolt*.
150 Similar taxes also dissuaded women from wearing jewellery and men from growing a moustache. The breast tax was abolished in 1812 (Nidhi Surendranath, '200 Years On, Nangeli's Sacrifice Only a Fading Memory').
151 Lavanya Shanbhogue Arvind, 'When Women Paid Tax to Cover Their Breasts'.
152 BBC, 'The Woman Who Cut off Her Breasts to Protest a Tax'.
153 R.N. Yesudas, *A People's Revolt*.
154 R.N. Yesudas, *A People's Revolt*.
155 R.N. Yesudas, *The History of the London Missionary Society*, p. 259, original translated from Malayalam.
156 Manoj Mitta, *Caste Pride*, pp. 21–2.
157 R.N. Yesudas, *Colonel John Munro*; *The History of the London Missionary Society*.
158 The primary objection to the shoulder cloth was that it was a caste marker of the upper castes (Manoj Mitta, *Caste Pride*).
159 R.N. Yesudas, *A People's Revolt*, p. 153; Manoj Mitta, *Caste Pride*, p. 25.
160 The letter by Governor Charles Trevelyan was dated 6 May 1859. Robert L. Hardgrave, *The Nadars of Tamilnad*; p. 67; Manoj Mitta, *Caste Pride*, p. 26.
161 R.N. Yesudas, *The History of the London Missionary Society*, p. 311.
162 Samuel Mateer, *The Land of Charity*; Manoj Mitta, *Caste Pride*.
163 On 28 September 2019, the Supreme Court had in a 4:1 majority verdict revoked a ban on the entry of women of reproductive age into the Sabarimala temple in Kerala. Despite the support of the Kerala government, for more than a month,

thousands of protestors physically barred female worshippers from entering the temple by resorting to vandalism.

164 In November 2019, the then chief justice Ranjan Gogoi headed a five-member bench which in a 3:2 judgement three days before his retirement referred to a larger bench of seven judges a batch of review petitions on the 2018 verdict allowing entry of women of all age groups into Kerala's Sabarimala Temple. The judgement did not stay the earlier order, but clubbed petitions on 'the entry of women into mosques and Parsi temples' which the dissenting judges objected 'aren't even before this court in the present batch of petitions in Sabarimala case' (Debayan Roy, 'Supreme Court Refers Sabarimala Review Petitions to Larger Bench in Split Verdict').

165 Kumari Jayawardena, *Feminism and Nationalism*, p. 113.

166 Kumari Jayawardena, *Feminism and Nationalism*.

167 At the twenty-fifth anniversary of the International Woman Suffrage Alliance Conference meeting in Berlin in 1929, the Women's Franchise Union of Ceylon was admitted as a member and represented by its President Lady Dias Bandaranaike. The first meeting of the Alliance was in 1904 in Berlin, and Indian delegates attended from 1913 at the Hungary conference (IWSA, *Call to the Ninth Congress of the International Women's Suffrage Alliance, Rome, 12–19th May 1923*).

168 Kumari Jayawardena, *Feminism and Nationalism*.

169 Special Commission on the Constitution of Ceylon (Donoughmore Commission): Written Representation. Volume VII, 279. Women's Franchise Union, Ceylon, letter dated 9th December 1927 based on resolution passed by the Union on 7th December 1927 (Colonial Office and Dominions Office records, The National Archives Library, Kew).

170 GoSL, *Women of Sri Lanka: A Special Publication on the Status of Women for International Women's Year*.

171 The Women's Franchise Association, Kandy, also submitted a memorandum dated 19 September 1928 to the Donoughmore Commission stating, 'The association is unanimously of the opinion that the age limit in the case of women should be

reduced to 21 years.' They added, 'The age restriction proposed would have the unfortunate and anomalous effect of shutting out a large percentage of the very section of our women best qualified by reason of their education and enlightenment to exercise this valued privilege.' Special Commission on the Constitution of Ceylon (Donoughmore Commission): Written Representation. Volume VII, 279. Women's Franchise Union, Ceylon, Letter Dated 9th December 1927 based on resolution passed by the Union on 7th December 1927 (Colonial Office and Dominions Office records, The National Archives Library, Kew).

172 Legend suggests that 2,500 years ago, Ceylon was ruled by a 'demon' queen Kuveni and through the millennia various queens have been anointed as regents (D. Rhys, *Psalms of the Early Buddhists*).
173 Inter-Parliamentary Union 2023.
174 S. Anandhi, 'The Women's Question', p. 390.
175 E.S.A. Vishwanathan, *The Political Career of E.V. Ramaswamy Naicker*.
176 Tali is a yellow thread or gold necklace worn by married women in south India similar to the mangalsutra in the north to signify their marital status.
177 S. Anandhi, 'The Women's Question'; Manoj Mitta describes in detail the legal battle to legalise Self-Respect Weddings which finally received legal acceptance after the enactment of the Special Marriage Act of 1954 (*Caste Pride*, pp. 134–47).
178 S. Anandhi, 'Sex and Sensibility in Tamil Politics', p. 4876.
179 GOI, 2022, *Periodic Labour Force Survey*.
180 Rex Casinader, 'Making Kerala Model More Intelligible'.
181 Rex Casinader, 'Making Kerala Model More Intelligible', p. 3086.
182 K.K. Pillay, *South India and Sri Lanka*.
183 'The introduction of paddy into Sri Lanka seems to have occurred from south India', while 'gems, conch shells or shanks, pearls and pearl shells moved into south India' (Dr Sudharshan Seneviratne, *Reading the Past in a More Inclusive Way*).

184 The Thiyyas are a group of Ezhavas, traditionally a toddy-tapping community in Kerala, who lived in Malabar.
185 Vaasanthi, *Cut-outs, Caste and Cine Stars*, p. 8.
186 Susantha Goonatilake, 'Sinhala Buddhist Roots of South Indian Tamil Chauvinism'.
187 Described by Theosophist Col. H.S. Olcott in G. Aloysius, *Iyothee Thassar*, p. 66.
188 G. Aloysius, *Iyothee Thassar*, p. 82–5.
189 Robert L. Hardgrave, *The Nadars of Tamilnad*.
190 Satia Vagiswara Aiyar, 'Well Attended Meeting of Malayalis: Under the Presidency of the First Indian Member'.
191 Nadars were a sub-caste which historically had the occupation of toddy tappers and made a living by climbing palmrya coconut trees, though many converted to Christianity in the nineteenth century.
192 R.N. Yesudas, *A People's Revolt*.
193 V.K. Ramachandran, 'On Kerala's Development Achievements'.
194 Harry Stevens, 'Seven Decades after Independence, Most Dalit Farmers Still Landless'.
195 UNDP, *Sri Lanka Human Development Report 2012*.
196 UNDP, *Sri Lanka Human Development Report 2012*.
197 Calculations from the 70th round of Land and Livestock Holdings Survey (L&LS) of the National Sample Survey Office (NSSO) seem to indicate that in terms of ownership of non-homestead land, in a highly urbanised state, 77 per cent of Dalits in Tamil Nadu are landless, compared to 58 per cent of OBCs and 72 per cent of forward castes (Ishan Anand, 'Dalit Emancipation and the Land Question').
198 K. Ravi Raman, *Development, Democracy and the State*.

8. THE PRICE OF INEQUALITY

1 Fernand Braudel, *A History of Civilizations*.
2 Life expectancy at birth, total (years) in WDI, World Development Indicators, June 2023.
3 Jagdish Bhagwati and Arvind Panagariya, *India's Reforms*, p. 233.

4   Naomi Hossain, *The Aid Lab*, p. 1.
5   Gosta Esping-Andersen, *The Three Worlds of Welfare Capitalism*.
6   Walter Korpi and Joakim Palme, 'The Paradox of Redistribution and Strategies of Equality: Welfare State Institutions, Inequality, and Poverty in the Western Countries'. Counter-intuitively, the 'paradox of redistribution' shows that countries with universal welfare systems, which tax everyone at an equal rate and also distribute benefits equally, have more effective redistribution than those that tax the rich to give to the poor. The reason is that while taxes are usually computed as a fixed percentage of income, benefits or services are usually fixed in nominal values (John Holt, *The Sri Lanka Reader*).
7   Across India 44 per cent of the rural households did not own any land other than their homesteads. Amongst rural Dalits, 58 per cent were landless, higher than all social groups. In rural Kerala, only 41 per cent of the households of the general population are landless, compared to 58 per cent of OBCs, 72 per cent of Dalits and 93 per cent of Adivasis (Ishan Anand, *Dalit Emancipation and the Land Question*).
8   As per the 2011 census, in Tamil Nadu 49 per cent of the population lives in urban areas, the highest in the country (GoI, 'Population Enumeration Data [Final Population])'.
9   B.R. Ambedkar, *Thoughts on Linguistic States*. In BAWS, 1(5), p. 164.
10 It is important to note that Babasaheb Ambedkar made this comparison in the context of the proposed post-Independence linguistic reorganisation of Indian states as he believed that it would result in the Balkanisation of the south and undue integrated dominance of the north (B.R. Ambedkar, *Thoughts on Linguistic States*, in BAWS Collection, 1(5)).
11 Christophe Jaffrelot, *India's Silent Revolution*.
12 Gail Omvedt, *Dalits and the Democratic Revolution*; Neil Selmer, *A Theory of Collective Behaviour*.
13 M.N. Srinivas, 'Mobility in the Caste System', p. 319.
14 Christophe Jaffrelot, *India's Silent Revolution*.
15 World Bank, *World Development Report 2006: Equity and Development*.

BIBLIOGRAPHY

Abed, Fazle Hasan, 'Bangladesh's Health Revolution', *The Lancet*, 382(9910), 2013, pp. 2048–49.
Acemoglu, Daron and James A. Robinson, *Why Nations Fail: The Origins of Power, Prosperity and Poverty* (Profile Books Ltd, London, 2013).
Acharya, Keshav, 'Evaluating Institutional Capability of Nepali Grassroot Organisations for Service Delivery Functions', *Dhaulagiri Journal of Sociology and Anthropology*, 11, 2017.
Acharya, Mosiqi, 'India's Newly Elected MPs: Almost 90 Per Cent Are Millionaires and 43 Per Cent Face Criminal Charges', *SBS Hindi*, 28 May 2019.
Adhikari, Krishna Kant, 'Criminal Cases and Their Punishments: Before and During the Period of Jang Bahadur', *Contributions to Nepalese Studies*, 3(1), January 1976 (Poush 2032), pp. 105–16.
AFP, 'Nepal Introduces Grants for Inter-caste Marriages', *Hindustan Times*, 13 July 2009.
Agha, Eram, 'Hindu Right Wrongly Says Muslims Brought Beef-eating—Hindutva History Is a Mystery: D N Jha', *The Times of India*, 9 October 2015.
Ahmad, Imtiaz, *Caste and Social Stratification among the Muslims* (Manohar Book Service, Delhi, 1973).
Ahsan, Syed Badrul, 'When Mr Jinnah Came to Dhaka', *Dhaka Tribune*, 4 March 2020.
Aiyar, Satia Vagiswara, 'Well Attended Meeting of Malayalis: Under the Presidency of the First Indian Member', *The Ceylon Indian*, 15 January 1928.

Ajay, T.G., 'How "Swachh Bharat" Is Being Forced Upon Chhattisgarh Villagers', *The Wire*, 15 December 2016.

Akmal, Maryam and Lant Pritchett, 'Learning Equity Requires More than Equality: Learning Goals and Achievement Gaps between the Rich and the Poor in Five Developing Countries', *International Journal of Educational Development*, 82(102350), 2021.

Ali, Hyfa M. and Leyanna S. George, 'A Qualitative Analysis of the Impact of Kudumbashree and MGNREGA on the Lives of Women Belonging to a Coastal Community in Kerala', *Journal of Family Medicine and Primary Care*, 8(9), 2019, pp. 2832–36.

Ali, Shaikh Maqsood, *From East Bengal to Bangladesh: Dynamics and Perspectives* (The University Press Limited, Dhaka, 2009).

Alkire, Sabina, Christian Oldiges and Usha Kanagaratnam, 'Examining Multidimensional Poverty Reduction in India 2005/6–2015/16: Insights and Oversights of the Headcount Ratio', *World Development*, 142, June 2021, 105454.

Alkire, Sabina, Usha Kanagaratnam and Nicolai Suppa, 'A Methodological Note on the Global Multidimensional Poverty Index (MPI) 2022 Changes Over Time, Results for 84 Countries', *OPHI MPI Methodological Note 54* (OPHI and UNDP, Oxford, 2022).

Aloysius, G., *Interpreting Kerala's Social Development* (Critical Quest, New Delhi, 2005).

Aloysius, G., *Iyothee Thassar and Tamil Buddhist Movement* (Critical Quest, New Delhi, 2015).

Ambedkar, B.R., *Dr Babasaheb Ambedkar: Writings and Speeches* (BAWS), edited by Vasant Moon, Dr Ambedkar Foundation, Ministry of Social Justice and Empowerment, Government of India, 2019.

Ambedkar, B.R., 'Social Stagnation', *Pakistan or The Partition of India*, https://franpritchett.com/00ambedkar/ambedkar_partition/, last accessed 24 October 2023.

Ameerudheen, T.A., 'NCERT Decision to Remove Chapter on Caste Struggle in Kerala from History Textbook Draws Criticism', *Scroll*, 22 March 2019.

Amin, Sonia, *The World of Muslim Women in Colonial Bengal, 1876–1939* (Brill, Leiden; New York; Koln: 1996)

Anand, Ishan, 'Dalit Emancipation and the Land Question', *Economic and Political Weekly*, 51(47), 2016, pp. 12–14.

Anandhi, S., 'Sex and Sensibility in Tamil Politics', *Economic and Political Weekly*, 40(47), 2005, pp. 4876–77.

Anandhi, S., 'The Women's Question', in Sumit Sarkar and Tanika Sarkar (eds), *Women and Social Reform in Modern India* (Indiana University Press, Indiana, 1991).

Ananthakrishnan, G., '200th Anniversary of Kerala's "Magna Carta of Education" Marked in Delhi', *The Indian Express*, 18 June 2017.

Annan, Kofi, 'Kofi Annan on Economic Inequality: "People Are Seduced by the Siren Songs of Cynical Populists"', *Quartz*, 2018.

APU, *State of Working India: One Year of Covid-19* (Centre for Sustainable Employment, Azim Premji University, 2021).

Arooran, K. Nambi, *Tamil Renaissance and Dravidian Nationalism: 1905–1944* (Koodal, Madurai, 1980).

Arvind, Lavanya Shanbhogue, 'When Women Paid Tax to Cover Their Breasts', *Madras Courier*, 1 April 2019.

Aryal, Urmila, 'All Nepal Women's Association', *Gender, Technology and Development*, 4(2), 2000, pp. 305–9.

Asaduzzaman, E.A.M., 'Women Language Movement Heroes of Nilphamari', *The Daily Star*, 19 February 2015.

Asher, Sam, Paul Novosad and Charlie Rafkin, 'Intergenerational Mobility in India: New Methods and Estimates across Time, Space, and Communities', G²LM|LIC Working Paper No. 66, *Gender, Growth and Labour Market in Low-Income Countries Programme*, IZA Institute of Labour Economics, June 2022.

Babajanian, B., 'Tackling Old Age Poverty and Vulnerability', *Poverty in Focus*, 25, 2013.

Banaji, Murad and Ashish Gupta, 'Estimates of Pandemic Excess Mortality in India Based on Civil Registration Data', *PLOS Global Public Health*, 2(12), 9 December 2022.

Banaji, Murad, 'Why India's Response to WHO on Excess COVID-19 Deaths Doesn't Hold Water', *The Wire*, 28 April 2022.

BANBEIS, 'Table 3.5.6: Number of Schools with Different Activities, 2016', *Bangladesh Bureau of Educational Information and Statistics*, 2016.

Baral, Biswas, 'What Is Delaying the Landmark Left Merger in Nepal?' *The Wire*, 28 April 2018.

Barik, R.K., *Land and Caste Politics in Bihar* (Shipra Publications, New Delhi, 2006).

Basham, A.L., *A Cultural History of India* (Clarendon Press, Oxford, 1975).

Basnett, Yurendra, *From Politicization of Grievances to Political Violence: An Analysis of the Maoist Movement in Nepal* (London School of Economics and Political Sciences, 2009).

BBC, 'Bangladesh Protests: How a Traffic Accident Stopped a City of 18 Million', BBC News, 6 August 2018.

BBC, 'Nepal blockade: Six Ways It Affects the Country', BBC News, 12 December 2015.

BBS, *Preliminary Report on Agricultural Census 2019* (Bangladesh Bureau of Statistics, Statistics and Informatics Division, Ministry of Planning, Government of Bangladesh, 2019).

Begum, Thaslima, "We Lay Like Corpses. Then the Raping began': 52 Years On, Bangladesh's Rape Camp Survivors Speak Out', *The Guardian*, 3 April 2023.

Behar, Anurag, 'The False Narrative of Teacher Absenteeism', *The Mint*, 27 April 2017.

Beverley, H., *Report of the Census of India 1872* (Bengal Secretariat Press, Calcutta, India, 1872).

Bhagwati, Jagdish and Arvind Panagariya, *India's Reforms: How They Produced Inclusive Growth* (Oxford University Press, New York, 2012).

Bhalla, Abhishek, 'Women Flock to Naxal Cause: Government Figures Reveal 60 Per Cent of Active Maoists Are Female', *Daily Mail Online*, 23 July 2013.

Bhalla, Surjit, 'Is Sri Lanka an Exception? A Comparative Study of Living Standards', *Rural Poverty in South Asia* (Columbia University Press, New York, 1985).

Bharti, Indu, 'Bihar's Bane: Slow Progress on Land Reforms', *Economic and Political Weekly*, 27(13), 1992, pp. 628–30.

Bhatia, Rahul, 'How India's Welfare Revolution Is Starving Citizens', *The New Yorker*, 16 May 2018.

Bhattacharya, Subhas, 'The Indigo Revolt of Bengal', *Social Scientist*, 5(12), 1977, pp. 13–23.

Bhattacharya, Sukanta, Sarani Saha and Sarmila Banerjee, 'Income Inequality and the Quality of Public Services: A Developing Country Perspective', *Journal of Development Economics*, 123, 2016, pp. 1–17.

Björkman, James Warner, 'Health Policy and Politics in Sri Lanka: Developments in the South Asian Welfare State', *Asian Survey*, 25(5), 1985, pp. 537–52.

Blunch, Niels-Hugo and Maitreyi Bordia Das, 'Changing Norms about Gender Inequality in Education: Evidence from Bangladesh', *Policy Research Working Papers* (The World Bank, 2007).

Borthwick, Meredith, *The Changing Role of Women in Bengal, 1849–1905* (Princeton University Press, Princeton, N.J., 1984).

Bose, Pradip, 'Mobility and Conflict: Social Roots of Caste Violence in Bihar', in D. Gupta (ed.), *Social Stratification* (Oxford University Press, New Delhi, 1991).

Boudet, Munoz, Ana Maria Petesch, Carolyn Turk and Maria Angelica Thumala, 'On Norms and Agency: Conversations about Gender Equality with Women and Men in 20 Countries', *Working Paper* 74191 (The World Bank, Washington, DC, 2013).

BP, 'Draft Law Forbids Private Tuition', *Bangladesh Post*, 15 February 2020.

BRAC, 'Annual Report 2020-21' (BRAC, Dhaka, 2021).

Braudel, Fernand, *A History of Civilizations*, translated by Richard Mayne, reprint edition (Penguin, London and New York, 1995).

Bühler, George, 'The Laws of Manu', *Sacred Books of the East* (Clarendon Press, Oxford, 1886).

Casinader, Rex, 'Making Kerala Model More Intelligible: Comparisons with Sri Lankan Experience', *Economic and Political Weekly*, 30(48), 1995, pp. 3085–92.

Chambers, Robert and Gregor Von Medeazza, 'Sanitation and Stunting in India: Undernutrition's Blind Spot', *Economic and Political Weekly*, 48(25), 2013, pp. 15–18.

Chancel, Lucas and Thomas Piketty, 'Indian Income Inequality, 1922–2014: From British Raj to Billionaire Raj?' *Working Paper Series* N° 2017/11, WID.WORLD (World Wealth and Income Database), 2017.

Chancel, Lucas, Thomas Piketty, Emmanuel Saez and Gabriel Zucman, *World Inequality Report 2022*, World Inequality Lab, wir2022.wid.world.

Chandra, Jagriti, 'Global Hunger Index Attempt to Tarnish India's Image: Centre', *The Hindu*, 15 October 2022.

Chang, Ha-Joon, 'Rethinking Development Economics: An Introduction', in Ha-Joon Chang (ed.), *Rethinking Development Economics* (Anthem Frontiers of Global Political Economy, Anthem Press, London, 2003).

Chang, Ha-Joon, 'The East Asian Experience', in Ha-Joon Chang (ed.), *Rethinking Development Economics* (Anthem Frontiers of Global Political Economy, Anthem Press, London, 2003).

Chasin, Barbara H. and Richard W. Franke, *Kerala: Radical Reform as Development in an Indian State* (Institute for Food and Development Policy, San Francisco, California, 1994).

Chatterji, Joya, *Bengal Divided: Hindu Communalism and Partition, 1932–1947* (Cambridge University Press, 2002).

Chattopadhyay, Dilip Kumar, 'The Ferazee and Wahabi Movements of Bengal', *Social Scientist*, 6(2), 1977, pp. 42–51.

Choudhury, Abhinash Dash, 'Jharkhand's Starvation Deaths Raise Questions About India's Welfare Schemes', *The Wire*, 11 January 2019.

Choudhury, Pranab, Rana Roy and Aswani Munnangi, 'Group Leasing Approach to Sustain Farming and Rural Livelihoods: The Journey of Women Farmers in Kudumbashree Kerala', *SSRN Scholarly Paper* 3803698 (Social Science Research Network, Rochester, NY, 2021).

Chowdhury, A.M.R. and Richard Cash, *A Simple Solution: Teaching Millions to Treat Diarrhoea at Home* (The University Press Limited, Dhaka, 1996).

Chowdhury, Abdul Momin, 'Reflections on Islamisation in Bengal', *Bangladesh E-Journal of Sociology*, 8(1), 2011, pp. 45–50.

Christophe Jaffrelot and A. Kalaiyarasan, 'Dominant Castes, from Bullock Capitalists to OBCs? The Impact of Class Differentiation in Rural India', in John Echeverri-Gent and Kamal Sadiq (eds), *Interpreting Politics* (Oxford University Press, Oxford, 2020).

Coffey, Diane and Dean Spears, 'Open Defecation in Rural India, 2015–16: Levels and Trends in NFHS–4', *Economic and Political Weekly*, 53(9), 2018, pp. 10–13

Coffey, Diane and Dean Spears, *Where India Goes: Abandoned Toilets, Stunted Development and the Costs of Caste* (Harper Litmus, New Delhi, 2017).

Coffey, Diane, Aashish Gupta, Payal Hathi, Nikhil Srivastav, Sangita Vyas, Nidhi Khurana and Dean Spears, 'Revealed Preference for Open Defecation', *Economic and Political Weekly*, 49(38), 2015, pp. 7–8.

Coffey, Diane, Angus Deaton, Jean Drèze, Dean Spears and Alessandro Tarozzi, 'Stunting among Children: Facts and Implications', *Economic and Political Weekly*, 48(34), 2013.

Colonial Office, *Report of the Commission on Constitutional Reform: Presented by the Secretary of State for the Colonies to Parliament by Command of His Majesty* (Colonial Office, London, 1945).

Coppedge, Michael, *Strong Parties and Lame Ducks: Presidential Partyarchy and Factionalism in Venezuela* (Stanford University Press, California, 1994).

Dale, Stephen F., 'The Mappila Outbreaks: Ideology and Social Conflict in Nineteenth-century Kerala', *The Journal of Asian Studies*, 35(1), 1975, pp. 85–97.

Das Gupta, Chirashree, 'Unravelling Bihar's "Growth Miracle"', *Economic and Political Weekly*, 45(52), 2010, pp. 50–62.

Das, Arvind, *Agrarian Movement in India: Studies in 20th Century Bihar* (Frank Cass, London, 1982).

Das, Maitreyi B., *Whispers to Voices: Gender and Social Transformation in Bangladesh*, Bangladesh Development Series, 22, The World Bank, 2008.

Dasgupta, Atis, 'Variations in Perception of the Insurgent Peasants of Bengal in the Late Eighteenth Century', *Social Scientist*, 16(8), 1988, pp. 30–43.

Dasgupta, R.K., *Peoples' Revolt in East Bengal* (Navana Printing Works, Calcutta, 1971).

de Silva, K.M., *A History of Sri Lanka* (Penguin India, New Delhi, 1981).

de Silva, K.M., *Social Policy and Missionary Organisations in Ceylon, 1840–1855*, Imperial Studies Series, No. 26, Oxford University Press, Oxford, 1965.

Deaton, Angus, 'The U.S. Can No Longer Hide From Its Deep Poverty Problem', *The New York Times*, 25 January 2018.

Deaton, Angus, *The Great Escape: Health, Wealth, and the Origins of Inequality*, reprint edition (Princeton University Press, Princeton, NJ, 2015).

Debayan Roy, 'Supreme Court Refers Sabarimala Review Petitions to Larger Bench in Split Verdict', *The Print*, 14 November 2019.

Deolalikar, Anil, 'Poverty and Child Malnutrition in Bangladesh', Working Paper No. 30866, World Bank, 2004.

Desai, Manali, 'Indirect British Rule, State Formation, and Welfarism in Kerala, India, 1860-1957', *Social Science History*, 29(3), 2005, pp. 457–88.

Desai, Manali, 'Party Formation, Political Power, and the Capacity for Reform: Comparing Left Parties in Kerala and West Bengal, India', *Social Forces*, 80(1), 2001, pp. 37–60.

Desai, Sonalde and Reeve Vanneman, *India Human Development Survey-II (IHDS-II), 2011-12* (Inter-university Consortium for Political and Social Research, Ann Arbor, MI, 2016).

Deshpande, Ashwini, *The Grammar of Caste: Economic Discrimination in Contemporary India* (Oxford University Press, Oxford, 2011).

Dhanda, Meena, 'Representation for Women: Should Feminists Support Quotas?', *Economic and Political Weekly*, 35(33), 2000, pp. 2969–76.

Domingo, Pilar, Rebecca Holmes, Anila Rocha Menocal, Nicola Jones, Dharini Bhuvanendra and Jill Wood, *Assessment of the Evidence of Links between Gender Equality, Peacebuilding and Statebuilding: Literature Review* (Overseas Development Institute, London, 2013).

Drèze, Jean and Amartya Sen, 'Public Action for Social Security: Foundations and Strategies', in Ehtisham Ahmad, Jean Drèze, John Hills and Amartya Sen (eds), *Social Security in Developing Countries*, United Nations University World Institute for Development (UNU-WIDER) (Clarendon Press; Oxford University Press, Oxford, 1991), pp. 1–41.

Drèze, Jean and Amartya Sen, *An Uncertain Glory: India and Its Contradictions* (Allen Lane, New Delhi, 2013).

Drèze, Jean and Amartya Sen, *India: Development and Participation* (Oxford University Press, Oxford, 2002).

Drèze, Jean and Amartya Sen, *The Political Economy of Hunger, Volume 1: Entitlement and Wellbeing* (Oxford University Press, Oxford, 2002).

Drèze, Jean and Mrilalini Saran, 'Primary Education and Economic Development in China and India: Overview and Two Case Studies', in K. Basu, P. Pattanaik and K. Suzumura (eds), *Choice, Welfare, and Development: Essays in Honour of Amartya Sen* (Clarendon Press, Oxford, 1995).

Drèze, Jean and Reetika Khera, 'Recent Social Security Initiatives in India', *World Development*, 98, October 2017.

Drèze, Jean, 'Bangladesh Shows the Way', *The Hindu*, 17 September 2004.

Drèze, Jean, 'Democracy and the Right to Food', *Economic and Political Weekly*, 39(17), 24 April 2004.

Drèze, Jean, 'On the Mythology of Social Policy', *The Hindu*, 8 July 2014.

Drèze, Jean, 'The Gujarat Muddle', *The Hindu*, 11 April 2014.

Drèze, Jean, Nirali Bakhla, Vipul Paikra and Reetika Khera, *Locked-out: Emergency Report on School Education* (The SCHOOL Team, Ranchi, 2021).

Eaton, Richard M., 'The Rise of Islam and the Bengal Frontier, 1204–1760', *Comparative Studies on Muslim Societies*, 17 (University of California Press, Berkeley, 1993).

Engels, Dagmar, *Beyond Purdah? Women in Bengal, 1890–1939* (Oxford University Press, New Delhi, 1996).

Esmé, Berkhout, Nick Galasso, Max Lawson, Pablo Andrés Rivero Morales, Anjela Taneja and Diego Alejo Vázquez Pimentel, *The Inequality Virus* (Oxfam International, 2021).

Esping-Andersen, Gosta, *The Three Worlds of Welfare Capitalism* (Polity Press, Cambridge, 1989).

FAO, *Guidelines for Measuring Household and Individual Dietary Diversity* (Food and Agriculture Organization of the United Nations, Rome, 2010).

FAO, IFAD, UNICEF, WFP and WHO, *The State of Food Security and Nutrition in the World 2023: Urbanization, Agrifood Systems Transformation and Healthy Diets across the Rural–Urban Continuum* (Rome, Food and Agricultural Organisation of the United Nations, 2023).

Feldman, Shelley and Florence E. McCarthy, 'Purdah and Changing Patterns of Social Control among Rural Women in Bangladesh', *Journal of Marriage and Family*, 45(4), 1983, pp. 949–59.

Ferguson, John, *Ceylon in 1884: Leading Crown Colony of the British Empire* (Sampson Low, London, 1884).

Firstpost, 'Nepal PM Oli Urges India to Lift Economic Blockade, Says It's Causing a 'Humanitarian Crisis', *Firstpost*, 16 November 2015.

Forbes, *Real-Time Billionaire List* and *Bloomberg Billionaire Index*, https://www.forbes.com/real-time-billionaires.

Fox, Justin, 'Is Mississippi Worse Off than Bangladesh?' *The Mint*, 16 March 2017.

Francis., W., Frederick Nicholson, C.S. Middlemiss, C.A. Barber, E. Thurston and G.H. Stuart, *Gazetteer of South India*, reprint edition (Mittal Publications, New Delhi, 1988).

Franz, Nathan and Dean Spears, 'What Can We Learn about Swachh Bharat Mission from NFHS-5 Factsheets?', *Ideas for India*, 2 February 2021.

Gail Omvedt, 'Women and PR', Round Table India, 13 October 2010.

Gautam, Shobha, Amrita Banskota and Rita Manchanda, 'Where There Are No Men: Women in the Maoist Insurgency in Nepal', in R. Manchanda (ed.), *Women, War and Peace in South Asia: Beyond Victimhood to Agency*, South Asia Forum for Human Rights (Sage India, New Delhi, 2001).

Gawande, Atul, 'Spreading Slow Ideas', *The New Yorker*, 22 July 2013.

GB, 'About Grameen Bank' (blog), Grameen Bank, Dhaka, 2020.

GDL, 'Subnational HDI—Global Data Lab', Institute for Management Research, Radboud University, Global Data Hub, 2021.

Gerbaudo, Paolo, 'The Pandemic Crowd: Protest in the Time of COVID-19', *Journal of International Affairs*, 73(2), 2020, pp. 61–76.

Ghosh, Arabinda, Dean Spears and Aashish Gupta, 'Are Children in West Bengal Shorter Than Children in Bangladesh?' *Economic and Political Weekly*, 49(8), 2014.

GoB, *Community Clinic Based Health Care (CBHC)*, DGHS (Ministry of Health and Family Welfare, Government of Bangladesh, Dhaka, 2017.

GoB, *Population and Housing Census, 2011: Analytical Report*, (Bangladesh Bureau of Statistics, Government of Bangladesh, Dhaka, 2017).

Goel, Kritika and Reetika Khera, 'Public Health Facilities in North India: An Exploratory Study in Four States', *Economic and Political Weekly*, 50(21), 2015.

GoI, 'Population Enumeration Data (Final Population)', *Census of India 2011* (Office of the Registrar General and Census Commissioner, Government of India, New Delhi, India, 2011).

GoI, 'The Causes and Nature of Current Agrarian Tensions', Ministry of Home Affairs, Government of India, 1969.

GoI, *Rural Health Statistics, 2020-21* (National Health Mission, Statistics Division, Ministry of Health and Family Welfare, Government of India, 2022).

GoN and UNDP, *Nepal Human Development Report 2014: Beyond Geography—Unlocking Human Potential* (National Planning Commission, Government of Nepal, Kathmandu, 2014).

GoN, *Nepal—National Population and Housing Census 2011, Marks 100 Years of Census Taking in Nepal* (Central Bureau of Statistics National Planning Commission Secretariat, Government of Nepal, 2011).

GoN, *Nepal—Nepal Living Standards Survey 2010-2011, NLSS Third*, Central Bureau of Statistics, National Planning Commission Secretariat, Government of Nepal, 2010.

GoN, New ERA and ICF Nepal, *Demographic and Health Survey 2016: Key Indicators Report* (Ministry of Health, Government of Nepal, Kathmandu, 2017).

Goode, Richard, *Government Finance in Developing Countries* (Brookings Institution Press, Washington, DC, 2010).

Goonatilake, Susantha, 'Sinhala Buddhist Roots of South Indian Tamil Chauvinism', *Lankaweb*, 23 August 2009.

GoSL, *Women of Sri Lanka: A Special Publication on the Status of Women for International Women's Year* (Colombo, Government of Sri Lanka, 1975).

Gupta, Aashish and Nikkil Sudharsanan, 'Large and Persistent Life Expectancy Disparities between India's Social Groups', *Population and Development Review*, 48(3), 2022.

Gupta, Aashish and Sangita Vyas, 'Is Open Defecation Still Prevalent in Rural North India?' *Ideas for India*, 20 January 2023.

Gupta, Aashish, Dean Spears, Diane Coffey, Nidhi Khurana, Nikhil Srivastav, Payal Hathi and Sangita Vyas, 'Revealed Preference for Open Defecation', *Economic and Political Weekly*, 49(38), 2014.

Gupta, Shaibal, 'Non-Development of Bihar: A Case of Retarded Sub-nationalism', *Economic and Political Weekly*, 16(37) 1981, pp. 1496–1502.

Gurung, Harka, 'The Dalit Context', *Occasional Papers in Sociology and Anthropology*, 9, 2005, pp. 1–21.

Gurung, Yogendra B., Bhim Raj Suwal, Meeta S. Pradhan and Mukta S. Tamang, *Nepal Social Inclusion Survey 2012: Caste, Ethnic and Gender Dimensions of Socio-economic Development, Governance and Social Solidarity* (Tribhuvan University, Kathmandu, Nepal, 2014).

Habib, Wasim Bin, 'Jail, Fine for Pvt Tuition', *The Daily Star*, 7 April 2016.

Hachhethu, Krishna, 'The Nepali State and the Maoist Insurgency, 1996-2001', in M. Hutt (ed.), *Himalayan People's War: Nepal's Maoist Rebellion* (Indiana University Press, Bloomington, Indiana 2004).

Haque, Shamsul, 'The Changing Balance of Power between the Government and NGOs in Bangladesh', *International Political Science Review*, 2002.

Hardgrave Jr, Robert L., 'Caste in Kerala: A Preface to the Elections', *Economic and Political Weekly*, 16(47), 1964, pp. 1841–47.

Hardgrave Jr, Robert L., *The Nadars of Tamilnad: The Political Culture of a Community in Change* (University of California Press, Berkeley and Los Angeles, 1969).

Hardy, P., *The Muslims of British India* (Cambridge South Asian Studies, Cambridge, 1972).

Haroon Habib, 'At Shahbagh, Bangladesh's Fourth Awakening', *The Hindu*, 16 February 2013.

Hassan, Mirza, 'Political Settlement Dynamics in a Limited-Access Order: The Case of Bangladesh', *Brooks World Poverty Institute Working Paper Series* (The University of Manchester, Manchester, 2013).

Heller, Patrick, *The Labor of Development: Workers and the Transformation of Capitalism in Kerala, India* (Cornell University Press, Cornell, 1999).

Himani Baxi, Social Expenditure and Human Development in Gujarat, *Economic and Political Weekly*, 54(14), 2019, pp. 58–64.

Hisila Yami, *Hisila: From Revolutionary to First Lady* (Penguin Random House, Gurugram, 2021).

Holt, John, *The Sri Lanka Reader: History, Culture, Politics* (Duke University Press, Durham NC, 2011).

Hossain, Begum Rokeya Sakhawat, 'The Worship of Women', in Sumit Sarkar and Tanika Sarkar (eds), *Women and Social Reform in Modern India: A Reader* (Indiana University Press, Bloomington and Indianapolis, 2008).

Hossain, Begum Rokeya Sakhawat, *Sultana's Dream and Padmarag: Two Feminist Utopias* (Penguin India, New Delhi, 2005 [republished]).

Hossain, Hameeda, 'Women's Movements in Bangladesh: The Struggle Within', *The Daily Star*, 5 February 2006.

Hossain, Naomi and Naila Kabeer, 'Achieving Universal Primary Education and Eliminating Gender Disparity', *Economic and Political Weekly*, 39(36), 2004, pp. 4093–100.

Hossain, Naomi, *The Aid Lab: Understanding Bangladesh's Unexpected Success* (Oxford University Press, Oxford, 2017).

HRW, 'Broken People: Caste Violence against India's "Untouchables"', *Human Rights Watch*, 1999.

HRW, 'Children in the Ranks: The Maoists' Use of Child Soldiers in Nepal', *Human Rights Watch*, 2007.

HRW, 'Hidden Apartheid: Caste Discrimination against India's "Untouchables"', *Human Rights Watch*, 12 February 2007.

HRW, 'Silenced and Forgotten: Survivors of Nepal's Conflict-era Sexual Violence', *Human Rights Watch*, 2014.

Hunter, W.W., *The Indian Mussalmans* (Trubner and Company, London, 1872).

Hutt, Michael, *Himalayan People's War: Nepal's Maoist Rebellion* (Indiana University Press, Bloomington and Indianapolis, 2004).

ICJ, 'Unprepared and Unlawful: Nepal's Continued Failure to Realise the Right to Health during the COVID-19 Pandemic', *International Commission of Jurists*, 2021.

iDE, 'A New Standard for Sanitation', *iDE*, 15 August 2022.

IE, 'Explained: Who are Mahadalits?' *Indian Express*, 20 October 2020.

IHME, *Global Burden of Disease*, 2019, Institute for Health Metrics and Evaluation (IHME), University of Washington, https://www.healthdata.org/research-analysis/gbd.

IIPS and ICF, *National Family Health Survey (NFHS-4), 2015-16: India*, International Institute of Population Sciences, Mumbai, 2017.

IIPS and ICF, *National Family Health Survey (NFHS-5), 2019-21: Bihar*, International Institute of Population Sciences, Mumbai, 2021.

IIPS and ICF, *National Family Health Survey (NFHS-5), 2019-21: India Report*, International Institute of Population Sciences, Mumbai, 2022.

ILO, *Labour Migration for Employment: A Status Report for Nepal 2014/2015* (International Labour Organisation, 2016).

IMF, 'Nepal: Poverty Reduction Strategy Paper Progress Report', *IMF Country Report No. 07/176, 2007* (International Monetary Fund, Washington, DC, 2007).

Inter-Parliamentary Union, Women in Parliaments: World Classification, 2023 (last checked 6 August 2023).

International IDEA, Gender Quotas Database, International Institute for Democracy and Electoral Assistance (International IDEA).

IPE Global, *National Annual Rural Sanitation Survey Data 2017-2018: Provisional Summary Results Report* (Ministry of Drinking Water and Sanitation, Government of India, New Delhi, 2018).

Iqbal, Iftekar, 'The Political Ecology of the Peasant: The Fairaizi Movement between Revolution and Passive Resistance', *The

Bengal Delta: Ecology, State and Social Change, 1840-1943 (Palgrave Macmillan, Dhaka, 2010).

IWSA, *Call to the Ninth Congress of the International Women's Suffrage Alliance, Rome, 12–19th May 1923*, International Women Suffrage Alliance, Rome, 1923.

Jaffrelot, Christophe and A. Kalaiyarasan, 'Dominant Castes, from Bullock Capitalists to OBCs? The Impact of Class Differentiation in Rural India', in J. Echeverri-Gent and K. Sadiq (eds), *Interpreting Politics: Situated Knowledge, India, and the Rudolph Legacy*, Oxford University Press, 2020, pp. 111–54.

Jaffrelot, Christophe, *India's Silent Revolution: The Rise of the Lower Castes in North India* (Hurst and Company, London, 2003).

Jain, Girilal, 'Response to the West: Hindu-Muslim Divergence in India', *The Times of India*, 11 February 1993.

Jalal, Ayesha, *The Sole Spokesman: Jinnah, the Muslim League and the Demand for Pakistan* (Cambridge University Press, Cambridge, 1994).

Janardhanan, Arun, 'Tamil Nadu's Caste Fields: In 1 Year, over 100 Murders in Two Southern Districts', *Indian Express*, 5 April 2015.

Jayasuriya, Laksiri, *Taking Social Development Seriously: The Experience of Sri Lanka* (Thousand Oaks, California, 2010).

Jayawardena, Kumari, *Feminism and Nationalism in the Third World* (Zed Books, London, 1986).

Jeffrey, Robin, 'Matriliny, Marxism, and the Birth of the Communist Party in Kerala, 1930–1940', *The Journal of Asian Studies*, 38(1), 1978, pp. 77–98.

Jeffrey, Robin, 'Testing Concepts about Print, Newspapers, and Politics: Kerala, India, 1800–2009', *The Journal of Asian Studies*, 68(2), 2009, pp. 465–89.

Jeffrey, Robin, *Politics, Women and Well Being: How Kerala Became a Model* (Oxford University Press, New Delhi, 2001).

Jeffries, Charles, *Ceylon: The Path to Independence* (Pall Mall Press, London and Dunmow, Essex, 1962).

Jha, Prabhat, Maya A. Kesler, Rajesh Kumar, Faujdar Ram, Usha

Ram, Lukasz Aleksandrowicz, Diego G. Bassani, Shailaja Chandra and Jayant K. Banthia, 'Trends in Selective Abortion of Female Foetuses in India: Analysis of Nationally Representative Birth Histories from 1990–2005 and Census Data from 1991–2011', *The Lancet*, 377(9781), 2011, pp. 1921–28.

Jinnah, Muhammad Ali, 'Address by Muhammad Ali Jinnah, Governor General of Pakistan, in Dacca, East Pakistan, 21st March', in *Quaid-e-Azam Mohammad Ali Jinnah Speeches: As Governor-General of Pakistan, 1947-1948* (Sang-e-Meel Publications, Lahore, 2004).

Jodhka, Surinder and Ghanshyam Shah, 'Comparative Contexts of Discrimination: Caste and Untouchability in South Asia', *Economic and Political Weekly*, 45(48), 2010, pp. 99–106.

Johanna Deeksha, 'The Caste of a Chair', *Scroll*, 23 August 2023.

John, Aparna, Nicholas Nisbett, Inka Barnett, Rasmi Avula and Purnima Menon, 'Factors Influencing the Performance of Community Health Workers: A Qualitative Study of Anganwadi Workers from Bihar, India', in Ashraful (Neeloy) Alam (ed.), *PLOS ONE*, 15(11), 2020, e0242460.

John, Aparna, *Performance of India's Community Nutrition Workers: Anganwadi Workers of the Integrated Child Development Services Scheme in Bihar* (Thesis, Institute for Development Studies, University of Sussex, 2017).

Jones, Stephen, 'The Politics of Social Rights', *Public Management Review*, 14(2), 2012, pp. 239–54.

Joseph, Anto P., 'How Kerala is Feeding Its 3.48 Crore Residents, Migrants amid the COVID-19 Lockdown', *The Caravan*, 26 April 2020.

Joseph, Tony, *Early Indians: The Story of Our Ancestors and Where We Came From* (Juggernaut, New Delhi, 2018).

Joshi, Murari Raj, *Community Forestry Programs in Nepal and Their Effects on Poorer Households* (Food and Agricultural Organisation [FAO], Quebec City, Canada, 2003).

Justino, Cardona, R. Mitchell and C. Müller, 'Quantifying the Impact of Women's Participation in Post-conflict Economic Recovery', *HiCN Working Paper*, 131, 2012.

Jutta, Bolt and Jan Luiten van Zanden, 'Maddison Style Estimates of the Evolution of the World Economy: A New Update', *Maddison Project Database, Version 2020* (Groningen Growth and Development Centre, University of Groningen, 2020).

Kabeer, Naila, 'The Rise of the Daughter-in-Law: Why Son Preference Is Weakening in Bangladesh', *Anokhi Magazine*, 2012.

Kabeer, Naila, *Minus Lives: Women of Bangladesh* (Change International Reports, London, 1983).

Kalaiyarasan, A. and M. Vijayabaskar, *The Dravidian Model: Interpreting the Political Economy of Tamil Nadu* (Cambridge University Press, Cambridge, 2021).

Kalid, Saif, 'India's 'Blockade' Snuffs Out Nepal's Medical Lifeline', *Al Jazeera*, 21 November 2015.

Kandiyoti, Deniz, 'Bargaining with Patriarchy', *Gender and Society*, 2(3), 1988, pp. 274–90.

Kannan, R., *MGR: A Life* (Penguin India, New Delhi, 2017).

Kapur, Avani and Devashish Deshpande, 'Swachh Bharat Mission (Gramin) 3 Years On', *Accountability Initiative*, 2017.

Karthikeyan, D., Hugo Gorringe and Stalin Rajangam, 'Dalit Political Imagination and Replication in Contemporary Tamil Nadu', *Economic and Political Weekly*, 47(36), 2012, pp. 30–34.

Karwa, Surbhi, 'Intersectionality, the Missing Link in the Women's Reservation Bill', BehanBox, 16 February 2023.

Kaur, Banjot, 'WHO Is Disputing India's COVID Death Numbers, So Govt Wants to Bury Global Report', *The Wire*, 18 April 2022.

Khan, Maulana Wahiduddin and Goodword, *Quran: A Simple English Translation* (Goodword Books, New Delhi, 2013).

Khatiwoda, Rajan, Simon Cubelic and Axel Michaels, *The Muluki Ain of 1854: Nepal's First Legal Code* (Heidelburg University Publishing, Heidelburg, 2021).

Kidd, Stephen, Rebecca Calder and Emily Wylde, 'Assessing Targeting Options for Nepal's Social Grants—What Does the Evidence Tell Us?' *Development Pathways*, 2011.

Klonner, Stefan and Christian Oldiges, 'The Welfare Effects of India's Rural Employment Guarantee', *Journal of Development Economics*, Vol. 157(C), 2022.

Kooiman, Dick, 'The Strength of Numbers: Enumerating Communities in India's Princely States', *Journal of South Asian Studies*, 20(1), 1997, pp. 81–98.

Korpi, Walter and Joakim Palme, 'The Paradox of Redistribution and Strategies of Equality: Welfare State Institutions, Inequality, and Poverty in the Western Countries', *American Sociological Review*, 63(5), 1998, pp. 661–87.

Kothari, Rajni, *Caste in Indian Politics*, 2nd revised edition, revised by James Manor (Orient Blackswan, Hyderabad, 2010).

Kumar, Abhay, 'Over 3,000 Teachers Surrender Fake Degrees in Bihar', *Deccan Herald*, 20 October 2019.

Kumar, Ashwani, *Peasant Unrest, Community Warriors and State Power in India: The Case of Private Caste Senas (Armies) in Bihar* (Thesis, The University of Oklahoma, Oklahoma, 2003).

Kumar, Awanish, 'A Class Analysis of the "Bihari Menace"', *Economic and Political Weekly*, 44(28), 2009, pp. 124–27.

Kumar, Awanish, 'Where Is Caste in Development?' *Economic and Political Weekly*, 50(45), 2015.

Kumar, Dhruba, *Social Inclusion, Human Development and Nation Building in Nepal* (Vajra Books, Kathmandu, 2013).

Kumar, Manish and Deepshika Ghosh, 'No Aadhaar, No Food? 11-Year-Old Girl Died "Begging for Rice", Says Jharkhand Family', NDTV, 17 October 2017.

Kumar, Manish, 'Temple Cleaned, Idols Washed after Bihar Chief Minister's Visit', NDTV, 28 September 2014.

Kumar, Radha, *The History of Doing: An Illustrated Account of Movements for Women's Rights and Feminism in India, 1800–1990* (Kali for Women, New Delhi, 1993).

Kumar, Rajiv, 'On an Average, India Reported 10 Cases of Rape of Dalit Women Daily in 2019, NCRB Data Shows', News18, 3 October 2020.

Kumar, Sanjay and Rakesh Ranjan, 'Bihar: Development Matters', *Economic and Political Weekly*, 44(39), 2009, pp. 141–44.

Kumarasingham, Harshan, '"The Jewel of the East Yet Has Its Flaws": The Deceptive Tranquillity Surrounding Sri Lankan Independence', Working Paper (University Library of Heidelberg, 2013).

Kumari, Saroj, *Role of Women in the Freedom Movement in Bihar, 1912–1947* (Janaki Prakashan, Patna, 2005).

Kundu, Tadit, 'Why Kerala Is Like Maldives and Uttar Pradesh, Pakistan', *The Mint*, 17 December 2015.

Kunnath, George J., *Rebels from the Mud Houses: Dalits and the Making of the Maoist Revolution in Bihar* (Social Science Press, New Delhi and Bengaluru, 2012).

Kunnath, George, 'Compliance or Defiance? The Case of Dalits and Mahadalits', *Journal of the Anthropological Society of Oxford*, 5(1), 2013, pp. 36–59.

Lata, Kusum, 'The Women's Question in the Naxalite Movement in Bihar: Experiences of Women Leaders of Nari Mukti Sangharsh Samiti (NMSS) and Nari Mukti Sangh (NMS)', Working Paper Series 2019/1 (Department of Sociology, South Asian University, New Delhi, 2019).

Leve, Lauren, '"Failed Development" and Rural Revolution in Nepal: Rethinking Subaltern Consciousness and Women's Empowerment', *Anthropological Quarterly*, 80(1), 2007, pp. 127–72.

Lieten, G.K., 'The Human Development Puzzle in Kerala', *Journal of Contemporary Asia*, 32(1), 2007, pp. 47–68.

Lijphart, Arend, 'Comparative Politics and the Comparative Method', *The American Political Science Review*, 65(3), 1971, pp. 682–93.

Limbu, Sangita Thebe, 'Nepal's House of Cards: Are Women Included or Co-opted in Politics?' *South Asia LSE Blog*, 2 February 2018.

Louis, Prakash, 'Bihar: Class War Spreads to New Areas', *Economic and Political Weekly*, 50(23), 2000, pp. 7–8.

Louis, Prakash, 'Lynchings in Bihar: Reassertion of Dominant Castes', *Economic and Political Weekly*, 42(44), 2007, pp. 26–28.

Luna, K.C. and Gemma Van Der Haar, 'Living Maoist Gender Ideology: Experiences of Women Ex-combatants in Nepal', *International Feminist Journal of Politics*, 21(3), 2019, pp. 434–53.

Mackay, F., M. Kenny and L. Chappell, 'New Institutionalism through a Gender Lens: Towards a Feminist Institutionalism?' *International Political Science Review*, 31(5), 2010, pp. 573–88.

Mahajan, Shobhit, 'Decay and Darkness in Bihar', *Economic and Political Weekly*, 50(2), 2015.

Mahat, A., M. Zimmerman, R. Shakya and R.B. Gerzoff, 'Medical Scholarships Linked to Mandatory Service: The Nepal Experience', *Frontiers in Public Health*, 8, 2020.

Mahmud, Wahiduddin and Simeen Mahmud, 'Development, Welfare and Governance: Explaining Bangladesh's "Development Surprise"', in Mahmud, Wahiduddin and Simeen Mahmud (eds), *Development and Welfare Policy in South Asia Development and Welfare Policy in South Asia* (Routledge, New York, 2014).

Mahurkar, Vaishnavi, 'Feminist Poetry: Contemporary Woman Poets Who Challenge Patriarchy in Hindi & Urdu', *Feminism in India*, 13 February 2017.

Mainali, Sujit, 'How Discriminatory Was the First Muluki Ain against Dalits?' *South Asia Check*, 21 August 2015.

Maiti, K.D. and Santosh Mehrotra, 'The Curious Case of India's Millions of "Missing" Poor People', *The Wire*, 12 January 2022.

Malla, Y.B., 'Changing Policies and the Persistence of Patron-Client Relations in Nepal: Stakeholders' Responses to Changes in Forest Policies', *Environmental History*, 6(2), 2001, pp. 287–307.

Mamoon, Muntassir, Mo Māhabubara Rahamāna and University of Dhaka International Centre for Bengal Studies, *Material Conditions of the Subalterns: Nineteenth Century East Bengal* (International Centre for Bengal Studies, 2009).

Manohar, Asit, 'Indian Billionaire Made More Money than Elon Musk, Jeff Bezos, Bill Gates in Q4', *The Mint*, 1 April 2022.

Manoj Mitta, *Caste Pride: Battles for Equality in Hindu India* (Westland Books, Chennai, 2023).

Marx, Karl, *Notes on Indian History* (664–1858) (Foreign Languages Pub. House, Moscow, 1900).

Masih, Niha, 'Who Is Gautam Adani? Asia's Richest Man Is Rocked by Fraud Claims', *Washington Post*, 28 January 2023.

Mateer, Samuel, *Native Life in Travancore* (W.H. Allen & Co, London, 1883).

Mateer, Samuel, *The Land of Charity* (John Snow and Company, London, 1871).

Mehrotra, Santosh and Richard Jolly, *Development with a Human Face: Experiences in Social Achievement and Economic Growth* (Oxford University Press, Oxford, New York, 2000).

Mehrotra, Santosh, 'Well-being and Caste in Uttar Pradesh: Why UP Is Not Like Tamil Nadu', *Economic and Political Weekly*, 41(40), 2006, pp. 4261–71.

Mehrotra, Santosh, *Integrating Economic and Social Policy: Good Practices from High-Achieving Countries* (United Nations Children's Fund [UNICEF], New York, 2000).

Menon, Nivedita, 'Elusive "Woman": Feminism and Women's Reservation Bill', *Economic and Political Weekly*, 35(43/44), 2000, pp. 3835–39, 3841–44.

Meyer, Eric, 'The Specificity of Sri Lanka: Towards a Comparative History of Sri Lanka and India', *Economic and Political Weekly*, 31(7), 1996.

Mill, John Stuart, *A System of Logic Ratiocinative and Inductive: Being a Connected View of the Principles of Evidence and the Methods of Scientific Investigation* (John W. Parker, West Strand, London, 1843).

Mint, 'How Much Did India's Richest Earn during the Pandemic?' *The Mint*, 26 March 2021.

Mishra, Girish, 'Review of the Internal Colony', *Sociological Bulletin*, 23(1), 1974, pp. 144–47.

Mishra, Satyavrat, 'Bihar's Bitter Lesson in Teacher Recruitment', *Business Standard*, 19 July 2014.

MoE, *Report on Unified District Information System for Education Plus (UDISE+), 2018-19* (English) (Ministry of Education Department of School Education and Literacy, Government of India, 2020).

Momin, A.R., 'Muslim Caste: Theory and Practice', *Economic and Political Weekly*, 10 (14), 1975, pp. 580–82.

Mondol, Martina, 'Women's Contribution in Language Movement', *Daily Observer*, 21 February 2016.

Mookherjee, Nayanika, 'Gendered Embodiments: Mapping the Body-Politic of the Raped Woman and the Nation in Bangladesh', *Feminist Review*, 88, 2008, pp. 36–53.

Mookherjee, Nayanika, *The Spectral Wound: Sexual Violence, Public Memories, and the Bangladesh War of 1971* (Duke University Press, Durham, 2015).
Muhammad, Anu, 'Rise of the Corporate NGO in Bangladesh', *Economic and Political Weekly*, 53(39), 2018, pp. 46–52.
Mukherjee, Gopal Maju, 'C.R. Das and the Bengal Pact', *Proceedings of the Indian History Congress, 2000-2001*, 61(1), pp. 739–46.
Mukherjee, S.N., 'Class, Caste and Politics in Calcutta 1815–38', in *Calcutta: Myths and History* (Subarnarekha, Calcutta, 1977).
Mulmi, Amish Raj, 'Codifying the Breaking of Wind', *The Kathmandu Post*, 8 July 2021.
Muni, S.D., *Maoist Insurgency in Nepal: The Challenge and the Response* (Rupa Publishers, New Delhi, 2003).
Murshid, K.A.S., K. Iqbal and M. Ahmed, 'A Study on Remittance Inflows and Utilization', United Nations Development Programme and International Migration Organisation, Regional Office for South Asia, Dhaka, 2002.
Murthy, Laxmi, 'The Birangana and the Birth of Bangladesh', *Himal Southasian*, 20 March 2012.
Narayan, Swati, 'Aadhaar-for-food Can't Be a Mandatory Requirement', *Hindustan Times*, 22 February 2018.
Narayan, Swati, 'Breaking New Ground: Women's Employment in India's NREGA, the Pandemic Lifeline', *Gender and Development*, 30(1–2), pp. 217–46.
Narayan, Swati, 'In Jharkhand, Suspected Starvation Death Sheds Light on Deprivation of a Whole Settlement', *Scroll*, 25 June 2018.
Narayan, Swati, 'India Surpassed: The Price of Inequality in South Asia', Doctoral Thesis, Tata Institute of Social Sciences, Mumbai, 2019.
Narayan, Swati, 'Towards Equality in Healthcare: Trends Over Two Decades', *Economic and Political Weekly*, 51(12), 2016.
Narayan, Swati, *Serve the Essentials: What Governments and Donors Must Do to Improve South Asia's Essential Services* (Oxfam International, New Delhi, 2006).
Nayak, Rajesh Kumar, 'Naxalism, Private Caste-based Militias and Rural Violence in Central Bihar', Proceedings of the Indian History Congress, 73, 2012, pp. 1303–12.

Newclick, 'Women Sanitation Workers Protest Against Govt "Lies" on Sewer Deaths', Newsclick, 28 August 2023.

Newman, S. Katherine and Sukhdeo Thorat, *Blocked by Caste: Economic Discrimination in Modern India* (Oxford University Press, New Delhi, 2012).

Nilsen, Alf Gunvald, 'India's Turn to Rights-Based Legislation (2004–2014): A Critical Review of the Literature', *Social Change*, 48(4), 2018, pp. 653–65.

Nisar, M. and Meena Kandasamy, *Ayyankali: A Dalit Leader of Organic Protest* (Other Books, Calicut, Kerala, 2007).

Office for National Statistics, 'How Has Life Expectancy Changed over Time?', Office of National Statistics, United Kingdom, 9 September 2015.

Omvedt, Gail, *Dalits and the Democratic Revolution: Dr Ambedkar and the Dalit Movement in Colonial India* (Sage, Newbury Park and New Delhi, 1994).

Oommen, T.K., 'Development Policy and the Nature of Society: Understanding the Kerala Model', *Economic and Political Weekly*, 44(13), 2009, pp. 25–31.

Osella, Filippo and Caroline Osella, *Social Mobility in Kerala: Modernity and Identity in Conflict* (Pluto Press, London, 2000).

Osmana, S., *Shree Narayana Guru* (Critical Quest, New Delhi, 2005).

Osmani, Siddiqui, 'Has Microcredit Helped the Rural Poor of Bangladesh? An Analytical Review of the Evidence So Far', Working Paper (Institute of Microfinance, 2014).

Oxfam and ANSISS, 'Mapping Inequality in Bihar' (Oxfam India and A.N. Sinha Institute of Social Sciences, Patna, 2020).

Oxfam, 'Inequality Kills, India Supplement 2022', Working Paper (Oxfam India, New Delhi, 2022).

Oxfam, 'Survival of the Richest: The India Story' (Oxfam India, New Delhi, 2023).

Oxford COVID-19 Government Response Tracker, https://covidtracker.bsg.ox.ac.uk.

Pal, Gobinda, 'Caste and Access to Public Services', *Economic and Political Weekly*, 51(31), 2015, p. 7.

Palacios, Robert, 'Universal Social Protection: Universal Old-age and Disability Pensions, and Other Universal Allowances in Nepal',

Social Protection in Asia (International Labour Organisation, 2016).

Pandian, M.S.S., 'Notes on the Transformation of Dravidian Ideology: Tamilnadu, c. 1900–1940', *Social Scientist*, 22(5–6), 1994.

Pandian, M.S.S., *Brahmin and Non-Brahmin: Genealogies of the Tamil Political Present* (Permanent Press, New Delhi, 2007).

Panikar, P.G.K. and C.R. Soman, *Health Status of Kerala: The Paradox of Economic Backwardness and Health Development* (Centre for Development Studies, Trivandrum, 1984).

Papada, Evie, David Altman, Fabio Angiolillo, Lisa Gastaldi, Tamara Köhler, Martin Lundstedt, Natalia Natsika, Marina Nord, Yuko Sato, Felix Wiebrecht and Staffan I. Lindberg, 'Defiance in the Face of Autocratization: Democracy Report 2023', Working Paper (University of Gothenburg: Varieties of Democracy Institute (V-Dem Institute), Sweden, 2023.

Paran, Amitava and Kanika Sharma, 'Where Are the Kids? The Curious Case of Government Schools in Bihar' (Jan Jagran Shakti Sanghatan, Patna, 2023).

Parth, M.N., 'In Kheri: Changing Sides for Health', *People's Archive of Rural India*, 24 February 2022.

Parvati, 'Women in the People's War in Nepal', *Economic and Political Weekly*, 40(50), 2005, pp. 5234–36.

Parvez, Saimum, 'Understanding the Shahbag and Hefajat Movements in Bangladesh: A Critical Discourse Analysis', *Journal of Asian and African Studies*, 57(4), 2022, pp. 841–55.

Paswan, Bhola, 'Data Reveals Local Elections a Disaster for Gender Equality', *The Record*, 14 October 2017.

Patel, Aakar, The *Price of the Modi Years* (Westland Books, Chennai, 2021).

Perappadan, Bindu Shajan, 'WHO Has Released the Excess Death Estimates without Adequately Addressing India's Concerns: Health Ministry', *The Hindu*, 5 May 2022.

Petesch, Patti, 'Women's Empowerment Arising from Violent Conflict and Recovery: Life Stories from Four Middle-Income Countries', *USAID Microlinks* (USAID, Washington, DC, 2011).

Pillay, K.K., *South India and Sri Lanka: Sir William Meyer Lectures (1958–59)* (University of Madras 2001).

Pokharel, Ridish K., 'Pro-poor Programs Financed through Nepal's Community Forestry Funds: Does Income Matter?' *Mountain Research and Development*, 29(1), 2009, pp. 67–74.

Pradhan, Gyan, 'Nepal's Civil War and Its Economic Costs', *Journal of International and Global Studies*, 1(1), 2009, pp. 114–31.

Pratham, 'Survey Process—Instruction Booklet', *Annual Status of Education Report* (ASER Centre, New Delhi, 2020).

Pratham, *Annual Status of Education Report (ASER) (Rural): 2017 Beyond Basics* (ASER Centre, New Delhi, 2019).

Pratham, *Annual Status of Education Report (ASER) (Rural): 2018 Provisional* (ASER Centre, New Delhi, 2019).

Pratham, *Annual Status of Education Report (Rural) 2022 Provisional* (ASER Centre, New Delhi, 2023).

Prodip, Mahbub Alam, 'Cultural Obstacles to Women's Political Empowerment in India and Bangladesh: A Comparative Perspective', *Asian Journal of Comparative Politics*, 7(9), 2022, pp. 449–65.

Prodip, Mahbub Alam, 'Exclusion Through Inclusion: Institutional Constraints on Women's Political Empowerment in India and Bangladesh,' *World Affairs*, 184(2), 2021, pp. 213–44.

Punjabi, Kavita, 'Otiter Jed or Times of Revolution: Ila Mitra, the Santals and Tebhaga Movement', *Economic and Political Weekly*, 14(33), 2010.

Pyakurel, Uddhab, *Maoist Movement in Nepal* (Adriot Publishers, New Delhi, 2007).

Quint, 'Dalit Youth Killed in Rajasthan for His "Good Looks", Say Kin; Cops Cite Rivalry', *The Quint*, 19 March 2022.

Rahman, Andaleeb, 'Universal Food Security Program and Nutritional Intake: Evidence from the Hunger Prone KBK Districts in Odisha', *Food Policy*, 63, pp. 73–86.

Raj, Prakash A., *Maoists in the Land of Buddha* (Nirala Publications, New Delhi, 2004).

Rajshekhar, M., *Despite the State: Why India Lets Its People Down and How They Cope* (Westland Books, Chennai, 2020).

Ramachandran, V.K., 'On Kerala's Development Achievements', in Jean Drèze and Amartya Sen (eds), *Indian Development: Selected Regional Perspectives* (Clarendon Press, Oxford, 1997).

Ramalingaswami, V., U. Jonsson and J. Rohde, 'Malnutrition: A South Asian Enigma', in Gillespie Stuart (ed.) *Malnutrition in South Asia: A Regional Profile, ROSA Publication, Report 5* (UNICEF Regional Office for South Asia, Kathmandu, Nepal, 1997).

Raman, K. Ravi, *Development, Democracy and the State: Critiquing the Kerala Model of Development* (Routledge, New Delhi, 2010).

Rao, Jammi N., 'Inconvenient Truth: Why the Modi Govt Is Choosing "Denial" as Its Response to WHO's Covid Death Toll', Newslaundry, 9 May 2022.

Rao, Kavitha, *Lady Doctors: The Untold Stories of India's First Women in Medicine* (Westland Books, Chennai, 2021).

Rashidnzzamn, M., 'Election Politics in Pakistan Villages', *Journal of Commonwealth Political Studies,* 4, 1966, pp. 192–4.

Rashmi Verma, 'Swachh Survekshan Gramin Reports 62% Toilet Coverage, Surveys 0.72% Villages in India', *Down to Earth*, 10 August 2017.

Rasul, Golam and Eklabya Sharma, 'Understanding the Poor Economic Performance of Bihar and Uttar Pradesh, India: A Macro-Perspective', *Regional Studies, Regional Science*, 1(1), 2014, pp. 221–39.

Rasul, Golam, Apsara Karki Nepal, Abid Hussain, Amina Maharjan, Surendra Joshi, Anu Lama, Prakriti Gurung, Farid Ahmad, Arabinda Mishra and Eklabya Sharma, 'Socio-Economic Implications of COVID-19 Pandemic in South Asia: Emerging Risks and Growing Challenges', *Frontiers in Sociology*, 6, 24 February 2021.

Ratcliffe, J., 'Social Justice and the Demographic Transition: Lessons from India's Kerala State', *International Journal of Health Services: Planning, Administration, Evaluation*, 8(1), 1978, pp. 123–44.

Ravelo, Jenny Lei, 'The World's Largest NGO Rethinks Its Future', *Devex*, 13 January 2021.

Ray, Jhilam and Rajarshi Majumdar, 'Snakes and Ladders: Intergenerational Income Mobility in India', *Indian Journal of Human Development*, 7(2), 2013.

Rege, Sharmila, 'Dalit Women Talk Differently: A Critique of "Difference" and Towards a Dalit Feminist Standpoint Position', *Economic and Political Weekly*, 33(44), 1998, pp. 39–46.

Rhys, D., *Psalms of the Early Buddhists: I. Psalms of the Sisters* (Oxford University Press, London, 1909).

Risley, Sir Herbert Hope, *The Imperial Gazetteer of India, Vol. 24: Travancore—Zira* (Clarendon Press, Oxford, 1908).

Robb, Peter, 'Peasants' Choices? Indian Agriculture and the Limits of Commercialization in Nineteenth-century Bihar', *The Economic History Review*, New Series, 45(1), 1992, pp. 97–119.

Rodgers, Gerry, Amrita Datta, Janine Rodgers, Sunil Mishra and Alakh Sharma, *The Challenges to Inclusive Development in Rural Bihar* (Institute for Human Development, New Delhi, 2013).

Rowbotham, Sheila, *Women in Movement: Feminism and Social Action* (Routledge, New York, 1992).

Rowlatt, Justin, 'The Woman Who Cut off Her Breasts to Protest a Tax', *BBC News*, 28 July 2016.

Roy, Archana K., R.B. Bhagat, K.C. Das, Sunil Sarode and R.S. Reshmi, *A Report on Causes and Consequences of Outmigration in the Middle Ganga Plain* (Department of Migration and Urban Studies, International Institute of Population Sciences, Mumbai, 2021).

Roy, Asim, *The Islamic Syncretistic Tradition in Bengal* (Princeton University Press, Princeton, NJ, 1983).

Roy, Prannoy and Dorab R. Sopariwala, *The Verdict: Decoding India's Elections* (Vintage, New Delhi, 2019).

Roy, Tirthankar, *The Economic History of India, 1857–1947*, 3rd edn (Oxford University Press, New Delhi, 2000).

Rukmini, S., 'India's Objections to WHO COVID-19 Mortality Estimates Are Misleading, Experts Say', *The Wire*, 28 April 2022.

Sadasivan, S.N., *A Social History of India* (APH Publishing Corporation, New Delhi, 2000).

Saikia, Yasmin, *Women, War, and the Making of Bangladesh: Remembering 1971.* (Duke University Press, Durham, 2011).

Sajjad, Mohammad, 'Atrocity against Dalits in Bihar', *Economic and Political Weekly*, 51(51), 2016.
Sajjad, Mohammad, 'The Shocking Silence of Muzaffarpur', *Rediff*, 2 August 2018.
Sakia, Yasmin, *Women, War, and the Making of Bangladesh* (Duke University Press, Durham, 2011).
Samarendra, Padmanabh, 'Between Number and Knowledge: Career of Caste in Colonial Census', in I. Banerjee-Dube (ed.), *Caste in History* (Oxford University Press, New Delhi, 2008).
Sanaullah, Muhammad, *A.K. Fazlul Huq: Portrait of a Leader* (Homeland Press Publications, 1995).
Santosh Singh, '"Fake" Degree Probe in Bihar: For 53,000 Contract Teachers, "Last Chance' to Prove Degrees Real, *The Indian Express*, 10 January 2021.
Sardesai, Shreyas, Sandeep Shastri, Sanjay Kumar and Suhas Palshikar, 'Decoding the Close Bihar Election 2020 Verdict', *The Indian Express*, 19 November 2020.
Schneiderman, Sara and Mark Turin, 'The Path to Jan Sarkar in Dolakha District: Towards an Ethnography of the Maoist Movement', in M. Hutt (ed.), *Himalayan People's War: Nepal's Maoist Rebellion* (Indiana University Press, Bloomington, Indiana, 2004).
Scroll Staff, 'West Bengal: 'Not Even a Bird Will Be Allowed from Across the Border If BJP Wins, says Amit Shah', *Scroll*, 18 February 2021.
Selin, Helaine, *Encyclopaedia of the History of Science, Technology, and Medicine in Non-Western Cultures*, 2nd edn (Springer Dordrecht, GX Dordrecht, The Netherlands, 2008).
Selmer, Neil, *A Theory of Collective Behaviour* (The Free Press, New York, 1965).
Sen, Amartya, 'Sri Lanka's Achievements: How and When', in T.N. Shrinivasan and Pranab Bardhan (eds), *Rural Poverty in South Asia* (Columbia University Press, New Delhi, 1985).
Sen, Amartya, 'Food, Economics, and Entitlements', in Jean Drèze and Amartya Sen, *The Political Economy of Hunger, Volume 1: Entitlement and Wellbeing* (Oxford University Press, Oxford, 1990), p. 48.

Sen, Amartya, 'Imperial Illusions', *New Republic*, 31 December 2007.
Sen, Amartya, 'What's Happening in Bangladesh?' *The Lancet*, 382(9909), 2013, 1966–68.
Sen, Amartya, *Development as Freedom* (Random House, New York, 1999).
Sewak, Ram, 'Congress Socialist Party in Bihar—1934-39', *Proceedings of the Indian History Congress*, 41, 1980, pp. 540–46.
Shah, Alpa and Judith Pettigrew (eds), *Windows into a Revolution: Ethnographies of Maoism in India and Nepal* (Routledge, New Delhi, 2012).
Shah, Alpa, 'Humaneness and Contradictions', *Economic and Political Weekly*, 52(21), 2017.
Shamasastry (tr.), *Kautilya's Arthashastra* (Government Press, Bangalore, 1915).
Sharma, Alakh and Jerry Rodgers, 'Structural Change in Bihar's Rural Economy', *Economic and Political Weekly*, 50(52), 2015.
Sharma, Jeevan, *Political Economy of Social Change and Development in Nepal* (Bloomsbury, New Delhi, 2021).
Sheoraj, S. 'Bechain', *Voices of Awakening*, Literary Review, *The Hindu*, 3 August 2008.
Shiga, Miwako, 'The Non-Brahmin Movement', in Noboru Karashima, *A Concise History of South India: Issues and Interpretations* (Oxford University Press, Oxford, 2014).
Shiva Kumar, A.K., Arnab Acharya, K. Nagaraj, Rama Baru and Sanghamitra Acharya, 'Inequities in Access to Health Services in India: Caste, Class and Region', *Economic and Political Weekly*, 45(38), 2010.
Shrivastava, Rahul, 'WHO "Excess Covid Death" Report: Govt Lens on Pharma Firms Denied Entry to India', *India Today*, 11 May 2022.
Sijapati, Bandita, 'The Quest for Achieving Universal Social Protection in Nepal: Challenges and Opportunities', *Indian Journal of Human Development*, 2017, 11(1), pp. 17–36.
Singh, Jagpal, 'Karpoori Thakur: A Socialist Leader in the Hindi Belt', *Forward Press*, 15 August 2016.
Singh, K.S., 'Solar Traditions in Tribal and Folk Cultures of India', *India International Centre Quarterly*, 19(4), 1992, pp. 28–39.

Singh, Pratibha, 'Women's Role in the Naxalite Movement', Centre for Land Welfare Studies (CLAWS) (blog), 27 April 2013.

Singh, Prerna, 'We-ness and Welfare: A Longitudinal Analysis of Social Development in Kerala, India', *World Development*, 39 (2), 2011, pp. 282–93.

Singh, Prerna, *How Solidarity Works for Welfare: Subnationalism and Social Development in India* (Cambridge University Press, Cambridge, 2016).

Singh, Santosh, *Ruled or Misruled: Story and Destiny of Bihar* (Bloomsbury, New Delhi, 2015).

Singh, Savita, 'Hindi *Kavita: Main Kiski Aurat Hun*', 2015, https://www.lyrikline.org/en/poems/12171.

Sinha, Indu and Arvind Sinha, 'Ranveer Sena and "Massacre Widows"', *Economic and Political Weekly*, 50(23), 2015, pp. 7–8.

Sinha, Indu B., '"Escape" and "Struggle": Routes to Women's Liberation in Bihar' (Dissertation, University of Bath, 2002).

Sinha, Sachchidanand, *The Internal Colony: A Study in Regional Exploitation* (Sindhu Publications, Mumbai, 1973)

Skocpol, Theda, 'Historical Institutionalism in Contemporary Political Science', in I. Katznelson (ed.), *Political Science: State of the Discipline* (W.W. Norton, New York, 2002).

Sobhan, Rehman, *Bangladesh: Problems of Governance, Governing South Asia* (Konark Publishers, Delhi, 1993).

Spears, Dean, 'Exposure to Open Defecation Can Account for the Indian Enigma of Child Height', *Journal of Development Economics*, 146, 2020, 102277.

Srinivas, M.N., 'A Note on Sanskritization and Westernization', *The Far Eastern Quarterly*, 15(4), 1956, pp. 481–96.

Srinivas, M.N., 'Mobility in the Caste System', in D. Gupta (ed.), *Social Stratification in India: Readings in Sociology and Social Anthropology* (Oxford University Press, Delhi, 1989).

Srinivas, M.N., *Caste in Modern India and Other Essays* (Asia Publishing House, New York, 1962).

Srivastav, Nikhil, 'Labelling versus Outcomes: On Swachh Bharat Mission', *The Hindu*, 15 November 2017.

Srivastava, Sumit S., 'Violence and Dalit Women's Resistance in Rural Bihar', *Indian Anthropologist*, 37(2), 2001, pp. 31–44.

Stepan, Alfred, Juan J. Linz and Yogendra Yadav, *Crafting State-Nations: India and Other Multinational Democracies* (Johns Hopkins University Press, Baltimore, 2011).

Stevens, Harry, 'Seven Decades After Independence, Most Dalit Farmers Still Landless', *Hindustan Times*, 31 February 2018.

Subrahmaniam, Vidya, 'There Can Be No Swachh Bharat Without Ending Institutional Discrimination against Dalits', *The Wire*, 31 October 2017.

Summerfield, Penny, *Women, War and Social Change: Women in Britain in World War II* (Palgrave Macmillan, London, 1988).

Surendranath, Nidhi, '200 Years On, Nangeli's Sacrifice Only a Fading Memory', *The Hindu*, 21 October 2013.

Tagade, Nitin, Ajaya Kumar Naik and Sukhadeo Thorat, 'Wealth Ownership and Inequality in India: A Socio-Religious Analysis', *Journal of Social Inclusion Studies*, 4(2), 2018, pp. 196–213.

Tanjeem, N. and R.E. Fatima, 'The 2018 Road Safety Protest in Bangladesh: How a Student Crowd Challenged (or Could Not Challenge) the Repressive State', in I. Rivers and C.L. Lovin (eds), *Young People Shaping Democratic Politics* (Palgrave Macmillan, Cham, 2023).

Tarique, Mohammed, 'How the Muzaffarpur Sex Scandal Was Unearthed', *Rediff*, 2 August 2018.

Teltumbde, Anand, 'No Swachh Bharat Without Annihilation of Caste', *Economic and Political Weekly*, 49(45), 2014.

Thapa, Shridhar and Sanjaya Acharya, 'Remittances and Household Expenditure in Nepal: Evidence from Cross-section Data', *Economies*, 5(16), 2017.

Thapar-Bjorkert, Suruchi, *Women in the Indian National Movement: Unseen Faces and Unheard Voices, 1930–42* (Sage, New Delhi, 2006).

Tharakan, P.K. Michael, 'History as Development Experience: Desegrated and Deconstructed Analysis of Kerala' (Dissertation, Mahatma Gandhi University, Kottayam, 1997).

The Lancet, 'Water with Sugar and Salt', *The Lancet*, 312(8084): 1978. pp. 300–1.

The Print, 'Nepal's Latest Crisis and Its Unstable Political History with 49 PMs in 58 Years', *The Print*, 23 December 2020.

The Wire Staff, '2 Dalit Children Beaten to Death for Defecating in Public in Madhya Pradesh', *The Wire*, 25 September 2019.

Thomas, Samuel V., *One Caste, One Religion, One God: A Study of Sree Narayana Guru* (Sterling Publishers, New Delhi, 1977).

Tilly, Charles, *Durable Inequality* (University of California Press, Los Angeles, 1999).

Tilly, Charles, *Social Movements, 1768–2004* (Routledge, Boulder, 2004).

Timberg, Thomas, 'Regions in Indian Development', *Pacific Affairs*, 53(4), 1980, pp. 643–50.

Tiwari, Bishwa Nath, 'An Assessment of the Causes of Conflict in Nepal', Himalayan Research Papers Archive, UNM Digital Repository, September 2007.

TOI, 'Imitate the English Suffragettes: Advice to Colombo Women', *The Times of India*, 30 March 1928.

Transparency International, *Corruption Perceptions Index: 2022*, Transparency International, 2023.

Tripathi, Salil, 'Bangladesh's Quest for Closure', *The Caravan*, 21 September 2012.

Tripathi, Salil, *The Colonel Who Would Not Repent: The Bangladesh War and Its Unquiet Legacy* (Aleph Book Company, New Delhi, 2014).

TRT, 'Bangladesh's History of Student Protest Movements', *TRT World*, 10 August 2018.

Tsujita, Yuko, Hisaya Oda and Prabhat Ghosh, 'Development and Intra-state Disparities in Bihar', *Economic and Political Weekly*, 45(50), 2010, pp. 13–15.

UNDESA, 'Poverty, Unemployment, and Development Policy: A Case Study of Selected Issues with Reference to Kerala', United Nations. Department of Economic and Social Affairs, 1975.

UNDP, *COVID-19 and Human Development: Assessing the Crisis, Envisioning the Recovery, Human Development Reports* (UNDP, New York, 2021).

UNDP, *Human Development Report 2005* (UNDP, New York, 2005).

UNDP, *Human Development Report 2013: The Rise of the South—Human Progress in a Diverse World* (UNDP, New York, 2013).

UNDP, *Human Development Report 2016: Human Development for Everyone* (UNDP, New York, 2016).

UNDP, *Human Development Report 2019: Beyond Income, beyond Averages, Beyond Today: Inequalities in Human Development in the 21st Century* (UNDP, New York, 2019).

UNDP, *Human Development Report 2020: The Next Frontier—Human Development and the Anthropocene* (UNDP, New York, 2020).

UNDP, *Human Development Report 2021-22: Uncertain Times, Unsettled Lives: Shaping our Future in a Transforming World* (UNDP, New York, 2022).

UNDP, *Sri Lanka Human Development Report 2012: Bridging Regional Disparities for Human Development* (UNDP, New York, 2012).

UNFPA, *Against My Will: State of the World Population 2020* (United Nations Population Fund, New York, 2020).

Vaasanthi, *Cut-outs, Caste and Cine Stars: The World of Tamil Politics* (Penguin India, New Delhi, 2006).

Verma, B.S., *Socio-religious, Economic and Literary Condition of Bihar* (Munshi Ram Manohar Lal, Delhi, 1962).

Vishwanathan, E.S.A., *The Political Career of E.V. Ramaswamy Naicker* (Ravi and Vasanth Publishers, Madras, 1983).

Viswanathan, P.K. and Chandra Sekhar Bahinipati, 'Growth and Human Development in the Regional Economy of Gujarat, India: An Analysis of Missed Linkages', *Journal of Social and Economic Development*, 23(1), June 2021, pp. 25–47.

Vivek, S., 'Understanding Public Services in Tamil Nadu: An Institutional Perspective', *Social Science: Dissertations*, 175, 2010, Syracuse University.

Vivek, S., *Delivering Public Services Effectively: Tamil Nadu and Beyond* (Oxford University Press, New Delhi, 2014).

Vogel, Ann and Kim Korinek, 'Passing by the Girls? Remittance Allocation for Educational Expenditures and Social Inequality in Nepal's Households 2003–2004', *International Migration Review*, 46(1), 2012, pp. 61–100.

WDI, World Development Indicators, World Bank, Washington, DC, June 2016.

WDI, World Development Indicators, World Bank, Washington, DC, June 2023.

Webb, Beatrice's Typescript Diary, 30 May 1929–25 December 1931 (LSE Digital Library, London, 1931).

WEF, *Global Gender Gap Report 2021* (World Economic Forum, Davos, 2022).

Whelpton, John, 'The Quest for "Development": Economy and Environment, 1951–1991', in John Welpton, *A History of Nepal* (Cambridge University Press, New Delhi, 2005).

WHO, '14.9 Million Excess Deaths Associated with the COVID-19 Pandemic in 2020 and 2021', Press Release, World Health Organisation, 5 May 2022.

Wilkinson, Richard and Kate Pickett, *The Spirit Level: Why Greater Equality Makes Societies Stronger* (Bloomsbury Publishing, New York, 2010).

Wilson, Bezwada, 'Will Swachh Bharat Abhiyan Be a Success?' *The Hindu*, 30 September 2017.

Wire Staff, 'Rajasthan: Nine-Yr-Old Dalit Boy Passes Away After Alleged Assault by Schoolteacher', *The Indian Express*, 14 August 2022.

World Bank, 'Moving Up the Ladder: Poverty Reduction and Social Mobility in Nepal', Working Paper 106652 (World Bank, Washington, DC, 2016).

World Bank, 'Treasures of the Education System in Sri Lanka: Restoring Performance, Expanding Opportunities and Enhancing Prospects', Working Paper 47034 (World Bank, Human Development Unit, South Asia Region, Washington, DC, 2005).

World Bank, *Migration and Remittance Flows: Recent Trends and Outlook, 2013-2016*, Report 105075, Migration and Development Brief 25, 2016.

World Bank, *Poverty and Shared Prosperity 2022: Correcting Course* (World Bank, Washington, DC, 2022).

Yadav, Punam, 'White Sari: Transforming Widowhood in Nepal', *Gender, Technology and Development*, 20(1), 2016, pp. 1–24.

Yadav, Punam, *Social Transformation in Post-conflict Nepal: A Gender Perspective* (Routledge, London, 2016).

Yadav, Shikhar, 'Dalit Billionaires & "De-Sanskritisation": Is India Ready to "Rap"?' *The Quint*, 9 July 2021.

Yadav, Yogendra, 'Ambedkar Said Tyranny of Majority Is No Democracy, Indians Must Read Him Again', *The Print*, 14 April 2021.

Yadav, Yogendra, *The Rise of State-Nations—Lecture Transcript* (Centre for International Governance Innovation, Balsillie School of International Affairs, 2011).

Yadavar, Swagata, 'Casteism Will Not Allow Swachh Bharat Abhiyan to Succeed', *IndiaSpend*, August 2017.

Yami, Hisila, *People's War and Women's Liberation in Nepal* (Purvaiya Prakashan, Kathmandu, 2006).

Yee, Amy, 'Profile: The Icddr,b—Saving Lives in Bangladesh and Beyond', *The Lancet*, 381(9875), 2013, p. 1350.

Yesudas, R.N., *A People's Revolt in Travancore* (Kerala Historical Society, Trivandrum, 1975).

Yesudas, R.N., *Colonel John Munro in Travancore* (Kerala Historical Society, Trivandrum, 1977).

Yesudas, R.N., *The History of the London Missionary Society in Travancore, 1806–1908* (Kerala Historical Society, Trivandrum, 1980).

Yunus, Muhammad, *Banker to the Poor: The Story of the Grameen Bank* (Aurum Press, London, 2003).

Zelliot, Eleanor, 'Gandhi and Ambedkar: A Study in Leadership', in Ishita Banerjee-Dube (ed.), *Caste in History* (Oxford University Press, New Delhi, 2008).

Zharkevich, Ina, *Maoist People's War and the Revolution of Everyday Life in Nepal* (Cambridge University Press, Cambridge, 2019).

ACKNOWLEDGEMENTS

From the unforgettable Ramzan iftar parties in the modest homes of Bangladeshi villagers to celebrating chhath in Bihar to enjoying the rural market fairs in Nepal, the journey of nearly a decade to complete this book has been as memorable and colourful as it has been insightful. Am eternally grateful for the depth of generosity, hospitality and compassion that families in the humblest of homes have showered on me.

From day one, this research owes immeasurably to the unparalleled inspiration, commitment and generosity of Jean Drèze, my co-guide from Ranchi University and the Delhi School of Economics—there are simply no words in the dictionary, in any language. Infinite gratitude for being the beacon of light at every step of this journey and for your indelible legacy much beyond.

As an anchor at the Tata Institute of Social Sciences (TISS), I am also thankful to Ashwani Kumar for his steadfast support as a guide, and to all the faculty and staff at the School of Development Studies and the Doctoral Student Office. This research has also been truly collaborative with local researchers in every country, shaping and enriching its texture. Five angels went out of their way to support the logistics—Abul Kalam Azad of BRAC and Md Harun Ur Rashid of Pally Sahitya

Sangstha in Bangladesh's Panchagarh district, Parbati Sunuwar of Village Women Consciousness Centre (VWCC) in Nepal's Sindhuli, Sanjay Sahni and all the saathis of Samaj Pragati Shakti Sanghatan (SPSS) in Bihar's Muzaffarpur, and Abodh Kumar of Project Potential in Kishanganj district. Special thanks also to the forty women across the four districts who conducted this survey in local dialects, and the host families of different religions, castes, communities and languages who opened their doors and hearts.

For generously accompanying me on my preliminary recces as interpreters, special thanks to Ram Narayan Shreshta and Mustafa Shabuj of South Asian University. For Hindi translations of the survey, I am thankful to Dheeraj Kumar and Snehil Mishra in Ranchi, for Bengali to the generous Pratichi team especially Kumar-da, Swagata Nandi, Toa Bagchi and Piyali Pal in Kolkata and for Nepali to Jagdish Gautam in Kathmandu. For the meticulous data entry, my thanks to Snehil Mishra.

For the fieldwork in Nepal, Bijeta Shreshta of Jawaharlal Nehru University was extraordinary as an interpreter and friend. The icing on the cake is that Bijeta and Ram, both of whom were my Nepali translators, have now tied the knot—the best gift of my Ph.D. Time flies so quickly that my wonderful translator from Dhaka University in Bangladesh, Safiqul Islam, is also now married and soon will be a father. In Bihar, the teams coordinated by Ashwini Kumar and Mohammed Ismail in Kishanganj and by Sunita Devi and her band of women in Muzaffarpur district were equally stellar.

Am also deeply thankful to my long-time activist colleagues and friends. Maria Lourdes Almazan Khan of ASPBAE, Saloni Pradhan Singh of Didi Bahini in Kathmandu, A.M.R. Chowdhury of BRAC, Rasheda K. Chowdhury and K.M. Enamul Hoque of CAMPE, and Chinmaya Kumar in Patna who kindly opened the doors to their large networks of friends in civil society, journalism, bureaucracy and academia across borders. Am also particularly grateful to economist Rehman Sobhan in Bangladesh for his generosity. Special thanks also to Aashish Gupta for being a pillar of statistical support, S. Vivek for his insights on Tamil Nadu, and Chinnaiah Jangam, Sambuddha Chaudhuri for their comments on specific chapters. Immeasurable thanks are also due to many other unnamed friends and colleagues who have anchored this journey along the way. Also, a special thank you to all my friends in the Right to Food Campaign and other civil society networks who have been an extended activist family.

For the memorable year spent at the London School of Economics and Political Science, am truly grateful to Naila Kabeer and the Gender Institute, and to Duncan Green's for his steadfast support across decades. I also deeply value the many unforgettable friendships forged through the SAVE FOOD network—your light shone brighter than the London skyline.

Libraries are amongst the most cherished sacred spaces, and hope scores more can be built, especially in rural areas and in every school. For this research, am grateful for the facilities at the British Library and LSE Library (including the iconic Women's Library) in London, the National Archives in Kew, Nehru Memorial Library and National Archives in Delhi, the TISS Library in Mumbai, Bangladesh Institute for Development Studies and Central Library in Dhaka, A.N. Sinha Institute of Social Sciences Library in Patna and SAARC Library in Kathmandu.

For their scholarships and travel grants, sincere thanks also to the International Relations Office at TISS, the Sir Dorabji Tata Trust and the Commonwealth Scholarship Commission. At my current university, am truly grateful to Stephen P. Marks for his kindness and support along with the wonderful cohort of faculty, friends and students.

Acknowledgements

The storms after completing my doctorate were unexpectedly the hardest. Infinite gratitude to my inspiring sister Anu, my ever-caring parents Jaya and S.A. Narayan, and my extended family who have supported me in untold ways, as only families can. This journey is inspired by the fortitude of my grandmothers.

This book would have never seen the light of day without Rahul Bhatia and his last-minute inputs, and Anish Chandy who has been an angel as a wonderful literary agent and friend and has taken a leap of faith in championing this book. Immense gratitude to Ajitha G.S., who has been a magnificently empathetic editor to work with, as has the entire dream team at Westland Books. Am also so grateful to the stalwart public intellectuals in the field who have so graciously provided endorsements and, even more importantly, moral support through their inspirational work.

Travelling by train with the wind blowing on your face is one of the best ways to gain perspective and also step into the shoes of your co-travellers. I am most grateful that this cathartic journey across borders has gone much further towards the horizon and truly transformed me.

In the end, I hope this book does justice to all the faith that so many have placed in it. Hopefully, too, the contrasting of India's blistering inequalities with those of its neighbours will clear some of the mist in our path ahead as a nation.

INDEX

A

Aama Samuhas, 97, 108, 109, 156
Aama Surakshya, 107
absenteeism, 55, 60, 220, 221, 298
accountability, 82, 311
Accredited Social Health Activists (ASHAs), 19, 61
Adani, Gautam, 11, 203, 314
adivasis, 12, 31, 141, 143, 145, 169, 203, 239, 243, 271
affirmative action, 13, 113, 117, 228
Afghanistan, 7, 32, 46, 224, 226, 229
Africa, 30, 37, 212, 261, 319
African-American, 8, 201
agrestic slavery, 161, 162, 179
agro-processing, 5, 95, 199
Airbnb, 47
Airtel, 4
Akbar, Emperor, 88
All India Anna Dravida Munnetra Kazhagam (AIADMK), 167, 293, 294
Ambedkar, B.R.,12, 14, 141, 142, 197, 204, 205, 229, 248–50, 257, 271, 296, 317, 329
American, 8, 24, 96, 201, 312, 313
anganwadi, 31, 58, 132–35, 153, 157, 158, 186, 222, 245, 310
Annual Status of Education Report (ASER), 37, 50, 206, 212, 213, 215, 216, 218, 283, 318
anti-caste movements, 15, 126, 160, 161, 163, 164, 167, 196, 245
anti-Brahmanism, 167, 188
anti-discrimination, 142
anti-Hindi, 167, 292, 293
Antyodaya Anna Yojana, 31
Arab, 32, 84, 85, 114, 224, 229, 256
Argentina, 114
Arthashastra, 139, 248, 323
Ashoka, Emperor, 84, 169, 187
'ashrafisation', 84, 85, 229
autocracy, 74, 163, 224, 318
Awami League (AL), 58, 71, 75, 77, 90, 225
Ayyankali, Mahatma, 160, 162, 257, 316

B

Bachchan, Amitabh, 35
Bahuns, 64, 100, 118, 119, 124, 125, 240

Bai, Rani Parvati, 183
Bakhtiyar, Mohammad, 228
Bandaranaike, Sirimavo R.D.,
    185, 268
Bangladesh, 1, 3–8, 11, 13–17,
    22–24, 26–31, 33–41, 43–58,
    60–62, 64–67, 69, 71–78,
    80–84, 86, 87, 90–96, 100,
    109, 115, 122, 147, 148,
    158, 159, 193–96, 198–201,
    205, 208–13, 215, 217–28,
    230–36, 242, 251, 252, 274,
    276, 278, 281, 282, 295–
    302, 304–7, 311, 314–17,
    319, 321, 322, 324–26,
    329–32
Banglabandha, 27, 75, 209, 210
Bangladesh Nationalist Party
    (BNP), 75
bhadralok, 88, 89, 136, 195, 231
bhadramahila, 93
Bhattarai, Baburam, 106, 239
Bhumihar, 141, 143, 150, 151
Bhutan, 6, 8, 22, 28, 33, 194,
    200, 201, 209, 210, 278
Bihar, 8, 10, 11, 13, 15, 17,
    19–22, 24, 26, 27, 29–31,
    36, 37, 39, 40, 45, 48–58,
    60–63, 65–67, 96, 115, 129,
    131–52, 156, 158, 197, 198,
    202, 206, 207, 209, 210,
    213, 215, 217–23, 228, 233,
    245–54, 274, 281, 282, 298,
    299, 301, 306, 308, 310,
    312, 313, 315–18, 320–24,
    326, 327, 330, 331
biogas, 34
birangana, 94, 235, 316
Bishwakarmas, 110
Bonaparte, Napoleon, 62
Brahmin, 13, 64, 100, 103, 111,
    141, 142, 151, 161, 162,
    165–67, 179, 181–83, 187,
    239, 256, 257, 259, 266,
    290, 292, 293, 317
Braudel, 194, 270, 299
Brazil, 30
British, 8, 27, 84–89, 93, 108,
    136, 139, 141, 144, 161,
    168, 170, 171, 178, 181,
    183, 184, 188, 209, 230,
    231, 233, 249–51, 256, 257,
    261, 264–66, 289, 299, 302,
    304, 306, 332
    census, 85, 141
    colony, 27, 85, 88, 89, 139,
        231, 261, 289
    empire, 88, 93, 261, 304
    India, 8, 230, 233, 306
    library, 85, 266, 332
Buddha, 85, 101, 110, 238–40, 319
Buddhism, 84, 110, 111, 139,
    169, 170, 172, 184, 187,
    188, 195, 228, 249, 256,
    259, 270, 296, 305, 321

C

caste, 9–12, 14–16, 30, 31, 46,
    51, 55, 56, 58, 59, 64, 66,
    67, 84–86, 88, 89, 92, 97,
    100, 101, 103–5, 108, 110–
    21, 125, 131–33, 136–46,
    148, 150–52, 158, 160–66,
    168–70, 178–84, 187, 188,
    195–98, 200, 203–6, 215,
    216, 222, 228–31, 239, 243,
    245, 247–51, 256, 257, 259,
    260, 262, 265–67, 269–71,
    275, 285, 287, 288, 290,
    292, 293, 295, 296, 298–
    302, 306, 307, 309, 310,
    312–17, 322–27, 329, 331

associations, 141
discrimination, 10, 15, 111, 118, 120, 133, 138, 160, 161, 249, 307
hegemony, 120, 166
hierarchy, 183, 245
Hindus, 89, 139, 183, 184
inequalities, 104, 114, 195
militias, 143, 150, 151
politics, 144, 251, 298
prejudice, 92, 138, 143, 163
quotas, 293
violence, 140, 143, 151, 168, 248, 250, 299, 307
casteism, 13, 103, 127, 152, 182, 214, 329
census, 4, 35, 45, 85, 87, 140, 141, 175, 178, 201, 206, 215, 228–31, 239, 242, 246–48, 271, 274, 281, 298, 305, 310, 322
centre-left, 106, 171
Ceylon, 155, 169, 170, 176, 177, 180, 184, 185, 188, 256, 260, 261, 263, 264, 268, 269, 289, 295, 302, 304, 305, 309
Ceylon Women's Franchise Union, 155, 260
Colebrooke-Cameroon reforms, 170
    Donoughmore commission, 170, 185, 260, 264, 268, 269, 289
    Donoughmore constitution, 177, 261, 264
Champaran satyagraha, 144
Chandragupta, Emperor, 141
Chang, Ha-Joon, 45, 215, 255, 300
Channars, 163, 181, 182, 188, 266, 290

Channar Upper Cloth Revolt, 163, 181, 182, 188, 266
Chatterji, Joya, 88, 230–32, 300
Chennai, 165, 172, 315, 318–20
Chhath, 147, 251, 330
Chhattisgarh, 210, 214, 246, 296
chhaupadi pratha, 127, 244
Chhetris, 100, 101, 118
children, 7, 8, 10, 13, 14, 16, 22, 31, 33, 34, 36–40, 44, 45, 50–52, 54–57, 60, 63, 64, 72, 75, 76, 78, 79, 81, 82, 96, 100–102, 107, 108, 110, 115, 118, 120, 125, 132, 134, 135, 139, 149, 153, 157, 158, 162, 167, 169, 172, 173, 177, 179, 180, 186, 187, 197, 200, 207, 208, 213–18, 220–23, 226, 227, 233, 237, 239–41, 244, 248, 252, 258, 265, 274, 276, 278, 280, 283, 302, 304, 307, 310, 314, 325, 326
childbirth, 37
childcare, 31, 167
childhood, 34, 49, 50, 63, 64, 222
child mortality, 213
child sex ratios, 13
China, 6, 26, 116, 139, 203, 205, 212, 239, 255, 303
Christian, 93, 161, 169, 170, 177–79, 181, 183, 188, 211, 238, 249, 256, 260, 267, 270, 290, 296, 311
Christian missionaries, 93, 161, 170, 177, 178, 181, 256, 290
Civil Disobedience Movement, 93, 149

civil society, 30, 47, 76, 82, 107, 171, 332
    movements, 30, 82
    organisations, 47, 82
Cochin, 153, 163, 175, 176, 178, 179, 291
Colombo, 155, 188, 254, 305, 326
Colonialism, 26, 27, 85, 88, 89, 135–37, 139, 169, 170, 176, 178, 188, 230, 231, 234, 246, 260, 261, 264, 268, 269, 289, 296, 301, 304, 315, 317, 322, 324
Communism, 29, 86, 93, 106, 107, 112, 116, 125, 126, 144, 160, 163, 164, 169, 171, 179, 188, 189, 243, 255, 258, 262, 291, 309
community clinics, 58, 74–76, 221, 305
community forestry, 108, 109, 238, 310, 318
community-managed schools, 34
conflict, 94, 105, 112, 116, 117, 120–22, 124, 127, 140, 144, 232, 236, 242, 244, 248–50, 256, 257, 299, 301, 317, 318, 326
Constituent Assembly, 107, 113, 120, 249
Constitution, 12, 105, 107, 113, 114, 123, 149, 177, 195, 207, 224, 228, 242, 243, 249, 260, 261, 264, 268, 269, 289, 292
contraceptives, 20, 22, 34, 58, 82
coronavirus, 201
COVID-19, 208, 311, 320, 323
corporal punishment, 51, 59
corporate, 158, 227, 315

corruption, 58, 73, 76, 78, 135, 167, 221, 224, 326
cow, 19, 37, 99, 100, 103, 119, 121, 134, 138, 141, 166
cultivators, 5, 87, 88, 102, 145, 156, 189
curriculum, 57, 119, 213, 266

D

Dahal, Pushpa Kamal, 22, 106
Dalit, 10–13, 31, 39, 59, 66, 91, 92, 100, 101, 103, 110, 112–15, 117, 121, 123, 124, 131, 132, 137, 138, 140–43, 145, 148, 150, 151, 164, 165, 168, 169, 180, 189, 196, 203–5, 214, 236–40, 242–48, 250, 252–54, 257, 260, 262, 270, 271, 297, 306, 311–14, 316, 317, 319–21, 324–26, 328, 329
Darjeeling, 4
Das, Chittaranjan, 89
Delhi, 9, 94, 135, 182, 228, 229, 262, 295–99, 301–5, 307–9, 311–13, 316–30, 332
democracy, 10, 14, 15, 72–74, 76, 77, 104, 105, 108, 112, 113, 120, 121, 123, 136, 163, 164, 189, 195, 196, 205, 209, 224, 227, 239, 270, 271, 289, 302, 308, 317, 318, 320, 324, 325, 329
Demographic And Health Survey (DHS), 199, 211, 216, 252, 276
demography, 26, 30, 199, 200, 210, 211, 213, 215, 216, 258, 260, 276, 280, 287, 305, 320

Index

Denmark, 14
Desai, Manali, 178, 258, 265, 266, 302
development studies, 258, 291, 310, 317, 330, 332
developed countries, 14, 158, 159
developing countries, 32, 37, 107, 134, 206, 213, 226, 262, 296, 299, 303, 305
developmental state, 105
Dhaka, 4, 46–48, 50, 69, 72, 73, 78, 80, 89, 90, 93, 191, 193, 199, 215, 226, 232, 233, 295, 296, 299, 300, 305, 306, 308, 314, 319, 331, 332
Dhaka University, 4, 69, 73, 90, 93, 191, 193, 331
Dharmapala, Anagarika, 170, 187
diarrhoea, 52, 81, 219, 226, 276, 300
dictatorship, 74, 76, 225
differently abled, 264
Dikshit, Madhuri, 38
Doha, 114
Dola Pratha, 148
domestic violence, 148
Doms, 9, 114, 118, 237
Dravida Munnetra Kazhagam (DMK), 167, 180, 292–94
Dravidian, 164–67, 169, 174, 180, 181, 188, 206, 259, 262, 292, 293, 297, 311, 317
Dravidian Self-Respect Movement, 180, 181
Drèze, Jean, 7, 59, 159, 200, 201, 204, 208, 212–14, 216, 222, 227, 255, 262, 263, 302, 303, 319, 322, 325, 330
Dusadh, 245, 250
Dussehra, 147
Dutch, 47, 170, 176, 261

E

East Asia, 114, 194, 212, 255
East Asian development, 32, 255, 300
East Bengal, 84–89, 93, 139, 195, 229–33, 296, 301, 314
East India Company, 85, 88, 182, 256, 261
East Pakistan, 8, 89, 90, 232, 233, 310
economic growth, 7, 8, 22, 30, 133, 137, 159, 190, 194, 210, 212, 215, 315
economic development, 134, 212, 215, 303, 327
economic discrimination, 206, 249, 302, 326
economic inequality, 207, 297
economic liberalisation, 6, 30, 246
ecotourism, 158
education, 7, 10, 14, 15, 21, 23, 30, 34, 36, 37, 40, 43, 44, 49–52, 54, 57, 60–62, 76–78, 88, 92, 104, 108, 112, 137, 141, 149, 161, 162, 164, 167, 170, 171, 173, 174, 176–81, 183, 197, 204–6, 212, 213, 215, 216, 218, 220–23, 225, 231, 235, 248, 249, 258, 262, 269, 276, 289, 290, 293, 297, 299, 303, 307, 315, 318, 328
educational expenditures, 238, 328
educational hypogamy, 62, 92
educational institutions, 228, 260, 292

egalitarianism, 85, 170, 290
elite, 15, 16, 78, 80, 88, 91, 136, 145, 178, 195, 229–31, 249
elite bias, 15
elite classes, 16
elite displacement, 15, 91, 195
Emperor, 84, 88, 141, 169, 187
English, 21, 49, 60, 88, 101, 104, 110, 177, 182, 206, 220, 254, 256, 265, 311, 315, 326
entitlement, 173, 174, 216, 263, 303, 322
equality, 3, 7, 14, 15, 24, 61, 65, 149, 162, 186, 205, 211, 213, 222, 223, 242, 243, 248, 249, 271, 274, 296, 299, 302, 311, 315, 316, 318, 328
equity, 45, 59, 213, 271, 296
equity-enhancing, 174
ethnic, 27, 99, 100, 113, 116, 117, 121, 188, 207, 239, 262, 306
ethnic communities, 100, 121, 188, 207
ethnicity, 105
ethnographies, 240, 322, 323
excess deaths, 9, 23, 202, 208, 328
Ezhavas, 161, 162, 166, 179, 182, 183, 256, 269, 290. *Also see* Izhavas

F

Fabian, 170, 171, 185, 264
Fa-Hien, 139
Fairaizi, 230, 308
Fakir rebellion, 85
Fazlul, A.K., 86, 89, 230, 231, 322
female, 13, 40, 47, 49–51, 61, 77, 92–94, 120, 121, 123, 127, 147, 148, 159, 186, 201, 204, 206, 208, 224, 241, 242, 244, 253, 254, 267, 278, 281, 298, 309
Female Secondary Stipend Programme (FSSP), 77
feminism, 151, 206, 243, 253, 263, 268, 309, 312, 314, 315, 321
festival, 27, 72, 94, 147, 245, 251
feudalism, 13, 87, 105, 127, 152
fieldwork, 11, 46, 48, 56, 64, 81, 87, 104, 114, 115, 131, 137, 148, 152, 193, 195, 199, 215, 220, 237, 331
FIFA World Cup, 114
Finland, 14
foreign, 46, 80, 81, 83, 104, 105, 109, 112, 115, 149, 156, 217, 228, 229, 314
foreign aid, 46, 81
foreign remittances, 83, 105, 109, 228

G

Gandhi, M.K., 144, 152, 162, 250, 257, 290, 325, 329
Ganga, 151, 251, 321
gender, 7, 10–16, 28, 32, 57, 59, 62, 65, 67, 72, 77, 93, 94, 110, 116, 122, 124, 127, 129, 149, 151, 180, 186, 189, 196, 198, 202, 204, 205, 208, 222–25, 234, 235, 239, 242, 243, 245, 275, 278, 297, 299, 301, 302, 306–8, 311, 313, 316, 318, 328, 329, 332
gender bias, 57
Gender Development Index (GDI), 32

gender discrimination, 13, 110
gender equality, 7, 149, 205, 223, 242, 243, 299, 302, 318
gender gap, 32, 204, 328
gender inequality, 12, 122, 222, 242, 299
gender norms, 62, 93, 222
gender perspective, 202, 205, 329
gender stereotypes, 15, 186
Gonoshasthaya Kendra, 80
graded inequality, 31, 131, 137, 211, 279
Grameen Bank, 81, 83, 226–28, 306, 329
Grameenphone, 81, 83, 228
Gujarat, 159, 245, 255, 298, 302, 327
Gurkha, 108

H

Hadith, 54, 64, 223, 229
Harijan, 138, 143
Haryana, 32, 135, 247
Hasina, Sheikh, 74, 75, 80
Hassan, Mirza, 76, 225, 227, 307
healthcare, 7, 8, 10, 15, 20, 21, 23, 28, 32, 34, 40, 52, 54, 58, 59, 74, 107, 108, 137, 164, 174, 196, 211, 219, 222, 223, 248, 289, 316
 centres, 174
 workers, 59
hegemony, 16, 88, 120, 137, 144, 145, 152, 165, 166, 259
Hindu, 46, 53, 58, 64–66, 84–86, 88, 89, 91, 101, 103, 105, 111, 138, 147, 148, 165, 183, 195, 203, 228, 230, 232, 234, 245, 248, 257, 261, 281, 295, 300, 302, 306, 315, 318, 323–25, 328

Hindu festivals, 101, 147, 245
Hinduisation, 111, 195
Hindu-majority, 45
Hindutva, 138, 248, 295
Hollywood, 81
Hossain, Naomi, 77, 78, 194, 225–28, 270, 307
human development, 3, 7, 9, 14, 24, 25, 27, 29, 33, 34, 44, 45, 49, 52, 54, 65, 66, 78, 104, 105, 109, 142, 158–60, 163, 164, 168, 171, 174, 176, 180, 187, 189, 194, 196, 199, 202, 205, 207, 208, 210–12, 216, 217, 220, 223, 236, 239, 250, 255, 256, 258, 270, 286, 298, 302, 305, 312, 313, 320, 321, 323, 326, 327, 329
Human Development Index, 29, 45, 52, 65, 202, 217
Human Development Report, 205, 208, 210, 211, 236, 239, 270, 305, 326, 327
human rights, 105, 113, 118, 142, 304, 307
human rights-based laws, 30, 82

I

immunisation, 174
India, 5–13, 15, 16, 19–24, 26–33, 35–38, 44, 48, 50, 53, 57, 59, 63–65, 71, 72, 74, 76, 79, 83–85, 88–91, 103, 109, 110, 113, 116, 122, 137, 139, 141, 142, 144, 146, 147, 149, 152, 158, 161, 163, 164, 166–70, 172, 173, 175, 178, 179, 182, 188, 194–218, 220–24, 228–30, 233, 236, 237, 240,

243, 245–51, 253–56, 258, 259, 261, 264–66, 269, 271, 274, 276, 278, 279, 281, 293, 295–98, 300–312, 314–21, 323–27, 329
Indian Constitution, 149, 292
Indians, 3–8, 10–12, 14, 16, 22–24, 27, 29, 31–33, 35–39, 45–48, 63, 79, 82, 88, 90, 91, 115, 121, 138, 142, 145, 148, 149, 158, 159, 164, 178, 179, 186, 188, 189, 194, 195, 200, 202, 203, 205, 207, 209, 210, 213, 214, 217, 221, 229, 230, 240, 243, 246, 247, 251, 253, 255, 259, 263, 268, 270, 271, 273, 274, 290, 292, 293, 295, 297, 299, 300, 305, 307–10, 312, 314–16, 319–26, 328, 329
indigenous, 33, 84, 100, 111, 117, 126, 136, 229, 249
Indigo Revolt, 86, 251, 299
industrialised countries, 122
inequalities, 8, 9, 11–16, 30, 31, 36, 45, 66, 67, 88, 96, 104, 112–14, 137, 145, 158, 160, 163, 173, 190, 195, 198, 205, 232, 239, 275, 285, 327, 333
inter-caste, 111, 119, 125, 126, 145, 166, 244, 252, 295
dining, 119, 145, 166
marriages, 119, 244, 295
Iraq, 114
Islam, 3, 46, 53, 54, 84, 85, 139, 195, 223, 228–30, 281, 300, 303, 321, 331
Izhavas, 161, 162.
See also Ezhavas

J

Jaffrelot, Christophe, 142, 168, 197, 205, 245, 248–51, 271, 300, 309
Jahan, Raunaq, 94, 95, 235
Janabadi Bibahs, 126
Janajati, 33, 100, 111, 119, 239
Japan, 255
Jayalalithaa, 165, 186, 262
Jharkhand, 11, 30, 31, 203, 210, 211, 246, 300, 312, 316
Jinnah, Mohammad Ali, 89, 232, 295, 309, 310

K

Kabeer, Naila, 77, 78, 92, 205, 225, 234, 235, 307, 311, 332
Kajoli Model, 50, 217
Kamaraj, K., 167, 180, 293
Kandy, 188, 268
Kathmandu, 10, 46, 104, 113, 115, 124, 127, 216, 238, 241, 244, 305, 306, 312, 316, 319, 329, 331, 332
Kayasthas, 141
Kerala, 8, 15, 25, 27, 30, 31, 153, 155–64, 166, 174–84, 188, 189, 196, 198, 201, 209–11, 249, 254–59, 262, 263, 265–71, 274, 290–92, 296, 297, 299–302, 306, 307, 309, 310, 312, 313, 317, 319, 320, 323, 325, 326, 329
Kerala Government, 157, 255, 267
Kerala Historical Society, 182, 329
Kerala–Sri Lanka Model, 158

Index

Keralopatti, 182
Kishanganj District 17, 19, 45, 58, 61, 67, 134, 137, 138, 202, 207, 209, 219–23, 245, 281, 331
Koeri, 141, 142
Kshatriya, 84, 100, 248, 260
Kudumbashree, 156–58, 254, 296, 300
Kumar, Nitish, 12, 51, 106, 133, 142, 143, 202–4, 219, 222, 230, 245, 247, 250, 253, 254, 300, 309, 312, 316, 322, 323, 325, 330, 331
kupayyam (jackets), 183
Kurmis, 141, 142, 151

L

labourers, 87, 114, 115, 143, 145, 164, 165, 260
labour force, 186, 206, 254, 269, 278
labour market, 186, 297
labour movements, 171, 188
Ladyland, 16
Lakshmanpur-Bathe, 150
landless, 78, 87, 143, 145, 147, 189, 196, 270, 271, 325
    labourers, 143, 145
landlords, 79, 84, 86, 87, 89, 136, 138, 145, 148, 150, 151
langars, 79, 91, 233
left movement, 164, 188
    coalitions, 171
    governments, 176
    ideologies, 169
    left-leaning, 105, 149
    parties, 105, 107, 169, 189, 258, 302
    left-wing, 15, 105, 106, 108, 125, 232
Liberation War, 8, 36, 78–81, 87, 90, 94, 193
Lichhavi dynasty, 111
local elections, 4, 83, 243, 318
local government, 6, 39, 71, 72, 79, 109, 123
Longue Durée, 194
Lumbini, 101, 110

M

Maddison Database, 23
Madhesis, 26
Madras, 27, 141, 163, 166, 168, 178–80, 184, 188, 249, 259, 261, 292, 293, 297, 318, 327
Madras Presidency, 163, 179, 259, 292
Maha Bodhi Society, 170
Mahadalit, 143, 144, 250, 308, 313
Mahato, 26, 239
Maithili, 26, 120
Malabar, 27, 163, 175, 176, 179, 187, 257, 269, 290
Malayalam, 63, 156, 162, 164, 166, 179, 182, 188, 267, 270, 290, 295
Maldives, 6, 22, 28, 30, 33, 200, 211, 276, 278, 312
Malla dynasty, 111, 238, 314
malnutrition, 37, 40, 137, 208, 213, 302, 319
Mandal Commission, 168, 293
Manjhi, Jitan, 33, 139, 144
Manusmriti, 148
Maoism, 15, 99, 102–8, 112, 113, 116–22, 124–28, 143, 232, 236, 238–45, 248, 253, 298, 304, 306–8, 313, 316, 319, 322, 323, 329

Maoist Party, 102, 124, 125, 244
  guerrillas, 15, 107, 118, 120, 124, 143, 244
  headquarters, 125
  movement, 117, 118, 128, 143, 236, 238, 240, 298, 319, 322
Marxism, 151, 258, 309
Marxist, 231, 232
matrilineal, 162, 163, 179, 181, 258
matriliny, 258, 309
matrilocal, 185
micro-credit, 15, 81, 83, 108, 121, 226, 235, 317
migration 26, 88, 109, 112, 114, 115, 122, 124, 146, 188, 228, 239, 291, 308, 319, 321, 328
minorities, 91, 117
Mississippi, 8, 201, 304
monarchy, 35, 104–6, 112, 123, 163, 239
Montagu–Chelmsford, 141, 166
Most Backward Classes (MBCs), 145, 169, 260
Mughal, 84, 139, 144, 229
Muluki Ain, 103, 111, 112, 236, 239, 287, 288, 311, 314
Munro, John, 161, 183, 257, 264, 265, 267, 329
Musahar, 55, 60, 114, 132, 135, 138, 139, 151, 222, 248
Muslim, 53, 54, 58, 59, 64–66, 84, 86, 88, 89, 93, 138, 147, 161, 169, 182, 183, 217, 223, 228–30, 232, 234, 249, 257, 290, 293, 296, 303, 309, 315
Mussalmans, 229, 307
Muzaffarpur, 45, 61, 131, 147, 152, 220, 222, 254, 281, 322, 325, 331
Myanmar, 115, 226

N

Nadar, 182, 188, 266, 267, 270, 290, 306
Nairs, 161, 162, 179, 181, 182, 256–58, 266
Namboodiri, 181, 258
Nangeli, 183, 267, 325
Narayan, Jayaprakash, 145
nari puja, 147, 148
National Archives, 182, 188, 260, 266, 268, 269, 332
National Family Health Survey (NFHS), 39, 135, 199, 200, 206, 211, 214, 216, 246, 251, 252, 274, 279, 308
National Food Security Act (NFSA), 30, 222, 255
National Rural Employment Guarantee Act (NREGA), 30, 152
Naxalism, 116, 143, 150, 232, 253, 254, 313, 316, 323
Nepal, 6, 8, 10, 11, 13–15, 21–24, 26–30, 32–35, 37, 39, 40, 45, 46, 48–53, 55–58, 60, 61, 63–67, 97, 99–117, 119–25, 127, 128, 143, 147, 148, 150, 156, 158, 159, 194–96, 198, 201, 202, 205–11, 213, 215, 217–23, 236–45, 252, 253, 276, 278, 281, 282, 287, 288, 295–98, 304–8, 310–14, 316–20, 322, 323, 325, 326, 328–31
Nepali, 6, 8, 10, 16, 21–23, 26, 27, 29, 31, 33–36, 39, 45, 55, 58, 60, 61, 65–67,

99–101, 103–6, 108–15, 120–24, 126–28, 206, 207, 216, 218, 237, 240–44, 287, 295, 306, 331
Nepalisation, 111
Newari, 64, 120
non-Brahmins, 162, 164, 166, 168, 180, 187, 249, 259, 260, 290, 292, 317, 323
Non-Cooperation Movement, 93
Non-Government Organisations (NGOs), 80
Norway, 14, 228
nutrition, 7, 38, 40, 52, 54, 156, 167, 174, 212, 219, 222, 245, 276, 304, 310

O

Odisha, 115, 211, 254, 274, 319
Open Defecation Free (ODF), 38, 39, 199, 200, 214, 216, 219, 223, 276, 301, 306, 325
oppressed castes, 91, 125, 131, 136, 139, 145, 150, 168, 179, 181–84
Oral Rehydration Salt (ORS), 20, 221
Other Backward Classes (OBCs), 31, 110, 123, 137, 138, 145, 168, 169, 203, 205, 228, 243, 249, 260, 270, 271, 300, 309
Oxfam, 103, 203, 303, 316, 317

P

Padmanabha temple, 182
Pahela Baisakh, 94
Pakistan, 7, 8, 28, 30, 31, 33, 74, 87, 89–91, 93, 94, 196, 211, 224, 231–33, 276, 278, 309, 310, 312, 320

Panchagarh District, 4, 5, 45–47, 50, 54, 65, 67, 86, 91, 92, 195, 199, 209, 212, 215, 217, 220–22, 227, 234, 281, 331
pandemic, 8, 9, 11, 23, 24, 30, 32, 36, 37, 83, 108, 109, 114, 133, 146, 157, 198, 200–202, 208, 210, 213, 218, 255, 297, 304, 307, 308, 316, 320, 328
Pariah, 188
Parliament, 16, 123, 206, 224, 242, 264, 301, 308
Parliamentarians, 14, 126, 185, 243, 278
Particularly Vulnerable Tribal Group (PVTG), 31
Pashupatinath temple, 113
Patna, 46, 139, 144, 147, 149, 248, 253, 312, 317, 318, 331, 332
patronage politics, 76
pension, 20, 107, 196, 236, 237, 317
People's War, 15, 102–5, 107, 112, 116, 117, 119, 121, 124, 239–41, 243–45, 253, 306, 308, 318, 322, 329
Persian, 88, 223
Phule, Savitribai, 149, 252
politics, 76, 83, 124, 133, 136, 144, 145, 160, 175, 185, 209, 231, 236, 237, 247, 249, 251, 256, 258, 259, 261, 262, 265, 269, 291, 297–99, 301, 307, 309, 310, 312, 313, 316, 319, 320, 325, 327
political activism, 126
political competition, 78

political elites, 77, 78, 82
political parties, 76, 82, 107, 108, 112, 113, 121, 123, 167, 170, 225, 259
political power, 189, 197, 258, 302
political science, 208, 225, 306, 313, 324, 332
political settlement, 77, 225, 227, 307
politicians, 53, 76, 87, 173, 174, 250
politicisation, 136
polygamy, 124
Portuguese, 170
poverty, 8, 9, 11, 12, 16, 28, 30, 34, 55, 81, 105, 109, 113, 133, 134, 137, 147, 150, 201–3, 208, 209, 211, 226, 236–38, 246, 254, 258, 263, 271, 289, 295–98, 302, 307, 308, 312, 322, 326, 328, 329
Pratham, 37, 50, 206, 212, 215, 216, 218, 318
Primary Education Stipend Programme (PESP), 77
Prophet Mohammad, 85, 224, 229
Pulaya, 161, 162, 179
Punjab, 135, 247
purdah, 65, 93, 95, 149, 223, 234, 235, 252, 303, 304

Q

Qatar, 114, 138
Quran, 54, 220, 311

R

Rahman, Sheikh Mujibur, 211, 235, 319
Rajasthan, 12, 39, 204, 210, 319, 328

Rajput, 111, 141, 151, 240
Ramzan, 64, 147, 217, 330
Ranas, 111, 112
Ranvir Sena, 143, 150, 151
Ready Made Garment Sector (RMGS), 95
refugees, 80, 81, 89–91
reservation quotas, 113, 166
rights-based laws, 30, 82
right-wing, 133, 171, 245
Royal Rescript on Education, 173

S

Sabarimala temple, 184, 267, 268
Safai Karmachari Andolan, 39
Saiyads, 71, 223, 229
Sampoorna Kranti, 145
sanitation, 6, 34, 39, 40, 53, 54, 91, 200, 214–16, 220, 276, 300, 308, 316
Sanskrit, 111, 120, 167, 259
Sanskritisation, 85, 119, 140, 197, 248, 324
Santhal, 86, 93, 144, 234
sari, 10, 51, 65, 75, 94–96, 132, 193, 223, 242, 243, 245, 329
Sarki, 110, 239
Savarnas, 120, 151, 182
Scandinavian, 14, 196
scholarships, 21, 51, 101, 177, 180, 207, 314, 332
Self-Help Groups (SHGs), 152, 156, 235
Self-Respect Movement, 166–68, 180, 181, 185, 187, 188, 292
Self-Respecters, 167, 169, 292
Self-Respect weddings, 126, 186, 269
Sen, Amartya, 7, 59, 200, 201, 204, 208, 222, 230, 262, 263, 266, 303, 319, 322

sex-selective abortion, 13, 32, 204
Shahbag, 78, 225, 306, 319
Shannar, 183, 184
sharecroppers, 87, 145, 146
Shudra, 111, 161, 228
Siliguri, 4, 27, 29, 209, 210, 281
Singh, Prerna, 27, 137, 148, 162, 210, 219, 221, 247, 248, 251–53, 257, 258, 323, 324, 331
Sinha, Sachinanada 135, 246, 253, 317, 324, 332
Sinhala 169, 185, 187, 256, 262, 270, 305
snakes and ladders, 101
social development, 6, 7, 9, 23, 80, 158, 169, 210, 247, 256, 258, 261, 262, 264, 296, 309, 323, 324
social discrimination, 116, 141
   disparities, 137
   distances, 59–61, 67, 84, 88, 110, 133, 195
   divisions, 91, 195, 229
   exclusion, 105
   hierarchies, 85, 86, 111, 195
   inequalities, 31, 67, 86, 96, 112, 113, 238, 328
   segregation, 165, 206
social equality, 15, 24, 61, 65
social achievements, 25, 54, 194, 215, 315
social action, 253, 321
social assistance, 107
social awareness, 80, 120
social capital, 122
social change, 15, 24, 95, 148, 196, 241, 242, 275, 308, 316, 323, 325
social class, 59, 231
social commitment, 78

social contract, 74, 78, 80, 83, 195, 197
social equity, 45, 59
social mobility, 12, 85, 115, 139, 140, 161, 231, 238, 256, 317, 329
social movements, 14, 15, 24, 83, 140, 160, 161, 163, 164, 166, 180, 190, 195, 198, 256, 262, 326
social pensions, 107, 236
social protection, 78, 107, 236, 317, 323
social reform, 149, 160, 162, 163, 198, 297, 307
social rights, 236, 237, 310
social security, 216, 262, 303
social solidarity, 116, 136, 239, 306
social stratification, 140, 229, 230, 295, 299, 324
social transformation, 91, 128, 202, 205, 222, 243, 244, 301, 329
social welfare, 74, 78, 176, 196, 198
social grants, 236, 237, 311
Socialism, 133, 135, 137, 144, 145, 171, 185, 251, 264, 323
social justice, 136, 161, 181, 258, 296, 320
social policy, 260, 261, 263, 302, 314
social sciences, 300, 302, 313, 316, 317, 328, 330, 332
sociologist, 23, 78, 93, 117, 139, 160, 178, 194, 197, 202, 248
South Asia, 6, 7, 9, 13–16, 22, 23, 26, 28–30, 32, 33, 36, 37, 46, 62, 73, 74, 123, 175, 194, 199, 201, 205, 212,

213, 223, 224, 230, 232,
261, 263, 273, 274, 278,
298, 299, 304, 306, 310,
311, 313, 314, 316, 319,
320, 322, 324, 329, 331
South India, 197, 264, 269, 270,
304, 305, 318, 323
sub-quotas, 123, 145, 243
sub-saharan Africa, 30, 37
subsidies, 34, 53, 109, 157, 165,
171, 174, 180, 246, 255,
262, 263, 294
subsidised foodgrains, 255
suffragettes, 155, 169, 170, 181,
184, 185, 254, 268, 289,
291, 309, 326
Sufism, 85
Sultana's Dream 16, 92, 206, 307
survey, 4, 5, 20, 21, 24, 27, 33,
34, 37, 39, 46–56, 58, 59,
62, 74, 84, 91, 92, 116, 127,
135, 142, 148, 194, 199,
200, 203, 206, 211–20, 222,
223, 236, 239, 241, 244–47,
251, 252, 255, 269, 270,
274, 279, 282–86, 299, 305,
306, 308, 318, 331
surveyors, 77, 92, 147, 218, 252
Swachh Bharat Abhiyan, 6, 199,
200, 214, 328, 329
Swachh Survekshan Gramin, 214,
327
Swasthya Sevikas, 34, 61
Sweden, 11, 14, 318
Switzerland, 11
syncretic, 85, 195

T

Taliban, 7
Tamil Nadu, 25, 27, 31, 126,
155, 157–60, 164, 165, 167–
69, 172–76, 179–81, 185,
186, 188, 189, 196, 198,
206, 209, 221, 254, 255,
259, 260, 262, 265, 266,
270, 271, 274, 292, 293,
311, 314, 327, 328, 332
Tamil Buddhist, 187, 259, 296
Tamil renaissance, 165, 259,
297
Tebhaga, 93, 234, 319
Telli caste, 132
Terai, 26, 29, 45, 65, 120, 237,
239, 281
textbooks, 36, 51, 56, 57, 101,
102, 104, 179, 182, 207,
212, 266, 296
Thakur, Karpoori 145, 251, 323
Thakuri Raj, 116
Tharu, 99, 236
Thass, Iyothee, 165, 187, 188,
259, 270, 296
Tinnevelly, 188
tourism, 155
tribes, 117, 150, 249, 260
Tripura, 91
Trivandrum, 258, 291, 317, 329
Travancore, 161–63, 174–79,
182, 183, 187, 188, 256,
257, 264–66, 290, 291, 314,
321, 329

U

Ujjwala Yojana, 34
underweight, 16, 37, 147, 200,
214, 223, 278, 280
unemployment, 147, 189, 246,
326
United Kingdom, 316
United Nations, 23, 29, 232, 258,
303, 304, 314, 319, 326,
327

United Nations Development
 Programme (UNDP), 202,
 205, 207, 208, 210, 211,
 236, 239, 270, 296, 305,
 326, 327
United Nations Educational,
 Scientific and Cultural
 Organization (UNESCO), 77
United States, 8, 14, 177, 201, 219
universal adult franchise, 261, 289
universal healthcare, 107
universal public services, 172,
 178, 190
universal social protection, 236,
 317, 323
untouchability, 103, 111–13, 116,
 118, 141, 142, 161, 170, 310
untouchables, 112, 131, 151, 187,
 249, 250, 256, 257, 307
upazila, 220–22, 225, 227, 230,
 232
upper castes, 12, 51, 59, 64, 88,
 100, 103, 111, 117, 137,
 140–42, 145, 150–52, 163,
 183, 184, 197, 243, 267
urban, 44, 63, 78, 99, 137, 170,
 231, 232, 245, 271, 273,
 274, 321
Urdu, 89, 93, 232, 252, 314
Uttar Pradesh, 8, 10, 30, 39, 59,
 139, 210, 211, 247, 254,
 266, 274, 312, 314, 320

V

vaccines, 75, 276
Vaikkom temple, 161–63, 187,
 257, 290
Vaikkom Temple Entry
 Satyagraha, 162, 187, 290
Vanniyars, 169, 260, 293

Varieties of Democracy (V-Dem)
 Index, 74, 224, 318
Vedic period, 139
Vidyasagar, Ishwar Chandra, 149

W

Wahhabi uprising, 86
Washington, 299, 305, 308, 314,
 318, 328, 329
wealth tax, 11
welfare, 15, 31, 58, 61, 65,
 74–78, 82, 105, 108–10,
 133, 134, 157, 165, 169–72,
 175–77, 186, 195, 196, 198,
 204, 210, 211, 226, 247,
 257, 258, 261, 270, 271,
 276, 294, 299, 300, 303,
 305, 311, 314, 323, 324
welfare investments, 105, 109, 195
welfare policies, 76, 77
welfare programmes, 176, 294
welfare services, 15, 31, 134,
 165, 171, 186, 195, 276
welfare state, 15, 108, 110,
 169–72, 175, 177, 196, 261,
 271, 299, 311
welfare workers, 61, 65, 75, 157

Y

Yadav, Yogendra, 27, 205, 209,
 324
Yami, Hisila, 121, 127, 240, 241,
 243–45, 253, 307, 329
 Parvati, Comrade, 121, 127,
 173, 183, 241, 244, 318

Z

zamindari system, 86, 87, 91,
 136, 145
zamindars, 87, 141, 144, 231, 251

www.ingramcontent.com/pod-product-compliance
Ingram Content Group UK Ltd.
Pitfield, Milton Keynes, MK11 3LW, UK
UKHW021058231224
3761UKWH00016B/68/J